T4-ATW-136

A CONCISE ENCYCLOPEDIA OF ANTIQUES

The Tapestry Room, Osterley Park, Greater London, c. *1780. The room was designed by Robert Adam and feature Paris-made Gobelins tapestry on the walls as well as on the seats and backs of the chairs. The design of the carpe reflects that of the ceiling, both also being the work of Adam. (Osterley Park, Greater London: The Nationa Trust. Photo: Cooper-Bridgeman Library)*

A CONCISE ENCYCLOPEDIA OF ANTIQUES

GEOFFREY WILLS

OSPREY

By the same author

Antiques
Collecting Copper and Brass
Country Life Book of English China
Jade
English Looking-Glasses
Country Life Pocket Book of Glass
English Life Series (6 vols.)
Book of Copper and Brass
Ivory
English and Irish Glass
English Pottery and Porcelain
Silver for Pleasure and Investment
Antique Glass for Pleasure and Investment
English Furniture 1550–1760
English Furniture 1760–1900
Jade of the East
Candlesticks
Craftsmen and Cabinet-Makers of Classic English Furniture
English Glass Bottles

ISBN 0 85045 063 2

This book was designed and produced by
Alban Book Services Limited,
147 London Road, St. Albans, Herts AL1 1TA

Printed in Great Britain

First published in 1975 by
Osprey Publishing Limited,
137 Southampton Street, Reading, Berks, England
Member Company of the George Philip Group

Set in 10pt Times New Roman 327
by Morrison & Gibb Limited,
Tanfield, Edinburgh, Scotland
A Member of the Oxley Printing Group Limited

LIST OF CONTENTS

FOREWORD

THIS book is a guide to many kinds of antiques; articles made and used in the past, principally in England but including those from foreign lands that influenced London and provincial craftsmen. In addition are those made by English and other migrants to America prior to the inauguration of the United States. The subjects discussed and illustrated are furniture, pottery and porcelain, glass, silver, and pewter and other metals, made between about 1500 and 1890.

An introductory section, divided into periods, outlines the changing background as the centuries progressed. It records artistic and other trends, followed in each instance by details of the careers of architects, painters and sculptors; no less than cabinet-makers, silversmiths and others, these men were influenced by successive styles. The various types of antiques are listed separately, each with entries in alphabetical order, all being cross-referenced in the index at the end of the volume.

ACKNOWLEDGEMENT

Illustrations appear by courtesy of the undermentioned:

National Gallery, London.
National Trust: Saltram, Devon, and Montacute, Somerset.
Victoria and Albert Museum, London.
H. Blairman & Sons, London.
Bonhams, Montpelier Street, London SW7 1HH.
Christie, Manson & Woods, Ltd., London SW1Y 6QT.
King & Chasemore, Pulborough, Sussex.
Phillips, London, W1Y, 0AS.
Sotheby & Co., London W1A, 2AA.
Sotheby Parke Bernet, New York and Los Angeles.

The five Roman Orders of Architecture

From left to right they are: Tuscan, Doric, Ionic, Corinthian and Composite, each of which varies in the proportions of its component parts as well as in details.

The examples illustrated are made of gold with columns of lapis lazuli mounted on a base of ormolu-mounted porphyry. This masterpiece, which stands 26·7 cm. in height overall, was made in about 1780 probably by the French goldsmith Robert-Arnould Drais, and is traditionally said to have been the property of Queen Marie-Antoinette. It is now in the Jones Collection, Victoria and Albert Museum.

PART I: DECORATIVE STYLES

TUDOR PERIOD: 1500-1600

BRITISH art has been stimulated continuously by foreign influences. This has occurred as a result of visits or settlement by artists and craftsmen, from the circulation of their designs, or as a result of journeys abroad made by inhabitants of the country.

In the sixteenth century a completely fresh artistic style which gradually affected everyone's life spread from Italy throughout Europe: it has become known as the Renaissance, or re-birth. It arose from a study of the long-neglected cultures of ancient Greece and Rome, and especially from acceptance of the classic Orders of architecture with their meticulously accurate proportions.

In England, Cardinal Wolsey, who had acquired Hampton Court in 1514, sent for Italian workers to provide the latest patterns of ornament as an enhancement of the plain brick building. Another survivor of the period is the tomb of Henry VII and Elizabeth of York, which was ordered to be placed in Westminster Abbey by their son Henry VIII. He commissioned the Italian sculptor, Pietro Torrigiano, to model the two figures and the plinth upon which they rest.

The most important building of Henry VIII's reign was Nonsuch, near Epsom, which was demolished soon after 1670 having stood for about 130 years. It was noted that the King 'invited thither, at the Royal expense, the most excellent artificers, designers, sculptors, and statuaries of different nations, Italians, Frenchmen, Hollanders and native Englishmen, and these presented a marvellous example of their art'. The architect as he is known nowadays, a man who plans and supervises the building from start to finish, was then unknown, and in his place was a skilled craftsman, either a stone-mason or a carpenter, who devised as well as worked on a project. He was responsible for the layout of the interior and the general appearance of the exterior, but carving and other embellishments inside and outside were designed and added by the various specialists concerned. As the century advanced, direct Italian influence became weaker, and features of the Renaissance style were more often taken from engravings by Hans Vredeman de Vries and others published in the Netherlands.

In the reign of Elizabeth I the men combining the roles of mason and architect included the Smythson family, who worked on many of the great mansions of the time. These, by whomever they were built, almost always had a central courtyard enclosed on three sides; an improvement on the earlier completely enclosed yard, and allowing much more light and air into the rooms. A striking feature of surviving examples (for instance, Wollaton Hall, Nottinghamshire) is the symmetrical appearance, with a careful balance in the arrangement of doors, windows and chimneys, in place of the less regular silhouettes of earlier date. Changes in living habits as well as the provision of an orderly exterior meant that the

Decorative Styles, Tudor Period (Continued)

lay-out of the rooms inside was affected, and the old-style hall dominating the planning gradually ceased to be built. There had been signs of this occurring from about 1500, when, instead of a vast room that was used for daily living, smaller rooms were provided. The hall

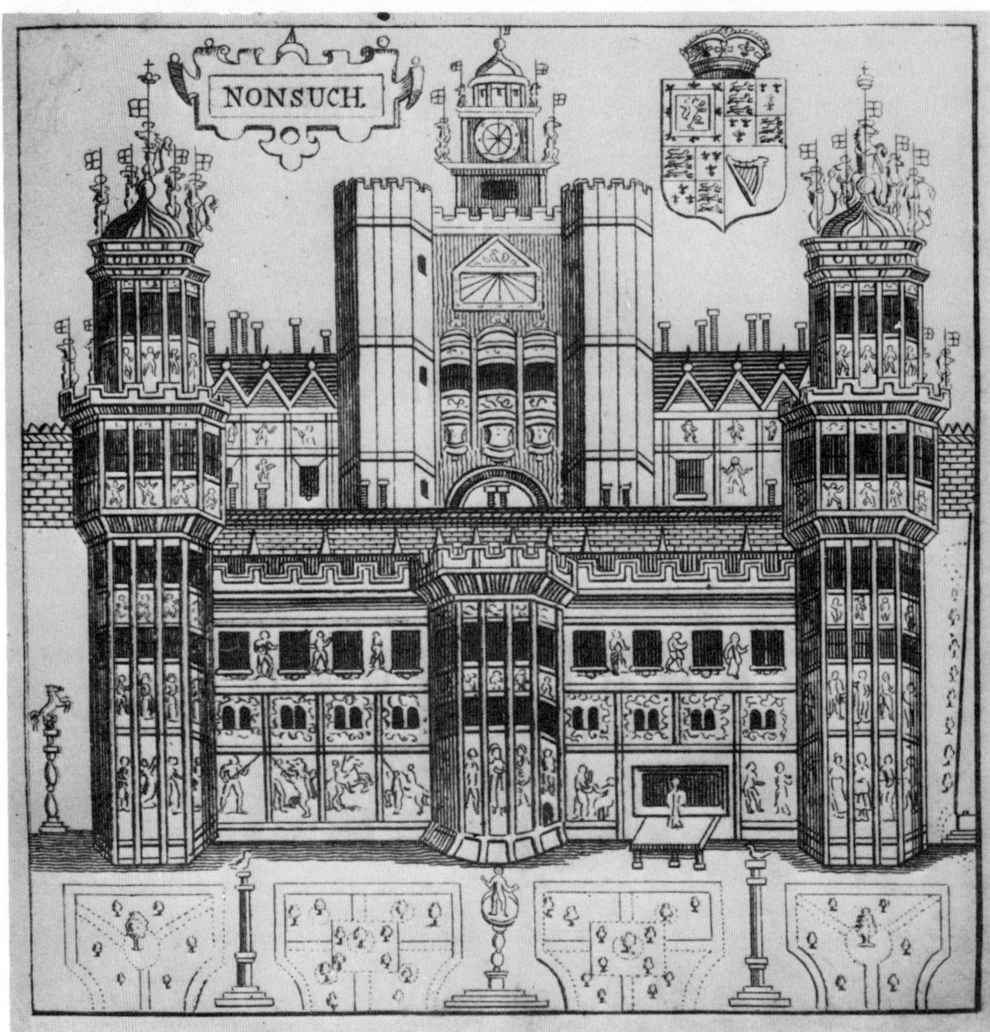

Nonsuch, near Epsom, Surrey, built in the reign of Henry VIII and demolished soon after 1670.

This, which no equal has in art or fame,
Britons deservedly do Nonsuch name.

The engraved illustration comes from the translation of Paul Hentzner's Travels, *1797, which was first published in German in 1598.*

Decorative Styles, Tudor Period (Continued)

became an entrance hall giving access to the rooms and was used occasionally for large-scale entertainments, but daily life was conducted in a dining-room and one or more parlours. Notable features were the principal staircase which was designed with much care, and a long gallery on an upper floor in which exercise could be taken during inclement weather.

Of the interior decoration of Elizabethan and earlier homes there is evidence remaining that the woodworker and the plasterer did not lack employment. Walls were frequently lined with oak panelling composed of small boards within frames held together with wood pins. The panelling usually did not rise to the ceiling and this left a space for the plasterer to show his skill. There and on the ceiling itself he would model in relief whatever was required of him to suit the taste of a patron. Often this would be one or more scenes illustrating Biblical passages or the works of classical writers, perhaps centred in the coat-of-arms of the owner. An exception was the wall which included the fireplace: a dominant feature of elaborately carved stone or wood, that usually reached from floor to ceiling and was proportionately of commanding width.

The homes of the majority of the people were constructed of wood and mud or plaster. However, a Spanish visitor remarked that 'These English have their houses made of sticks and dirt, but they fare commonly as well as the king'. By modern standards gloom prevailed indoors, for although glass became more plentiful and cheaper in time, windows remained small. The dimness was countered by the use of bright colours, so that a lack of daylight was less noticeable.

As for paintings, these were uncommon except in the great houses. Religious pictures, which had for long been the constant preoccupation of artists, were frowned upon following the recognition of Henry VIII as Head of the Church of England in 1531. Thenceforward an interest began to be shown in portraits, and surviving examples depict the faces, figures and costume of many of the personalities of the time.

One commentator wrote in the mid-century of the prosperity of much of the nation:

> The furniture of our houses also exceedeth, and is grown in manner even to passing delicacy: and herein I do not speak of the nobility and gentry only, but likewise of the lowest sort in most places of our south country that have anything at all to take to.

ARCHITECTS

The names of most of the master-masons and carpenters responsible for designing the buildings of the period are no longer remembered. One man whose name has been recorded is *Robert Smithson* or *Smythson*, who lived between 1535 and 1614. He is known to have been employed on two Wiltshire mansions, Longleat House and Wardour Castle. In the Midlands his name has been associated with several great houses, particularly Wollaton Hall, Nottinghamshire, and Hardwick Hall, Derbyshire. His son *John* (died 1634) and his grandson *Huntingdon Smithson* (died 1648) were also men who combined the roles of mason and architect, as was the custom of their times.

Tudor Period (Continued)

PAINTERS

Hans Eworth (*flourished 1540–74*)

Eworth was born in Antwerp, but the date of his birth is unknown. He signed work with his initials, but there is uncertainty about the spelling of his surname and it is confusingly rendered in half-a-dozen different ways in documents of the period. He was in London

Chimneypiece, c. *1570; the mantel supported on Corinthian columns, and the coats of arms in the upper stage flanked by atlantes and caryatids.*

Painters, Tudor Period (Continued)

Miniature painting of James I of England, James VI of Scotland, by Nicholas Hilliard, c. *1610.*

by 1549 and remained in England for the next twenty-five years, painting Mary Tudor in about 1553 and Elizabeth I in 1569. The latter is depicted in a painting at Hampton Court *Elizabeth confounding Juno, Minerva and Venus*, where the artist flatteringly shows the Queen awarding herself the Golden Apple instead of giving it to Venus!

Nicholas Hilliard (*1547–1619*)

The son of an Exeter goldsmith, Hilliard is recorded as having painted full-size portraits, but it is on miniatures that his fame rests. He has been described as 'the only English painter whose works reflect, in its delicate microcosm, the world of Shakespeare's earlier plays'. A portrait of his Royal patron, Elizabeth I, together with one of Sir Walter Raleigh, is in the National Portrait Gallery, while portraits of his father, his first wife, and the artist himself are among others in the Victoria and Albert Museum.

Hans Holbein (*1497–1543*)

The greatest painter in Britain in the sixteenth century was Hans Holbein, born in Augsburg, Germany, in 1497. He went to Basle, Switzerland, in 1519, but despite his prowess found it difficult to earn a living there and made a visit to England lasting from 1526 to 1528. He returned in 1532 to settle for the remainder of his life in London, where he painted Henry VIII, some of the latter's wives, members of the Court and others. Two of his best-known works are in the National Gallery: a full-length portrait of Christina, Duchess of Milan, painted for Henry when he was considering marrying her, and *The Ambassadors*, with its meticulously rendered accessories in the background and an intriguing elongated skull in the foreground. Holbein also designed jewellery and silverware, and painted

Painters, Tudor Period (Continued)

Miniature painting of an unknown young woman by Hans Holbein the Younger (1497–1543).
Sotheby's.

miniatures. A dozen or so of these are attributed to him with confidence, including likenesses of Anne of Cleves, fourth wife of Henry VIII, and Mrs. Pemberton, the twenty-three-year-old wife of a country landowner (both miniatures in the Victoria and Albert Museum). Holbein's miniature of Thomas Wriothesley, first Earl of Southampton, grandfather of Shakespeare's patron, the third Earl, is in the Metropolitan Museum of Art, New York.

Hans (*or Jan*) *Vredeman de Vries* (*1527–?1608*)

Like many other sixteenth century artists de Vries combined the rôle of painter with that of designer. He was born at Leeuwarden, Holland, studied in Amsterdam, Antwerp and Malines, and gained a reputation for his paintings with architectural backgrounds, some of them showing scenes inside churches and cathedrals. Not only did he provide interior decorations for buildings, but he also designed open-air decorative works for the triumphal entry into Antwerp of the Emperor Charles V. It is for his ornamental designs that the name of de Vries is remembered, for his working period coincided with great activity on the part of engravers and printers in spreading information. His book entitled *Différents pourtraicts de menuiserie*, which was published in about 1580, contained a series of fashionable designs for the use of furniture makers and others. It shows panels, pilasters and pieces of furniture embellished with male and female heads and whole figures, grotesque animals, swags of fruit, bosses, fluting and, most distinctively, scrolls resembling curled cardboard. While de Vries was not by any means the only man to publish work of this kind in the late sixteenth century, his was the first to be issued in the Netherlands and it would appear to have enjoyed a particularly wide circulation. His son, Paul Vredeman de Vries (1567–?1630) followed in the footsteps of his father and published works of a similar character.

Federico Zuccaro (*1543?–1609*)

Among other artists who were active in Britain during the period must be included the Italian, Zuccaro. He came to London at the end of 1574 and returned to his native land in the following year, but his impact was such that many more paintings than he could possibly have executed in the time bear his name in error. This was once excusable because it was

Painters, Tudor Period (Continued)

thought that he had stayed in the country for several years, but it is now known that he came and went within little more than twelve months. It is recorded that he painted portraits of Elizabeth I and the Earl of Leicester which have disappeared, and all that has been traced at present of his output in England are two drawings in the British Museum.

SCULPTORS

Giovanni da Maiano (*born 1438*)

Giovanni da Maiano was the son of a stonemason. Of his relatives, Giuliano was an architect and Benedetto a sculptor, and together they were employed in the building of the cathedral at Faenza. Giovanni modelled in terracotta (red or buff-clay that was modelled while soft and baked in a kiln until hard) and supplied for Cardinal Wolsey at 'Anton Court' ten roundels with busts of Roman emperors. Of the original number, six remain at Hampton Court today. A letter from da Maiano regarding the roundels is in the British Museum, dated 18 June 1521; it contains the information that he charged for them 26/8d. (£1.33p) apiece.

Designs for caryatids, an atlantes and (second from left) a combination of both by Hans Vredeman de Vries, from an engraving published at the end of the sixteenth century.

Sculptors, Tudor Period (Continued)

Pietro Torrigiano (*1472–1528*)

Torrigiano was born in Florence and learned the art of bronze sculpture in that city. It is recorded that while he was there he gained more fame because he assaulted the great Michelangelo and broke the latter's nose, than on account of his artistic prowess. Nevertheless he continued in his chosen career by working in Rome and elsewhere in Italy. He spent some time fighting with the forces of Cesare Borgia, then in 1509 was in the Netherlands. From there Torrigiano went to London and on 23 November 1511 contracted to execute the tomb of Lady Margaret Beaufort in Westminster Abbey. He received other commissions while in England, culminating in one to provide the tomb of Henry VII and

The Monument of K. HENRY VII in Westminster Abbey.
J. Mynde sc.

Engraving depicting the tomb of Henry VII and his Queen, Elizabeth of York, by Pietro Torrigiano; started in 1512 it was completed in 1517 and stands in Westminster Abbey, London. Clear signs of Renaissance design are to be seen in the frieze of scrolling leaves immediately below the recumbent figures, and in the lower panels of wreath-framed figures.
Mansell Collection.

Sculptors, Tudor Period (Continued)

Elizabeth of York, also in the Abbey. It was begun in 1512 and completed seven years later. Torrigiano's group of the two recumbent figures and the ornamental plinth on which they rest, show many features of the Renaissance in contrast to those of the ancient structure in which the tomb is placed. The sculptor did more work in England, went back to Florence and returned to London again before journeying to Spain in 1522. He died there six years later.

EARLY STUART PERIOD: 1600-1660

THE reigns of James I and Charles I, which followed that of Elizabeth, lasted from 1603 to 1649. From about 1620 the lessons learned in Italy by Inigo Jones began to take effect. He wholeheartedly adopted the system of strict proportions recommended by the Italian, Andrea Palladio, and initiated a profession by becoming the first British architect: designing a building and supervising its erection from start to finish.

Earlier, the general outline of a structure had been symmetrical, but now more attention began to be paid to the balancing of details. A fashionable new home presented to the observer a series of carefully-spaced windows of matching size broken by a ground floor central doorway and perhaps, in the centre of the first stage, by a window framed differently from the others. No longer were there romantic-looking turrets disturbing the line of a roof, or bays jutting forward to break the straight ground-line, and windows ceased to vary in size from floor to floor.

The regular façade posed problems which had earlier been commented on by the essayist Francis Bacon, who had written: 'let use be preferred to uniformity'. The enormous medieval chamber that served for all daytime purposes evolved into a smaller space immediately within the doorway, while leading off it were rooms for various purposes and a staircase giving access to upper floors. As not all the rooms were required to be of the same size, it was often a task for the designer to arrange that windows internally and externally were suitably positioned. The difficulties were gradually overcome, and remaining examples of the work of Jones and his followers show that in most instances it was found possible to equate use and uniformity with complete success.

The Banqueting House, Whitehall, London, is a surviving example of an important building of the time, having been erected to the design of Inigo Jones between 1619 and 1622, and is all that was carried out of a projected Royal Palace. Jones was responsible also for a type of smaller house that set the pattern for some years to come. It was neat and box-like in shape, having a sloping roof with plain chimneys and a deep cornice where roof and walls met.

Interior decoration of the sober-fronted houses was contrastingly showy, with the chimneypiece continuing to be an elaborately ornamented focal point and the ceiling heavy with modelled plaster. With changes in joinery methods, wall panelling comprised panels of larger size but framed as before.

The period is notable for the interest shown in collecting works of art, an interest that emerged in the early years of the seventeenth century. The eldest son of James I, Henry,

Decorative Styles, Early Stuart Period (Continued)

The Banqueting House, Whitehall, London, designed by Inigo Jones and erected between 1619 and 1622. The ceiling in the interior was painted by Rubens and installed in 1636. Mansell Collection.

Prince of Wales, acquired old paintings, and when he died at the age of only eighteen in 1612 these passed to his brother, Charles. The latter, who became King Charles I, added to the collection and was encouraged to do so by some of his subjects. Prominent among them was Thomas, Earl of Arundel, who was especially famed for his collection of carved marbles, being described at the time as the man to whom 'this angle of the world oweth the first sight of Greek and Roman statues'. Much of his collection was destroyed in later years, but most of the remainder was given to the University of Oxford in 1667.

Like their forbears, James and Charles encouraged visits to England by foreign artists, notable among them being Rubens and van Dyck. Both men were rewarded with knighthoods, and their work greatly influenced that of English painters.

Following the execution of Charles I in 1649, an event that took place outside Inigo Jones's Banqueting House, there followed a period in which little or no attention was paid to artistic matters. The Civil War and the ensuing political troubles, together with the

Decorative Styles, Early Stuart Period (Continued)

prevailing influence of the Puritans, did nothing to encourage the arts; for most people there was time only for consideration of the bare bones of existence. However, even in such disturbed days, fortunes were made as well as lost, and homes were built even if they were few in number.

ARCHITECTS

Inigo Jones (*1573–1652*)

The son of a London clothworker, Inigo Jones visited Italy in 1601, and it is not unreasonable to assume that this might well have been at the expense of a patron. During his travels he became interested in design and especially in architecture, which resulted in his employment for a few years by Christian I, King of Denmark. The monarch's brother-in-law was James I of England, and when Jones returned to his native land he found employment as a designer of masques: entertainments for the Court and nobility in which the performers danced, acted and sang, the participants sometimes being amateurs with, on one occasion, the Queen herself taking part. Inigo Jones designed scenery, costumes and stage machinery for masques written by Ben Jonson and others, and many of his original drawings for them are preserved at Chatsworth, Derbyshire. In addition to his appointment as Surveyor of the King's Works, which he gained in 1615, Jones practised as an architect, often in collaboration with his pupil, John Webb. His most famous extant building is the church of St. Paul, Covent Garden, with its many-pillared portico, scene of the opening act of Shaw's *Pygmalion* (*My Fair Lady*). The original structure was, in fact, burned down in 1794 and rebuilt to the design of Jones in the following year, so the present church may be termed his own. In conjunction with Webb he designed the Double Cube room at Wilton House, Wiltshire (Earl of Pembroke), which has been described as 'one of the most magnificent rooms in England'. Both architects were so steeped in Italian ideas that they went so far as to attribute the building of Stonehenge to the Romans! This earned them a measure of contempt, which was shouldered by Webb; the latter publishing their shared theory in 1655, three years after Jones had died. In spite of this lapse Inigo Jones was remembered with respect, gaining for himself the title of the 'English Palladio': from Andrea Palladio (1518–80), whose printed work was translated by Jones and whose buildings were the Englishman's inspirations.

John Webb (*1611–72*)

After leaving Merchant Taylor's school, London, Webb became a pupil of Inigo Jones, and later married his master's niece. He assisted Jones for many years, and as a result the work of the two men is very similar. John Webb is known to have been employed at The Vyne, Hampshire, in about 1655, when he designed the portico added to the front of the Tudor building.

PAINTERS

Samuel Cooper (*1609–72*)

Cooper enjoyed a considerable reputation in his day as an accomplished miniaturist. He

Painters, Early Stuart Period (Continued)

Charles II, a miniature painting by Samuel Cooper; dated 1661, the year in which he was crowned.
Christie's.

painted likenesses of Oliver Cromwell and his associates, but despite this was appointed Limner to Charles II. His miniatures of women do not flatter them so much as was customary at the time, and because of the surviving number of unfinished works it has been suggested that Cooper's draughtmanship was deficient except with regard to faces. His work is to be seen in many museums.

John de Critz (before 1552–1642)

The son of an Antwerp goldsmith who settled in England in about 1550, John de Critz became Serjeant Painter to James I. He was connected by marriage with Marcus Gheeraerts (1561/2–1635/6) of a family from Bruges, and with Isaac Oliver (1568–1617) from Rouen. All three of them, and the Englishman Robert Peake (died 1626), painted portraits which are more remarkable for depicting details of costume and accessories than for revealing any depth of character in the sitters. Attributions to one or the other of the artists are not always possible, but some of the surviving works bear dates and initials ensuring positive identification. Other foreign-born painters who worked in England during the period included Paul van Somer (1577?–1621/2) and Daniel Mytens (1610–?48), the latter becoming 'Picture Drawer' to Charles I in 1625. Examples of the work of all the above-named, fully documented or only attributed, are to be seen in the National Portrait Gallery, London, and in collections up and down the country.

William Dobson (1610–46)

William Dobson had a well-to-do father who spent all his money in good living, and for that reason the son took up painting to provide an income for himself. Despite the turmoil of the Civil War, Charles I continued commissioning portraits of himself and his family, whom Dobson painted in the years between 1642 and 1646, although he does not appear

Painters, Early Stuart Period (Continued)

Portrait of a young lady, said to be Lady Mary Howard, wearing a dress with a fine lace collar, painted by Marcus Gheeraerts and dated 1592. Sotheby's.

Painters, Early Stuart Period (Continued)

Charles I dressed in armour and on horseback painted by Sir Anthony van Dyck in the 1630s. The picture is on canvas and stands about 12 ft. (about 3·65 metres) in height.
National Gallery, London. (*Reproduced by courtesy of the Trustees*)

Painters, Early Stuart Period (Continued)

to have painted the King. His portrait of Charles II as Prince of Wales is in the Scottish National Portrait Gallery, Edinburgh.

Sir Anthony van Dyck (1599–1641)

Like Rubens, van Dyck lived in Antwerp, came to England and duly received a knighthood from Charles I. He was in London briefly in 1620 and finally settled there in 1632, receiving numerous marks of the Royal favour including frequent visits by the King and Queen to his studio. Van Dyck's portraits were an inspiration to other artists then and later. His great equestrian painting of Charles I, his group of the silk-clad George and Francis Villers, and the smiling *Lady and Child* (all in the National Gallery, London) show his diverse skills and bear witness to his ability in capturing animation on canvas.

Cornelius Johnson (1593–?1664)

Born of Dutch parents, Cornelius Johnson, sometimes called Cornelis Jonson, was born in England and worked there for much of his life. He painted portraits, often setting his subject in a feigned oval: the rectangular canvas painted with an oval framing sometimes in imitation of marble. He was possibly trained for his art in Holland, and his sitters sometimes appear more Dutch-looking than English. At the outbreak of the Civil War his wife's fears for their safety caused the Johnsons to depart for the safety of the Netherlands, where he later died. Examples of his work are to be seen in the National Portrait Gallery, London, and in many other cities.

Isaac Oliver (1568–1617)

Isaac Oliver was born in Rouen, the son of a Huguenot goldsmith who fled from France to escape religious persecution. He was apprenticed to Nicholas Hilliard and the similarity between much of their work has caused confusion. Oliver painted full-sized portraits, but is famed for his miniatures, some of which show the subject at full length. There is a fine collection of his work in the Victoria and Albert Museum. Isaac Oliver's son by his first wife, Peter Oliver (1594–1647), assisted his father for some years, painting portraits and making copies in miniature of Italian paintings.

Sir Peter Paul Rubens (1577–1640)

Although he cannot be considered an artist of the English School, Rubens visited the country and his work greatly influenced its painters. He came to London on a diplomatic mission in June 1629 and stayed about nine months, receiving a knighthood from Charles I just before he returned to Antwerp. He painted the King as St. George (Buckingham Palace), and is thought at the same time to have given attention to the possibility of providing decoration for the ceiling of the recently completed Banqueting House. In 1636 the paintings he had completed for the purpose were installed and remain there to-day.

SCULPTORS

Edward Marshall (1598–1675)

Marshall was Master of the Masons' Company in 1650, emphasizing the fact that there was little division between masons who carved ornament for buildings, and sculptors who

Sculptors, Early Stuart Period (Continued)

executed figures and objects in stone, marble and bronze. Edward Marshall made tombs differing little from others of his day, and examples are to be seen at St. Michael, Withington, Gloucestershire, and at St. Peter, Ightham, Kent.

Nicholas Stone (*1586–1647*)

The son of a Devonshire quarryman, Stone was apprenticed to a London mason, and in 1603 went to Holland to work with a sculptor. He returned to London in 1613, when he established a workshop at Southwark and James I duly appointed him Master-Mason at the Banqueting House. Nicholas Stone is best known for the numerous tombs he provided in churches in many parts of England, his best work showing Renaissance influence and breaking away from the earlier style of stiffly-modelled figures either kneeling or lying flat on their backs. Among his tomb sculptures are those to Francis Holles (died 1622: at Westminster Abbey), Dr. John Donne, Dean of St. Paul's and poet (died 1631: at St. Paul's Cathedral), and Sir Thomas Bodley (died 1613: at Merton College Chapel, Oxford). Stone's three sons, Henry (1616–53), Nicholas (1618–47) and John (1620–67) were also sculptors.

Hubert le Sueur (*active 1610–43*)

Born in France, le Sueur came to England in 1625 and was employed by Charles I. He made a bronze bust of the monarch (Stourhead, Wiltshire) and the equestrian figure of him

Trafalgar Square, London, showing the National Gallery in the background, le Sueur's equestrian statue of Charles I at right of centre and the portico and spire of St. Martin's-in-the-Fields to the right of the statue, an oil-painting by James Pollard probably executed in about 1838. Christie's

Sculptors, Early Stuart Period (Continued)

at Charing Cross, London. This last was cast in 1633, but had not been erected before the start of the Civil War. It was sold for scrap to a brazier, who concealed it until about 1678 when it was at last placed on view. Le Sueur was among the first to make portrait busts suitable for display in houses, and he carved in marble instead of stone or alabaster which had usually been employed. His work was much praised in his lifetime, an English writer calling him 'the most industrious and excellent statuary in all materials, that ever this country enjoyed'. Later opinions of his merits are less fulsome, although it is agreed that he was responsible for the introduction to England of fresh forms and techniques.

LATE STUART PERIOD: 1660-1714

ON 8 May 1660 Charles II was proclaimed King, and on the 25th of the month he returned to his native land from an exile that had lasted nearly a dozen years. During that time he had stayed in France and Holland and in 1662 married the Portuguese, Catherine of Braganza, so that the artistic insularity of the Commonwealth was replaced by tastes acquired across the Channel. In addition, the long period of stagnation in many spheres of daily activity was quickly countered by a thirst for luxury, and extravagance obliterated the miseries of recent years.

There was a wave of house-building, in some instances with the formal exteriors introduced by Inigo Jones modified by Dutch influences. These included facing a principal frontage with a row of tall pillars supporting a triangular pediment placed at roof height; this and other details often subsequently being termed 'Queen Anne', although they had been introduced into England much earlier.

From the end of the century there survive a number of buildings by William Talman, who favoured French models of the time. The results show a massiveness typical of the Louis XIV or baroque style. The severe outline of a building was sometimes embellished with carved garlands and bouquets of flowers and fruit in relief. These, together with balanced curves, cupids and leaves, appear frequently on furniture as well as on other suitable surfaces.

The most esteemed architect of the period was Sir Christopher Wren, whose reputation in his lifetime remains amply justified by his many buildings still standing. Of them all, St. Paul's Cathedral, built between 1675 and 1710, is his greatest achievement, and the numerous churches erected in the City following the Great Fire of 1666 testify to his inventiveness. The calamity of the fire, which laid waste an area of over 400 acres and more than 13,000 dwellings, drew attention to the dangers of wood-framed houses ranged along narrow streets. The city was rebuilt with wider thoroughfares and the use of inflammable materials kept to a minimum. Nicholas Hawksmoor served as Wren's assistant, worked at some projects on his own account and then assisted the playwright and architect, Sir John Vanbrugh.

All of these men held one or more offices under the Crown; a lucrative distinction for which there was keen competition. Such positions gave the holder not only an assured

Decorative Styles, Late Stuart Period (Continued)

income, albeit sometimes only a small one, but the opportunity to exchange ideas with fellow-professionals, meet influential persons, and obtain worthwhile contracts. Throughout the eighteenth century almost every noteworthy architect was indebted to his post in the Office of Works for his important commissions.

From the 1680s fashionable new buildings had sash windows in place of the earlier casement type. At first these were made to slide from side to side, but later versions opened and closed vertically. Most older houses have been brought up-to-date in this respect at one time or another, so that very few of them now retain their original casements.

Interior decoration of large mansions often incorporated elaborate wood carvings with which the name of Grinling Gibbons is invariably associated, although he was not the sole producer of them. Another feature was the use of painting in place of panelling and plaster-work, staircase walls and the ceilings of principal rooms being favoured for such treatment. Among the executants were the Italian, Antonio Verrio, the Frenchman, Louis Laguerre, and the Englishman, Sir James Thornhill.

Smaller buildings also had their share of rich ornamentation, as can still be seen at Ham House, near Richmond on Thames, which was decorated and furnished between 1637 and

The North Drawing Room, Ham House, Surrey, of which the plaster-work was executed in about 1637. The chair with arms carved as dolphins is one of a set of twelve covered in their original brocade (c. *1675) and the ebony table in the centre has silver mounts* (c. *1670*). Victoria and Albert Museum.

Decorative Styles, Late Stuart Period (Continued)

1675. Much of the remaining contents can be identified from inventories that were taken in 1679 and 1683. While time has faded the fabrics and mellowed the woodwork, the original sumptuous effect requires little imagination for its re-creation.

The published engravings of Daniel Marot, who worked in France and Holland before coming to England, had a considerable influence on the design of furniture. In addition, the Orient began to play an increasing part. Imported articles were eagerly bought as soon as they reached the country, and home-made imitations quickly came on the market. The French mirror-lined *Galerie des Glaces*, at Versailles, was admired and emulated. More than one room in London, admittedly on a much smaller scale than the *Galerie*, was lined with looking-glass and commented on at the time.

The period saw foreign travel becoming gradually more common, and the Grand Tour of foreign lands was a normal termination to a gentleman's education. The travellers invariably purchased paintings and other works of art that were brought back to England to enhance their homes, giving visible proof of the breadth of the owners' interests not only to their contemporaries but to later generations. The paintings frequently showed real or imaginary scenery, and during this period there came to the fore a school of English landscape artists. The Dutch-born Jan Wyck was among the first to produce such works, and his pupil John Wootton started a long-lived vogue for pictures of sporting subjects.

ARCHITECTS

Nicholas Hawksmoor (*1661–1736*)

When only about eighteen years of age, Hawksmoor's architectural abilities came to the notice of Sir Christopher Wren, who gave him employment. He assisted in designing St. Paul's Cathedral and many others of Wren's buildings, and in 1689 Wren, who held the post of Surveyor-General, was able to recommend Hawksmoor to that of Clerk of the Works at Kensington Palace and later to the same office at Greenwich Hospital. Early in the 1700s Hawksmoor became associated with Vanbrugh and remained his assistant until the death of the latter in 1726. Nicholas Hawksmoor designed a number of buildings in various parts of the country, and it has been suggested that he may have played a greater part in the work attributed to his more famous masters than was acknowledged. He was said in his lifetime to have been very modest about his achievements, a fellow-architect remarking of him that 'he never talked with a more reasonable man, nor one so little prejudiced in favour of his own performances'.

Daniel Marot (*1663?–1752*)

Born in Paris, Daniel Marot had begun studying art when he had to leave France on account of his Protestant beliefs. Arriving at The Hague, he became architect and designer to the Stadtholder, William of Orange, and when the latter became King of England in 1689 Marot duly followed him to London. There, he is known to have designed some of the gardens at Hampton Court, where it is probable that he worked on the interior of the palace before returning to The Hague in 1698. His published designs include a variety of pieces of furniture as well as suggestions for the interiors of rooms; all of them characterized

Architects, Late Stuart Period (Continued)

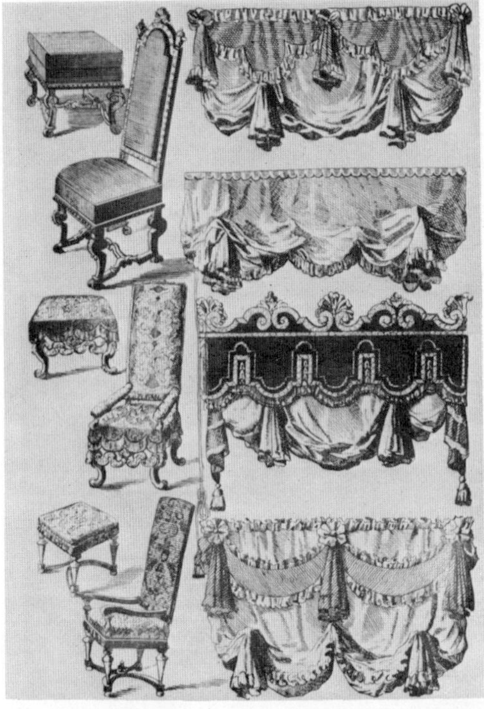

Engraving of designs for chairs, stools and curtain valances by Daniel Marot published in about 1700.

by florid ornament and extravagant upholstery and hangings, but surviving examples in his manner testify to the fact that the designs were practical.

Hugh May (1622–84)

He was born near Chichester, Sussex, and his early life is obscure beyond the knowledge that Pepys recorded May as being in the service of the Duke of Buckingham from about 1650. Following the accession of Charles II, he was in charge of finances connected with restoring the Royal palaces, and in 1673 became responsible for the reconstruction of Windsor Castle. His work there, and almost all his work elsewhere, has been destroyed, and none of his plans has been preserved. It was to May that Grinling Gibbons owed his first important commission. Hugh May's portrait was painted by Lely, and in his Will the architect included among his bequests the sum of £100 to Chichester Cathedral.

William Talman (1650–1719)

Talman is known to have been born in Wiltshire, but there is no record of his early years or where he may have been trained. In 1689 he was appointed Comptroller of the King's Works. His surviving buildings include Dyrham Park, Gloucestershire (National Trust), and parts of Chatsworth, Derbyshire (Duke of Devonshire), both of which show French influence in their design. William Talman would seem to have been a quarrelsome man, disagreeing with his fellow-architects as well as with some of his clients.

Architects, Late Stuart Period (Continued)

Sir John Vanbrugh (*1644–1726*)

The grandson of a Ghent merchant who fled to England to avoid religious persecution, John Vanbrugh was one of nineteen children, and little more is known about him until he received a commission in the army in 1686. He then turned to playwriting, his *The Relapse, or Virtue in Danger* and *The Provok'd Wife* being highly successful at the time and subsequently, their combination of wit and immorality earning them applause or abuse according to the outlook of the audience. Soon after 1696, when the second of his best-known plays had been produced in London, Vanbrugh had taken up a further career causing Jonathan Swift to write a few years later:

Van's genius, without thought or lecture,
Is hugely turned to architecture.

In 1702 he became Comptroller of the Royal Works, following in Talman's footsteps, and in 1705 the playwright was chosen to design Blenheim Palace, Oxfordshire, the nation's gift to the Duke of Marlborough, vanquisher of the armies of Louis XIV. The erection of the mansion commenced in 1705, but when the Duchess fell out of favour with Queen Anne, payments from the Treasury grew less and then ceased altogether. With the accession of George I work began again, but in 1716 Vanburgh was accused of mismanagement and his direction of the great project ceased. His other work on a comparable scale was Castle Howard, Yorkshire, which was erected between 1699 and 1726, and he designed and altered buildings in various parts of the country

The front of Blenheim Palace, Oxfordshire, designed by Sir John Vanbrugh and built between 1705 and 1720. It was a gift from the nation to the first Duke of Marlborough and bears the name of his most famous victory.

Sir Christopher Wren (*1632–1723*)

Wren was the son of the Rector of Knoyle, Wiltshire, later Dean of Windsor, and went to Westminster School, London. In due course he went up to Oxford, where he stayed studying science after taking his degree, before being appointed Professor of Astronomy at Gresham College, London. It was in his rooms at Gresham College that the foremost

Architects, Late Stuart Period (Continued)

The river Thames from Somerset House showing St. Paul's Cathedral and the spires of Wren's City churches on the skyline, painted by the visiting Italian artist, Antonio Canale, known as Canaletto, who came to England on more than one occasion between about 1746 and 1756.
Christie's

scientists of the day met to form the nucleus of what later became the Royal Society. In 1661 Charles II offered him the appointment of Surveyor-General of the Royal Works as well as another post, but both were declined despite the fact that Wren had already begun to take an interest in architecture. However, after designing some buildings at Oxford (including the Sheldonian Theatre) and acting as one of the three men appointed to survey and report upon the restoration of London following the Great Fire, Wren became Surveyor-General. He was responsible for the rebuilding of the fifty-two City churches that had been destroyed, and from 1675 was occupied for the ensuing thirty-five years in the erection of St. Paul's Cathedral. He was responsible also for many other buildings, including the basic design for the original William and Mary College, at Williamsburg, Virginia, built in 1695. Appropriately his epitaph is carved over a doorway in St. Paul's: *Si monumentum requiris, circumspice* (If you seek a monument, look about you).

PAINTERS

Francis Barlow (*1626?–1704*)

Little definite is known about Barlow's early years and even the place and date of his birth are uncertain. Apparently he achieved fame early in his career, for when the artist was aged about thirty, John Evelyn referred to him as 'the famous painter of Fowle, Beasts & Birds'. His compositions of those subjects, painted in oils, are rare and include one of *An Owl mocked by small Birds*, painted in about 1673, at Ham House, Surrey. Best known are his etchings made to illustrate *Aesop's Fables*, first published in 1666, for which most of his original drawings are in the British Museum.

Painters, Late Stuart Period (Continued)

Sir Godfrey Kneller (1646?–1723)

Kneller came to England from his birthplace, Lübeck, north Germany, after working in the Netherlands and Italy, arriving in London in 1674. He became the foremost portrait painter in the country, leaving for future generations likenesses of many of the notabilities of his day. Of his output, two series are remarkable: the *Hampton Court Beauties* (Hampton Court) and the *Kit Kat Portraits* (National Portrait Gallery). The former depict the ladies of the Court of Charles II, while the latter portray members of a literary and political club that included in its numbers many of the prominent men of the years about 1700. Kneller's paintings show their subjects with lifelike expressions, his best work revealing much of their character.

Portrait of Diana Kirke, Countess of Oxford by Sir Peter Lely; a good example of the artist's treatment of the beauties of his day.
Christie's.

Painters, Late Stuart Period (Continued)

Louis Laguerre (*1663–1721*)

Louis Laguerre came to London from his birthplace, Paris, in about 1683, where he began to work for Antonio Verrio. Between 1689 and 1694 the two men painted the ceilings of a number of the principal apartments at Chatsworth. His most important work was in the Saloon at Blenheim Palace, where he painted the ceiling and walls, the latter decorated with simulated columns flanking groups of figures seen against cloudy skies. The persons portrayed include the Duke of Marlborough's Chaplain and the artist himself.

Sir Peter Lely (*1618–80*)

Lely was born at Soest of Dutch parents, and after training as a painter at Haarlem came to London. The date of his arrival is not known, but it is assumed to have been either 1641 or 1643, and in due course he channelled his talents principally into portraiture. He pre-dated Kneller as the leading recorder of likenesses of the men and women of England, and his industry was such that his sitters had to make appointments well in advance. With the working day beginning at 7 a.m. Lely had a highly organized studio with numerous assistants, and it has been pointed out that he is the first painter in England of whom a large amount of work survives: 'for it would not be difficult to make a catalogue of four or five hundred pictures more or less painted by Lely himself . . .'. Like Kneller, he is well represented by two series of portraits: *The Windsor Beauties* (Hampton Court), and *The Admirals* (National Maritime Museum). While in many instances he probably flattered the looks of his sitters, this was not invariably required of him, Oliver Cromwell having been reported as requesting:

> Mr. Lely, I desire you would use all your skill to paint my picture truly like me, and not flatter me at all; but remark all these roughnesses, pimples, warts, and everything as you see me, otherwise I will never pay a farthing for it.

Sir James Thornhill (*1675?–1734*)

A Dorset man, Thornhill was apprenticed to a distant relative, a painter of no great distinction, but by 1706 he was working at Chatsworth and following in the footsteps of Verrio and Laguerre. In the year following he began his greatest work, the decoration of the Painted Hall at Greenwich Hospital, in which he imaginatively mingled allegory and realism. The work was not completed until 1727, and as visitors obviously found the scene confusing, Thornhill wrote for them *An Explanation of the Painting in the Royal Hospital at Greenwich*. At the time same as he was employed at the Hospital, he was busily engaged in decorating rooms at Hampton Court, Blenheim Palace and elsewhere. From 1714 to 1721 he painted the cupola, lantern and Whispering Gallery of St. Paul's Cathedral where, as at other places, he had help from assistants. He was appointed History Painter in Ordinary to George I, and in 1720 became the first British artist to receive the honour of knighthood.

Antonio Verrio (*1639?–1707*)

The Italian, Verrio, was apparently working in England by 1671, and employed by the Crown from 1676. He was a Catholic and refused at first to work for William III, who came to the throne in 1689, but from 1690 to 1698 was busy at Chatsworth and Burghley. At the former he painted the Great Staircase, the State Dining Room, the ceiling of the present Library and provided an altarpiece for the Chapel. Later, he worked at Hampton Court,

Painters, Late Stuart Period (Continued)

where his output included the Great Staircase. Verrio has been censured on the ground that his draughtmanship failed to rise to the power of his imagination. It was also written of him that 'his exuberant pencil was ready at pouring out gods, goddesses, kings, emperors and triumphs, over those public surfaces on which the eye never rests long enough to criticize, and where one should be sorry to place the works of a better master . . .'.

John Wootton (1686?–1756)

This artist's career spans the period under consideration as well as that which follows. He specialized in paintings of horses, with and without an accompanying hound or two, and produced many pictures of the famous racehorses of his day. In addition to paintings in which the animal almost fills the canvas, he produced landscapes in which humans and animals are less dominant. His work may be seen in public galleries and in houses; the entrance halls at Longleat, Althrop and Badminton contain fine examples of his equestrian studies.

SCULPTORS

John Bushnell (died 1701)

John Bushnell was apprenticed to a sculptor named Burman, but because of his involvement in an intrigue fled overseas before he had served his full term of seven years. After some twenty years he came back to England, rather full of self-importance as a result of his success in Italy, and was soon busily engaged carving statues of the King and Queen and others. In Westminster Abbey is Bushnell's monument to the poet, Abraham Cowley, and in the church at Ashburnham, Sussex, is what has been described as his most dramatic work: 'the great baroque group of William Ashburnham and his wife . . . with its kneeling figure of the husband, his hands outstretched in agonized entreaty towards the dying woman, whom cherubs beckon to the skies'.

Caius Gabriel Cibber (1630–1700)

He was the son of a cabinet-maker employed at the Danish Court, and travelled in Italy and the Netherlands before coming to England in the late 1650s. After some years he was appointed Sculptor in Ordinary to William III, by whom twelve months earlier he had been paid £100 for executing over the windows on the south front of Hampton Court 'two great coats of arms with two boys to each, bigger than the life'. One of his most highly praised works is the monument to Thomas Sackville (who died in 1767) at Withyam, Sussex, in which 'the look of frozen sorrow on the father's face makes this group one of the most moving in England'. It cost £300 and was to be subject to the approval of 'Mr. Peter Lilly [Lely] his Maty's painter. . .'. Cibber carved the relief at the base of the Monument, designed by Wren to commemorate the Great Fire of London and sited close to where the blaze began.

Grinling Gibbons (1648–1720)

Gibbons was born at Rotterdam of English parents and came to England in about 1670. John Evelyn recorded in his diary how he found the young man living alone at Deptford,

Sculptors, Late Stuart Period (Continued)

Marble figure of a boy playing bagpipes carved by Caius Gabriel Cibber, who was born in Germany and was in the Netherlands and Italy before settling in England probably in the 1650s. The figure dates from c. *1680.*
Victoria and Albert Museum.

close to the diarist's home, carving a Crucifixion in wood. This occurred in January 1671, and in March of the same year Evelyn took the lad with the completed carving to Whitehall, so that the King should see it. Charles II inspected it and requested it should be shown to the Queen, but she was preoccupied in buying trifles from 'a French peddling woman' and the latter, thinking her own business might suffer, diverted the Queen's attention from Gibbons's work and he left unrewarded. He later sold the carving, and Evelyn was able to persuade Sir Christopher Wren to employ him and mention to the King that he might find work for him in Hugh May's restoration of Windsor Castle. Although the fame of Grinling Gibbons rests on his brilliance as a wood-carver, and this was his own favourite medium, he also carved in stone and marble. He executed a number of monuments (that of Robert Cotton in the church at Conington, Cambridgeshire, is signed), and carried out work at Blenheim Palace as well as supplying chimney-pieces for Dalkeith Palace, Midlothian. Carvings in wood attributed to Gibbons are far more in number than any one man could have executed in a lifetime, but those at Petworth House, Sussex, are fully documented. The oak-panelled room has portraits inset in the walls, each painting being framed with skilfully carved groups of cherubs, baskets of flowers, birds, fishes, and much more. His work is so fine that it was said of some flowers he carved over a doorway in Ludgate Hill, London, 'that the coaches passing made them shake surprisingly'.

Late Elizabethan Room, c. *1600. The plain oak panelling of the walls contrasts with the elaborate chimney-piece. The furniture, all made of oak, includes armchairs, chests, stools and a cradle. Standing on the rush-strewn floor is a salt-glazed stoneware jar. (Geffrye Museum, London. Photo: Cooper-Bridgeman Library)*

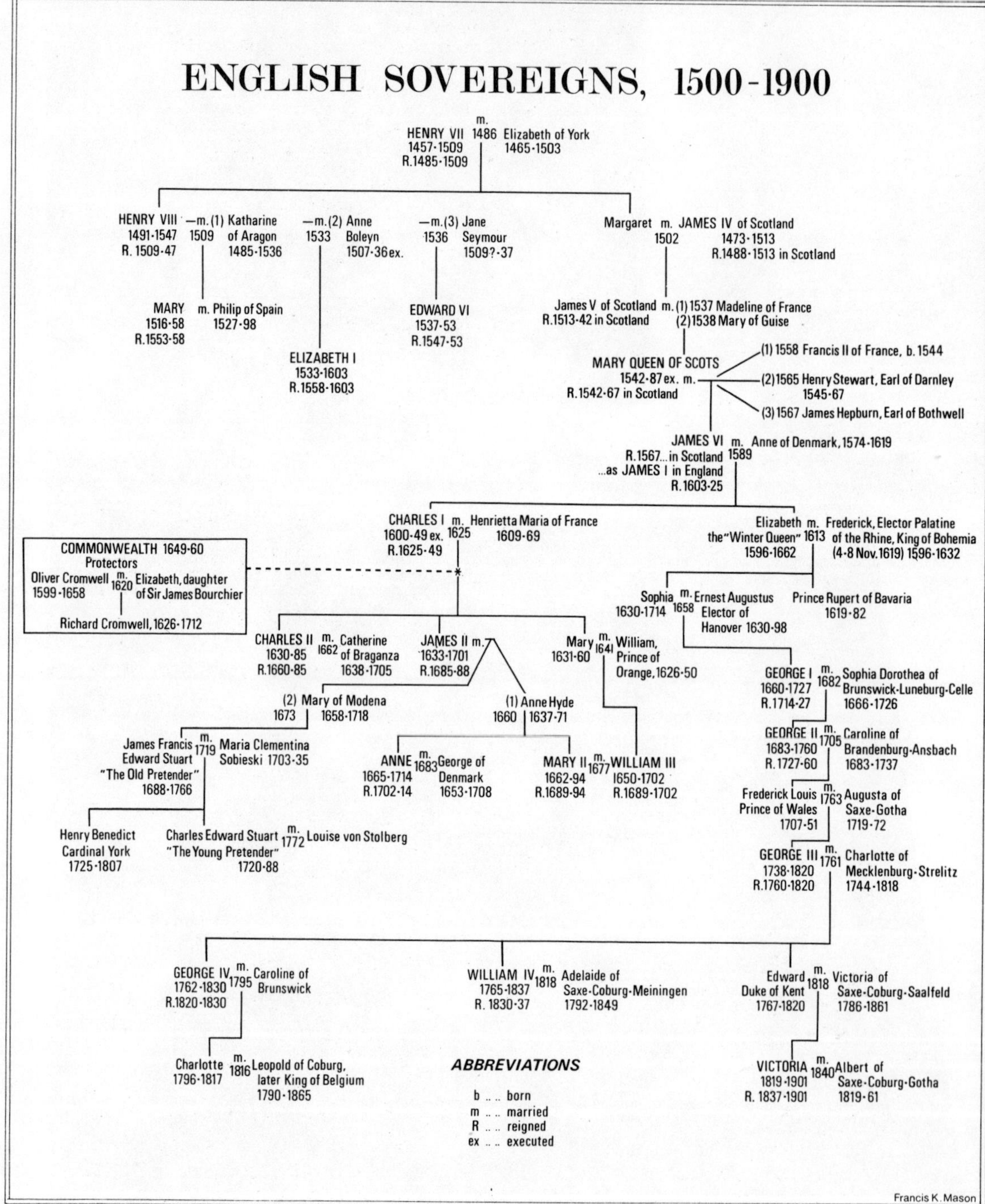
ENGLISH SOVEREIGNS, 1500-1900
HENRY VII m. 1486 Elizabeth of York
1457-1509 R.1485-1509
1465-1503
HENRY VIII 1491-1547 R. 1509-47
—m.(1) 1509 Katharine of Aragon 1485-1536
—m.(2) 1533 Anne Boleyn 1507-36 ex.
—m.(3) 1536 Jane Seymour 1509?-37
Margaret m. 1502 JAMES IV of Scotland 1473-1513 R.1488-1513 in Scotland
MARY 1516-58 R.1553-58 m. Philip of Spain 1527-98
EDWARD VI 1537-53 R.1547-53
ELIZABETH I 1533-1603 R.1558-1603
James V of Scotland R.1513-42 in Scotland m. (1) 1537 Madeline of France (2) 1538 Mary of Guise
MARY QUEEN OF SCOTS 1542-87 ex. R.1542-67 in Scotland m.
(1) 1558 Francis II of France, b. 1544
(2) 1565 Henry Stewart, Earl of Darnley 1545-67
(3) 1567 James Hepburn, Earl of Bothwell
JAMES VI R.1567... in Scotland ...as JAMES I in England R.1603-25 m. 1589 Anne of Denmark, 1574-1619
CHARLES I 1600-49 ex. R.1625-49 m. 1625 Henrietta Maria of France 1609-69
Elizabeth the "Winter Queen" 1596-1662 m. 1613 Frederick, Elector Palatine of the Rhine, King of Bohemia (4-8 Nov.1619) 1596-1632
COMMONWEALTH 1649-60
Protectors
Oliver Cromwell 1599-1658 m. 1620 Elizabeth, daughter of Sir James Bourchier
Richard Cromwell, 1626-1712
Sophia 1630-1714 m. 1658 Ernest Augustus Elector of Hanover 1630-98
Prince Rupert of Bavaria 1619-82
CHARLES II 1630-85 R.1660-85 m. 1662 Catherine of Braganza 1638-1705
JAMES II 1633-1701 R.1685-88 m.
Mary 1631-60 m. 1641 William, Prince of Orange, 1626-50
GEORGE I 1660-1727 R.1714-27 m. 1682 Sophia Dorothea of Brunswick-Luneburg-Celle 1666-1726
(2) 1673 Mary of Modena 1658-1718
(1) 1660 Anne Hyde 1637-71
GEORGE II 1683-1760 R. 1727-60 m. 1705 Caroline of Brandenburg-Ansbach 1683-1737
James Francis Edward Stuart "The Old Pretender" 1688-1766 m. 1719 Maria Clementina Sobieski 1703-35
ANNE 1665-1714 R.1702-14 m. 1683 George of Denmark 1653-1708
MARY II 1662-94 R.1689-94 m. 1677 WILLIAM III 1650-1702 R.1689-1702
Frederick Louis Prince of Wales 1707-51 m. 1763 Augusta of Saxe-Gotha 1719-72
Henry Benedict Cardinal York 1725-1807
Charles Edward Stuart "The Young Pretender" 1720-88 m. 1772 Louise von Stolberg
GEORGE III 1738-1820 R.1760-1820 m. 1761 Charlotte of Mecklenburg-Strelitz 1744-1818
GEORGE IV 1762-1830 R.1820-1830 m. 1795 Caroline of Brunswick
WILLIAM IV 1765-1837 R. 1830-37 m. 1818 Adelaide of Saxe-Coburg-Meiningen 1792-1849
Edward Duke of Kent 1767-1820 m. 1818 Victoria of Saxe-Coburg-Saalfeld 1786-1861
Charlotte 1796-1817 m. 1816 Leopold of Coburg, later King of Belgium 1790-1865
ABBREVIATIONS
b ... born
m ... married
R ... reigned
ex ... executed
VICTORIA 1819-1901 R. 1837-1901 m. 1840 Albert of Saxe-Coburg-Gotha 1819-61
Francis K. Mason

Sculptors, Late Stuart Period (Continued)

John van Nost (*died 1729*)

John van Nost came to England from the Netherlands and was employed in London as foreman by Arnold Quellin, son of a well-known Antwerp sculptor, Artus Quellin. Arnold Quellin died when he was only twenty-three and van Nost married his widow. Van Nost carved figures and so forth in stone and marble, and also executed work in lead; much of his work in the latter medium remaining at Melbourne Hall, Derbyshire, for which it was supplied from 1699 onwards. John van Nost worked at Hampton Court and many other important mansions but much of his output has been destroyed over the years. After his death his wife advertised the sale of his remaining works, adding that Mrs. Nost 'designing to go beyond the seas, will dispose of them at reasonable rates at her house near Hyde Park where attendance will be daily given'.

EARLY GEORGIAN PERIOD: 1715-1750

WHEN Queen Anne died in 1714 she left no living children, so the crown went to George, Elector of Hanover, grandson of James I.

George I was a German by both birth and residence, whose command of the English tongue was ridiculed and one of whose most memorable utterances was to state that he hated 'all Boets and Bainters'. Nevertheless, the arts flourished no less during his reign than they had under more encouraging monarchs.

The outstanding architectural influence of the period was that of Richard Boyle, Earl of Burlington, who was responsible for encouraging acceptance of the strictly classical designs of Palladio. This he advocated not only as regards the proportions of the buildings and their components, as had been done earlier by Inigo Jones, but he went so far as to have reproduced on English soil close copies of the Italian's work. Lord Burlington more or less standardized the country mansion with its central principal block flanked by wings for subsidiary rooms; an arrangement arousing much comment because it invariably meant that the kitchen was far away from the eating room, with exhausted servants carrying chilled food to the patient diners.

Lord Burlington's protégé was William Kent, whose name is linked closely with that of his patron, and whose talents extended so far as to design furniture for the rooms he created. Other men who interpreted Palladio included Colin Campbell, and two who are remembered more for the books of designs they published than for their buildings: Isaac Ware and Robert Morris. Less affected by the prevailing style were James Gibbs and Nicholas Hawksmoor.

Houses in cities and towns showed few signs of Palladianism. Space was limited, regulations were strict as a result of fire and plague, and the majority of urban houses were small and functional with only a minimum of external ornament to reveal the individuality of their designer. In many places rows of houses were built to appear as a single unit; the separate homes linked externally by an overall façade. Some of the London squares were successfully executed in this manner, each side looking as if occupied by a single imposing building, and at Bath a similar style was adopted when it was laid out by John Wood from

Decorative Styles, Early Georgian Period (Continued)

View of Bloomsbury Square, London, an engraving published in 1787. The Duke of Bedford's house is in the middle background, it was demolished in the 1800s. The rows of houses seen at each side of the picture were built in 1662, but Henry Flitcroft and other architects replaced some of them at later dates.

the late 1720s onwards. In Scotland, William Adam earned praise as a 'strictly classical architect'.

Large sums were spent on interior decoration, with gilded furniture and silk fabrics creating a sumptuous impression. In the great mansions, reception rooms were arranged to open one into another for special occasions, and these, with a gallery for sculpture in part replacing the Elizabethan long gallery, served for the display of paintings together with other esteemed possessions. Painted walls and ceilings grew less popular and were largely replaced by moulded plaster, which was frequently the work of Italian craftsmen.

Following the success of the three immigrant sculptors, Roubiliac, Rysbrack and Scheemakers, sculpture became less confined to church or outdoor monuments. Bust portraits were in demand and were not confined to the living, but might be of past celebrities for the decoration of a gentleman's library or a public room. Ancient Roman statuary was imported, together with copies for those who could not afford, or were unable to obtain, original examples.

The most notable English painter of the period was William Hogarth. He was far above contemporary rivals, his fellow-artists including Thomas Hudson, Philip Mercier and Allan Ramsay. Among other achievements, Hogarth was instrumental in popularizing the 'Conversation' picture: a small-sized portrayal of persons in their normal surroundings probably introduced by Mercier.

Decorative Styles, Early Georgian Period (Continued)

Chinese porcelain reached the West in a flood, stimulating efforts by all nations to find a substitute or something better. The Germans succeeded in 1710 at Meissen, near Dresden, and by 1745 the Chelsea factory on the fringe of London had been started.

There were people in England who disputed the right of George I to the throne, in favour of the son of James I, Prince James Francis Edward Stuart, known as 'The Old Pretender'. The Pretender and his son, 'The Young Pretender', had followers united in religion as well as politics. The movement had an artistic offshoot in the form of commemorative drinking glasses, of which the surviving numbers perhaps give an impression that those supporting the cause of the two Princes were more numerous and influential than was really the case.

ARCHITECTS

William Adam (*1689–1748*)

William Adam has been described as 'the first strictly classical architect that Scotland produced', and his surviving work shows that there is truth in the words. He designed a number of mansions including Hopetoun House, situated outside Edinburgh, where he enlarged the earlier building. The central block was extended and the wings added, so that the east façade is entirely his work. He did not live to complete the task, which was finished by two of his sons, Robert and John Adam. William Adam held the post of Master Mason in North Britain to the Board of Ordnance, and was responsible for the chain of forts in the Highlands built following the 1745 Rebellion. Some of his designs for buildings were engraved and appeared in parts between 1720 and 1740, and in a single volume in 1810 under the title of *Vitruvius Scoticus*: named after the Roman architect and engineer, Vitruvius, who wrote a celebrated work on architecture.

Richard Boyle, *Earl of Burlington* (*1694–1753*)

Richard Boyle succeeded to the title and estates of his father when he was ten years of age, and in 1714 set out for Italy. He returned there a few years later in order to make a close study of Palladio's buildings, and came back to England accompanied by William Kent. Before long, Lord Burlington was successfully adapting the work of Palladio, and in some instances erected close copies of the Italian originals (Chiswick House, London; Assembly Rooms, York). It has not always proved possible to decide whether Burlington or Kent was responsible for certain buildings, as they co-operated very closely. Lord Burlington admired the work of Inigo Jones and assisted William Kent in publishing a volume of Jones's designs, and he himself published a book of the designs of Andrea Palladio.

Colin Campbell (*died 1729*)

A Scot by birth, nothing appears to be known of his early years. In about 1719 he was employed by Lord Burlington to remodel Burlington House, Piccadilly, in the Palladian style. Campbell had shown his grasp of this in his recently-published book of designs, *Vitruvius Britannicus*, which had almost certainly instigated Burlington's lifelong interest in the Italian architect. Colin Campbell designed a number of mansions, including Stourhead,

Architects, Early Georgian Period (Continued)

Wiltshire, but only the present central block was his and this was burned down in 1902 to be rebuilt more or less to the original design. The wings were added to the house in 1793.

James Gibbs (1682–1754)

Also from Scotland, James Gibbs toured the mainland of Europe and decided to take up the profession of architect. His first public building was the church of St. Mary-le-Strand, London, built between 1714 and 1717, and soon afterwards his design for St. Martin in the Fields, Trafalgar Square, was accepted. He built other churches in London and the provinces, as well as houses which have mostly been demolished. Between 1737 and 1749 James Gibbs built the Radcliffe Camera, Oxford, to which he bequeathed his books, prints and drawings. Much of Gibbs's earlier work is in an Italianate baroque style, but later in his career he designed simpler buildings conforming more to the prevailing English Palladian.

William Kent (1685?–1748)

Kent was born at Bridlington, Yorkshire, and apparently had his talents recognized by some local gentry who paid for him to study in Italy. He learned painting there, and in that rôle returned to England with the Earl of Burlington who obtained for him a commission to paint some mural decorations in Kensington Palace. In about 1730 Kent turned to architecture, and in his position as Master Carpenter in the Office of Works, secured for him by his patron, he was able to bring the influence of Palladio into the design of public buildings. Painting was not forgotten and in 1739 George II appointed Kent Portrait Painter to the King, and to add yet a further accomplishment he became an influential designer of gardens. Later in the century Horace Walpole summed up William Kent's career as follows:

> He was a painter, an architect, and the father of modern gardening. In the first character he was below mediocrity; in the second, he was a restorer of the science; in the last, an original, and the inventor of an art that realizes painting, and improves nature.

It was he who assisted, and often outshone, Lord Burlington in adapting Palladio to English soil. Kent built a number of mansions, but is equally remembered for his designs for interiors and their furniture (Houghton Hall and Holkham Hall, Norfolk). He also designed silverware, and the Royal State Barge, built in 1732 for Frederick, Prince of Wales (National Maritime Museum).

Robert Morris

Morris is often confused with his kinsman who had the same initials, Roger Morris (1695–1749). The latter was on friendly terms with the Duke of Argyll and the Earl of Pembroke, and for the last named he supervised the Palladian Bridge at Wilton, which the Earl designed and had erected in 1736–7. Roger Morris designed a number of other buildings in various parts of the country. On the other hand, Robert Morris is known almost exclusively for a number of books on architecture he published between 1728 and 1759. His *Select Architecture* (1755) circulated as far afield as America, where it inspired the design of Monticello, near Charlottesville, Virginia, home of the President of the country, Thomas

Architects, Early Georgian Period (Continued)

Chiswick House, Lord Burlington's imitation of Andrea Palladio's Villa Capra, or Rotonda, at Vicenza, about 40 miles west of Venice. The latter house was built in the 1560s, and the English one in the 1720s with its furniture and interior decoration designed by William Kent. The engraved view was published in 1827. Mansell Collection.

Jefferson. In about 1730 Robert Morris established a Society for the improvement of knowledge in Arts and Sciences. The dates of his birth and death are apparently unrecorded, but he is said to have lived in Twickenham.

Isaac Ware (*died 1766*)

Ware is stated to have had a romantic life story. He was apparently a chimney sweeper's lad who was found making a sketch of the Banqueting House, Whitehall, and as a result was given a good education, sent to Italy, and returned as a polished architect. The fairy godfather who found him in Whitehall is said to have been Lord Burlington, who certainly gave him patronage. Such houses as Ware designed have now vanished and he is remembered by the books on architecture bearing his name.

PAINTERS

William Hogarth (*1697–1764*)

Born in London and the son of a schoolmaster, Hogarth began his artistic career as apprentice to a silversmith for the purpose of learning to engrave coats of arms and ornament. In the early 1720s he began to engrave book illustrations, and painted portrait-

Painters, Early Georgian Period (Continued)

groups on a small scale in the manner of Philip Mercier. He was responsible for a number of series of paintings, of which *The Harlot's Progress* was the first, followed by *The Rake's Progress* (Sir John Soane's Museum) and *Marriage à la Mode* (National Gallery). These were issued also as engravings, both at the time and later, and popularized the work of a man whose power of invention in composing a story suitable for illustration was equalled by his skill with the brush. Hogarth painted a number of portraits (*The Shrimp Girl*, National Gallery: *The Graham Children*, Tate Gallery) with success, but his attempts at what was known at the time as 'History Painting', historical subjects treated in a grandiose manner, did nothing to enhance his reputation. Most of his portraits are of friends, and he did not have, or perhaps never sought, sitters among contemporary notabilities. He produced a number of attractive paintings of theatre scenes. William Hogarth was a combative man, one of his longest-lasting quarrels being conducted with picture-dealers; those who imported Old Masters, more often than not third-rate works by fourth-rate artists which he referred to as 'shiploads of dead Christs, Holy Families and Madonnas', rather than sell the work of talented moderns. He was responsible for establishing in 1735 the St. Martin's Lane Academy, in St. Martin's Lane, London, where young artists were taught to draw and where new ideas and styles spread among them. Hogarth married the daughter of Sir James Thornhill, and died childless. His grave is in Chiswick churchyard with an epitaph by

Conversation picture by William Hogarth, showing a family taking tea and playing a game in a room of the time, c. *1740*. Christie's.

Painters, Early Georgian Period (Continued)

Garrick on the tomb, not far from the small red-brick house in which he spent summers away from his Leicester Square home.

Thomas Hudson (*1701–79*)

Hudson came from Devonshire to London, where he acquired a reputation as a portrait painter of fashionable ladies and gentlemen. It has been said of him that 'he drew the face well, and his unaffected representations pleased the gentry of his time, but he had little ability to paint more than the face, the rest was left to the drapery man'. This alludes to the practice, not uncommon throughout the history of portraiture, of an esteemed artist concentrating his skill on his sitter's likeness and leaving the clothing and background to an assistant. Hudson's paintings can be described as competent but normally uninspired, and his principal claim to notice is that the young Joshua Reynolds was his pupil from 1741 to 1743.

Philip Mercier (*1689–1760*)

The son of French refugee parents, Mercier was born in Berlin, and in due course went to Hanover. By about 1725 he was working in England, and painted what are considered to be the forerunners of 'Conversation' pictures. A few years later, Frederick, Prince of Wales, son of George II, who had known Mercier in Hanover, appointed him Painter to the Prince of Wales, and followed this with further honours. His portrait of the Prince is in the National Portrait Gallery, together with a group entitled *Frederick and his Sisters at Concert*: the latter possibly being intended as a punning satire in view of the strained relations between them. In due course, Mercier quarrelled with his Royal patron, and took to painting what are called 'Fancy' pictures, designed to provide innocent pleasure and without any moral or satire in them. Nine of them were engraved in 1739, and possibly they were produced with this end in view, making good use of the engraver's skill and benefiting from the market for prints. Soon afterwards Mercier went to live in Yorkshire and examples of his work are to be found in that county (*Portrait of Viscount and Viscountess Irwin*, Temple Newsam House), and elsewhere.

Allan Ramsay (*1713–84*)

Ramsay was born at Edinburgh, came to London for tuition in drawing and then worked in Rome. He returned by 1739, established himself in London, but often visited his birthplace. His portraits reflect his Italian tuition, and the sitters are given a grandeur that is lacking in the work of his nearest rival, Thomas Hudson. His portrait of his wife (National Gallery of Scotland, Edinburgh) was painted in about 1755. Soon afterwards, the Prime Minister, the Earl of Bute, a fellow-Scot, introduced Ramsay to the King and he spent much of the remainder of his life painting likenesses of George III and Queen Charlotte (National Portrait Gallery, and elsewhere).

SCULPTORS

Benjamin Carter (*died 1766*)

Benjamin Carter often worked in association with his elder brother, Thomas, although

Sculptors, Early Georgian Period (Continued)

each of them had his separate establishment. Both specialized in making marble mantlepieces, but also carved monuments. The model of a lion above the river front of Syon House, Isleworth, was modelled by Benjamin Carter in 1752; it originally stood above the main doorway of Northumberland House, Charing Cross, demolished in 1874.

Sir Henry Cheere (*1703–81*)

He is said to have been a pupil of John van Nost and later entered into partnership with Henry Scheemakers, brother of the better-known Peter Scheemakers. Cheere's workshop was near Hyde Park Corner, where he produced all kinds of statuary in marble, stone, bronze and lead, and also made chimneypieces. A number of Cheere's monuments are in Westminster Abbey, and in 1758 he supplied one commemorating Charles Apthorp to King's Chapel, Boston, Massachusetts.

Louis-François Roubiliac (*1705?–62*)

As his name suggests, Roubiliac was a Frenchman. He was born at Lyons, worked at Dresden and is supposed to have come to London in about 1732. He was engaged as

Bust of Isaac Ware, architect, carved in marble by Louis-François Roubiliac in about 1755. Christie's.

Sculptors, Early Georgian Period (Continued)

assistant by one of the Carter brothers and then by Sir Henry Cheere, and in 1737 carved a statue of the composer, Handel, which was placed in the pleasure park, Vauxhall Gardens (the statue is now in the Victoria and Albert Museum). Roubiliac carved a monument to the Duke of Argyll in 1748 (Westminster Abbey), which a contemporary observed 'outshone for nobleness and skill all those before done by the best sculptors this fifty years past'. He executed other monuments, statues and portrait busts. These last were of men and women of his own day and before, including one of himself which is in the National Portrait Gallery.

Michael Rysbrack (1694–1770)

He was born in Antwerp and came to England in about 1720. He executed monuments, statues, busts, and panels for incorporating in and above chimneypieces. Like those of Roubiliac, his portrait busts included former notabilities as well as those of his own day. There are a number of examples of Rysbrack's work at Stourhead, Wiltshire, including his statue of *Hercules*, commenced in 1747, which was said to have taken the sculptor 'the study and labour of five years to complete'.

Peter Scheemakers (1691–1781)

Like Rysbrack, Scheemakers came from Antwerp and arrived in England in about 1720. He produced a large quantity of statues, busts, monuments and relief panels, his most familiar work being the statue of William Shakespeare which he carved in 1741 from the design of William Kent (Westminster Abbey). He was said to have undercut the prices of his fellow-sculptors and to have had his head turned by the praise he received for his Shakespeare. A contemporary quoted Scheemakers as saying: 'I am a little impudent fellow, no matter, I can't help it'.

MID-GEORGIAN PERIOD: 1750-1765

WHEREAS George II, who succeeded his father on the throne in 1727, was little devoted to the arts, his son extended patronage to painters and others. The son, Frederick Louis, Prince of Wales, died in 1751 at the age of forty-four. For most of his comparatively short life he had behaved in the manner of many sons, before and since his day, by quarrelling with his parents and encouraging almost everything and everybody anti-establishment. It was this Prince's eldest son, the grandson of George II, who came to the throne as George III in 1760.

Architecture altered little from that of previous decades, subtle differences in ornament being the main observable variation. The principal designers of buildings were Henry Flitcroft and James Paine, while Sir William Chambers was active during this and the succeeding period.

In the interiors of houses great changes were to be seen as regards both the decoration of rooms and their contents. In the 1740s engraved designs by Matthias Lock and Henry Copland had been issued. These small booklets brought to notice a fresh style of ornamentation that had been current in France for some time previously. It became known as the

Decorative Styles, Mid-Georgian Period (Continued)

Mid-eighteenth-century plasterwork overmantel of rococo design, the mantelpiece is of about the same date but the grate and surround are much later.

Louis XV style in France and the rococo style in England; the latter derived from *rocaille*: rock-work, an allusion to the oddly-shaped rocks, groups of seashells and other natural objects linked with scrolls in the form of a capital 'C' featured in the style. Above all the rococo is distinguished by its asymmetry: the lack of balance visible between one portion of a design and another. It is a feature more noticeable in French and German versions of the style, but almost always present to some degree in the English.

By 1750 the rococo style was beginning to be seen everywhere: on the plasterwork of ceilings and walls, the shapes and carving of chairs and tables, the frames of paintings and looking-glasses, and in the forms and decoration of silverware. Further, it was frequently combined with two other current decorative styles: the Gothic and the Chinese. The former was an adaptation of that to be seen in old churches, particularly the tall and pointed lancet window and the leafy crocket; while the Chinese influence was clearly visible in rectangular fretwork, pagoda shapes and figures in Oriental costume. The various motifs were employed by innumerable craftsmen in many trades, and in furniture their use was illustrated by the cabinet-maker, Thomas Chippendale.

Sculpture gained no important exponents, with Roubiliac, Rysbrack and Scheemakers continuing their successful careers. A fresh field for their fellow-sculptors opened in the

Decorative Styles, Mid-Georgian Period (Continued)

mid-1740s, when the manufacture of porcelain was introduced at Chelsea and Bow. Among the many who were to be employed over the years in modelling original figures for the industry was Joseph Willems, the first name to be recorded in England in this connexion.

The three outstanding painters of the century (not forgetting a fourth, William Hogarth), Reynolds, Gainsborough and Richard Wilson, did much of their finest work during the period. In each instance they continued their careers for some decades afterwards, but their fame rests principally on the impact of their earlier productions. The ever-increasing popularity and ease of foreign travel meant that more and more British artists went abroad to study, and there was less need to rely on immigrants for the introduction of fresh ideas.

After some years of failed attempts, the end of the period saw the formation of the Royal Academy of Arts, which was founded in 1768 'for the purpose of cultivating and improving the arts of painting, sculpture and architecture'. George III gave the proposed Academy his patronage, nominated the first thirty-six members and agreed to make good any financial losses from his own purse. For twelve years he was called upon to do so, but subsequently the body was self-supporting. Since 1869 the Academy has occupied a portion of Burlington House, Piccadilly, the former town house of Richard Boyle, Earl of Burlington, where there are schools for potential artists, and exhibitions of the work of members, associates and others are held annually. Full members are given the initials R.A. after their names, associates have A.R.A., while the President has P.R.A.

The activities of the radical John Wilkes gained him a popular following while causing concern to the government. In 1763, his notorious contribution to No. 45 of his journal, *The North Briton*, gained him punishment but resulted finally in greater freedom for the Press. A side effect of the affair was a demand for glass and chinaware suitably inscribed with 'Wilkes and Liberty' and similar sentiments.

ARCHITECTS

Sir William Chambers, R.A. (*1723–96*)

He was born at Gothenburg, Sweden, of Scottish parents, and was educated in England. Chambers entered the service of the Swedish East India Company and during nine years travelled far and wide, leaving in 1749 for Paris to study architecture. Then he went to Italy for a few years, and finally settled in London, becoming architectural tutor to the future George III. Most of his buildings were designed and erected after 1765, but those finished earlier included the tall Pagoda in Kew Gardens, which was one of his few excursions from the severely classical. More typical is his later building, Somerset House, Strand, erected between 1776 and 1786, to which wings were added by others at later dates.

Henry Flitcroft (*1697–1769*)

Flitcroft is said to have had an unusual start to his career. The story goes that he was working as a carpenter on some alterations to Burlington House, Piccadilly, when he fell from the scaffolding and broke his leg. The event came to the notice of the Earl of Burlington 'who interested himself with much humanity concerning the sufferer', and when he discovered that Flitcroft had abilities as a draughtsman gave him employment. The last part of the tale is certainly true, for Flitcroft was working for the Earl by 1720, and six

Architects, Mid-Georgian Period (Continued)

years later his patron had obtained for him the post of Clerk of the Works at Whitehall. Further posts followed, and the holder earned for himself the nickname 'Burlington Harry'. Flitcroft's work is similar to that of Kent, in the English baroque or Palladian style, and he also has been credited with the design of furniture. His houses include Woburn Abbey, Bedfordshire, which he rebuilt between 1747 and 1761. At Stourhead, Wiltshire, he provided the Pantheon, and later the Temple of Apollo and Alfred's Tower. Earlier, in 1731–4, he built the church of St.-Giles-in-the-Fields, London, and that at Wimpole, Cambridgeshire, in 1748–9.

James Paine (*1717?–89*)

The early life of James Paine has eluded research, but he is said to have studied at the St. Martin's Lane Academy. By about 1736 he had begun work at Nostell Priory, Yorkshire, where building continued for a further fifteen years. Paine was concerned there principally with the interior decoration, which shows his interest in the rococo style, and it has been suggested that while in the house he met the young Thomas Chippendale, persuading him to go to London to study the latest styles. As a result, it is mooted, the future cabinet-maker went to the St. Martin's Lane Academy, where he gained his skill at draughtsmanship and acquired his understanding of the fashionable mode. Paine's buildings were mostly in the Palladian manner, although he was fully capable of forgetting his early training when it came to interiors: he was responsible for the Gothic Library at Felbrigg Hall, Norfolk, and a bridge in the same style at Syon House, Middlesex. He designed the Town Hall at Doncaster, Yorkshire, and the bridge over the River Thames at Richmond, Surrey, both of which have been altered since they were built.

PAINTERS AND DESIGNERS

Thomas Chippendale (*1718–79*)

Chippendale published designs which played a notable part in propagating the rococo style. It has been argued that Chippendale's own part was that of an agent: in effect, commissioning designs from others and putting his own name to them. The men thus employed are said to have been Henry Copland and Matthias Lock, but there is as yet no proof that this was the case. Chippendale's book of designs is entitled *The Gentleman and Cabinet-Maker's Director*, published in 1754, with a second edition in the year following and a third, revised one, in 1762.

Henry Copland (*died ?1761*)

Nothing is known about Copland, except that on his own and in partnership with Matthias Lock he published some engravings in the rococo style. The first appeared in 1746 in the form of a booklet named *A New Book of Ornaments by H. Copland*, a title re-used jointly with Lock in 1752. The earlier designs show a variety of patterns incorporating rococo motifs: shells, leaves and 'C'-scrolls, which could be adapted by carvers and others to suit their needs. The suggestion has been made that Copland was responsible for making many of the designs used by Chippendale in his book, *The Gentleman and Cabinet-Maker's Director*, but no proof of this has been forthcoming.

Painters and Designers, Mid-Georgian Period (Continued)

Painting of the Cruttenden sisters, Elizabeth and Sarah, by Thomas Gainsborougn, a charming picture by an artist who was at his best with the likenesses of women and children. Sotheby's.

Thomas Gainsborough, R.A. (*1727–88*)

This Suffolk-born artist was one of the nine children of a Sudbury cloth-merchant, who was sent to London to learn to paint in about 1740. From a few years afterwards he was engaged in painting in his native town, at Ipswich in 1752–9, Bath in 1759–74 and then London. His earlier pictures include *Mr. and Mrs. Andrews* (National Gallery) and others set in the Suffolk countryside, his landscapes causing a later artist to remark that 'we find tears in our eyes, and know not what brings them'. *The Painter's Daughters chasing a Butterfly* (National Gallery), dating from about 1755, is a further example of his style unfettered by not having to please a client, a masterpiece created for the pleasure of his family and himself. From 1760 Gainsborough was a popular painter of portraits, his most typical depicting the ladies and gentlemen of the time posed at full-length against vaguely rustic backgrounds; these last described by a writer as being 'as artificial as the Victorian photographer's backdrop'. While still at Bath, in 1768, his reputation was already so high that he was invited to become a member of the newly-instituted Royal Academy. It was a unique honour for a painter of portraits working away from the capital.

Painters and Designers, Mid-Georgian Period (Continued)

Matthias Lock (died 1770)

Like his fellow-designer Copland, Lock is rather an obscure figure, and few details of his life have been discovered. It is known that he was a carver as well as a draughtsman, and some of his designs were published in the form of engravings. A quantity of his original drawings are in the Victoria and Albert Museum, and a few are in the Metropolitan Museum of Art, New York. Some of his sketches bear notes recording the time taken to produce the article depicted and the cost of doing so, and a few surviving pieces of his furniture have been identified. It is thought that Lock may have been employed by Thomas Chippendale, and it is certain that he worked for other cabinet-makers. He was an early master of the rococo style in England, both as regards its design as well as its execution.

Sir Joshua Reynolds, P.R.A. (1723–92)

Reynolds was the son of a schoolmaster at Plympton, Devon, and at the age of seventeen

The actress, Mrs. Abington, as Miss Prue in Congreve's play 'Love for Love', painted by Sir Joshua Reynolds; pensive, she turns to face the artist, who has included the sitter's pet dog peering through the chair-back. Christie's.

Painters and Designers, Mid-Georgian Period (Continued)

The head of Lake Nemi, south-east of Rome, by Richard Wilson; a souvenir of a famous beauty-spot. Christie's.

went to London to serve an apprenticeship in the studio of Thomas Hudson. He left his master after just over two years, working on his own partly in London and partly in Devon. Then he went to Italy, returning after three years of study and settling in London. Within a few years he had acquired such a reputation for his portraits that he had to raise his charges to keep sitters away, and he was employing an increasing number of assistants. His paintings of men and women are justly famous internationally. When the Royal Academy was founded in 1769 it was fitting that he should be its first President.

Richard Wilson, R.A. (1713–82)

Richard Wilson was born in Montgomeryshire, and left Wales to come to London to learn portrait-painting. He executed a few portraits (among them *Admiral Thomas Smith*, National Maritime Museum), but in 1750 went to Venice and then to Rome, making a decision to become a painter of landscape. By 1758 he had returned to London, and was painting views in Italy for those who had been there and wanted mementoes—or had not been, and perhaps wanted to pretend that they had. He also painted views of mansions and scenes in England and Wales, but these mostly fall outside the period under review. Wilson's work was unappreciated in his lifetime, and he returned to Wales a year prior to his death. An eighteenth-century critic wrote of him: 'But, honest Wilson, never mind, immortal praises thou shalt find'; which was a true prophecy, unrealized until a century or more after the artist had passed away.

LATE-GEORGIAN PERIOD: 1765-1810

THE period included the French Revolution, which confirmed the fears and suspicions of many Englishmen, and started the country on a long and anxious wait for a cross-Channel invasion that never materialized. At about the same time, a more peaceful unheaval, the Industrial Revolution, was taking place, with factories replacing innumerable backyard workshops. The system received no more than a slow start, and it took several decades before it was accepted as normal practice.

Across the Atlantic, Thomas Jefferson's Declaration of Independence was signed on 4 July 1776, with the participators describing themselves in it as 'The Thirteen United States of America'. In 1783, following the earlier surrender of the British force at Yorktown, a peace treaty was ratified and the country gained freedom from the rule of George III and his ministers.

The classic Palladian architecture of previous years continued with little alteration except in ornamental details, but interior decoration changed with the same apparent rapidity as had occurred earlier with the rococo. In retrospect, such innovations in style seem to have been immediate in their effect, but careful research shows them to have been becoming visible over a period running to decades. This was the case with the new style that came to fruition in England in the early 1760s, and of which the origins have been traced back in time as well as place.

The style is known as the neo-classic, and the name of Robert Adam is inseparably linked with it, for he was foremost in its application and popularization. The principal source of neo-classicism was the series of excavations conducted on the sites of Herculaneum and Pompeii, near Naples. Found accidentally early in the eighteenth century, it was only after systematic exploration was undertaken in 1738 and 1763 that the world at large knew what had been discovered. To these sources were added details from ancient Greece, owing their introduction to the investigations of James Stuart.

As a result, the abandon and extravagance of rococo curves was replaced by neatly ordered and austere motifs from classical sources. These were moulded in plaster on ceilings and walls, carved and inlaid on tables and other furnishings, and employed to decorate silverware and much else.

Robert Adam was the innovator, assisted by his brother, James, and they were soon followed by other designers. Chief among them were Thomas Leverton and James Wyatt, but the Adams resourcefulness and capacity for work kept them ahead of rivals. It was not until the mid-1780s that a challenge to their supremacy appeared in the person of Henry Holland.

Sculptors of the time included Joseph Wilton, Joseph Nollekens and John Flaxman, but many ready-made figures and groups were being imported from Italy. There, a number of Scotsmen and Englishmen earned their living by escorting their countrymen in Rome and elsewhere, and assisting them in the purchase of mementoes of their Tour. In addition to paintings, these often took the form of excavated ancient sculptures, sometimes heavily restored, which were sent home to adorn the Sculpture Gallery now considered an essential requisite for a gentleman's mansion.

In portrait painting, Reynolds and Ramsay continued their rivalry, and were joined by

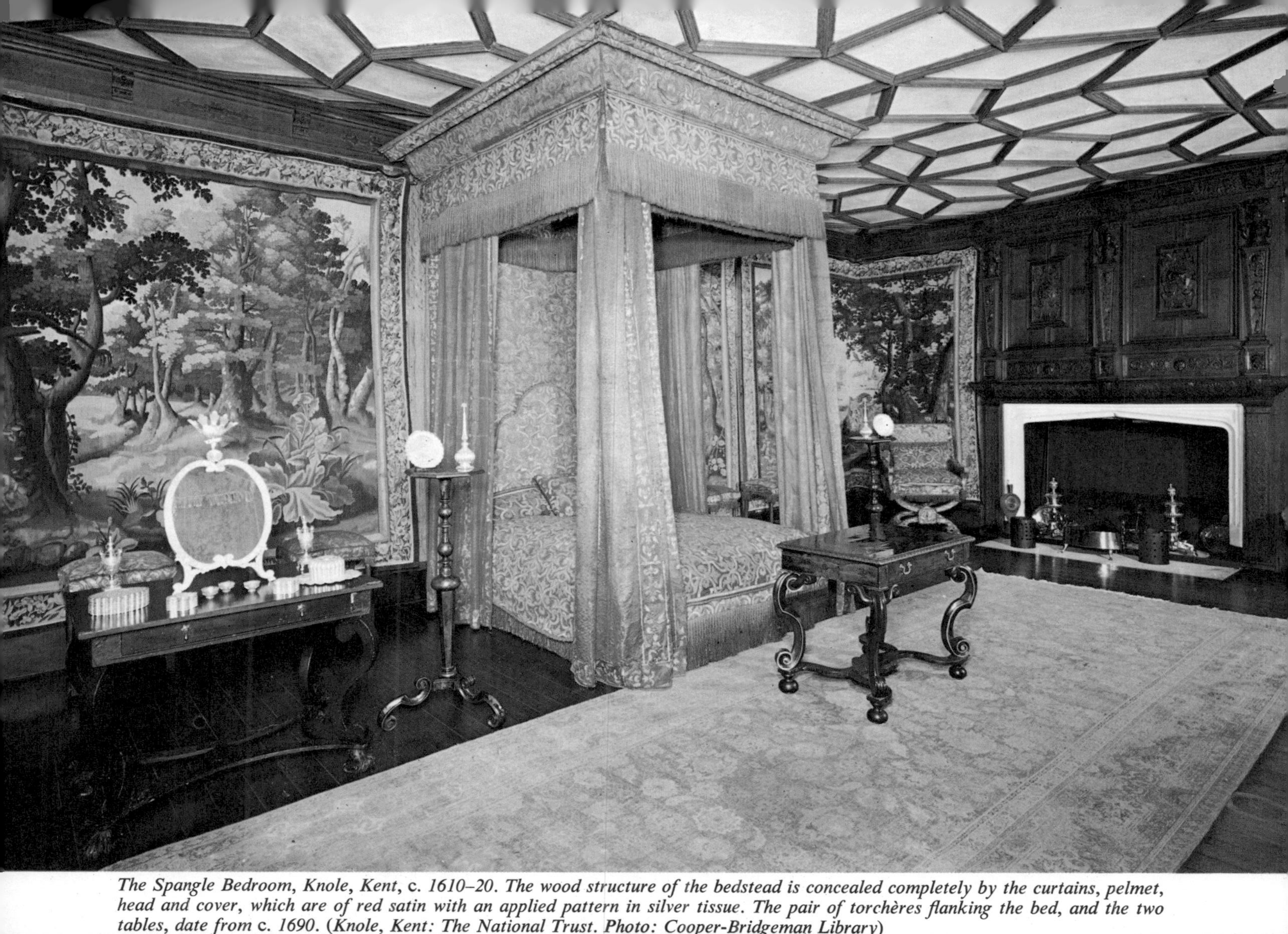

The Spangle Bedroom, Knole, Kent, c. *1610–20. The wood structure of the bedstead is concealed completely by the curtains, pelmet, head and cover, which are of red satin with an applied pattern in silver tissue. The pair of torchères flanking the bed, and the two tables, date from* c. *1690. (Knole, Kent: The National Trust. Photo: Cooper-Bridgeman Library)*

Decorative Styles, Late Georgian Period (Continued)

The Saloon, Saltram, Devon, decorated by Robert Adam in 1768; it is in the neo-Classical style and shows its complete contrast with the preceding rococo.
Saltram, Devon: The National Trust.

Decorative Styles, Late Georgian Period (Continued)

George Romney. Open-air pictures were contributed by George Morland and George Stubbs, the latter's studies of horses being noteworthy. At the end of the century came William Blake, poet as well as painter, whose visionary work was a foretaste of the intense romanticism of the years ahead. Some of this was to be seen, too, in the watercolour views by Paul Sandby, Thomas Girtin and others. While the foregoing depicted the idyllic world of Nature, man and his foibles were equally well portrayed by Thomas Rowlandson and, with greater satire, by James Gillray.

The art of miniature-painting reached great heights, and the numerous surviving examples portray men and women from many walks of life. The work of John Smart, Ozias Humphry and George Engleheart was particularly well regarded, and is often found carefully framed in gold with a lock of the sitter's hair preserved at the back.

The age did not lack its characters. The greatest was probably Samuel Johnson (1709–84), the author of numerous essays and compiler of an English dictionary, whose life and times were vividly recorded by his Scottish-born biographer, James Boswell. Boswell's *Life of Samuel Johnson* was first published in three volumes in 1791, and unwittingly revealed no less about the author than it did about his subject. Others deserving mention were the dilettante, Horace Walpole (1717–97), who succeeded to the title of Earl of Orford when he was seventy-four, and the energetic Mary Granville, better known as Mrs. Delany (1700–88). The letters of both have been collected and printed to provide remarkable pictures of the world in which they lived.

ARCHITECTS

Adam Family

William Adam, the architect, had four sons: (John (1721?–92), who succeeded to his father's Scottish practice but was content in the main to lead the life of a gentleman in Scotland; and Robert (1728–92), James (1730–94) and William (1738–1822), all three of whom worked together in London. The presiding genius was Robert Adam, who was educated at Edinburgh and in 1754 travelled through France to Italy. From there he went in 1757 to Split, Dalmatia, where he joined with other draughtsmen in exploring, measuring and drawing the ruins of the great palace of the Emperor Diocletian. He returned to London in 1758 and after settling into a house in Lower Grosvenor Street, was joined by his brother James and his two sisters. Adam was aided by the Prime Minister, a fellow-Scot, the Earl of Bute, who used his influence to obtain for him the post of Architect to the King's Works. His practice quickly grew and in 1762 he was at work on Lansdowne House, Berkeley Square, for Lord Bute, who sold it prior to completion to the first Marquis of Lansdowne. A vestige of the building remains, and the drawing-room is now in the Philadelphia Museum of Arts, U.S.A. The library at Kenwood, Hampstead, is one of his most striking and successful rooms, while the suite of apartments at Saltram, Devon, is a typical example of his treatment of a country mansion. From about 1760 onwards Robert Adam was continually designing buildings and reconstructions, so that the total list of his firm's achievements is a formidable one. Their own publication, *Works in Architecture of Robert and James Adam*, appeared in three volumes in 1773, 1779 and 1822, while a more modern assessment is that of A. T. Bolton, *The Architecture of Robert and James Adam*, in two

The Double Cube Room, Wilton House, Wiltshire, c. *1650. The room was designed by Inigo Jones, and still contains the series of paintings by Vandyck in the spaces originally intended for them. The carved giltwood settees date from* c. *1730 and were possibly designed by William Kent. (Wilton House, Wiltshire: the Earl of Pembroke. Photo: Cooper-Bridgeman Library)*

Architects, Late Georgian Period (Continued)

volumes, 1922. James Adam did not attempt to challenge Robert's leadership in the firm, although he was responsible personally for a few designs; notably the façades of the houses they built in Portland Place. The third of the brothers, William, would appear to have overseen the business side of the partnership and to have had little or nothing to do with the architectural work. Robert Adam's contribution to the arts is principally his introduction and continued use of neo-classical motifs, which he had the skill to employ with great effect. Within a few years the style had completedly routed rococo, but in turn it, too, was thought to be outmoded. In 1785, Horace Walpole was writing complainingly of what he termed 'Mr. Adam's gingerbread and sippets of embroidery'.

Henry Holland (*1745–1806*)

He received training while working for his father, a Fulham, London, master-builder, and duly was employed as assistant to Lancelot 'Capability' Brown, the landscape gardener. He became acquainted with Brown's clients and after designing Brooks's Club (60 St. James's Street, London) did work for many of its members, who were in the circle of the Prince of Wales, later George IV. For the latter, he altered Carlton House (now demolished, but the portico fronts the National Gallery), and for the Duke of Bedford he carried out

Roll-front bureau made of rosewood inlaid with ivory and with ivory knobs on the drawers; in the manner of Henry Holland and made in about 1820. H. Blairman & Sons.

Architects, Late Georgian Period (Continued)

much work at Woburn Abbey. For the same client he built the George Inn at Woburn and the Swan Inn at Bedford. Henry Holland also designed furniture, much of which showed French influence; with dark woods contrasting with gilt-metal mounts, and a use of Greek motifs such as the anthemion.

Thomas Leverton (*1743–1824*)

Thomas Leverton was born in Essex, but little is known about him until the early 1770's. He has been described as one of the Adam brothers' most successful imitators, and he was responsible for the interiors of many of the houses in Bedford Square, London.

James Stuart (*1713–88*)

He was the son of a Scotsman but born in London, early in life showing an aptitude for learning and drawing. Although lacking money, he set out for Rome in 1742, covering much of the journey by foot, and it is thought that when there he paid his expenses by acting as a guide to English visitors. In 1748 Stuart's name was appended to *Proposals for publishing an Accurate Description of the Antiquities of Athens*, and as a result finance was forthcoming for an expedition to the Greek capital. The first volume of *The Antiquities of Athens* was published in 1762 and gained Stuart considerable fame, and thenceforward he was dubbed 'Athenian'. He designed a number of houses as well as some furniture but had a reputation for indolence, and it is said that he preferred 'an easy and convivial life to the exacting routine of a busy architect's office'. His buildings in the park at Shugborough, Staffordshire, erected between 1764 and 1770, are among his best-known surviving works. Typically, the second volume of his *Antiquities* did not appear until twenty-six years after the first, and when almost ready for publication was further delayed by Stuart's unexpected death.

James Wyatt (*1746–1813*)

James Wyatt belonged to a Staffordshire family which included several architects among its members. He spent six years in Italy and became a pupil of a Venetian architect while there, but although it is known he was back in England in about 1768 there is no record of what he was doing. Then, in 1772, his design for the Pantheon or 'Winter Ranelagh', an indoor pleasure park, was selected, and at the early age of twenty-six he was entrusted with erecting the building in Oxford Street, London. It earned him fame, with Horace Walpole going so far as to remark that it was 'the most beautiful edifice in London'. Notwithstanding, in 1867 it became a depot for storing wine and in about 1936 was entirely demolished to make way for a chain-store. Wyatt was kept busy reconstructing mansions, building churches and providing interior decoration in the neo-classic style. One of his most successful houses was Heveningham Hall, Suffolk, erected in 1788–99, but the list of his works is a long one and a fair proportion survives. Wyatt is credited with being the first English designer to employ *scagliola*: a mixture of plaster and isinglass, stained and polished to imitate marble.

Late Georgian Period (Continued)

PAINTERS

William Blake (*1757–1827*)

Blake combined painting and poetry and is sometimes given the label 'eccentric genius', probably because he lived for his work and cared little for reward. He was born in London, and, showing promise at drawing, was apprenticed to an engraver. In 1789 he printed by an original process his *Songs of Innocence*, followed by other works, all of which he illus-

One of William Blake's engraved illustrations to his edition of the Book of Job, in which he illustrates in his individual manner the words 'When the morning Stars sang together, and all the Sons of God shouted for joy'. Sotheby's.

Painters, Late Georgian Period (Continued)

trated. He drew a number of imaginative religious pictures, and illustrated Dante's *Divine Comedy* and other works. Many books have been devoted to the life of Blake; his coloured engravings have been carefully reproduced in facsimile and his work has been deeply studied. There is a fine collection of William Blake's drawings at the Tate Gallery, London, and examples are to be seen in the principal galleries of the world.

James Gillray (*1757–1815*)

An etcher and engraver, James Gillray caricatured the Royal family, politicians and anyone else of prominence. He seldom spared his victims, particularly George III, and although much of his work shows an unequalled savagery it has wit.

Thomas Girtin (*1775–1802*)

One of the pioneers of painting in watercolours, Thomas Girtin painted scenery in many parts of England and Wales. He died of consumption at the early age of twenty-seven, his friend J. M. W. Turner remarking 'If Tom Girtin had lived I should have starved'. Girtin's work may be seen at the Victoria and Albert Museum, and in many other galleries.

George Morland (*1763–1804*)

George Morland enjoyed the doubtful honour of having his works forged during his lifetime and for many years afterwards. He specialized in country scenes with rustics and animals, and his work varies in quality. It has been remarked that 'the piggishness of his pigs and the dampness of his wet woodlands are very complete', while his men, women and children are outstandingly bucolic. His paintings are well-known from the numerous engravings of them that have been made from his lifetime onwards, and examples are to be seen in the National Gallery and elsewhere. Morland spent much of his time in gin-shops and ale-houses, painting during his sober intervals, and from 1799 to 1802 was in prison for non-payment of debts.

Sir Henry Raeburn, R.A. (*1756–1823*)

Born in Edinburgh, Raeburn was orphaned early in life and at the age of fifteen was apprenticed to a goldsmith. He showed an aptitude for miniature-painting and from that graduated to oils, in which he received encouragement from his employer. In 1778 he was asked to paint the portrait of a young lady with whom he fell in love; they married within a month and the two set out for Italy. On his return to Edinburgh he established himself as an artist and quickly became so popular as to become known as the 'Reynolds of the North'. Raeburn's portraits have a freshness that renders them attractive, although their colouring is sometimes harsh. Examples are to be seen in many galleries in England, Scotland and other countries.

George Romney (*1734–1802*)

Romney was the son of a Lancashire cabinetmaker, and after apprenticeship to an itinerant artist set up his studio in Kendal, Westmorland. By 1762 he was working in London, where he pursued a successful career as a fashionable portraitist despite his private ambition to paint 'History' pictures. During the 1780s he painted as many as fifty pictures

Painters, Late Georgian Period (Continued)

of Emma Hart, later Lady Hamilton and Nelson's mistress. Romney featured her posed as various legendary and other characters, including Joan of Arc and the Magdalene. Romney's portraits are in major galleries, his *Mrs. Robinson*, in the Wallace Collection, London, is representative of his work.

Thomas Rowlandson's rendering of a happy scene, showing a family setting off to market. Christie's.

Thomas Rowlandson (1756–1827)

Rowlandson was a Londoner who went to Paris when he was sixteen, and studied drawing. A French relative left him a legacy, whereupon he soon gave up his interest in art and took to gaming, but after a time poverty caused him to halt his dissipated existence and take to caricature and book-illustration. His tinted pen-and-ink drawings of town and country scenes all over the British Isles mock daily life, as do his numerous engravings. His large drawing of *Vauxhall Gardens*, exhibited at the Royal Academy in 1784, typifies him at his best. The drawing was lost for a considerable time, and re-appeared some years ago in a shop in Essex when it was bought for £1. It is now in the Victoria and Albert Museum.

Paul Sandby, R.A. (1725–1809)

Often termed 'the father of watercolour art', Paul Sandby was born at Nottingham

Painters, Late Georgian Period (Continued)

and worked in the Tower Drawing Office, London, the ancestor of the Ordnance Survey. He was a very early exponent of pure watercolours, not just tinted pencil drawing, and his scenes are obviously truthful. His *Twelve Views in South Wales*, published in 1775, is the first use of a variety of engraving known as aquatint, which reproduces the soft effect of watercolour by copperplate printing.

John Smart (*1742/3–1811*)

John Smart was one of the most skilful of British miniature-painters, and with his fellow-workers, Ozias Humphry, R.A. (1742–1810) and George Engleheart (1750–1829) practised his art when it was at its peak of perfection. The best work of all three is so perfect, and appears to have been executed so effortlessly, that it might be thought to have been done by machine. All three were kept busy by innumerable sitters, and Smart and Humphry spent some time in India painting likenesses of officials and military men and their ladies.

Portrait of an unknown man painted in miniature by John Smart in 1779.
Sotheby's.

George Stubbs, A.R.A. (*1724–1806*)

The fame of Stubbs rests on his great ability as a painter of horses, although he was equally skilled with other animals and not untalented with human beings. He was born at Liverpool and until he went to Italy in 1754 spent his life painting in the north of England. On his return he lived in Lincolnshire, where from about 1756 to 1759 he spent most of his time making drawings for his book *The Anatomy of the Horse*, which was published in 1766. Typical of his work are his *Lady and Gentleman in a Carriage* (National Gallery), and *Cheetah and Stag with two Indians* (City Art Gallery, Manchester).

John Zoffany (*1733?–1810*)

Zoffany, sometimes referred to as Johann Zauffely, was born at Frankfort, Germany, and after some years in Italy came to England. In the early 1760s, soon after his arrival,

Painters, Late Georgian Period (Continued)

he began painting scenes from theatrical successes of the day showing popular actors and actresses in their stage parts. Later, he turned to family portraits in domestic settings, 'Conversation' pictures, executed with a meticulous regard for detail.

SCULPTORS

John Flaxman, R.A. (*1755–1826*)

Born in York but brought to London by his parents when he was six months old, John Flaxman was the son of a sculptor of the same name. Both men prepared designs for Josiah Wedgwood, the potter, and in 1787 the latter assisted Flaxman in going to Rome. There, he continued to work for Wedgwood, while carving statues, designing monuments and drawing illustrations for books. Back in London by 1797, Flaxman spent the majority of his remaining years carving monuments, which are to be seen in cathedrals and churches in England, Scotland and Wales; others as far afield as Madras and Quebec. Among others by him in St. Paul's Cathedral, London, is the monument to Admiral Lord Nelson.

Joseph Nollekens, R.A. (*1737–1823*)

In 1750 Nollekens was apprenticed to Scheemakers and in 1760 went to Rome, where he produced sculptures as well as dealing in excavated fragments which he restored and sold to English visitors. On his return to London in 1770, he soon became the equivalent in sculpture to Reynolds in painting, with a continual procession of sitters from the ranks of the personalities of the time. His bust of William Pitt, Prime Minister at the age of twenty-five, executed in 1806, was so widely approved that he was reported to have made seventy-four replicas of it which sold for £120 each. Nollekens also carved statues and monuments, some of which are in Westminster Abbey (among them, Oliver Goldsmith, the author) and others are in churches in many parts of England. The sculptor was the subject of a biography entitled *Nollekens and his Times*, written by John Thomas Smith, who began his career by spending three years as a pupil in his studio. The book first appeared in 1828 in a single volume, and in the following year came a second edition with a further volume of short biographies of artists and others. The book revealingly details the daily life of Mr. and Mrs. Nollekens ('wedded and childless misers') and their contemporaries, with valuable descriptions of London scenes. It is a malicious biography, 'a strange budget of animus and anecdote' and has been reprinted in modern times, but mostly without the second volume of 1829.

Joseph Wilton, R.A. (*1722–1803*)

Wilton was born in London and received training as a sculptor in the Netherlands and Paris. He travelled to Italy with Roubiliac, and for a few years was busy making copies of antique statues before returning to London. Joseph Wilton designed and carved some of the ornament of George III's State Coach, used at the Coronation in 1761, and was later appointed Sculptor to His Majesty. He did much work at Somerset House, Strand, including chimney-pieces, vases and two 'colossal lions'. In a competition Wilton's design for a monument to General Wolfe was selected, and is to be seen in Westminster Abbey, along with other monuments he executed.

Decorative Styles (Continued)

REGENCY AND GEORGE IV PERIOD: 1810-1830

GEORGE, Prince of Wales, became Regent in 1811; on account of his father's severe illness he ruled in his stead. A controversial figure he was described by one contemporary as 'a well-bred accomplished gentleman', and by another as 'a spoiled, selfish, odious beast'. His reign as Regent and King is commemorated for many by his Pavilion at Brighton, by his judicious purchases of French furniture and paintings which remain in the Royal collection, and by the almost legendary way in which he spent money.

The Prince Regent, however, was not alone in his generous expenditure; he lived in lavish times and many of his subjects did not hesitate to follow his lead or encourage him in his habits. For example, although glass bore a substantial excise duty this did not prevent the heaviest pieces being fashionable; silverware of the period was comparably weighty despite the duty levied on every ounce of the metal, and porcelain bore elaborate painting with lavish gilding.

The austerities forced on the nation by Napoleon's campaigns were temporarily relieved by Nelson's victory at Trafalgar in 1805, and finally ended by Wellington's rout of the French at Waterloo ten years later. In the interim there had been the abdication and exile of the Emperor, and his dramatic escape from captivity. All these were stirring events involving the entire nation, so that every phase of the war was reflected in daily life. The contrasting horrors and celebrations had their counterparts in frequent and sudden changes in fashions, and the dreary outlook was punctuated by bursts of luxury.

The period is notable for the variety of fashions prevailing. Grecian, Indian, Egyptian, Chinese, Tudor and Gothic vied with one another for popularity, while rustic simplicity, wild Nature or the picturesque, were equally in demand. Each might be employed on its own or in conjunction with one or more of the others, the Prince himself having a pseudo-Chinese interior for his pseudo-Indian Pavilion. The demand for revived Tudor or Elizabethan was stimulated by the success of Sir Walter Scott's romantic tales set in the period.

The general employment of painted cement, or stucco, for all or part of the fronts of houses and the use of cast-iron balcony railings are familiar figures of Regency terraces at London, Cheltenham and elsewhere. In Scotland, the second New Town in Edinburgh was planned and built between 1800 and 1825.

The work of the sculptor was not outstanding during the period, either as regards originality or quantity. The names of Sir Francis Chantrey and Sir Richard Westmacott were prominent, while those unable to afford real marble or stone could still adorn their homes with Coade's artificial stone which had been in production since 1769.

Painting in England at the time undoubtedly owed some of its inspiration to the rise of London as the centre for dealing in Old Masters, which were brought there from the ravaged countries of the European mainland. A number of highly important collections were dispersed, with English homes and in due course public galleries becoming enriched by the acquisition of masterpieces. In 1824 the first English public gallery, the National Gallery, was opened in Trafalgar Square, the Government having voted the sum of £57,000 to buy a ready-formed collection for its inauguration.

Regency and George IV Period (Continued)

A caricature of the Prince Regent by George Cruikshank, showing the Prince on the lid of a teapot with a view of Brighton Pavilion on its side. It was published in 1820.

ARCHITECTS

John Nash (*1752–1835*)

A Londoner, Nash worked in an architect's office, set up on his own but went bankrupt and re-started his career in Wales. By 1796 he was again in London, and two years later gained the patronage of the Prince of Wales. He held a number of posts, and as Architect to the Department of Woods and Forests laid out Regent's Park and Regent Street. At he north end of the latter he designed the church of All Souls, Langham Place, which remains with its finely tapering spire, but his colonnaded Quadrant in Regent Street was rebuilt in the present century. John Nash was responsible for remodelling the Royal Pavilion, Brighton, between 1815 and 1821, and he also reconstructed Buckingham Palace. His work on the latter has been twice changed and substantially all that remains is the

Architects, Regency and George IV Period (Continued)

NASHIONAL TASTE !!!
(Dedicated without permission, to the Church Commissioners —
Providence sends meat.
The Devil sends cooks –
Parliament sends Funds –
But, who sends the Architects ?_!!!

John Nash, the architect, pilloried on the spire of All Souls, Langham Place, London, which he designed. The church was built between 1820 and 1824, the print was issued in the latter year and the lines below read
Providence sends meat, the Devil sends cooks—
Parliament sends funds—but, who sends the Architects?

Marble Arch, which was originally built in front of the Palace where the present Victoria Memorial now stands. On the death of George IV in 1830, Nash fell from favour and his reputation shared the public censure accorded to that of his Royal Patron.

William Wilkins (1778–1839)

William Wilkins was born at Norwich, and following five years at Caius College, Cambridge, went to Greece and other Mediterranean countries. He came back to Cambridge, where his knowledge of Greek architecture appealed to Thomas Hope and others who were eager to see a revival of the style. Wilkins designed Downing College, Cambridge, as well as some other buildings in the city, and in London built the National Gallery in the front of which he incorporated the columns formerly at Carlton House. He built a number of country mansions in various parts of the country from Scotland to Cornwall, ranging in style from Grecian to Tudor and Gothic.

Sir Jeffry Wyatville, R.A. (1766–1840)

He was the son of an architect, Joseph Wyatt, and a nephew of James Wyatt. After training with his uncle, Jeffry Wyatt set up on his own and was kept busy designing country houses in various styles. In 1824 he began to rebuild Windsor Castle, the sum of £150,000 having been voted for the task by the Government. By 1830 the total had reached over

Architects, Regency and George IV Period (Continued)

£500,000, and with the addition of a like sum the work was finally completed soon after 1837. George IV authorized his architect's use of the surname Wyatville, knighted him and granted him quarters in the Castle.

PAINTERS

John Constable, R.A. (*1776–1837*)

Son of a Suffolk mill-owner, John Constable tried for a year to follow his father's trade, but gave it up for his true bent: painting. He attended the Royal Academy Schools in 1799 and duly painted some portraits, but his vocation was depicting landscape. At this he excelled, but public appreciation was rarely forthcoming in his own land. Some of his works were sold in France, and *The Hay Wain* (now in the National Gallery, London) was particularly well received, the treatment and colouring of the scene arousing comment from French artists and winning the painter a gold medal. Constable's style developed slowly and recognition was accorded him at an equal pace; he was elected A.R.A. in 1819, but did not become a full Academician until 1829. This last event occurred a year after his wife had died, a shock from which he never recovered, causing him to remark that the honour had come too late. When Constable died a group of his friends and admirers subscribed to buy his painting *The Cornfield,* which they presented to the National Gallery. There is an important collection of his work in the Victoria and Albert Museum. It is apposite to recall what Constable himself wrote in 1803: 'I feel now, more than ever, a decided conviction that I shall some time or other make some good pictures; pictures that shall be valuable to posterity, if I do not reap the benefit of them'. His prophetic words came true.

Dedham Vale from East Bergholt by John Constable. This is a view in Suffolk, the county in which the artist was born. Bearnes and Waycotts.

Painters, Regency and George IV Period (Continued)

John Sell Cotman (*1782–1842*)

Cotman's father was a silk mercer in Norwich, and like Constable it was supposed that he would enter his parent's business, but he preferred painting. He went to London in 1800, returning to his home town by 1807. There, he became a member and secretary of the recently-formed Norwich Society of Artists, with whom he exhibited his work. In 1825 he was elected to associate membership of the Society of Painters in Watercolours in London, and later moved to the capital to teach drawing. Cotman painted in both oils and watercolours, and also lithographed and etched architectural subjects. It was said of his work that 'his light and shade were good, the masses broad and simple . . . his colour rich . . . his figures were well placed, and the details of his architecture well understood'. Examples of Cotman's work are to be seen in many galleries, including the Victoria and Albert Museum.

George Cruikshank (*1792–1878*)

Son and grandson of artists, George Cruikshank was born in London and his future career was in little doubt. He received no academic training, but by 1811, the year in which his father died, Cruikshank was already established. He produced hundreds of etched satires on all aspects of social and political life: 'for a generation he delineated Tories, Whigs and Radicals with fine impartiality'. He also illustrated a number of books, amongst them *Sketches by Boz*, *Oliver Twist* and *Nicholas Nickleby*, by Charles Dickens. George Cruikshank was a fervid advocate of total abstinence, and used his art to assist the movement. It would appear that temperance agreed with his constitution, for he lived to the age of eighty-six. He was buried in St. Paul's Cathedral.

William Etty, R.A. (*1787–1849*)

Born in York, the son of a miller, William Etty was apprenticed to a printer, but an early ambition to become a painter eventually triumphed when an uncle assisted him to study art. He decided to devote his talents to what he termed 'God's most glorious work, Woman', and after a long struggle for recognition he achieved his purpose. He went abroad to visit galleries and almost to the end of his days attended the life-classes at the Academy schools. An admirer wrote: 'Look for a while at Mr. Etty's pictures, and away you rush, your "eyes on fire", drunken with the luscious colours that are poured out for you on the liberal canvas, and warm with the sight of the beautiful sirens that appear on it'. William Etty's works include *Youth on the Prow and Pleasure at the Helm* (Tate Gallery, London), *Pandora* (City Art Gallery, Leeds), and *The Three Graces* (Metropolitan Museum of Art, New York), while there is a representative selection of his sketches and other work in the City Art Gallery, York.

Sir Thomas Lawrence, P.R.A. (*1769–1830*)

Undoubtedly the greatest portrait painter of his time, Lawrence was born at Bristol and in 1787 became a student in London at the Royal Academy. Four years later, although only twenty-two years old, he was selected an Associate, and in 1792 George III appointed him Painter-in-Ordinary. To the esteem he enjoyed in England was added international

Painters, Regency and George IV Period (Continued)

William Etty's painting of a Classical scene showing the god, Pluto, carrying off Proserpine; a typical example of the artist's 'constellations of naked women'.
Sotheby's.

appreciation when he was selected by the Prince Regent to paint portraits of the many eminent statesmen and soldiers whose efforts had led to Napoleon's downfall. These portraits are in the Waterloo Chamber, Windsor Castle, while his likenesses of the eminent and not so eminent of his day are to be seen in galleries throughout Europe and in America. Lawrence formed a large collection of drawings by Old Masters on which he spent much of his income.

Sir David Wilkie, R.A. (1785–1841)

The Scottish village of Cults, Fifeshire, was the birthplace of David Wilkie, whose early talent at drawing caused his father to send him for training in Edinburgh. He then attended the Academy Schools in London and was soon exhibiting his work at the annual exhibitions, where they attracted favourable notice. The paintings he produced were full of interest for the general public; life-like scenes with plenty of ordinary people and a title explaining the circumstance. Wilkie's work in this vein included *Chelsea Pensioners Reading the Gazette of the Battle of Waterloo* (Wellington Museum, Apsley House) which he painted for the Duke in 1822, and *The Scottish Toilet* (Wallace Collection). His *Entry of George IV into Holyrood House* (Scottish National Portrait Gallery) records the visit of the monarch to Edinburgh in 1822.

Regency and George IV Period (Continued)

SCULPTORS

Sir Francis Chantrey, R.A. (1781–1841)

Chantrey was born in Sheffield and began his working life by assisting a grocer, then he became apprenticed to a carver and gilder. In due course he turned to sculpture, later stating 'that he had never had an hour's instruction from any sculptor in his life'. In the early 1800s he came to London and struggled to gain recognition, which came his way following exhibition of a bust of Horne Tooke, the radical politician, at the Royal Academy in 1811 (now at the Fitzwilliam Museum, Cambridge). He carved statues and busts of many notabilities, as well as numerous monuments, receiving particular praise for the manner in which he conveyed the softness of flesh. Sir Francis worked hard in his profession and left all his money to his wife for life, after which it was to go to the Royal Academy. To that body it was left in trust, with the income to be spent on the encouragement of British painting and sculpture, by 'the purchase of the finest works of fine art of the highest merit'. Strict rules were laid down for the application of what remains known as the Chantrey Bequest, which became available after Lady Chantrey died in 1875. The work of Sir Francis Chantrey is to be seen in many galleries, while his statues include George Washington (State House, Boston, Mass.), James Watt (Westminster Abbey, Handsworth Parish Church, Birmingham, and elsewhere), and William Pitt (Hanover Square, London). Probably his best-known monument is that to the children of the Rev. W. Robinson, in Lichfield Cathedral, Staffordshire.

Sir Richard Westmacott, R.A. (1775–1856)

Unlike Francis Chantrey, Richard Westmacott was able to study sculpture with thoroughness. He began under his father in London, and then spent four years in Rome before coming back to London and setting up his studio. He carved a great number of monuments, including those of the politicians William Pitt, Charles James Fox and Spencer Perceval, in Westminster Abbey. Westmacott also made some chimneypieces, among them one for the Music Room at the Royal Pavilion, Brighton, for which he received no less than £1,244.2s.6d.; it is now in Buckingham Palace. His most familiar work is the colossal bronze statue of the nude Achilles, subscribed for by the Ladies of England as a compliment to the Duke of Wellington. It was erected in 1822, on the seventh anniversary of the Battle of Waterloo, and stands in Hyde Park close to Apsley House, the Duke's London home. Westmacott also carved the group of figures representing the progress of civilization on the pediment of the portico of the British Museum. His work was summed up by a critic, who wrote: 'his figures, if not attaining a high degree of refinement, are never wanting in grandeur of proportions and solidity'.

WILLIAM IV AND EARLY VICTORIAN PERIOD: 1830-1860

THE reign of George IV closed with his death in 1830, when he was succeeded by his sixty-five-year-old brother, William. He reigned as William IV, and was known as the 'Sailor King' because he had held the rank of Admiral of the Fleet. The new King has been

Decorative Styles, William IV and Early Victorian Period (Continued)

described as 'blundering, though well-intentioned', and whatever his personal shortcomings his reign was not long enough for him to have had any noticeable effect on the Arts. It is not apparent that he had any particular interest in painting or any other form of art, and contrary to his predecessor on the throne his patronage was very limited.

The same applied when William's successor, his niece Princess Victoria, was proclaimed Queen in 1837. She was only seventeen years of age at the time, but after she married her cousin, the German-born Prince Albert of Saxe-Coburg-Gotha in 1840, there came a

Inside the Crystal Palace, 1851, the Main Avenue looking east.

Decorative Styles, William IV and Early Victorian Period (Continued)

change. The Prince Consort was keenly interested in art and industry and their inter-relation, and an opportunity for him to apply his energies in that direction came when he was invited in 1843 to become President of the Society for the Encouragement of Arts, Manufactures and Commerce; a body still active and known since 1908 as The Royal Society of Arts. He accepted the invitation, and in conjunction with the Secretary, Henry Cole, the idea of the Great Exhibition of 1851 became a reality.

The Exhibition was held in Hyde Park, London, inside a great iron and glass building aptly named by *Punch* the 'Crystal Palace'. It was international in scope, with over 100,000 contributions from all over Europe, North and South America and Asia submitted by 13,937 exhibitors. The undertaking proved a great success, with no fewer than 6,039,195 visitors passing the turnstiles and leaving the Commissioners in charge with a profit on their hands of £186,437.

The lessons learned from a study of the British and foreign exhibits were applied in the formation of a Museum of Ornamental Art, opened temporarily in Marlborough House, St. James's, loaned for the purpose by the Queen. It was initiated by a grant of £5,000 from the Government in order to purchase from the Exhibition suitable examples of good design and craftsmanship 'as well for the use of Schools of Ornamental Art as for the improvement of the public taste in Design'. In due course the temporary museum was removed to South Kensington where it became the Victoria and Albert Museum, built on land purchased by the Commissioners of the Great Exhibition.

By bringing the merits of good design to the attention of artists and manufacturers it was hoped that standards might be improved. The nineteenth century had seen a gradual improvement in the welfare of the people, with a consequent demand for more wordly goods, hitherto met largely by articles of indifferent design.

Henry Cole, under the trade name 'Felix Summerly', had pioneered in the 1840s the design and manufacture of better articles in china, glass and silver, but the venture failed. The Art Schools and the Museum of Ornamental Art more successfully exerted a similar influence and continued doing so for the remainder of the century and beyond.

Architectural design in the period was a comparable mixture to that seen in other forms of art. The many styles current during the preceding Regency and George IV period remained in demand, but had become coarsened in line and usually overladen with ornament. There was a continued liking for Elizabethan and Gothic, both of which received official approval when the rules were announced for those wishing to enter designs for a Houses of Parliament to replace the building burned down in 1834. In addition to the conventional architects designing decorative buildings, were the engineers. The work of these men was contrastingly purely functional, using iron and steel according to careful calculations and often with a minimum of added ornament.

Opposite: *Restoration Room*, c. *1665. The panelled walls and the ceiling with its modelled plaster are typical of the time, and the design of the chimney-piece is more restrained than in former years. The furniture includes a wood-seated settle, a table with carved front and a chair with back and seat covered in leather. In the fireplace are cast-iron andirons and a fireback, and on one wall hangs a panel of crewelwork.* (*Geffrye Museum, London. Photo: Cooper-Bridgeman Library*)

Decorative Styles, William IV and Early Victorian Period (Continued)

The conventional painters of the day were briefly challenged by the members of the Pre-Raphaelite Movement. The work of these idealists was assisted in print by the critic John Ruskin, who was himself an able draughtsman. A greater challenge to artists lay in photography, which was brought to a practical state more or less simultaneously in England and France in 1839. It was constantly improved over the years, with the greatest advance coming in 1854 when the dry glass plate was introduced. This replaced a clumsy process in which the plate had to be coated with a solution prior to use and exposed before it dried. Glass supplanted negatives of paper and gave much better positive prints, but it was not until towards the end of the century that photographs could be reproduced in print other than by hand-chiselled woodcuts, hand-drawn lithographs, or hand-engraved metal plates. The new 'art', whatever its effect on oil-painting in general, quickly killed the miniature and silhouette which could not compete in accuracy or cost.

Continued improvements in the printing-press and the increased employment of steam-power meant that newspapers achieved wider circulation, and there was a further gain when the tax on them was repealed in 1855. Illustrations in books and periodicals became more common, woodcuts often being used because they could be printed at the same time as the text. Advantage was taken of these changes when the *Illustrated London News* began to appear weekly from 14 May 1842, printing news alongside pictures of the events described.

Group of articles manufactured for Summerly's Art Manufactures under the direction of Henry Cole. The venture was in being for a few years from about 1847, when Cole terminated it and turned his attention to the forthcoming Great Exhibition. Victoria and Albert Museum.

Decorative Styles, William IV and Early Victorian Period (Continued)

Cheap printing was also a considerable aid in circulating the works of the most popular writer of the time, Charles Dickens. His books were issued in weekly parts, each of them including half-a-dozen or so woodcut illustrations to help bring the written words to life.

The attention of many more people was directed to sculpture by a new type of unglazed white porcelain named after the Greek marble, Parian. Parian china was used for small-sized copies of sculptures, resulting in reduced versions of busts, figures and groups suitable for the average home. They spread a knowledge of sculpture just as engravings and lithographs did of painting, by introducing the work of the foremost artists to thousands who would otherwise never have seen them.

ARCHITECTS

Sir Charles Barry, R.A. (1795–1860)

Charles Barry was born into comfortable circumstances, and after being articled to a firm of London surveyors travelled abroad studying architecture for a few years. On returning to London he began his career by designing some churches in the Gothic style (for example, St. Peter, Victoria Gardens, Brighton—although it was altered in 1900). Following the accidental burning of the old House of Commons in 1834, a competition for a new building was announced, with entries to be in 'Gothic or Elizabethan' style. Barry's design was accepted, and he employed A. W. N. Pugin to assist him in drafting many of the details; the building was still unfinished at his death in 1860, his son being thenceforward employed in its completion. Barry's other work included the City Art Gallery, Manchester, and the original layout and fountains for Trafalgar Square, London (the present fountains date from 1948). That he was not exclusively an adherent to Gothic is proved by his Classical-style building for the Travellers' Club, in Pall Mall, London.

Isambard Kingdom Brunel (1806–59)

Brunel was the son of Sir Marc Isambard Brunel, a French engineer who fled from the Revolution to America and came to England in 1799. Isambard Kingdom Brunel assisted his father in some of his works, including the Thames Tunnel. He was foremost an engineer, his output including such projects as the Clifton Suspension Bridge, Bristol, and the layout of the Great Western Railway (now incorporated in British Rail, Western Region). He designed many bridges, docks and other constructions, some of which may be thought to entitle Brunel, no less than Sir Joseph Paxton, to be included under the same heading as conventional architects.

Decimus Burton (1800–81)

The tenth son (hence his forename) of a builder, Decimus Burton was practising as an architect by the time he was twenty-four. Most of his work was in the Regency classical style. He designed houses erected in many parts of England, while his public buildings in London attest his ability in that sphere. They include the Athenaeum Club, Pall Mall (top storey added in 1899), the Screen giving entry to the park at Hyde Park Corner, and the archway at the top of Constitution Hill. This last was first erected in 1828 to form a Royal

Architects, William IV and Early Victorian Period (Continued)

entrance to Hyde Park, outside which it stood. In 1846 a large statue of the Duke of Wellington on horseback was placed on top of it, but this was taken to Aldershot in 1883 when the arch was removed to its present site. Eventually the well-known figure of Peace in a chariot was substituted for that of the Duke.

William Butterfield (*1814–1900*)

Butterfield was the son of a London chemist, and after receiving training began his architectural career in Worcester. He was a member of the Cambridge Camden Society, known after 1845 as the Ecclesiological Society. It was one of several concerned with ecclesiology, the science of the building and decoration of churches, which was a hotly debated subject from the late 1830s. His work was in the Gothic style and concerned almost exclusively with churches, parsonages and schools, and of the first-named All Saints, Margaret Street, London, is the most typical. His use of contrasting brick, tiles, stone and alabaster, the brick in various colours, was copied by some and has been criticised by many.

Sir Joseph Paxton (*1801–65*)

Joseph Paxton was employed by the Duke of Devonshire as Superintendent of the

The main entrance in the south side of the Great Exhibition building, the Crystal Palace, which was sited almost opposite Prince of Wales Gate leading into Hyde Park from Kensington Road.

Architects, William IV and Early Victorian Period (Continued)

gardens at Chatsworth, Derbyshire, duly becoming House Steward, manager of the estate and the Duke's confidential adviser. At Chatsworth in 1836–50 he built iron and glass conservatories, as well as other garden buildings at various dates. The Executive Committee of the Great Exhibition had set a competition in 1850 for a building to be situated in Hyde Park, but none of the 245 designs submitted was considered satisfactory. Paxton heard of the dilemma, promised to send his own design, and while at a meeting at Derby of the Midland Railway, a company of which he was a director, doodled on a blotting-pad the idea that soon became the Crystal Palace. Following his successful combination of iron and glass for conservatories, he proposed a similar, but gigantic structure for the exhibition building, and the suggestion was accepted. Clearing of the site began on 30 July 1850 and the building was finished in the following May, the structure containing about 4,500 tons of iron, 293,500 panes of glass and twenty-four miles of guttering. After the Exhibition had ended, on 15 October 1851, the building was dismantled and re-erected some miles away in Sydenham, South London. There, it was put to numerous uses until, on 30 November 1936, it caught fire and was destroyed, leaving its name attached to the area where it had stood. Paxton designed a few conventional buildings, including one in France.

PAINTERS

Sir Edwin Landseer, R.A. (1802–73)

Edwin Landseer was the son of an engraver, and responded to his father's encouragement to study drawing. Fond of animals, by the age of eighteen he had won prizes for his likenesses of horses and dogs. Before long, he had an opportunity of dissecting and studying a dead lion, enabling him to increase his repertoire and render the animal with great accuracy and realism. His steady output was very popular with the public, whether those who attended exhibitions or those who bought engraved or lithographed reproductions of the works. Landseer posed his subjects as if they were human models, and most of his pictures point a simple moral or tell a simple story; features that irritate many observers, and invoke criticism of the artist despite his great ability with the brush. One of his typically sentimental pictures is *The Old Shepherd's Chief Mourner* (Victoria and Albert Museum), with the faithful dog resting its head on the blanket covering the coffin of his master, the latter's hat, stick and Bible in the foreground, and the entire scene faultlessly drawn and painted. Landseer produced some etchings and also modelled the four bronze figures of lions at the base of Nelson's Column, in Trafalgar Square. A painting of him by John Ballantyne shows him in his studio at work on one of the lions, while two completed ones are in the background (National Portrait Gallery).

Pre-Raphaelite Brotherhood (1848–52)

In 1848 there was a general fear that revolution might break out in England, with the Chartists clamouring for reforms for the working class. The spirit of revolt penetrated to art circles, and from it grew what was called the Pre-Raphaelite Brotherhood. It comprised a group of seven men: William Holman Hunt (1827–1910), John Everett Millais (1829–96), Dante Gabriel Rossetti (1828–82) and his brother William Michael Rossetti, Thomas

Painters, William IV and Early Victorian Period (Continued)

A painting by Sir John Millais in which every detail is rendered realistically. It depicts a Huguenot on St. Bartholomew's Day refusing to allow the young woman to tie a scarf around his arm; the scarf would have proclaimed him to be Catholic and assured his life being spared. Christie's.

Woolner (1825–92), F. G. Stephens (1828–82) and James Collinson (1825–81). Of them, the first three were the most active and talented as painters: Woolner was a sculptor, Stephens destroyed most of his paintings and took to the pen, and W. M. Rossetti was neither painter nor sculptor but acted as secretary to the others. Their objective was to look back in time and emulate the artists prior to the fifteenth/sixteenth century painter Raphael, and to rescue art from the failed state into which they considered it had declined. The result was a series of paintings resembling brightly-coloured and well-focussed photographs of people in costume, telling either a secular or a religious story. Typical of them are Hunt's *May Morning on Magdalen Tower* (Museum and Art Gallery, Birmingham), and *The Light of the World* (City Art Gallery, Manchester), Millais's *The Woodman's Daughter* (Guildhall Gallery, London), and *Ophelia* and *Christ in the House of His Parents* (Tate Gallery), D. G. Rossetti's *The Childhood of Mary, Virgin* (Tate Gallery) and Collinson's *The Empty Purse* (Tate Gallery, painted in 1857, but earlier versions elsewhere). The Brotherwood kept more or less intact until 1852, having published its own journal, *The Germ*, which ran for four issues. Ruskin defended the group against the attacks of Charles Dickens and others, but although they themselves did not endure, their style was contagious and they had numerous followers during the ensuing years.

Painters, William IV and Early Victorian Period (Continued)

Augustus Welby Northmore Pugin (1812–52)

A. W. N. Pugin was the son of a Frenchman who came to London and worked as an architectural draughtsman for John Nash. The younger Pugin was trained by his father, and making for him a large number of drawings of Gothic details, he retained a lifelong interest in the style. In 1827 he designed some furniture for Windsor Castle, and in 1835 published a book of designs entitled *Gothic Furniture* (examples of some of his furniture are in the Victoria and Albert Museum). Pugin assisted Sir Charles Barry on the drafting of Gothic details for the Houses of Parliament; a matter that was later a subject of argument as to which of the two men was mainly responsible for these important features. Pugin was a convert to the Roman Catholic faith, designing for its adherents a number of places of worship, including: St. Chad's Cathedral, Birmingham; St. Mary's Cathedral, Derby; St. Peter, Marlow, Buckinghamshire, and St. Giles, Cheadle, Staffordshire. He was critical of the design of recently-built Anglican churches, writing to a friend that he was 'perfectly convinced the Roman Catholic Church is the only true one, and the only one in which the grand and sublime style of church architecture can ever be restored'. Pugin designed church vestments and ornaments and was responsible for the Medieval Court at the Great Exhibition, where his ideas reached a wide public. He was married three times, his first two wives dying and the third surviving him. A. W. N. Pugin died tragically, in a private asylum, mentally deranged from pressure of work.

A. W. N. Pugin was responsible for the display in the Medieval Court at the 1851 Great Exhibition, of which this is a view published at the time.

Painters, William IV and Early Victorian Period (Continued)

J. M. W. Turner's watercolour view of Geneva and Mont Blanc with the lake of Geneva in the foreground. Sotheby's.

John Ruskin (1819–1900)

Ruskin is seldom considered as an artist, although he could draw well, but his eminence as a critic caused him to play an important part in artistic matters from the mid-century onwards. John Ruskin was the only child of a successful wine merchant, and was considered to be in poor health; to safeguard him his anxious mother took lodgings in Oxford when he was at the University. Soon after he was twenty-four he published the first volume of *Modern Painters* containing a strong defence of J. M. W. Turner, which prompted much comment from readers. He then paid a visit to northern Italy, studying painting, architecture and sculpture, resulting in the book *The Seven Lamps of Architecture*. This came from the press in 1849, and was illustrated by his own etchings. He continued to publish books and to lecture, wrote in support of the Pre-Raphaelites and taught classes at the Working Men's College, Great Ormond Street, London. His father's death in 1864 left him a wealthy man, and he started a number of philanthropic projects including the founding of a museum at Sheffield and the initiation of a guild to run on co-operative and Socialist principles. His written and spoken pronouncements were taken most seriously when they were made, and undoubtedly had an effect on the art world of his time.

Joseph Mallord William Turner, R.A. (1775–1851)

J. M. W. Turner was born in London, the son of a barber from Devonshire. After a rudimentary education the boy had drawing lessons, did an assortment of jobs such as colouring engravings, and then attended the Academy Schools. He was commissioned to

Painters, William IV and Early Victorian Period (Continued)

make drawings of scenes in various parts of England and Wales, and walking from place to place carrying his baggage was able to do the work. From 1793 he exhibited oil-paintings at the Academy and by the end of the century was experimenting with the effects of light and shade that were to be characteristic of much of his future work. Being introspective by nature, he was always fully absorbed in whatever he was engaged on, and as his personal appearance was not attractive led rather a solitary existence. Many of his views were engraved and reached a wide audience, but his controversial impressionistic scenes required the writings of Ruskin before they gained acceptance. He spent his last years living in secret under an assumed name at Chelsea, and was buried in St. Paul's Cathedral. His Will was not clearly expressed, but after litigation the Royal Academy received £20,000 for its funds and his paintings and drawings went to the nation. They may be seen in the Tate Gallery, while other examples of his work are in galleries in many countries.

SCULPTORS

Edward Hodges Baily, R.A. (1788–1867)

Baily was born at Bristol and eventually took up art as a career, receiving training at the Academy Schools. In 1816 he became chief modeller to the firm of Royal silversmiths,

Venus, John Gibson's representation in marble of the goddess of Love. Bonhams.

Sculptors, William IV and Early Victorian Period (Continued)

Rundell, Bridge and Rundell, designing for them soup tureens and much else during the next thirty years. His statues included that of *Nelson* which surmounts the column in Trafalgar Square, and *Eve at the Fountain* (City Art Gallery, Bristol). Baily executed numerous monuments, and although he must have made money during a busy career spent his last years in comparative poverty.

John Gibson, R.A. (*1790–1866*)

The son of a Welsh market-gardener, Gibson was first apprenticed to a cabinet-maker in Liverpool and then obtained work with a local firm of statuaries, who made chimney-pieces and monuments. He eventually went to London and in 1817 to Rome, where he received further training and remained working there until 1844. In that year he was summoned by Queen Victoria to make a statue of her, which he embellished with tints of colour—much to the surprise and horror of some critics. He returned to Rome, visiting his native land only twice again for short stays. In about 1855 he began the *Tinted Venus* (Walker Art Gallery, Liverpool), of which he wrote 'How can I ever part from her?', and kept the figure in his studio for four years before finally sending it to the client who had given him the commission. Gibson's *Grazia* and his *Pandora* (both, Victoria and Albert Museum) are typical of his work: 'his subjects were gleaned from the free actions of the splendid Italian people he noticed in his walks, and afterwards baptized with such mythological names as best fitted them'.

LATER VICTORIAN PERIOD: 1860-1890

DURING the final decades of Queen Victoria's reign the Gothic style continued to be employed. It would seem to have been considered suitable for almost every purpose, ranging from churches where it was debatably appropriate to town halls where it was completely unjustified. Early signs of a change in taste came with the building of the Red House, Bexley Heath, Greater London, in 1859, designed for William Morris by Philip Webb.

The new and simple designs slowly gained ground during the remainder of the century, although there was no lack of support for what many still considered to be conventional architecture. There was a continued demand for buildings in variations of Italian styles, and the reign closed with the ornamented old and the plain new jostling for attention.

The Prince Consort died suddenly at the age of forty-two in 1861, having been taken ill while making arrangements for a forthcoming international exhibition. This duly took place in London in 1862, and although it was attended by more people than had visited the display of eleven years earlier, the death of the Prince overshadowed it and it was considered to have been less successful. Other, comparable exhibitions had also been held, at New York and Dublin in 1853 and at Paris in 1855, all of which had stimulated competition and assisted in spreading ideas from one country to another.

Decorative Styles, Later Victorian Period (Continued)

Prevailing styles in merchandise were assorted, with an emphasis on eye-catching ornament. The ever-expanding markets at home and abroad demanded goods that were both plentiful and cheap, causing designers to work with the machine foremost in mind and cut costs by keeping hand workmanship to a minimum.

On the other hand there was, as at any time, a minority of buyers who were more discerning than most and willing to pay for the privilege of owning something superior in design and workmanship to mass-produced goods. Earlier, Henry Cole had attempted to cater for such people, and from 1862 the task was shouldered by William Morris and his associates.

They were responsible for designing sober-looking, functional furniture, akin to that traditionally made by country joiners; furniture of straightforward construction with a minimum of ornamentation. When decoration did appear it took the form of painting executed by first-class artists, leading a sarcastic critic to suggest framing the work of the latter and discarding the remainder.

The influence of Morris led in the early 1880s to the founding of a number of groups to foster the individual craftsman and protect him from the machine. The first display organized by the Arts and Crafts Exhibition Society was held in 1888, others following at intervals, and the public was enabled to see carefully designed and produced objects of all kinds from furniture to silver.

A 'fairy' painting of the type popular during the period 1840–71. This example depicts the wedding of Oberon and Titania and was painted by J. A. Fitzgerald (1832–1906). Christie's.

Decorative Styles, Later Victorian Period (Continued)

A Drawing Room, 1887; The writing table to the left and the scroll picture hanging over it are the result of the keen interest in Japanese art at the time. Most of the china in the room is Oriental.

There were as many current styles in painting as in other forms of art. The majority of people would seem to have enjoyed colourful scenes with clear explanatory titles that circulated widely as prints. There was a more limited popularity for pictures of fairies, which first made an appearance in the 1840s and continued to come and go during the ensuing thirty years. Shakespeare's works, to which attention was directed afresh by the tercentenary celebrations of 1864, inspired scenes featuring Titania and her winged subjects as well as numerous other characters from the plays.

The Pre-Raphaelite artists left a legacy in the shape of an interest in the medieval, and there was further a school of prolific painters who concentrated their attention on the ancient Greeks and Romans. These were portrayed, wearing togas or in the nude, in scenes that have been compared with coloured 'stills' from Hollywood epics.

Decorative Styles, Later Victorian Period (Continued)

Photography claimed a number of skilled artists who took up the rapidly improving science, joining a never-ending argument as to whether it was that or an art. Conversely, many painters employed photography to assist them in their work and this, also, was the subject of debate.

The influence of Japanese art is discernible from the 1860s onwards, when increasing quantities of examples reached Europe. Fans and other motifs soon appeared on English chinaware, which was manufactured in shapes and colours more or less simulating that of the Far East. Anglicized versions of Japanese furniture were made on a commercial scale and it was suggested that a profusion of potted ferns and other plants would give a room a truly Oriental air. Not least, the work of a few artists, notably that of Whistler, was markedly affected, with models posing in kimonos, and occasionally a Nankin blue-and-white vase was carefully introduced.

ARCHITECTS

William Morris (1834–96)

Morris was born at Walthamstow, Essex. His father died when the boy was only thirteen but left the family comfortably provided for, enabling William to be sent to

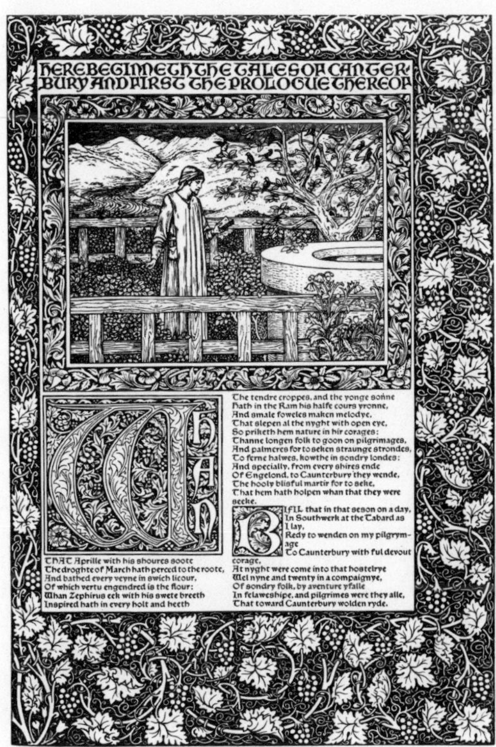

HEREBEGINNETHTHETALESOFCANTER
BURYANDFIRSTTHEPROLOGUETHEREOF

WHAN THAT Aprille with his shoures soote
The droghte of March hath perced to the roote,
And bathed every veyne in swich licour,
Of which vertu engendred is the flour:
Whan Zephirus eek with his swete breeth
Inspired hath in every holt and heeth
The tendre croppes, and the yonge sonne
Hath in the Ram his halfe cours yronne,
And smale foweles maken melodye,
That slepen al the nyght with open eye,
So priketh hem nature in hir corages:
Thanne longen folk to goon on pilgrimages,
And palmeres for to seken straunge strondes,
To ferne halwes, kowthe in sondry londes:
And specially, from every shires ende
Of Engelond, to Caunterbury they wende,
The hooly blisful martir for to seke,
That hem hath holpen whan that they were seeke.

BIFIL that in that seson on a day,
In Southwerk at the Tabard as I lay,
Redy to wenden on my pilgrymage
To Caunterbury with ful devout corage,
At nyght were come into that hostelrye
Wel nyne and twenty in a compaignye,
Of sondry folk, by aventure yfalle
In felaweshipe, and pilgrimes were they alle,
That toward Caunterbury wolden ryde.

A page from The Works of Geoffrey Chaucer, with illustrations by Sir Edward Burne-Jones, printed at William Morris's Kelmscott Press.

Architects, Later Victorian Period (Continued)

Marlborough and Exeter College, Oxford. While at the latter he met a group of students who were interested in ecclesiastical history, medieval verse and kindred subjects. He had intended taking holy orders, but changed his mind and decided that he would be of greater service to the world as an architect; a profession in which, he considered, he might best apply his zeal for social reform. Morris entered the office of G. E. Street, and soon afterwards, when he had formed a friendship with D. G. Rossetti, was persuaded to exchange architecture for painting. He then married and had a house built at Bexley Heath, Greater London, which, with much of its contents was designed by his friend Philip Webb, who had also worked with Street. Within a short time Morris set off on another tack; he became a decorator, and in 1862 started a firm with premises in London for the supply of distinctive stained glass, furniture and fabrics. In spite of the care lavished on it, the house at Bexley proved unhealthy in occupation; a move to London occurred and a country home, Kelmscott Manor, near Oxford, was taken on a joint-tenancy with D. G. Rossetti. In 1877 Morris and Webb founded the Society for the Preservation of Rural England. For a few years he became enthusiastically enmeshed in the realities of politics, first as a Liberal and then as a Socialist. For his new friends he wrote some battle-songs, *Chants for Socialists*, and treated them to a lecture on 'Art, Wealth and Riches'. Finally, he found, as others have subsequently, that the more extreme members of the movement were outpacing a comparative moderate and he ceased to play an active part. His final activity was to set up a printing-press, named the Kelmscott Press, on which he printed poems and prose works of his own composition as well as those of other writers. The carefully-produced books are typical of Morris's thoroughness at whatever he attempted, the work of a man who stated 'Have nothing in your house that you do not know to be useful or believe to be beautiful'.

Sir George Gilbert Scott, R.A. (*1811–78*)

He was born in Buckinghamshire, and after a period of training set up in practice with a fellow-pupil. Scott's career opened with the building of churches, and after being roused to enthusiasm by some of A. W. N. Pugin's writings and the papers of the Cambridge Camden Society, he eagerly studied medieval principles. In 1841 he designed the Martyrs' Memorial, Oxford, in the style of the late thirteenth century and was soon accepted as one of the chief workers in the medieval manner. He was a prolific builder and restorer of churches; in the latter rôle, in company with other men of his time, he has been accused of wantonly destroying old work and replacing it with his own. His churches include: Christ Church, Turnham Green (chancel added later), St. Mary, Hanwell, and St. Mathias, Richmond, all three on the outskirts of London. Between 1862 and 1872, Scott was occupied with the design and erection of the Albert Memorial, Kensington, which has been described as 'a magnified thirteenth century reliquary' by one writer and in much less complimentary terms by others. Towards the end of that commission he built the Home Office and the Foreign Office, Whitehall, but on the insistence of the Prime Minister, Viscount Palmerston, he was not allowed to employ Gothic. Scott is said to have been concerned, in one way or another, with more than 700 buildings and projects ranging from cathedrals to ecclesiastical accessories. He served as Professor of Medieval Architecture at the Royal Academy and President of the Royal Institute of British Architects, and is buried in Westminster Abbey, where a brass plate engraved by G. E. Street marks his grave.

Architects, Later Victorian Period (Continued)

Richard Norman Shaw, R.A. (*1831–1912*)

Born at Edinburgh, Shaw studied at the Royal Academy Schools, London, and in 1858 was working in Street's office. After a period in partnership, he set up in practice on his own and specialized in designing large houses and blocks of offices. His first work was highly individual, with a use of timbering, hung tiles and a profusion of projecting gables and big chimneys, quite different from anything else at the time. Later he modified his style, but his buildings almost always have a marked individuality. His work in London includes: Albert Hall Mansions, Kensington, the Piccadilly Hotel, Piccadilly, and Nos. 170 and 185 Queen's Gate, Kensington. Shaw also designed furniture, although most of it seems to have disappeared, perhaps temporarily (a large cabinet-bookcase and a cradle are in the Victoria and Albert Museum). Norman Shaw designed much of the 'garden city' of Bedford Park, Chiswick, where the neat red-brick buildings, commonplace to-day, must have been in dramatic contrast to conventional villas when they were erected in the late 1870s.

George Edmund Street, R.A. (*1824–81*)

Street was born at Woodford, Essex, and in 1855 established his practice in London after earlier ventures at Wantage, Berkshire, and Oxford. He was a member of the Ecclesiological Society and a deeply religious man, believing that a pure Gothic setting was beneficial to worship. His first essay in church building was St. Mary, Biscovey, Par, Cornwall, erected in 1849, and in due course he designed others including St. James-the-Less, Thorndike Street, Westminster, and St. Philip and St. James, Oxford. He also provided furnishings for these and other churches. Apart from ecclesiastical work, Street built the Royal Courts of Justice (The Law Courts), Strand, after gaining the commission in competition. He served as President of the Royal Institute of British Architects and as Professor of Architecture at the Royal Academy, and was buried in Westminster Abbey. It has been remarked that Street's office was a nursery of the Arts and Crafts movement, as so many of its prominent members started their careers with the architect.

PAINTERS

Lord Leighton of Stretton, P.R.A. (*1830–96*)

Frederic Leighton was born at Scarborough, Yorkshire, and trained as an artist in Italy, Germany and France. He travelled and worked in several countries before settling in London in 1860. Along with Sir E. J. Poynter, P.R.A. and Sir Lawrence Alma-Tadema, R.A., he specialized in what may be termed 'reconstructions' of real and mythological scenes in ancient Greece and Rome. They featured pretty models, often nude, with titles like *Perseus and Andromeda* (Walker Art Gallery, Liverpool) and *The Bath of Psyche* (Tate Gallery). Leighton also drew illustrations for books and executed sculpture, his best-known works in the latter medium being *Athlete with a Python* and *The Sluggard* (both, Tate Gallery). He was described as having a 'fine presence and manners at once genial and courtly', and spoke several languages fluently. Leighton was raised to the peerage only a few days prior to his death, and was the first British painter to be so honoured. From 1866 he lived at 2 Holland Park Road, Kensington, in which there remains his tile-lined Arab Hall.

Painters, Later Victorian Period (Continued)

An imaginary scene in Classical times showing a procession in honour of the season of Spring, painted by Sir Lawrence Alma-Tadema. Sotheby Parke Bernet, Los Angeles.

Sir John Everett Millais, P.R.A. (1829–96)

Millais was born at Southampton, his father being one of a family originating in Jersey. By the time he was eleven years of age the boy was in London attending the Academy Schools, and in 1849 he joined with D. G. Rossetti and others in the Pre-Raphaelite Brotherhood. A year later, in the Royal Academy exhibition of 1850, he showed *Christ in the House of His Parents* (*The Carpenter's Shop*) (Tate Gallery) and drew down upon himself and his circle a storm of abuse led by Charles Dickens. The realistic painting was considered to be

Painters, Later Victorian Period (Continued)

just as blasphemous as it was inartistic, but when Ruskin sprang to the defence of the Brotherhood the criticism abated. In due course came *Ophelia* (Tate Gallery), equally true to life in every minute detail, 'selecting nothing, rejecting nothing', as was *The Woodman's Daughter* (Guildhall Art Gallery, London); for the latter the strawberries were purchased out of season at Covent Garden market, and they are depicted being proffered to a child whose boots were painted from a pair borrowed from 'a little country girl named Esther'. The Brotherhood did not endure long, and Millais set off after fame and fortune soon after marrying Effie Ruskin, who had obtained a decree of nullity against her husband, the critic John Ruskin. Over the years Millais painted those popular favourites *The Boyhood of Raleigh* and *The North-West Passage* (both, Tate Gallery) and *Bubbles*, the last being firmly associated with the brand of soap it was so effectively used to advertise. He also painted a number of portraits, including those of Lord Beaconsfield, Carlyle and Sir Arthur Sullivan (all, National Portrait Gallery). Millais, a handsome and successful man, built himself a mansion in Palace Gate, Kensington, and when he died was buried in St. Paul's Cathedral.

Sir William Quiller Orchardson, R.A. (*1835–1910*)

Born at Edinburgh and trained there before settling in London in 1862, Orchardson painted pictures of popular subjects such as *Napoleon on Board the 'Bellerophon'* (Tate Gallery). He is best known for his sentimental scenes of 'High Life', which include *The First Cloud* (National Gallery of Victoria, Melbourne, Australia and a smaller replica at the Tate Gallery), and *Mariage de Convenance* (City Art Gallery and Museum, Glasgow). The last-named depicts a young wife seated thoughtfully and sadly at one end of a long laden dining table, at the other end of which is her elderly husband for whom a butler pours wine. Orchardson was meticulous in portraying the well-furnished surroundings of his subjects, and liked to introduce old spinets, old French and English furniture and other period accessories. They reflect the interest that was then beginning to be shown in studying and collecting furniture and other antiques.

George Frederick Watts, R.A. (*1817–1904*)

Watts was born in London, the son of a Welshman and from an early age was encouraged to study art. In 1842 the Royal Commission appointed for the decoration of the new House of Commons offered prizes for suitable fresco paintings. Watts won £300, used the money to go to Italy to further his studies and in later years was successful in other competitions of the same kind. He was befriended by Lord and Lady Holland, the former serving as ambassador at Florence and then Paris, and by other wealthy patrons, so was able to spend almost the whole of his life free from economic worries. His paintings range from portraits of prominent people of the time (many in the National Portrait Gallery) to a series of allegorical subjects that have been both praised and adversely criticized. He has been described as 'a preacher in paint', and once stated 'My intention has not been so much to paint pictures that charm the eye, as to suggest great thoughts that will appeal to the imagination and the heart, and kindle all that is best and noblest in humanity'. The attempts of Watts to carry out this ideal varied in their success and may be seen in many galleries; his thoughts like his colouring were often somewhat blurred, but his drawing and composition were sound. He lived a secluded, almost unworldly life, which led him at the age

Painters, Later Victorian Period (Continued)

of forty-seven to marry the sixteen-year-old actress Ellen Terry. The marriage quickly terminated and he re-married some twenty years later. Many of Watts's allegorical paintings are in the Tate Gallery, and a selection of his work is to be seen at the Watts Gallery, Compton, Surrey, which was built and opened by the artist in 1904. Like Leighton, he also executed some sculpture, an example being the group *Physical Energy*, which stands in Kensington Gardens.

James Abbott McNeill Whistler (1834–1903)

Whistler was born at Lowell, Massachusetts, and by 1857 was in Paris studying art. Two years later he came to London and made a series of etchings of Thames-side scenes that were praised at the time and have retained general admiration. Whistler was by nature an extrovert, and liked publicising his frequent quarrels although he gained little personal credit from them. In 1877 he took John Ruskin to court, the critic having described his painting *Nocturne in Blue and Gold: the Falling Rocket* (Institute of Arts, Detroit) as 'a pot of paint flung in the public face'. Whistler made the most of his appearance in the witness box, winning the case but gaining a reward of a mere farthing damages and duly becoming bankrupt as a result of the legal costs. He did not give his paintings the descriptive titles popular with his contemporaries, but preferred to employ musical ones, such as Nocturne, Harmony or Arrangement. This did not please a public familiar with paintings and titles that told a story, and his use of an unorthodox signature in the form of a butterfly weighed against him with some people; Whistler was continually going against the tide, saving himself often only by his sarcastic tongue. The first American-born artist to gain international prominence, his paintings are distributed all over the world. The complete room he decorated for the shipowner F. R. Leyland and his painting *The Princess of the Land of Porcelain* are with a large collection of his works in the Freer Gallery of Art, Washington, D.C., and his many memorable pictures include also: *Arrangement in Grey and Black, No. 1: the Artist's Mother* (Louvre, Paris), *Arrangement in Grey and Black, No. 2: Thomas Carlyle* (City Art Gallery and Museum, Glasgow) and *Harmony in Grey and Green: Miss Cicely Alexander* (Tate Gallery).

Cabinet decorated by J. A. McNeill Whistler with Japanese-style cloud motifs and butterflies. It was exhibited in 1878. Christie's.

PART II

1. FURNITURE

AN old dictionary defines furniture as 'Movables: goods put in a house for use or ornament'. Modern usage of the term limits it, on the whole, to movable articles found in the home and which are constructed of wood.

WOODS

Many different timbers, home-grown as well as imported from the tropics, were employed from time to time in making furniture:

Alder The newly-cut wood is white, but turns deep red when exposed to the air and stabilizes to flesh colour. It was used by rural craftsmen who appreciated its resistance to decay. In Scotland, alder that has been immersed in a peat bog to acquire a dark red colour is termed 'Scots mahogany'.

Amboyna A close-grained hard wood, light brown in colour with innumerable small curly markings. It was used in the eighteenth century and after as a veneer. Amboyna was imported from the Moluccas, in the East Indies, the islands of Amboyna and Ceram being the sources of supply and the former giving the wood its name.

Apple The wood of this tree, whether wild or cultivated, was used by country craftsmen from the seventeenth century onwards. Apple-wood is hard, has a close grain and is light brown in colour.

Ash The wood is white with yellow-brown streaks, the grain resembling that of oak. It is hard, strong, heavy and resilient, but prone to attack by wood-worm. Ash was used for making furniture in rural districts from early times, and was employed for the seats of Windsor chairs. John Evelyn pointed out that certain cuts of the timber are unusually figured and greatly in demand by cabinet-makers; 'and when our woodmen light upon it, they make what money they will of it'.

Bamboo In China the woody stems of this giant type of grass were used to make chairs and settees which were exported to Europe. Sheraton noted in 1803: 'They are in some degree imitated in England by turning beech in the same form, and making chairs of this fashion, painting them to match the colours of the reeds and cane.' English cabinet-makers made many

Furniture, Woods (Continued)

other pieces of furniture, including tables, sets of bookshelves and whatnots in simulated bamboo during the late eighteenth and early nineteenth centuries. Bamboo was again fashionable from the 1880s.

Baywood Honduras mahogany, so-called because it was exported from the Bay of Honduras.

Beech The beech tree is quick-growing and produces a tough wood ranging in colour from near-white to pale brown. It turns well and has a long history of popularity. Writing in the seventeenth century of humble dwellings, a poet noted

> 'Beech made their Chests, their Beds
> and the Joyn'd-stools,
> Beech made the Board [table], the
> Platters and the Bowles'.

On the other hand, John Evelyn, who wrote a book on trees, entitled *Sylva*, published in 1664, complained that the wood was frequently attacked by woodworm: 'I wish the use of it were by a law prohibited all joyners, cabinet-makers, and such as furnish tables, chairs, bedsteads, coffers etc. They have a way to black and polish it so as to render it like ebony, and with a mixture of soot and urine imitate the walnut.' Beechwood was frequently employed for making the frames of bedsteads and chairs, mahogany chairs incorporating it wherever upholstery hid the woodwork from the eye. In the late eighteenth century, when painted chairs were fashionable, they were usually made of beech throughout. See Bentwood.

Bentwood A German, Michael Thonet (1796–1871), born at Boppard, near Koblenz, Germany, with a furniture factory in Vienna, developed a process for steam-bending Carpathian beechwood. By this means he was able to make chairs and tables of very simple construction and light weight in great numbers to sell cheaply. He showed examples in the London 1851 and 1862 International Exhibitions, and very quickly established a world-wide business. For inexpensive and practical chairs the name of Thonet (*Gebrüder Thonet:* Thonet Brothers) was synonymous with highly successful forerunners of the modern pressed metal and fibreglass articles.

Birch John Evelyn wrote: 'Though Birch be of all other the worst of timber, yet has it its various uses'. It is whitish in colour, and has been employed in place of many other woods. Not least, in the late eighteenth century it sometimes did duty as an inexpensive and easily obtained substitute for satinwood.

Bird's Eye A marking of tiny curls and dots resembling the eye of a bird. Some varieties of maple, amboyna and thuya show bird's eye figure.

Boxwood A particularly close-grained and hard wood, with qualities for carving and turning that have been compared to those of ivory. In medieval times boxwood was used for combs, later it was employed for mathematical instruments where a good straight edge was vital, and for nutcrackers in which the strength of the wood allied to the leverage of the handles produced a force no nut could resist. It was employed, too, for cutting printing blocks, the finest woodcuts being made from box cut on the fine end grain. The wood is unique in being the only one of European growth that sinks in water.

Furniture, Woods (Continued)

Brazil Brazil wood was imported from South America as well as from the West Indies. It is hard, and red in colour with distinct markings. The wood served as an inlay in the late seventeenth century, but it was principally used by dyers who extracted the colour from it.

Burr Wood A burr is a wart-like lump on a tree, formed where it has been injured, or has had its branches cut off (pollarded). Some trees are prone to form burrs when mistreated, among them being walnut, maple, yew, elm and mulberry. When sliced across, the burr reveals a distinctive pattern comprising a multitude of tiny curls making a highly decorative veneer. The best-known use of burr wood was in the Queen Anne/George I period, when veneers of burr walnut were placed within borders of herring-bone inlay and an outer framing of cross-banding. In America the word burl is used in preference to burr.

Calamander An East Indian timber deriving its name from the Singhalese *Kalu-mindrie:* black flowering. It is a variety of ebony, close-grained, hard and of a hazel-brown colour striped with black. Calamander was used during the Regency period as a veneer and for cross-banding. It is very similar to Coromandel wood.

Casuarina This is known also as Beef-wood and Iron-wood. It is hard, close-grained and dark or brick-red in colour.

Cedar Varieties of the tree are indigenous to North America and the West Indies, as well as to many other parts of the world. The timber is aromatic, and is mentioned in the Bible. Specimens of furniture made from it prior to the eighteenth century exist, but are scarce. Georgian boxes and travelling chests have survived, as well as cedar drawer linings. In America the wood was also employed for minor purposes, and sometimes as a principal wood in New England. Cedar-wood chairs, tables and other articles were made on the island of Bermuda from the mid-seventeenth century onwards.

Cherry This fruitwood is of a reddish colour and can be easily made to resemble mahogany. John Evelyn stated that the black cherry tree sometimes grows to a size sufficient to make tables and cabinets from the wood. Cherry wood was much employed by eighteenth century American cabinet-makers, especially in New York and Connecticut but less often elsewhere.

Chestnut The Sweet or Spanish variety was often employed in place of oak for all kinds of furniture. The two woods are alike in appearance, except that chestnut lacks the silvery markings distinctive in riven oak. It has been alleged that spiders will not spin their webs on chestnut, but this is untrue and an absence of spiders' webs means only that someone has recently been active with a duster. In the late eighteenth century veneers of both sweet chestnut and horse chestnut were occasionally used as a substitute for satinwood, in the same manner as birch. Horse chestnut wood tends to be soft and rather 'woolly'.

Coromandel A type of ebony imported from the Coromandel Coast of south-east India. Thomas Sheraton noted in 1803 that it was 'lately introduced into England and is much in use by cabinet-makers for banding'. It closely resembles Calamander wood.

Crotch or ***Curl*** Mahogany cut from

Furniture, Woods (Continued)

the junction of a branch and the trunk or from where a trunk divides into two.

Cypress John Evelyn wrote in 1664 that the cypress had not long been introduced into England and was a delicate plant to be given every attention. He added 'We see it now in every garden rising to as goodly a bulk and stature as most which you shall ever find in Italy'. He recommended its use especially for making chests, which would resist 'the worm and moth and all putrefaction to eternity'. Cypress wood was used by American makers, especially in the south of the country.

Deal A board or plank, usually of pine or fir, cut to a width of about 9 in. (23 cm.) and between 2 in. and 4½ in. (5–11·5 cm.) in thickness. It is used loosely to describe the actual timbers from which deals are cut. The word deal comes from the German *diele* and Dutch *deel*: a board or plank.

Dogwood A shrub that is common in Britain. One species produces wood with a bright yellow heart surrounded by lighter-coloured sap wood, and is said to have been used for inlaying furniture in the sixteenth and seventeenth centuries. Another species yields a white wood used for ladder rungs, skewers and other implements. In both instances the wood is noticeably hard.

Ebony Ebony is the name given to wood from a number of different species of trees. Their timber is black, very heavy and durable, and can be given a smooth, highly-polished surface. In the later seventeenth century it was very fashionable for mirror frames, clock cases and cabinets. Carved ebony chairs were made in the East in the eighteenth century and exported to England, where they were for long mistakenly described as 'Elizabethan'.

Elm Elm is a wood with many properties, both good and bad. The tree is subject to disease and a branch will fall without warning, or the whole tree can be uprooted in a storm. The wood is hard yet flexible, difficult to work and liable to attack by woodworm. Nevertheless it was widely used for furniture of many kinds, much of which has vanished long ago. Burr elm was occasionally employed as a veneer.

Fiddle Back Mahogany veneer with a flame-like marking, resembling the figuring of sycamore used for the backs of violins.

Harewood The name given to sycamore or maple stained with oxide of iron. When prepared it was a grey colour, but with time this has usually changed to a dull greenish-brown. In the eighteenth century it was known as aire wood or airs wood, an English version of the German *ehrenholz*: maple. The corruption of its name into harewood did not occur until the nineteenth century.

Hickory The tree is a native of North America, acquiring its name from *pohickery* which was given to it by the American Indians. The wood is a pale red in colour and although hard and tough is liable to be attacked by woodworm. Its resilience led to its use by makers of Windsor chairs, especially in the neighbourhoods of New York and Philadelphia.

Holly This common European tree yields a hard, white timber with an even grain. The wood was used for inlay from Tudor times, sometimes stained for special effects. Evelyn said that it was occasionally placed under inlays of ivory 'to render it more conspicuous'. The diarist should have had a good knowledge of the tree, for at his house at Deptford there was a hedge of holly 400 ft. long, 9 ft. high and 5 ft. broad (122·00 × 2·74 × 1·52 metres).

Kingwood This is the name given, probably in the nineteenth century, to a wood known two centuries earlier as Prince Wood or Prince's Wood. It is similar in appearance to rosewood, with blackish narrow stripes on a brown ground. It came from Brazil and the West Indies. In France, kingwood is known as *palissandre*.

Laburnum The ornamental laburnum tree gives a wood of a reddish-brown colour within a yellow outer sapwood. It would seem to have been first used in the late seventeenth century, particularly on the doors of cabinets. For the purpose veneers were sliced transversely from branches, the pieces being laid close together to form a repeat pattern. Because of the shape and marking of the components, this is often known as 'oyster veneer'.

Larch The wood of this tree varies noticeably according to the soil on which it has been grown. In the healthiest specimens it varies between a deep reddish colour and a brownish-yellow, while trees from rich soils or sheltered conditions yield a softer and lighter-coloured wood. When well seasoned, larch neither splits nor shrinks but it has an unfortunate tendency to warp. It was sometimes used in the late eighteenth century for the carcasses of furniture. When growing, the tree secretes a type of turpentine known as 'Venice turpentine', which is a deep yellow-coloured thick and tenacious fluid.

Lignum Vitae This wood was introduced into the West by the Spaniards in the early sixteenth century. It was welcomed for its medical properties by the doctors of the time, and in 1517 it was stated that some 3,000 persons had been restored to health by it in Spain. The wood was boiled and the decoction prescribed for numerous diseases from gout to epilepsy, but principally it was thought to be infallible as a cure for syphilis. The wood is very hard, and black with dark brown markings. In the late seventeenth century it was occasionally employed as a veneer, but was also of value to the turner who made from it bowls and drinking cups, the former of larger size than had hitherto been managed with available woods. Drinking from vessels made of lignum vitae was supposed to be a painless way of imbibing the medicinal value of the wood. The correct name of the tree is the *Guaiacum*, and the Latin name given in the West to the timber, *lignum vitae*, means wood of life.

Lime The wood is cream coloured or white, soft and close-grained. It was much in favour with the late seventeenth-century carvers, of whom Grinling Gibbons is the best known. He executed some of his realistic groups of flowers, fruit and other objects in limewood.

Mahogany The most esteemed of all woods for cabinet-making. Its existence was known in England by about 1670, but it was another fifty years before it reached the country in any quantity. Supplies came from the Spanish settlement of San

Furniture, Woods (Continued)

Domingo, in the Bahamas, and from the other West Indian island of Jamaica. The timber from the two sources varied somewhat in appearance, but both shared the familiar red-brown colour, hardness, and straightness of grain. The finished wood darkened with age, and well-carved examples have been not unreasonably compared to chiselled bronze. This timber is often referred to as Spanish mahogany, despite the fact that Jamaica was a British possession. An alternative source of supply was the nearby island of Cuba, from which the mahogany shared most of the attributes of the Spanish variety, but did not darken as much. In addition, the Cuban, especially, was available not only with a straight grain but could be found with highly attractive figuring. This included burrs, curls, fiddle back, roe and plum markings.

In the second half of the eighteenth century another variety of mahogany began to be imported from the mainland of Central America. It came from Honduras, and being loaded on to ships in the bay of that name was sometimes known as Baywood. The timber was softer, less likely to be attractively marked than the other kinds, and it faded on exposure to light. In its favour was the fact that it could be obtained in planks of notable width. These were in demand for the tops of dining-tables, so much so that 'the mahogany' served often as an alternative term.

The introduction of mahogany duly affected both the design and construction of many pieces of furniture. Apart from its use in large cabinets, tables and so forth, its strength allowed the making in solid wood of, for instance, the narrow mouldings in glazed bookcase doors. These and similar details had hitherto had to be made from oak veneered to match the rest of the article, involving more labour and expense. Equally, for the same reason, it was possible to make open fretting without difficulty, and thin rims or galleries could be cut out from layers of veneer glued together with their grains crossing: an ancestor of the present-day plywood. Chairs benefited from mahogany, not only because they could be carved so effectively and given openworked backs, but the latter could be constructed lightly without loss of strength.

Maple There are numerous varieties, of which the common maple (*Acer campestris*) produces a white timber that can be attractively veined and takes a good polish. Several types of maple were used in America, and on both sides of the Atlantic the sugar maple, with its distinctive bird's eye marking on a buff ground, was very popular.

Mulberry Although there are several species of mulberry, the timber they produce is not greatly dissimilar. When first cut, the colour is a brilliant gamboge yellow which turns to a golden brown. The wood is strong and durable, and was occasionally employed as a veneer in the early eighteenth century.

Oak The oak, besides being a tree of majestic appearance, produces a hard and durable timber that has been used for making furniture during many centuries. When cut down, the trunk can be split, or riven, without difficulty into quarters, which can then be further split into thin lengths. This timber is pleasingly figured with silvery markings and in addition shrinks and warps less than saw-cut wood. Boards that have been riven are necessarily

Furniture, Woods (Continued)

slightly thicker along one edge than the other and would often have been trimmed to an even thickness with an adze: a variation of the axe, but with the blade at right angles to the handle instead of along it.

Riven oak was imported into England from at least the sixteenth century, much of it coming from the Baltic forests, and it is often found to have been referred to as 'clapboard'. The term is derived from the German verb *klaffen*, meaning to split asunder. Alternatively it was known as 'wainscot', a word debatably of Dutch origin, at first used to describe the wood itself but later a term for wall-panelling, whether of oak or any other timber.

Much surviving early oak furniture is of simple construction, large in size and heavy to lift, but no doubt there were innumerable smaller pieces that have disappeared over the years. While it is a strong wood and seldom subject to woodworm attack, oak is not everlasting and continual daily use will have the inevitable result.

Dark-brown-coloured oak furniture is traditionally known as Jacobean, whether it is earlier or later in date than the reign of James I. In a similar manner many black wooden objects are said to have been made from Bog Oak, although other woods are sometimes so described in error. True bog oak results from fragments or complete trees that have lain in peat bogs for a considerable period, sometimes as long as several centuries, during which moisture and minerals have changed the appearance of the wood. The dense black material was frequently used for crudely carved small souvenirs, but an exception was a suite of furniture shown by an Irishman at the Great Exhibition in 1851. This was designed and made by Arthur James Jones, of Dublin, and the twenty or so pieces were carved to illustrate the 'history, antiquities, animal and vegetable productions, &c., of Ireland'.

Bog oak was used occasionally as an inlay, as was a natural bright green oak. The latter acquired its distinctive colour from an attack by a fungus known as *Chlorosplenium aeruginosum*, which is a sign of decay. The wood in that condition is unusable for most normal purposes, but was employed by craftsmen who boasted that they used only naturally coloured woods in their work.

Until the end of the seventeenth century oak was the principal timber in use for furniture-making in England, but its employment to a lesser degree has continued down to the present day. In the remoter provincial and country areas, where imported timbers were difficult or impossible to obtain, oak continued to be used during the eighteenth century, and pieces in current styles were made from it. It is not unusual to find, for example, a mid-eighteenth century sloping front bureau made of oak and exactly matching in every other way a London mahogany example. In the latter, much of the carcase and the interiors of the drawers would be of oak in better-quality bureaus and many other pieces.

Olive The tree, which is so highly valued for its oil-bearing fruit, produces a timber that is yellow or greenish-brown in colour with dark cloudy markings. It was used in the form of veneer in the seventeenth and eighteenth centuries and sometimes during the Regency.

Padouk The wood is very hard and noticeably heavy, ranging in colour from brown to purplish-brown. It was used in England very occasionally early in the eighteenth century. Most surviving pieces of padouk furniture of about that date, and later, although English in appearance were made by East Indian craftsmen. As padouk seldom shows signs of wear, it can be difficult to date articles made from it.

Partridge A Brazilian wood, marked in red and brown with a pattern somewhat resembling the feathers of the bird from which it gained its name. It was occasionally used in the form of a veneer.

Pear Like some other fruit woods, pear is hard and has been used in making furniture in rural areas. It is a pink-brown in colour, and one of its uses was for picture frames. Pear wood was sometimes stained black and varnished in imitation of ebony; occasionally it was carved and left in its natural state so that it contrasted with the mahogany to which it was applied.

Pine The most popular softwood, ranging in colour from a red tint to a yellow one. From the late seventeenth century pine was used for furniture that was finished with painting, japanning, or gesso with gilding. It was also made into wall panelling. The American yellow pine was employed in England after about 1760 for the carcasses of chests and other articles.

Plane The plane, which lines so many London streets, has a close-grained white wood. Thomas Sheraton wrote in 1804 that country cabinet-makers used plane wood 'instead of beech for painted chairs'; as they were finished with paint and varnish no one need be the wiser. He also said that the same men employed the wood for the under-frames of card tables and Pembroke tables. In Scotland the sycamore is called a plane.

Plum Pudding The name sometimes given to a mahogany veneer figured with a pattern of plum-like dark marks.

Prince Wood See Kingwood.

Purpleheart Imported from the West Indies, this wood acquired its name because of the colour it assumes when it has been cut. With age it resembles rosewood. It was occasionally used as a veneer in the late eighteenth century.

Roe Mahogany veneer figured with dark flakes and spots giving a mottled effect somewhat like fish roe.

Rosewood This timber was brought from the East Indies and Brazil, and is heavy and durable. In colour it is a warm brown with stripes of blackish-brown, so it can be confused with kingwood. Rosewood was especially popular for furniture in the Regency period.

Sabicu A wood imported mainly from Cuba in the mid-eighteenth century, used as a veneer and very occasionally in the solid. It is very hard and heavy and of a colour like that of rosewood. Sabicu was used for the stairs in the 1851 Great Exhibition building, and 'notwithstanding the enormous traffic which passed over them, the wood at the end was found to be little affected by wear'.

Satinwood Two species of this wood were employed during the eighteenth century: the East Indian and the West Indian. The West Indian variety was the first to reach England and Sheraton acclaimed it 'because of its breadth and general utility'. The other, he wrote, 'runs narrow and is used only for cross-bandings'.

Furniture, Woods (Continued)

Both types are of a distinctive yellow colour, varying from a plain grain to rich figuring. They were used principally as veneers, but sometimes chairs and parts of larger articles were made from the solid wood. Chestnut, sycamore and birch were occasionally used as substitutes.

Shavings Thick wood shavings were sometimes used in the seventeenth century as a decorative inlay. The shavings were glued into a hollowed space with their narrow edges uppermost, so that they form an unusual worm-like pattern.

Snakewood A rare import from South America. It is a wood of rich brown colour marked with darker mottled veins, and is hard and durable. It was used principally during the Regency.

Stinkwood A South African timber that acquired its unlovely name because it exudes an offensive smell when newly cut. It is alternatively referred to as Cape Walnut, Cape Laurel and Laurel wood. Stinkwood is extremely hard and durable, and in colour ranges from black to dark walnut or reddish-brown with yellow markings. Furniture was made from the wood at Cape Town and elsewhere in the country, and is sometimes to be met with in Europe.

Sycamore A hard wood, usually creamy-white in colour when first cut and then darkening to a golden brown. It sometimes has mottled markings, but is more often straight grained. Sycamore was used in marquetry in the seventeenth century, and later occasionally took the place of satinwood. Dyed sycamore is known as harewood. In Scotland the snuff boxes and other souvenirs made at Mauchline and Cumnock, in Ayrshire, were made of sycamore.

Thuya A North African timber of a brown colour, of which the burr is used as a veneer. It is heavily marked with bird's eyes and has a similar appearance to amboyna. Thuya was employed in the late eighteenth and early nineteenth centuries. It should be noted that Thuja is a cedar and quite different from Thuya.

Tulip A hard wood with reddish and other stripes on a lighter coloured ground, somewhat resembling rosewood. It was imported from Brazil from the second half of the eighteenth century. Tulip wood was used in England for cross-banding, but was more popular in France where it is known as *bois de rose*. In Germany it is referred to as *Rosenholz*, in Portugal as *Pao de Rosa*, and sometimes as Pinkwood in America. Tulip wood has no connexion with the decorative Tulip tree.

Walnut This familiar wood has black markings on a brown ground, the contrast increasing and becoming more attractive with age. The tree grows in many lands and comprises about ten species. Its timber was employed in the solid and as a veneer, the burr veneer being particularly well figured and therefore esteemed. Walnut is known to have been used for much of the best furniture in the late sixteenth century, but few examples have survived and the evidence is mainly to be found in inventories.

Late in the seventeenth century more extensive use was made of the wood, the technique of veneering was practised widely and advantage was taken of the more strikingly marked veneers. English-grown timber was occasionally employed,

Furniture, Woods (Continued)

but most wants were supplied from across the Channel; the walnut from Grenoble, France, being highly esteemed. A very severe winter in 1709 destroyed the majority of European walnut trees, and by 1720 the wood had become so scarce that the French prohibited its export.

A variety known as black walnut, native to the eastern states of America, was exported to England. The wood was often free of the distinctive markings of European walnut, and with age can closely resemble slightly faded mahogany. Sheraton noticed it in 1803, when he wrote: 'the black Virginia was much in use for cabinet work about forty or fifty years since in England, but is now quite laid aside since the introduction of mahogany'. Walnut was unfashionable by 1740, but there was a revival of furniture made from it in about 1850 when boldly figured wood was again in demand.

Yew The yew grows wild in many parts of the world. Its wood is hard, durable and a golden-brown colour often marked with patches of reddish-brown and purple. It was used occasionally as a veneer, but also in the solid, and it played a part in the construction of Windsor chairs.

Zebra A hard, durable wood from South America, alternately striped in light and very dark brown. Or, as Sheraton wrote in 1803, 'streaked with brown and white as the animal is, whence it has its name'. It was occasionally employed in the late eighteenth century as a cross-banding, and in the Regency period it was used as an all-over veneer. In 1820 a lady mentioned in a letter that she had seen a table in a house, 'of wood from Brazil, Zebra-wood, and no more of it to be had for love or money'.

ORNAMENT AND STYLES

Few makers of furniture were content to leave their handiwork free of ornament of one kind or another. Materials and techniques were allied to reproduce decorative forms, many of them revivals from the classical past and others freshly introduced. Widely accepted combinations of such motifs acquired the names of the designers and craftsmen who popularized them, usually by way of pattern-books.

Acanthus The rough-edged leaf of the acanthus plant, used as a decorative motif by the ancient Greeks, was revived in the sixteenth century and provided inspiration for a long time after. It was a particular favourite with carvers, but equally effective when inlaid.

Anthemion A formal motif resembling a honeysuckle flower and probably based on the flower of the acanthus. It was used by the Greeks and Romans and later popularised by Robert Adam.

Antique Once used to define ancient Greek and Roman objects, but now applied to articles of a hundred years old and sometimes less.

Applied Work Shaped pieces of wood were applied with glue and nails to the

Furniture, Ornament and Styles (Continued)

Armchair from a set designed by Robert Adam and made by Thomas Chippendale in 1764. The motifs include anthemions at the top of the back and on the knees, and acanthus on the arm supports and the back.
Christie's.

surfaces of furniture, especially between 1600 and 1660. They took the form of triangles, squares and lozenges, lengths of turning split lengthwise, and strips of moulding.

Apron The horizontal section between the legs of a chair, table or stand of a cabinet, often shaped and carved or pierced.

Arabesque Decoration based on Arabic art forms with complex patterns of interwoven flowing lines.

Arcading Panels framed with arched tops, often found on late sixteenth/early seventeenth century chests and other articles.

Arts and Crafts The name given to the revival of handiwork that took place in England from about 1875. The designers of the furniture ignored the machine, aiming for and achieving a basic simplicity and allowing the craftsman due credit by permitting him to sign his work. Members of the movement considered that furniture, along with other handicrafts, should be accorded the same recognition as the pictorial arts. As there was little or no possibility of their showing their work at the Royal Academy, they organized their own display, the Arts and Crafts Exhibition. This took place in London in 1888 and was subsequently held there annually as well as at various provincial centres.

Atlantes A support in the form of a male figure. Compare Caryatid.

Ball and Claw See Claw and Ball.

Baluster A turned column. It was sometimes cut lengthwise and applied to a piece of furniture to become known as a split baluster.

Bantam Lacquer See Lacquering.

Barley Twist The name given to twist turning resembling a stick of barley sugar, popular for the legs of chairs, tables and cabinets, and on the hoods of longcase clocks, in the reign of Charles II. It is a modern term.

Baroque A decorative style affecting furniture from about the mid-seventeenth

Furniture, Ornament and Styles (Continued)

A Charles II period walnut armchair with caned seat and back, the legs, stretchers and back supports of barley-twist turning.
Christie's.

century. It incorporated the human figure, cartouches, scrolls, leaves and much else in balanced patterns, typically seen in the carved cresting of Charles II tallback chairs. Much of the work of William Kent and his followers is in the baroque style, which was replaced by rococo from about 1740. In France, baroque is usually referred to as the Louis XIV style.

Beading A moulding in the form of a series of half rounds. A bead and reel moulding has alternate round beads and narrow discs.

Bellflower See Husk.

Biedermeier A florid variation of the French Empire style popular in Germany between about 1851 and 1860. It took its name from that of a caricature character, a well-to-do citizen notoriously lacking in culture, appearing in the journal *Fliegende Blätter*.

Block Front The upright fronts of chests and other pieces made with two projecting flat sections and a central hollowed section divided by narrow in-curved spaces, often topped by arcading carved with formal shells. A feature of furniture made in New England, particularly at Newport, Rhode Island, between about 1755 and 1785. It was described at the time as 'swel'd front'. Chief exponents of the style were John Goddard (1723–85), his relative, John Townsend (1721–1809) and members of their families.

Bombe A piece of furniture with a swelling front, and sometimes also sides. *Bombé* shaping was favoured in France under Louis XIV and Louis XV.

Bonnet Top See Pediment.

Boulle A type of marquetry associated with the eminent French cabinet-maker, André-Charles Boulle (1642–1732). He specialized in covering surfaces with patterns executed in brass and tortoiseshell, the latter often over a red backing, and sometimes with additions of pewter, mother-of-pearl and other materials. When the pattern is in brass on a tortoiseshell ground it is known as *première partie*, and when in tortoiseshell on brass as *contre partie*. Boulle marquetry is occasionally referred to as Buhl.

Furniture, Ornament and Styles (Continued)

Mahogany block-front desk attributed to a member of the Goddard-Townsend families of Newport, Rhode Island. The shell-like carvings are also typical features of furniture made by these cabinet-makers.
Sotheby Parke Bernet, New York.

Bow Front The convex curve on the front of a chest, sideboard or other piece of furniture.

Bracket Foot A low support found on chests, cabinets, clocks and other articles. It extends a short distance along the front and side at either corner, and can be straight or curved.

Breakfront A bookcase, wardrobe or other piece of furniture with a projecting centre section is described as breakfront.

Buhl See Boulle.

Bun Foot A late seventeenth century low support in the form of a flattened sphere, known in America as an onion foot.

Cabinet-maker A craftsman who specialized in the making of case furniture. He made his appearance when the introduction of veneering in the late seventeenth century called for special skills beyond those of the joiner.

Cable Cable or rope was imitated in carving, often featuring as the centre rail in the back of a Regency chair.

Cabochon A plain oval or round convex motif.

Cabriole A leg with a double curve, projecting at the knee and foot.

Caning Woven cane for the seats and backs of chairs was introduced in the mid-seventeenth century. It was appreciated for the comfort it gave, and because it was light in weight while it did not harbour dust or bugs. The mesh was large at first, but diminished after a decade or two. There was a revival of caning during the Victorian period.

Cartouche A decorative feature based on a partly unrolled scroll. It takes the form of an oval or oblong plaque with the top and bottom curled over. A cartouche was often the central feature in the cresting of a looking-glass frame.

Gilt cresting of a looking-glass frame of c. *1740, the swan-neck pediment centred in a cartouche.*
Christie's.

Furniture, Ornament and Styles (Continued)

Caryatid A support in the form of a female figure. Compare Atlantes.

Case A term used to describe chests, bookcases and similar containers.

Cavetto A moulding hollowed in a quarter circle, used frequently for cornices.

Chamfer An edge bevelled or cut at a slight angle.

Chinoiserie European versions of Chinese articles and motifs. Examples are japanned furniture and Thomas Chippendale's designs in the Chinese style.

Chip Carving Facets cut into the wood to form geometrical patterns. A simple type of carving going back to medieval times.

Chippendale Thomas Chippendale (1717–79), born in Yorkshire, was in London by 1748. Six years later he published an ambitious book of engravings, *The Gentleman and Cabinet-Maker's Director*, containing 160 large pages of plates depicting furniture designs. They show examples of all kinds that were then fashionable, the styles including French rococo, Chinese and Gothic, singly or intermixed. Some pieces of furniture, fully documented as coming from Chippendale's

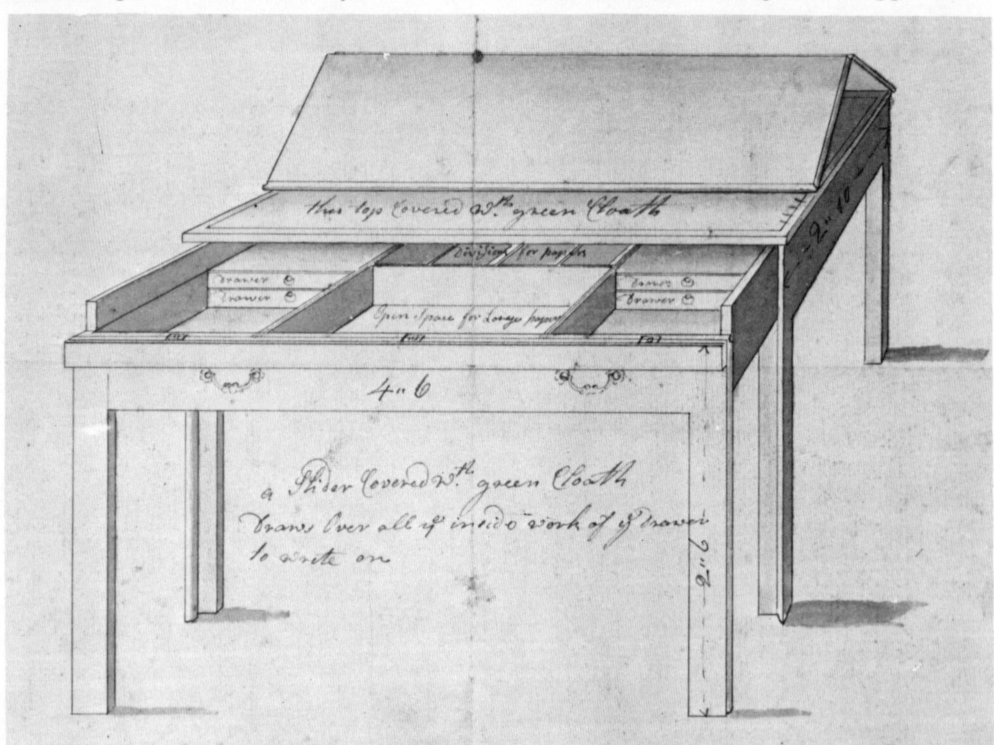

A design drawn by Thomas Chippendale. It is for a draughtsman's table; the pull-out interior fitted with drawers and spaces for keeping papers, and the folding top concealing a cloth-covered surface. Measurements and other details are on the drawing. Sotheby's.

Furniture, Ornament and Styles (Continued)

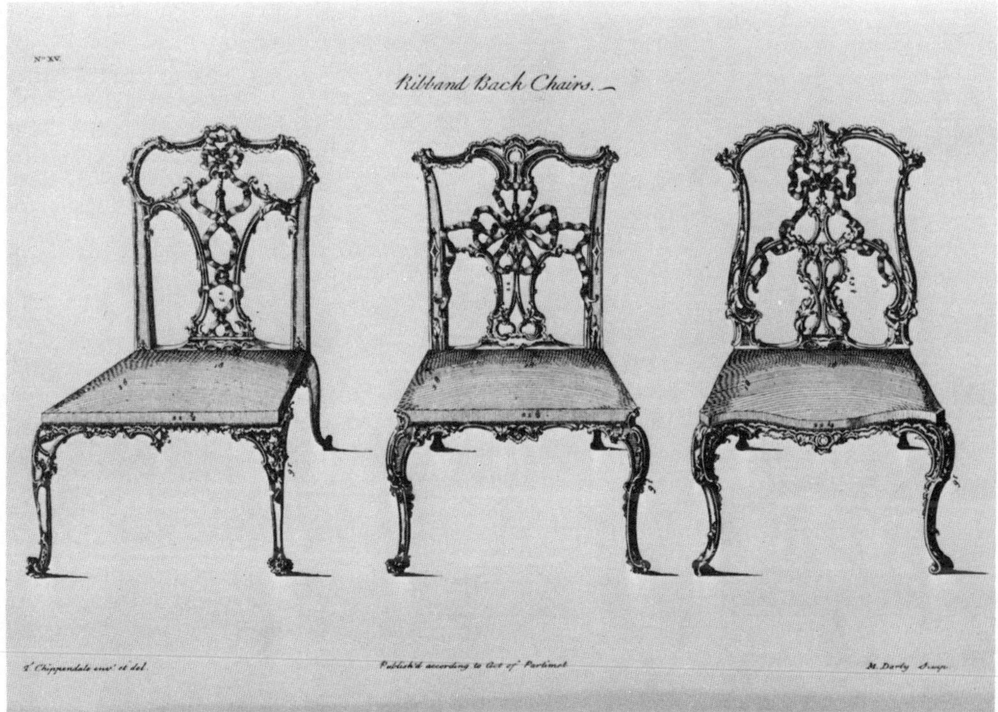

'*Ribband Back Chairs*' *designed by Thomas Chippendale and engraved in his book of designs*, The Gentleman and Cabinet-Maker's Director, *published in 1754. The author wrote: 'Several sets have been made, which have given entire satisfaction*'.

premises in St. Martin's Lane, London, remain in the houses for which they were originally supplied, and others are positively traceable to the same source. A third group resembles some engraved in the *Director*, but as the book was on open sale for anyone to buy and copy from it cannot be stated with certainty that such furniture was made by Thomas Chippendale. In 1762 he published a revised edition of the *Director*, in which some of the designs conformed to the newly introduced neo-classical style. The term Chippendale has, over the years, become applied to the majority of remaining mid-eighteenth century English mahogany furniture without seriously implying that it came from his workshop, but because it appears to be more or less similar to examples in his book. Furniture supplied by Thomas Chippendale and authenticated by the original accounts is to be seen at Nostell Priory, Wakefield, West Yorkshire (National Trust), and Harewood House, near Leeds, West Yorkshire (Earl of Harewood). Following Chippendale's death, the business was continued by his son, also named Thomas, who died in 1828. At Stourhead, Wiltshire (National Trust), there is a considerable quantity of furniture, together with the bills for it, from the workshop of Thomas Chippendale, Junior.

Furniture, Ornament and Styles (Continued)

Claw and Ball A foot carved in the form of talons grasping a sphere.

Cluster Column A support or decorative feature in the form of a group of slender columns.

Cock Bead A thin moulding projecting in a half-circle round the front of a drawer.

Composition A substitute for carved wood made from whiting with resin and size. It was heated and pressed into moulds, and when cooled was fixed in position with pins or glue or both. It is sometimes referred to as compo.

Cornice The projecting moulding along the top of a bookcase, wardrobe or other large piece of furniture.

Coromandel Lacquer See Lacquering.

Cresting Carved or other ornament at the top of a chair-back, above a cabinet and surmounting the frame of a looking-glass.

Crocket A Gothic feature in the form of a small bunch of leaves.

Cross-banding A strip of veneer cut across the grain often found edging a panel, table top or drawer front.

Cusp The point made by the meetin of two curves. A feature of Gothic design.

Cyma Curve A double curve, propounded by the artist, William Hogarth (1697–1764) as 'The Line of Beauty'. It is a *cyma recta* or ogee when the upper part is concave and the lower convex, a *cyma reversa* or reverse ogee if convex above and concave below.

Dentil A small rectangular block repeated with intervening spaces, often part of the moulding of a cornice.

Eastlake Charles Locke Eastlake (1836–1906) was keeper and secretary of the National Gallery, London, between 1878 and 1898. In 1868 he published a book that was very popular in its day: *Hints on Household Taste*, in which he strongly advocated sturdy, simple furniture. He showed designs by himself and others and the book, of which there was a fourth, revised, edition in 1878, influenced the taste of makers and buyers. Eastlake has suffered an understandable confusion with his near-namesake and uncle, Sir Charles Lock Eastlake (1793–1865) whose career as a painter culminated in his becoming President of the Royal Academy and director of the National Gallery. Sir Charles was not concerned professionally with the design of furniture, whereas C. L. Eastlake was.

Egg-and-Dart A pattern of upright ovals separated by dart or spear-like forms carved as a moulding.

Egyptian Motifs Napoleon's campaign in Egypt in 1798–1801 was followed by the publication of a book depicting the art and antiquities of the country. In both France and England furniture was made soon afterwards incorporating sphinxes, female heads wearing headdresses, lotus buds and crocodiles in carved wood, composition or ormolu.

Elizabethan The outstanding features of furniture during the reign of Queen

Furniture, Ornament and Styles (Continued)

A wash-stand designed by Charles Locke Eastlake and illustrated in his book Hints on Household Taste, *first published in 1868.*

Elizabeth I are the predominance of oak—although this may be because almost all else has perished—and the large bulbous turnings in the supports of tables and cupboards.

Empire The French Empire style was at its height between 1804 and 1815, continuing in vogue for a further ten years or so after Napoleon's banishment in 1815. The style was a painstaking revival of classical Greek and Roman styles, fostered by the published designs of Pierre-François-Léonard Fontaine (1762–1853) and Charles Percier (1764–1838). Furniture of the period tends to be severe in outline and much of it was massive. Well-figured mahogany veneers and solid mahogany were used in contrast with ormolu mounts of high quality.

Escutcheon A key-hole plate.

Espagnolette A French ormolu mount in the form of a female head used, for example, at the corners of writing tables. They were current during the *Régence* and early Louis XV periods.

The Heaven Room, Burghley House, Northamptonshire, c. *1695. The walls and ceiling are painted overall with mythological scenes in an architectural setting. The artist was Antonio Verrio.* (*Burghley House, Northamptonshire: the Marquess of Exeter. Photo: Cooper-Bridgeman Library*)

Furniture, Ornament and Styles (Continued)

Fall Front A hinged upright panel forming the front of a cabinet or other article. It is usually supported by two lopers.

Fauteuil An open-armed armchair originating in France.

Feather Banding A decorative inlay formed by placing two narrow strips of veneer alongside one another with the grain of one making an angle with the grain of the other. The result resembles a feather or the backbone of a herring. It was much used on walnut drawer fronts,

Corner of a drawer-front veneered with walnut, showing (A) principal surface, (B) herring-bone or feather banding, (C) cross-banding, and (D) moulded edge.

Furniture, Ornament and Styles (Continued)

table tops and other flat surfaces and is alternatively termed herring-bone inlay.

Fluting A row of closely cut parallel grooves.

French Foot A slender outward-curving type of bracket foot.

French Polish This shiny finish came into general use early in the nineteenth century. After filling the grain of the wood, a mixture of methylated spirits and shellac is applied with a pad until a smooth coating has been built up.

Fret Relief or pierced ornament in the form of geometrical patterns of Chinese inspiration.

Gadroon A series of splayed finger-like reedings carved on the edges of chests and

Caricature of a Gothic room engraved by A. W. N. Pugin and published in 1841. He remarked that: 'Anyone who remains any length of time in a modern Gothic room, and escapes without being wounded by some of its minutiae, may consider himself extremely fortunate'.

Furniture, Ornament and Styles (Continued)

tables. Gadrooning appears on Elizabethan bulbous supports, as well as on eighteenth-century mahogany. It is known also as nulling.

Gesso Prior to gilding, woodwork was given a preparatory coating of gesso. This was a mixture of chalk or plaster with size, applied in successive layers and allowed to dry before being carved and rubbed down to provide an acceptable surface.

Gilding A process of great antiquity. There are two distinct types: water gilding and oil gilding; the former of which needs a ground prepared with gesso or some other composition. For water gilding the gesso is moistened to hold the gold leaf, which is carefully applied. Oil gilding uses an oil-based size for the leaf. Water gilding is a more complicated and expensive process, as a laboriously prepared ground is essential and the effect can be enhanced by burnishing suitable areas in contrast to the general matt effect. On the other hand, oil gilding does not respond to the burnisher.

Giltwood A term used to describe gilded wood, usually pine.

Gothic Mock medieval forms and decoration of furniture came and went at intervals from the mid-eighteenth century. Noticeable signs are the inclusion of the lancet, cusp and crocket.

Gouge Carving Carving executed with a gouge: a round-bladed chisel. Fluting was done in this way.

Graining Painting a commonplace wood to look like a better one was achieved by graining, and skilled men were able to produce good imitations. They used hogs' hair brushes and flexible metal combs of various degrees of fineness, together with a rag for wiping out. In the early nineteenth-century beechwood chairs were grained to look like rosewood, and later in the century cheap pine furniture was similarly treated to improve its appearance.

Greek Key A running pattern formed of lines interlacing at right angles.

Grisaille Painting executed in shades of grey, occasionally used on satinwood furniture in the late eighteenth century.

Guilloche Ornament comprising two or three bands interlaced so that they form a continuous line of circles, sometimes having the centres filled with flowerheads. It is of Greek origin and there are many variations in its design.

Hepplewhite It is known that George Hepplewhite was a cabinet-maker with premises in Redcross Street, London, but no article from his workshop has been identified. He died in 1786, and two years later his widow, Alice, issued a book entitled *The Cabinet Maker and Upholsterers' Guide* containing about 300 furniture designs. Further editions were issued in 1789 and 1794. The plates show various items in the prevailing style, to which the name of Hepplewhite has long been loosely applied although it cannot be stated with certainty whether he personally had anything whatever to do with the designs. Chairs with shield-shaped backs, sideboards and tables with inlaid ornament, and other pieces to be made in satinwood or painted beech are shown. Many of them

Furniture, Ornament and Styles (Continued)

Chair with a shield-shaped back of the type engraved in Hepplewhite's book of designs.

incorporate neo-classical motifs, while others are quite plain. The last edition of the book includes a number of square-shaped chair backs to conform with changes in taste since the volume had first appeared eight years earlier.

Herring-bone See Feather Banding.

Honeysuckle See Anthemion.

Husk The dry outer casing of certain seeds and fruit, used in the form of festoons as a decorative motif by Robert Adam and his followers. It has been suggested that such festoons may have been based on the long catkins of *Garrya elliptica*, an American shrub.

Inlay Executed by cutting shallow cavities into the surface of woodwork and filling the spaces with suitable wood or other materials to form patterns.

Intarsia An Italian word describing perspective pictures made from veneer, taking advantage of their different colours and grains to gain the effect.

Irish Chippendale The name given to mahogany furniture made in Ireland during the mid-eighteenth century. The pieces are distinguished by the prolific and noticeably flat carving on many examples, all of which bear little or no resemblance to designs in Thomas Chippendale's *Director*.

Jacobean Refers to the reign of James I of England during which oak was the timber most commonly used. Ornament was less bold than in the preceding reign of Elizabeth I, and there was an increased use of chairs in place of stools.

Japanning True lacquer from the East became fashionable in Europe towards the end of the seventeenth century. Exact copying was impossible to make because of an absence of the basic material, so it was simulated with coloured varnishes. Decoration was executed in the Oriental style, but can be distinguished from the genuine work by an experienced eye. The ground colours employed were red, blue, green and tortoiseshell. Black, and very occasionally white, were included, the latter usually ageing to a cream colour

Furniture, Ornament and Styles (Continued)

because the varnish turns a shade of brown. Japanning was practised in many European countries, and sometimes it is difficult to be certain of the exact origin of an example.

Kent William Kent sometimes designed furniture for the principal apartments of mansions where he had been employed as architect. His tables and chairs were on a scale to match the rooms in which they stood, earning the criticism of being 'immeasurably ponderous' but certainly dignified when seen in their correct settings. Kent's furniture is characterised by heavily carved masks and foliage executed in gilt pine-wood, and examples may be seen at Holkham Hall, Norfolk (Earl of Leicester) which he designed in the early 1730s.

Lacquering The sap of the lacquer tree was collected in China and Japan, to be used on woodwork in the manner of gesso. It dried to form a very durable surface that could be given a high gloss and was decorated in gold and colours, often with parts of the design in relief. Another variety is known as Coromandel or Bantam lacquer, in which the patterns are incised into a black ground and then tinted. It gained its name because of its importation by the Dutch East India Company from their port of Bantam in Java in the seventeenth and eighteenth centuries. Lacquered furniture of many kinds, especially two-door cabinets, were brought to the West from the Orient. Some of it was of local design and some made to suit the European buyer, also a certain amount of ready-made furniture was sent to the East to be decorated. Lacquered panels, sometimes from the leaves of folding screens, were incorporated in European pieces.

Carved and gilt wood console table designed by William Kent for Chiswick House in about 1727.

Lancet The Gothic arch with a pointed top.

Linenfold A pattern resembling loosely-folded cloth or parchment carved on wall panelling or other flat surfaces. Used in England in the fifteenth century.

Lion Monopodium An early nineteenth century table support or ornament in the form of a lion's leg surmounted by the animal's mask.

Loper A pull-out support to take the weight of a fall-front, a loper being fitted at the front corners of the carcase.

Louis XIV The furniture style current

Furniture, Ornament and Styles (Continued)

during the long reign of Louis XIV of France, which lasted from 1643 to 1715, can be summed up as lavish. Carved and gilt pieces vied with elaborate marquetry by Boulle and others, all being of a high standard of workmanship. Baroque design was favoured, with the published engravings of Jean Bérain (1638–1711) exerting considerable influence.

Louis XV The reign of Louis XV, great-grandson of Louis XIV, lasted from 1715 to 1774. Furniture design during the period was characterized by the introduction and development of the Rococo.

Louis XVI Louis XVI was on the throne from 1774 until his execution in 1793. Furniture design altered radically early in the reign, with replacement of the asymmetrical curves of the rococo by the severe straight lines of neo-classicism.

Lyre The lyre, a musical instrument known to the ancients, was used as a decorative motif in the early nineteenth century. It is found adapted as a chair back or as end supports for sofa and other tables.

Marble Marble slabs were used as table tops from the sixteenth century. Great trouble and expense were often involved in importing such breakable

Box with hinged lid, veneered with oysters of walnut and with shaped panels of floral marquetry in various woods. Victoria and Albert Museum.

Furniture, Ornament and Styles (Continued)

material over great distances, but this did not prove a deterrent. In France, not only tables but commodes were similarly provided with marble tops. The marbles used included:

Breccia A type of marble with variously coloured fragments embedded in a reddish base. It is found in France and Italy.

Bardilla A dove-coloured or blue-grey marble marked with white and darker blue streaks. From Tuscany, Italy.

Carrara White or whitish marbles from quarries near Carrara, Italy.

Porphyry A dark red marble plentifully marked with small white and pink fragments.

Verde antico A marble of dark and light green colours mottled and veined with white.

Yellow Siena A yellow marble with black veining, from Italy.

Marbles quarried in various parts of England were also used. In some instances the slabs were solid, but in others the marble was veneered on a slab of concrete-like material. See *Pietre Dure*; Scagliola.

Marquetry A patterned veneer formed from two or more contrasting veneers, sometimes with the addition of other materials. In England, marquetry was introduced in the late seventeenth century. See Boulle.

Mask The term describing the face of a human or animal when used as a decorative motif.

Mother-of-pearl The pearly inner lining of certain sea shells sometimes used as an inlay.

Muntin A vertical member between panels.

Nulling See Gadrooning.

Ogee See Cyma Curve.

Onion Foot See Bun Foot.

Ormolu Gilded bronze, used on furniture usually in place of carving. It was favoured in France from the late seventeenth century onwards, and came into fashion in England about 100 years later. Ormolu was used on corners, feet and in the form of decorative plaques, as well as for handles and escutcheons.

Oyster Pattern Patterns resembling a series of oyster shells were fashionable during the late seventeenth century, when laburnum and olive were especially popular for the purpose. The wood was cut across a branch or the stem of a small tree, the resulting sections of veneer being trimmed so that they fitted together to form the design.

Pagoda The Chinese canopied roof was adapted for the tops of cabinets, top rails of chairs and occasionally elsewhere.

Parquetry Veneers arranged in a geometrical pattern.

Patera A circular or oval disc carved with ornament, much used by Robert Adam and his followers.

Patina A surface acquired by age and occasionally attempted by artifice.

Paw Foot A foot carved to simulate the paw of a lion, and sometimes that of a bear. The device is probably owed to the ancient Egyptians and has come into and out of fashion over the succeeding centuries.

Furniture, Ornament and Styles (Continued)

Panel of pietre dure: *shaped pieces of coloured marbles inset in a piece of white marble with natural tree-like markings.*

Pediment The architectural triangular feature surmounting cabinets, bookcases and clocks. With a space at the centre it is known as a broken pediment, and when curved it is a swan-neck pediment. A comparable shaping is known in America as a bonnet-top.

Pennsylvania Dutch The late seventeenth century emigrants from parts of Central and Western Europe who settled in Pennsylvania transplanted some of their native culture in their new homes. Their furniture was of simple type and strongly made, usually brightly decorated with painted flowers and other motifs. The alternative name for the style is Pennsylvania German, the term Dutch being a corruption of *Deutsch*: German.

Pietre Dure Designs formed by inlaying coloured marbles into a slab of marble so as to form pictures, either flat, in relief or both. In the late sixteenth century the craft was centred in Florence by the Medici, and many visitors to the city purchased specimens of the work. Among them was John Evelyn, the diarist, who returned to England with nineteen panels which he had inset into a cabinet.

Prince of Wales's Feathers The three ostrich plumes forming the crest of the Prince of Wales, eldest living son of the sovereign, were used as a decorative motif in chair backs, and on a small scale in the backs of Windsor chairs.

Quartering Four panels of veneer laid so that they form a symmetrical pattern. Frequently used on walnut furniture in the early eighteenth century.

Queen Anne Style Synonymous with

Furniture, Ornament and Styles (Continued)

walnut furniture of restrained design made between about 1700 and 1730. The Queen's reign, in fact, lasted from 1702 to 1714.

Reeding A series of closely-placed parallel convex mouldings of the same width, the opposite of fluting.

Régence Style Although the period when the Duke of Orléans was Regent of France covered the years 1715 to 1723, the *Régence* style was current between about 1700 and 1720. Decoration of the time bridged the baroque and rococo, and mingled the light-hearted characters of the Italian Comedy with the more formal motifs of the earlier age. The graceful *espagnolette* is typical of the period.

Regency Period Strictly speaking, the Regency period in England began when George, Prince of Wales, was made Regent in 1811. It terminated on the death of his father, George III, and his own succession to the throne as George IV in 1820. In fact, like all 'periods', this one is blurred in outline and is generally accepted as covering the years 1795–1830. During that time a number of different styles competed for interest: Greek, Egyptian, Chinese and Gothic. French influence in a general use of gilt metal was apparent, spread by the refugee craftsmen who fled from Paris to London during the Revolution. There was a liking for dark-coloured woods and for exotic timbers with striking markings, and probably at no other period was the finish of both wood- and metal-work brought to such a high standard.

Renaissance Literally translated the word means re-birth, and is used to describe a widespread cultural movement initiated in Italy in the fourteenth century. Then, scholars turned back to ancient times, discarding Gothic in favour of a revival of the classic orders of architecture as a basis for building and the other arts. The Renaissance spread throughout the civilized world and reached England in the mid-sixteenth century.

Ribband The eighteenth-century spelling (and doubtless also pronunciation) of ribbon. Used to describe chair backs designed with a central motif in the form of a carved and pierced bow of ribbon.

Rococo A word deriving from the French *rocaille*: rock-work. It is applied to a style developed in France during the late *Régence*/early Louis XV period and reaching England in the 1740's. The style is characterized by a use of scrolls, foliage, shells and other motifs arranged asymmetrically to give a sense of movement.

Rose and Ribbon A narrow band of carving showing rose-like flowerheads in between angled short lengths of crumpled ribbon, often found on the edges of eighteenth-century mahogany card tables.

Sabre Leg In the early nineteenth-century concave curved legs were often used on chairs, copied from those of ancient Greece. The term has been applied because of the likeness of such a leg to a military sabre. Alternative names are scimitar leg and Trafalgar leg, and it may be noted that sabre is spelt saber in America.

Sarcophagus An ancient stone coffin. The name given, it may be thought inappropriately, to an early nineteenth-century box-like wine cooler.

Scagliola A composition of plaster and other substances imitating marble. It was made in and around Florence in the

Furniture, Ornament and Styles (Continued)

eighteenth century and there are records of Englishmen ordering table tops from there designed to suit their requirements. Later, a similar material was made in London. Scagliola could be made to resemble a plain marble or one inlaid with a coloured pattern resembling *pietre dure*.

Scimitar Leg See Sabre Leg.

Scroll The scroll, either single like a 'C', or double like an 'S' was a feature of the baroque and rococo styles.

Serpentine Front A convex curve flanked by two concave curves was used as the front shaping of a proportion of mahogany furniture in the second half of the eighteenth century. It required extra labour and material to make, as well as demanding skilled craftsmanship.

Regency mahogany chair with sabre legs, the cross-member in the back carved to resemble rope.

Shaker Style The Shaker communities in America, which emigrated from England in the 1770s made distinctive furniture of starkly simple design. Most surviving pieces date from the nineteenth century, and in the 1870s members of the sect established a large-scale commercial production of chairs.

Sheraton Most of the furniture made in England in the years 1790–1805 is named after Thomas Sheraton (1751–1806). He was trained as a cabinet-maker in the North of England, but did not have a workshop and spent his time in London teaching drawing and publishing books of furniture designs. Of these, the principal one was *The Cabinet-Maker and Upholsterer's Drawing Book*, published in 1793. Many of the pieces illustrated were acknowledged by Sheraton to have been designed and executed by his contemporaries. The furniture he showed was often made of satinwood decorated with inlay or painting, and much of it was influenced by French work in the Louis XVI style. The chairs depicted are of smaller size than earlier examples, and have rectangular backs. In America, the Sheraton style was interpreted by the Scottish-born cabinet-maker, Duncan Phyfe (1768–1854), who emigrated to New York in 1783.

Shield Back A chair back in the form of an heraldic shield fashionable in about 1780–90.

Splat The central vertical member in a chair back.

Furniture, Ornament and Styles (Continued)

'Backs for Parlour Chairs', from Thomas Sheraton's Drawing-Book, *1793.*

Strapwork A decorative motif in the form of a band or strap, introduced into England in the mid-sixteenth century and popular for the next hundred years.

Stringing A narrow inlaid line.

Term A pillar, pedestal or support designed as a human head and shoulders rising from a tapering pillar, sometimes with feet at the base.

Thrown Made on a lathe: for example, thrown chairs of which all the members were turned.

Top Rail The horizontal member at the top of a chair back.

Trafalgar Leg See Sabre Leg.

Tunbridge Wells Tunbridge Wells, Kent, where there was a spa from the seventeenth century, was the source of a special kind of veneering. At first a chequer-like marquetry of assorted woods was employed as a decorative finish, but in time this was supplanted by a fine mosaic. Most surviving examples of the work are of the latter variety and date from the mid-nineteenth century onwards. They are usually in the form of small souvenirs that were bought by health-seeking visitors to the Wells, but larger objects such as tables were occasionally made. At the Great Exhibition in 1851 Edmund Nye, of Tunbridge Wells, showed what he called a Chromatrope Table veneered with 129,500 pieces of various woods 'in their natural colours'.

Upholstery Padded backs and seats for chairs, settees and stools were uncommon until after 1660, cushions having been used prior to that time. Coiled steel springs were incorporated with padding from the mid-nineteenth century.

Veneer A thin sheet of wood, usually carefully selected for its markings, glued to a piece of lesser distinction.

Vernis Martin The French brothers, Guillaume, Simon-Etienne, Julien and Robert Martin patented a fine varnish in 1730, and the description *vernis Martin* has subsequently been freely applied to varnish of the time and later. The Martins

Furniture, Ornament and Styles (Continued)

decorated rooms, sedan chairs, coaches, snuff boxes and much else.

Vitruvian Scroll A decorative pattern in the form of a wave-like series of scrolls.

Small box decorated with Tunbridge Wells veneer in various woods.

ARTICLES OF FURNITURE

The list comprises mostly pieces that were made in England, some made in America, and quite a number that originated on the mainland of Europe and in one way or another influenced the furniture produced elsewhere.

Armchair A chair with arms is a direct descendant of a throne. Prior to the late sixteenth century all chairs had arms. See Chairs.

Armoire French term for a large cupboard or wardrobe.

Bachelor's Chest A small chest of drawers with a hinged double top, the latter opening on to lopers to form a table. They were made during the first half of the eighteenth century, usually veneered with walnut and are occasionally found in other woods. It is not known exactly when or why they acquired their name.

Back Stool Alternative name for a single chair, a stool with a back, used from the sixteenth to mid-eighteenth centuries.

Basin Stand A mid-eighteenth century type is a mahogany stand supported on a short tripod base, the top an open ring to hold the basin, while midway down is a shelf with a spherical soapbox and a small drawer. In the recent past some romancer called these articles wig stands; the description is completely wrong but it continues to be used. Another basin stand of later date was made to fit in the corner

Articles of Furniture (Continued)

of a room, has a folding splash shield at the top and a cupboard below the basin space. Finally, in the later nineteenth century came the table with a marble top, a gallery at back and sides and drawers in the frieze, which was usually referred to as a Wash-stand.

Bed The bed was usually by far the most valued article of furniture in a home, and of its value the greater proportion was in the curtains surrounding it and the bedding materials. Surviving late sixteenth-century beds are made of oak, and are of four-poster type; the name being often a misnomer because many boast only two posts, one at either corner of the foot. The posts are decorated with carving and embody the large bulbous turnings typical of the period. Equally ornamental is the headboard, which runs the full height to support the panelled tester enclosing the

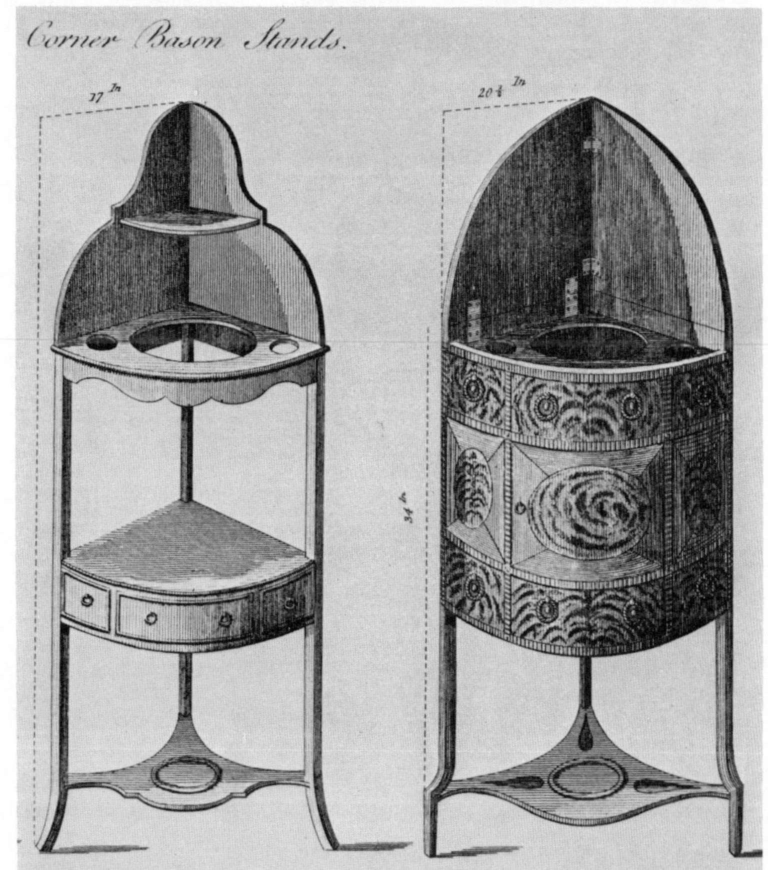

Two 'Corner Bason Stands' from Sheraton's Drawing-Book; *regarding the right-hand example, he wrote: 'by the top folding down the bason is inclosed and hid when it is not in use'.*

Articles of Furniture (Continued)

top of the bed. By a century later, the woodwork was completely concealed; the posts, headboard and tester being draped in fabric. In the mid-eighteenth century, with the use of mahogany, carved woodwork, sometimes enriched with gilding, re-appeared. About a hundred years later, the half-tester bed without bedposts came into fashion. See *Duchesse*; Field Bed; Truckle Bed.

Bed Steps Simple two- or three-tread bed steps, for easing the climb into a bed, were made in the eighteenth century. Later, they were enclosed to form a cupboard to hold a bidet or a chamber-pot. Despite their earlier usage, the majority of this last type have been, or are about to be, converted into drinks cabinets.

A Louis XVI period bonheur-du-jour; *the straight lines and square tapered legs of the piece are typical of the period and should be compared with the curves of the earlier table in the next illustration.* Christie's.

Bedside Cupboard A small-sized cupboard for holding a chamber-pot, and sometimes a close stool sliding away out of sight. Surviving eighteenth-century examples are mostly of mahogany, often with a gallery round the top pierced with hand holes. Later ones have marble tops and are frequently cylindrical in form like a short column, with a full-length door.

Bergère An armchair introduced in France in the reign of Louis XV. The *fauteuil en bergère* is characterized by upholstery filling the spaces below the arms, and the seat has a loose cushion. Some English armchairs of the 1760s were fashionably termed 'burjairs', but had open-spaced arms.

Bible Box Oak boxes of seventeenth-century date are often referred to by this term. Boxes of the type would have held all manner of things, including Bibles.

Bonheur-de-Jour A lady's writing table of small size with a set of shelves or a small cupboard forming a superstructure, introduced in France during the reign of Louis XV in 1750–60. Similar pieces were made in England in the later eighteenth century when they were known as Cheverets.

Bookcase Books were once kept on open shelves, the volumes being attached by chains to prevent their unauthorized removal. Closed cases came into use during the seventeenth century, when they were made with glazed doors. During the second half of the eighteenth century there was a fashion for large breakfront book-

Articles of Furniture (Continued)

A Louis XV period bureau plat *with ormolu mounts; the latter as well as the curved legs and general shaping being typical of the period.* Sotheby's.

cases, some of them 4m. in width, the centre section containing a secretaire drawer above plain drawers and with cupboards at each side. At the same date smaller secretaire-bookcases were made, resembling the centre sections of the foregoing and measuring about 1·5m. in width.

Breakfast Table In the mid-eighteenth century this was a small table of Pembroke type with hinged flaps, with or without an undershelf enclosed by fretwork. Later, it was a rectangular- or oval-topped table supported on a turned stem with three or four curving legs resting on castors.

Brewster An armchair of turned construction that once belonged to Elder William Brewster (1560–1644), and now in Pilgrim Hall, Plymouth, Massachusetts. Somewhat similar in appearance to the Carver chair, the Brewster boasts spindles at each side below the arms and in front below the seat.

Buffet A term formerly used for what is now called a Court Cupboard.

Bureau A piece of furniture with a writing space formed by a hinged flap resting at an angle of 45° when closed and on lopers when open. The flap conceals pigeon-holes, drawers, a cupboard and a well beneath a sliding cover; all or some being present according to the desire of the maker or purchaser. The design was current from the late seventeenth century, when such articles were raised on tall legs. Beneath the top writing section would be

Articles of Furniture (Continued)

two or three shallow drawers, the top one being a dummy to accommodate the well. By the mid-eighteenth century, the number and depth of the drawers increased until they reached almost to the ground and the whole was supported on bracket feet.

Bureau-Cabinet The bureau supporting a cabinet is usually of a type with drawers in the base, and it made its first appearance in the late seventeenth century. The cabinets are fitted with pairs of panelled or mirrored doors enclosing small drawers, filing spaces and a cupboard. The tops often have two curved cornices, when the articles are termed double-domed, these being surmounted by wood finials or with small shelves for displaying china. Examples dating from about 1720–30 are flat-topped or with a single dome, and may be no more than 65–70 cm. wide.

Bureau Dressing Table This takes the form of the early type of sloping-front bureau with two or three drawers below and raised on tall cabriole legs, but surmounted by a looking-glass supported at either side by uprights. A few examples of early eighteenth century date are known.

Bureau Plat The *bureau plat* (flat writing-table) was made in France from the early eighteenth century. It almost always has three drawers in its longest side and sometimes also pull-out slides at either end. Whereas earlier examples were given cabriole legs, those made during the reign of Louis XVI conformed to the prevailing style with straight legs.

Burgomaster Chair Name given to an armchair with a rounded carved back, circular caned seat and cabriole legs, often made of padouk or some other heavy timber. They were produced in the Dutch East Indies in the eighteenth century.

Butterfly Table In use during the late seventeenth/early eighteenth centuries in America. The table has hinged falling leaves raised on pivoted shaped supports, and when these are in position they resemble a butterfly's wings.

Cabinet The cabinet doubtless began as a functional storage place and developed into a decorative piece of furniture. Examples dating from about 1660 have pairs of doors enclosing drawers and are supported on stands with turned legs or on bases in the form of chests of drawers. Lacquered and japanned cabinets were given elaborately carved and gilt pinewood stands. The display of small specimens of chinaware called for cabinets with glazed doors, which began to be made late in the seventeenth century. Others of later date were made for specific purposes, such as to contain jewels, coins and mineralogical specimens.

Caddy See Tea Caddy.

Canterbury According to Thomas Sheraton, writing in 1803, this was a partitioned tray raised on tall legs, 'made to stand by a table at supper'. Modern usage of the term applies to a music holder (nowadays more often with newspapers and magazines in it), with vertical divisions, a drawer and short legs, dating from the first half of the nineteenth century. Earlier examples are made of mahogany and later ones of rosewood.

Caquetoire Name given to a type of chair made in the sixteenth century. In France it was low and small in size, and in England an armchair derived from a French type with a narrow back and outwardly-angled seat and arms.

Carlton House Table A writing-table with a superstructure containing small

The State Bedroom, Nostell Priory, Yorkshire, c. 1750. The ceiling is moulded with rococo ornament and the walls are hung with imported Chinese printed paper. The furniture, japanned in green with gilt decoration, was made by Thomas Chippendale and supplied in 1771. (Nostell Priory, Yorkshire: The National Trust. Photo: Cooper-Bridgeman Library)

Articles of Furniture (Continued)

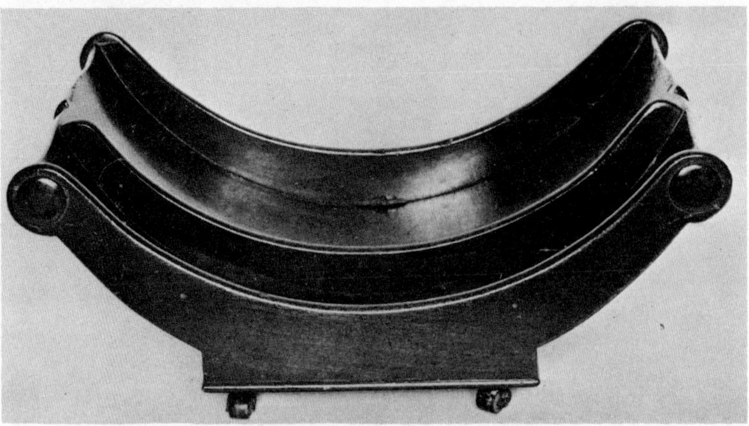

Late-eighteenth-century mahogany cheese coaster. It held a round of cheese on its side, conveniently placed for cutting wedges from it.

drawers at the back and each side of the writing space, with drawers in the frieze and the tall legs square or turned according to date. The first publication of the design was in 1792 and four years later it had acquired its name, doubtless because one had been supplied to the Prince of Wales at Carlton House.

Carver An alternative modern term for an armchair. In America it is the name for a particular type of rush-seated armchair with a turned framework, named after John Carver (1575?–1621), first Governor of Plymouth Plantation. It is now in Pilgrim Hall, Plymouth, Massachusetts. The Carver resembles the Brewster chair, but the former has spindles only in the back.

Cellaret A box in which bottles of wines and spirits might be kept. Cellarets were of various shapes, on tall or short legs according to taste, and sometimes brass-bound. The hinged lid reveals a divided space lined with lead foil

Chair The chair began its existence as a throne, a place of honour, and this it retained until the late sixteenth century. Until that date there were only chairs with arms and rigid etiquette prevailed as to their use. Single chairs were at first called Backstools, being in fact stools with backs. The design of chairs varied greatly as the years passed: styles changed and habits altered, different timbers became available and craftsmanship improved.

Chair-back Settee The name applied to a settee of which the back is composed of two or more matching conjoined chair-backs. See Settee.

Chair Table A chair with a back that pivots and can be lowered on to the arms to form a table. Examples of early seventeenth century date survive.

Chaise Longue This translates literally as 'Long Chair', and is the French equivalent to the English Day Bed. The *chaise longue* comprises an armchair and matching stool, which are placed together to provide a full-length piece of furniture. Sheraton wrote of them: 'Their use is to

Articles of Furniture (Continued)

rest or loll upon after dinner'. See Day Bed.

Chamber Horse A device enabling the user to have the benefits of horse-riding within doors. It comprises a series of strong springs in a leather casing on which the 'rider' sits while grasping two wooden arms and jerking himself up and down. It was introduced during the eighteenth century.

Cheese Coaster A small trough on castors, in which a round of cheese might rest and be passed about the table.

Chest A low container for storage dating from medieval times. It takes the form of a long rectangular box with a hinged lid, the earliest examples being simply hollowed-out tree trunks. Many seventeenth century and later examples have a small lidded compartment at one end, known as a till, to hold valuables and small articles.

Chest of drawers The chest fitted with a number of sliding drawers evolved from the simple chest, early examples having a hinged top above the rows of drawers. During the eighteenth century the most usual type had three full-length drawers below two narrow ones. The shape of the front varied according to taste, and might be straight, bowed or serpentine.

Chesterfield A double-ended couch with the frame concealed by luxuriant upholstery, often buttoned and of leather. A nineteenth century introduction, it is unknown whether it owed its name to an Earl of Chesterfield or to the Derbyshire town.

Cheval Glass A full-length mirror supported between uprights on a base equipped with castors. It was known in the late eighteenth century as a Horse Glass.

Cheveret See *Bonheur-du-Jour*.

Chiffonier A late eighteenth century cabinet in the form of a cupboard surmounted by open bookshelves.

Claw Table An eighteenth century name for a table with a tripod base.

Close Stool A box-like stool enclosing a pottery or pewter vessel, kept in a room before water-closets were installed in homes. Close stools must have been very numerous but are now scarce.

Clothes Press A cupboard for the storage of clothing, and sometimes with drawers in the base. See Gentleman's Wardrobe.

Cock-Fighting Chair A chair with a small desk fitted on top of the back, the user sitting astride the seat and facing the reverse way to normal. Such chairs were designed for reading or writing, and the term cock-fighting has been applied to them erroneously. See Conversation Chair; *Voyeuse*.

Coffin Stool A term at one time used to describe a Joined Stool.

Commode A French word literally meaning 'useful', and applied in France from about 1700 to a decorative chest of drawers. In England such pieces began to be made in about 1740 and the same name was used for them. English examples were mostly raised on short legs and usually had wooden tops, whereas the French had marble.

Commode Desserte A type of side table made in France during the reign of Louis XVI. The top is straight-fronted with curved ends and fitted with drawers in the frieze, while beneath are two open shelves.

Regency Room, c. *1815. The convex looking-glass, the settee, the chair with its painted decoration and the zebra-wood card table are all typical of the period. Equally so are the striped fabric on the settee and the patterned wallpaper. (Geffrye Museum, London. Photo: Cooper-Bridgeman Library)*

Articles of Furniture (Continued)

Mid-eighteenth-century reading chair on which the user sat astride facing the back. There is a hinged flap behind the back that could be fixed to support a book or to rest paper on when writing. Sotheby's.

Oak court cupboard of early-seventeenth-century date. Sotheby's.

Confidente Introduced in France in the eighteenth century, the *confidente* is a large sofa which included triangular seats attached at each end. In 1788 Hepplewhite's book of designs showed one, mentioning that 'an elegant drawing-room with modern furniture is scarce complete without a confidante'. In crossing the Channel, the design remained unaltered but the spelling of its name suffered a change.

Connecticut Chest A type of chest made in the seventeenth century mainly in the state of Connecticut. It had inset panels carved with floral motifs flanked by applied split balusters and bosses.

Console Table A table with one or more legs, but supported in part by being screwed to a wall.

Conversation Chair Similar to the 'Cock-Fighting' chair but without the desk and used in the same manner. Sheraton illustrated one in 1803 but added that he thought it was 'by no means calculated to excite the best of conversation'.

Corner Chair An armchair with a curved back, the rectangular seat placed angle forward and with a leg at each corner. In England its vogue lasted from about 1730 to 1750 but in America it retained its popularity for a further twenty-five years. Sometimes referred to as a Writing Chair.

Articles of Furniture (Continued)

Corner Cupboard A cupboard made to stand in the corner of a room was first made probably in the early eighteenth century, with a glazed door in the upper part and a plain door in the lower. Hanging cupboards of the same type, with glazed or plain doors, were also made and slightly pre-dated the full length variety.

Court Cupboard The court cupboard was used for the display of family plate and in its simplest form comprised a set of open shelves with decorative pillars at the front corners and plain ones at the back. Other examples included a cupboard between the upper shelves, with a central door flanked by canted sides to leave the pillars standing free. They were made from the late sixteenth century and went out of fashion a hundred years later.

Credence Table A Victorian or later name for a folding-top table of small size that was the forerunner of the gate-leg table.

Credenza An Italian low cabinet fitted with cupboards and drawers that served as a sideboard, introduced in the mid-sixteenth century. In modern times the term is used for a type of English late nineteenth century drawing-room display cabinet.

Cupboard The word originally meant a board, or table to hold cups, and now describes an enclosed storage space fitted with one or more doors.

Davenport A writing desk with a sliding, sloping and rising top above a series of drawers. On the right-hand side there is usually a small drawer for inkwell and pens. It was introduced in the late eighteenth century, and the first example was seemingly made for a Captain Davenport who is otherwise uncommemorated.

Day Bed A full-length seat with an adjustable back at one end, of which surviving examples date from the seventeenth century. In most instances the seat and back were caned. The French equivalent was the *chaise longue*.

Desk A piece of furniture designed for writing. Various types have existed, many of them remaining popular over a long period. The earliest had a sloping surface, which persisted into the nineteenth century Davenport, and of which a vestige is perhaps to be seen in the hinged sloping front of the bureau. From the eighteenth century, writing tables often had their tops lined with leather: a popular variety having drawers in the friezé and tall legs. An alternative was the pedestal desk with a similar top to the preceding, but supported on box-like pedestals fitted with drawers or cupboards leaving a leg space between them. Large examples of these have been given the name Partners' desks, because two people might use them seated opposite one another. See Bureau; *Bureau plat*; Davenport.

Dresser A wide and shallow piece of furniture fitted with drawers and raised on legs, often surmounted by rows of open shelves. Of early origin, the dresser persisted in country homes throughout the eighteenth century, when town houses had replaced it with the sideboard.

Dressing Table A rectangular table fitted with a drawer and with a separate swing-frame mirror standing on it was in use in England from the late seventeenth century. About 1720 a modified table with more drawers and a central recess for the knees was introduced, and a similar type was used in America where it is known as a Lowboy. About the mid-eighteenth century there were chests of drawers, of

Articles of Furniture (Continued)

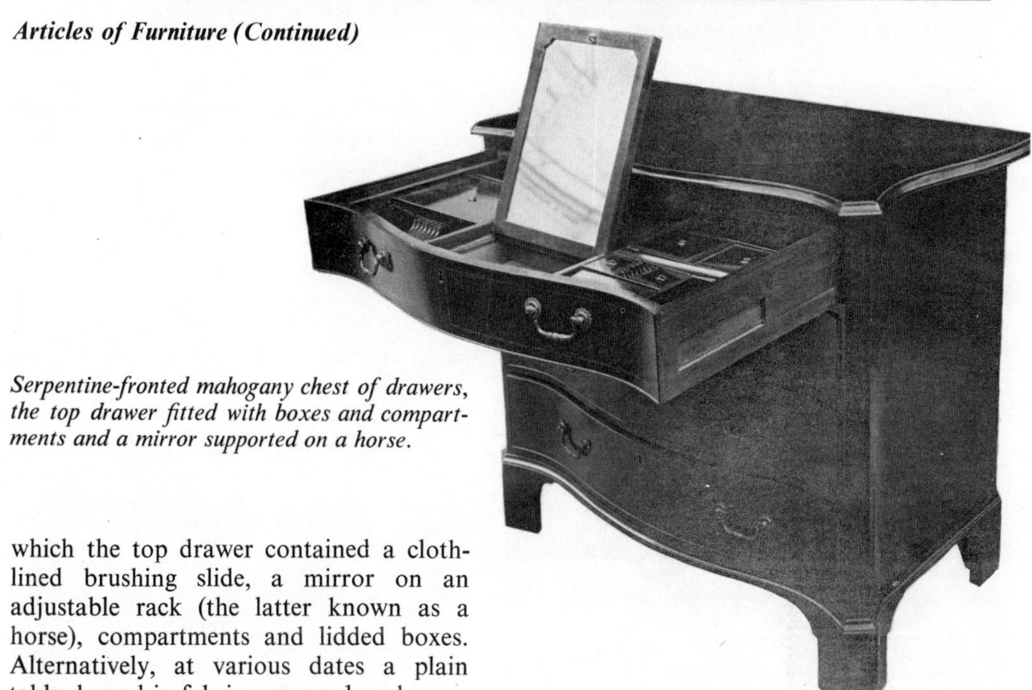

Serpentine-fronted mahogany chest of drawers, the top drawer fitted with boxes and compartments and a mirror supported on a horse.

which the top drawer contained a cloth-lined brushing slide, a mirror on an adjustable rack (the latter known as a horse), compartments and lidded boxes. Alternatively, at various dates a plain table draped in fabric was employed.

Drum Table A table with a leather-lined octagonal or circular top fitted with drawers in the frieze and made to revolve on a tripod base. Drum tables were made between about 1770 and 1820.

Duchesse A French bed of which the canopy or tester is affixed to the wall and not raised on posts. An English *Duchesse* illustrated by Hepplewhite comprised two armchairs with a matching stool between them.

Dumb Waiter A stand fitted with two or more trays revolving on a central column which usually terminates in a tripod base. It dates from the eighteenth century.

Escritoire See Secretaire.

Etagere A set of shelves on legs, known in France as an *étagère* and in England as a Whatnot.

Farthingale Chair An early seventeenth century chair with a broad upholstered back and seat, so-called because it was thought to have been of a convenient shape for use by wearers of farthingales: wide hooped dresses. It is a modern term as applied to a chair.

Fauteuil A French armchair with open spaces beneath the arms. Compare *Bergère*.

Field Bed An eighteenth-century term for a small four-post bedstead used when travelling.

Gate-Leg Table A table with two hinged leaves to be supported by pivoted 'gates' that swing out from the central framework. It was used throughout the seventeenth century in England and was made in oak, elm and occasionally in yew.

Gentleman's Wardrobe It takes the

Articles of Furniture (Continued)

Carved and gilt wood girandole of rococo design, composed of 'C'-scrolls, acanthus leaves and dripping water across the upper centre.

form of a cupboard fitted with sliding shelves raised on a chest of drawers. With variations in design it was made during much of the eighteenth century and later, usually being referred to at the time as a clothes press.

Girandole The name given to a wall candle-holder for one or more lights. Carved giltwood examples were fashionable in the mid-eighteenth century.

Gout Stool A stool designed that the sufferer might rest his foot at an angle to alleviate pain. Most surviving examples are of nineteenth-century date.

Guéridon A French occasional table of small size current during the later eighteenth century and Empire.

Hall Chair A chair with a wood seat, often painted on the back with a crest, coat of arms or monogram. The hall chair was described by Sheraton as 'for the use of servants and strangers waiting on business'.

Highboy An American piece of furniture which takes the form of a chest of drawers mounted on a stand fitted with a row or two of drawers and raised on legs. It was made throughout the eighteenth century in various woods and styles.

Joined Stool A stool of joined construction, the various parts held tightly together with wooden pegs (dowels). It is sometimes referred to as a Joint stool or a Coffin stool. The majority of surviving specimens are of seventeenth-century date. American examples dating from the late seventeenth/early eighteenth centuries are closely similar to English ones, but are usually distinguishable because they were made from local timbers.

Kas A large-sized cupboard with a distinctive overhanging cornice, popular in northern Europe from the seventeenth century. The *Kas* was made of oak, sometimes veneered and further embellished with ebonized columns and other features. The cupboards were constructed to take apart without difficulty, and many a toe has been inadvertently crushed when a pediment was raised releasing without warning a heavy pivoted door. The *Kas*

Articles of Furniture (Continued)

was also made in America to suit the needs of immigrant communities, for whom they were made of similar pattern to those in Europe and usually brightly painted.

Knife Box A container made in pairs for placing at either end of a sideboard. Each has a sloping hinged lid with a serpentine-shaped front, the interior being provided with shaped spaces for cutlery

Philadelphia mahogany highboy on cabriole legs with claw and ball feet and a swan-neck pediment. Parke-Bernet Galleries, New York.

Pair of inlaid mahogany vase-shaped knife cases.

and small plate. Many boxes have had these fittings removed so that they might be used for storing stationery or other items. An alternative pattern, reflecting the neo-classical style, took the form of an urn, the lid rising on a central post and the interior fitted similarly to the box.

Knole Settee An early seventeenth-century upholstered settee at Knole Park, Kent (National Trust), that has served as a prototype for many thousands of later examples. The original has ends adjustable by means of metal ratchets, but the copies have the hinged ends held by looped cords. See Settee.

Library Table A term sometimes applied to a large-sized table with drawers in

Articles of Furniture (Continued)

the frieze, raised on tall legs. Alternatively called a Writing table.

Linen Press A cupboard in which to store linen. Also, an appliance for pressing linen by placing it between two boards, one of which is fixed and the other screws down by means of a handle.

Loo Table The name given to a circular-topped table dating from the first half of the nineteenth century. The top often hinges for storage and is supported on a turned or shaped stem with a flat base raised on low feet. The name comes from a card game, abbreviated from lanterloo, that is of much earlier date and was presumably played on a table of this type during the Regency and later.

Looking-Glass In the past a looking-glass was a wall mirror, whereas the term mirror was used for a hand-held glass. Looking-glasses became popular in the later seventeenth century, and from then onwards much thought was given to framing them suitably. At first their usual place was over a mantel, but by about 1700 it had become fashionable to hang them on the piers, or wall spaces between windows, later above a matching table. The styles of frames varied over the years, many seventeenth-century examples being of carved giltwood and others having the main plate of glass outlined with narrow strips of bevelled mirror. Throughout the eighteenth century there were continual changes in shape and size, with carved giltwood proving the most popular material, although in 1740–50 it vied with a combination of walnut or mahogany with gilt mouldings and carving. Chippendale illustrated designs for rococo frames in his *Director*, and Thomas Johnson (born ?1714), a practical carver as well as a designer, issued some of his designs in book form between 1755 and 1760. Johnson's work, which includes other articles as well as frames, is in an extreme rococo style and has been scorned as being impossible to execute, but in recent years a number of eighteenth-century pieces conforming to his designs have come to light to confound the scoffers. In the third (1762) edition of his book, Thomas Chippendale included some neo-classical frames, but many other designers worked in the same vein with greater effect. Wall-glasses were duly designed for the Regency interior, incorporating some of the numerous motifs then current. From about 1800 the circular bulging convex mirror enjoyed a widespread popularity. Framed within a deep gilt moulding ornamented with small spheres, it was often topped by a carved gilt eagle holding in its beak a

Convex looking-glass in a circular deep-moulded frame and an inner band of ebony, the eagle holding in its beak a chain with two gilt balls echoing those surrounding the glass. Phillips.

Articles of Furniture (Continued)

ball on a chain. After that there were few innovations, but many earlier designs were re-used and their true age can now prove difficult to determine.

Love Seat Name given to a wide arm-chair, suggesting coyly that a couple sat close together on it. It is not an old term.

Lowboy See Dressing Table.

Manx Table An occasional table with a turned stem, of which the tripod base has legs carved to represent human male legs wearing buckled shoes and knee breeches. It takes its name from the three-legged symbol on a pillar cross in the churchyard at Maughhold, Isle of Man, which has been adopted as the arms of the island.

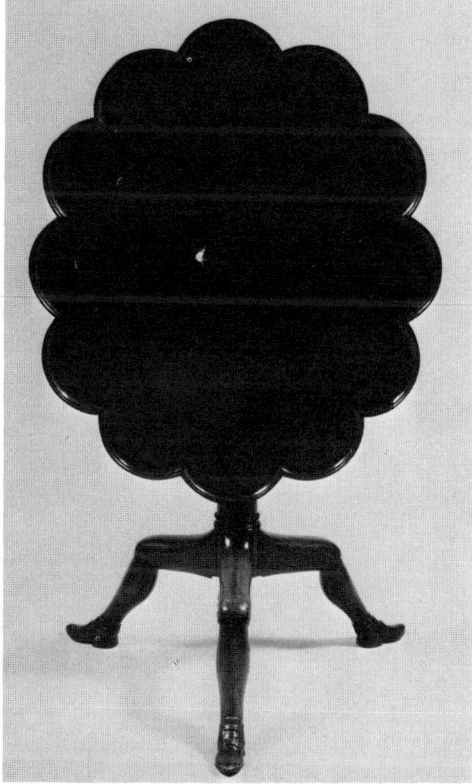

Tripod table with scalloped top; the legs in the shape of human limbs have earned this type the name of Manx tables in allusion to the three legs in the coat of arms of the Isle of Man. Sotheby Parke Bernet, Los Angeles.

Marquise A wide-seated French arm-chair comparable to the Love Seat.

Mendlesham Chair A type of Windsor chair having four rails in the back, a wide solid seat and turned legs, said to have been a speciality of Daniel Day, of Mendlesham and Stonham, Suffolk, in the first half of the nineteenth century.

Military Chest Two-part chests of plain form, brass-bound at the corners, were made for officers of the Army and Navy and civilian travellers. Some of the chests were fitted in the upper section with a secretaire drawer, and the majority of surviving examples date from the mid-nineteenth century.

Music Stool Circular-topped music stools with threaded centre posts for adjusting their height, were introduced in the early nineteenth century. At first they were made of mahogany, but later walnut was used.

Nonsuch Chest Late sixteenth-century chests decorated with inlay of pinnacled buildings are called Nonsuch chests. It is probably only a coincidence that the buildings bear a resemblance to the one-time Nonsuch Palace in Surrey, of which the erection began in 1538. The chests were almost certainly imported from Germany, but there is a possibility that some were made in England by German craftsmen.

Ottoman Introduced from Turkey in

Articles of Furniture (Continued)

Late-sixteenth-century chest, the front inlaid with various patterns including views of domed and turreted buildings. These last have been supposed to represent Nonsuch, near Epsom, Surrey, and the chests are often referred to as Nonsuch chests. Victoria and Albert Museum.

the early nineteenth century, the Ottoman was a long and low stuffed seat for several people. In time, there were various changes in its form. By the end of the century it was sometimes no more than a chest with a hinged top, differing from other chests in that it was entirely covered in cloth and the top was padded to form a seat.

Partners' Desk See Desk.

Pembroke Table A small table, usually with a single drawer in the frieze, the top having hinged side pieces to be raised and held on hinged brackets. It was introduced in the late eighteenth century, and the origin of its name remains unknown. The design of the Pembroke table varies principally in the shape of the top, which can be oval or rectangular; the latter either with rounded corners or of serpentine outline. Some examples have cabriole legs, but the majority are raised on tapering square supports with brass cap castors.

Piano Stool See Music Stool.

Piecrust Table The name applied to a mahogany table on a turned stem and tripod base, the top with a scalloped rim resembling the edge of a pie.

Pier Table A table designed to stand against a pier, the wall-space between windows.

Plate Pail A round or polygonal bucket with a swing handle at the top, for carrying plates from room to room. It was made with an opening about 12 cm. in width from top to base so that the plates could be removed easily. Plate pails were made from the mid-eighteenth century.

Articles of Furniture (Continued)

Portfolio Stand A stand for holding a portfolio of prints or drawings, adjustable for their removal or examination.

Pot Cupboard See Bedside Cupboard.

Poudreuse A dressing table current in France in the eighteenth century. The flat top is divided into three lidded sections, the central lid rising to reveal an adjustable mirror, while the flanking lids cover wells for toilet articles.

Press Bedstead A cupboard that converts into a bedstead has a history going back at least to the seventeenth century. Later, there were similarly adaptable chests of (dummy) drawers, and settees.

Prie Dieu Originally a prayer desk, having a low platform on which to kneel facing an upright section topped by a book rest. The name was applied in the nineteenth century to a tall-backed chair with a low seat, both back and seat often being upholstered in *gros point* needlework.

Mahogany Pembroke table, the edges of the top and drawer-front cross-banded with tulip wood. King & Chasemore.

Purdonium A wooden coal container in the form of a lidded box complete with a shovel and a place to keep it. The interior was given a removable metal liner and the article came into use in the second half of the nineteenth century.

Quartetto Table A set of four tables, the tops graduated in width and height so that they slide one beneath another for compact storage. The Quartetto Table was mentioned under that name by Sheraton in 1803, and was then a recent introduction.

Refectory Table A long and narrow table, usually of oak and of heavy construction used in a sixteenth/seventeenth-century hall or dining-room. It has acquired its name because of a supposed connexion with the refectories of religious establishments.

Rent Table A variant of the Drum table, but with the drawers initialled. A till in the centre of the top communicates with a cupboard forming the base.

Rocking Chair A chair with or without arms but with curved rockers on the legs, supposed to have been devised by Benjamin Franklin and much favoured in America.

Rudd's Table A toilet table with a fitted central drawer flanked by drawers supporting folding hinged mirrors. It was illustrated by Hepplewhite in 1788, and is supposed to have acquired its name from that of a notorious Mrs. Rudd who was tried and acquitted for forgery in 1775.

Secretaire A drawer with a hinged fall-front for writing, the interior with

Articles of Furniture (Continued)

Elaborately carved sideboard and wine cooler exhibited at the 1862 International Exhibition.

small drawers and pigeon holes. It was introduced in the eighteenth century and is found principally in chests and bookcases.

Secrétaire à abbatant A tall cabinet of which the front of the upper part falls down to form a writing surface, the interior being fitted with drawers and pigeon holes. The *secrétaire à abbatant* is the French equivalent of the English writing cabinet, and it came into fashion in the mid-eighteenth century.

Settee The words settee and sofa are nowadays interchangeable and apply to a seat with arms for more than one person. The articles were upholstered according to fashion and might display carved woodwork and caning, or needlework and a minimum of timber. The settee was introduced in the seventeenth century, whereas the word sofa did not come into use until later. See Chair-Back Settee; Knole Settee.

Settle An un-upholstered seat for several people, similar to a settee but without the comfort of the latter. Late eighteenth/early nineteenth-century examples were sometimes made with very tall backs, and drawers beneath the seats.

Side Table Literally a table to stand at the side of a room, against a wall. From the early eighteenth century, when the tables were mostly of giltwood expense was lavished on their tops, with rare marbles being sought for the purpose of providing attractive and unusual surfaces. Later in the century, with the increased use of mahogany, solid or inlaid wood tops became common. From the 1770's the side table did duty in the dining-room, where it was flanked by a pair of matching pedestals. See Sideboard.

Sideboard The sideboard for use in a dining-room was introduced in the third quarter of the eighteenth century. It formed a compact and convenient unit for table requirements, with drawers for cutlery, small plate and glass, bottles of wine, and in some instances an isolated compartment in which to keep a chamber pot. In the course of the nineteenth century the sideboard was made with

Articles of Furniture (Continued)

pedestals flanking a section containing a drawer, the whole becoming heavier in appearance as the century progressed. Sometimes it was surmounted by a large mirror at the back, while in the 1850's it was a favourite objective of ambitious carvers.

Sofa Table A wide variation of the Pembroke table with similar hinged ends, but raised on flat supports with splayed legs. The frieze usually has two drawers, with dummy drawer-fronts at the back. It was introduced at the end of the eighteenth century. Some examples have in the top a sliding reversible centre section marked on the back for chess, with the well it conceals for playing backgammon.

Stool A backless seat for one person.

Sutherland Table An early nineteenth-century two-flap table characterized by a long and narrow centre section.

Tallboy In effect a tallboy is a chest of drawers standing upon another, and it was introduced in England in about 1700.

Tea Caddy Tea caddies were known as Tea Chests until towards the end of the eighteenth century, when the term caddy came into use. Designs for chests were shown in Chippendale's *Director* of 1754, and they were made then and later in numerous forms and many styles.

Teapoy The late eighteenth century

Rosewood sofa table on flat end supports with curved legs. Bonhams.

Articles of Furniture (Continued)

saw the introduction of the teapoy, a tea caddy supported on a pillar and base.

Toilet Glass A looking-glass for use at the toilet table, with a mirror pivoted between uprights on a base fitted with drawers. It was an early eighteenth-century introduction, and was made in successive styles during the ensuing years.

Treen The word means literally made from trees, and is used to describe any small article of domestic ware made from wood.

Tri-Darn A Welsh cupboard topped by a row of three shelves dating from the mid-seventeenth century.

Tripod Table A table, usually of mahogany, on a turned stem with a three-legged base. It was made in quantity in the mid-eighteenth century, when it was referred to as a Claw table.

Truckle Bed A low bed on wheels which, when not in use, could be stored under the principal bed.

Urn Stand A small table with a square, circular or oval top and tall legs, for holding an urn. A small slide pulling out from beneath the top was used for the teapot while it was being re-filled. It came into use in the mid-eighteenth century.

Voyeuse A chair of which the back is topped by a padded rail, the sitter resting astride with his arms on the rail while watching a game of cards or conversing. A lady had a *voyeuse à genoux* on which she kneeled in much the same position, as it was considered indelicate for a lady to sit astride. The chairs were introduced in France just prior to the mid-eighteenth century. Compare Cock-Fighting Chair.

Windsor armchair, the back with pierced Prince of Wales's feathers and the arm supports similarly decorated.
Montacute, Somerset: The National Trust.

Wash Stand See Basin Stand.

Wellington Chest A tall and narrow chest of drawers that can be locked by a hinged flap down one side of the front. The Wellington chest dates from the early nineteenth century.

Welsh Dresser The term Welsh Dresser is often applied indiscriminately to dressers

Articles of Furniture (Continued)

originating in the North of England as well as to those from Wales. See Dresser.

Whatnot See *Etagère.*

Wig Stand See Basin Stand.

Windsor Chair A chair of stick construction. The Windsor chair has an arched back with upright sticks, a shaped solid seat and turned legs, each part made from timbers suited to the particular purpose. The chairs were made from at least the early eighteenth century. Many were produced in the area of High Wycome, Buckinghamshire, and others were made in Nottinghamshire and elsewhere, including America.

Wing Chair An upholstered tall-backed armchair with 'wings' at head level to protect the occupant from draughts. It was introduced in the late seventeenth century.

Writing Chair See Cock-Fighting Chair; Corner Chair.

Zograscope A mirror and lens supported on a turned stand with a circular base, overall about 60 cm. in height, used for viewing prints. The Zograscope was made in the eighteenth century, but its use has long been forgotten and surviving examples give rise to speculation as to their purpose.

2. POTTERY AND PORCELAIN

POTTERY

POTTERY is little more than natural clay baked in a kiln, and glazed if it is required to be impervious to liquids. Variations in its quality are due to the degree of heat to which it has been subjected, determining whether the result is straightforward pottery or hard semi-vitreous stoneware. The appearance of pottery can be affected in several ways: by shaping it or incising patterns in it prior to firing, by coating it with tinted glazes, or by painting it with suitable pigments. Pottery is opaque.

METHODS AND MATERIALS

Agate Ware Coloured clays mixed so as to produce the effect of agate. Alternatively a similar appearance was gained by trailing coloured slips over an article and combing them.

Arcanist Arcanists were the men who possessed manufacturing secrets. They were especially active in the eighteenth century, some of them going from country to country offering to establish factories, especially for porcelain-making, and not always succeeding in carrying out their ambitious promises.

Basaltes A hard black stoneware introduced by Josiah Wedgwood in about 1769 and named by him after the stone, basalt, which it resembled.

Bat Printing See Transfer Printing.

Pottery, Methods and Materials (Continued)

Bust of Venus in Wedgwood's basaltes ware. Sotheby's.

Bellarmine Stoneware jugs moulded below the neck with the head of a bearded man were known as bellarmines or greybeards. They were made in the Rhineland from the fifteenth century, and acquired their name in ironical reference to Cardinal Roberto Bellarmino (1542–1621), an Italian theologian who advanced arguments opposed to Protestantism and was bitterly disliked by non-Catholics.

Bianco sopra bianco Literally means white over white, and is used to describe an opaque white decoration on a faintly tinted ground. It was employed at the Rörstrand factory in Sweden by 1745 and brought to England soon afterwards by a man named Magnus Lundberg. It was used at Lambeth and Bristol, and possibly at Liverpool.

Biscuit Although the word literally means twice-fired, it was applied to ware that had been only once subjected to the heat of the kiln and was unglazed.

Bleu Persan The name given to a type of pottery painted with patterns in white and orange on a deep blue ground. It was at one time thought erroneously to have been made in Persia, but actually came from Nevers, France, and was copied at Delft, Lambeth and elsewhere.

Blue Blue, from the mineral cobalt, was extensively used for decorating pottery. It was mixed with glaze or slip to form an all-over colouring, and painted in patterns on its own or in conjunction with other colours. See Colours.

Blue Dash Late seventeenth/early eighteenth century chargers with an outer border of slanting blue dashes were given the name of Blue Dash chargers. It is common to several English factories of the time.

Boccaro Name given to a red pottery imported from Mexico by the Portuguese. Later, in the seventeenth century, it was used for Chinese red stoneware from Yi-Hsing. The word is alternatively spelt *buccaro*.

Casting Wares were cast by pouring slip into moulds made of plaster of Paris. Being porous, the plaster absorbed much of the water, and after the surplus slip had

Pottery, Methods and Materials (Continued)

been poured off a shell of clay remained for removal from the mould. The mould was made in parts that could be separated to permit withdrawal of the clay undamaged.

Colours The colours used in decorating pottery can be divided into cold and fired, the former being comparatively seldom used, and comprising the oil-based paints used on canvas. As they cannot be fixed by baking they soon wore away. Fired colours withstood the heat of the kiln, were durable and further divisible into high temperature and low temperature colours. The high temperature ones included red, blue and turquoise-blue, yellow, and purplish-brown, all of which could be baked in the kiln at the same time as the glaze. On the other hand, low temperature colours, known as enamels, were applied after firing of the glaze, and comprised a more or less full range of tints. The enamel colours had to be mixed with a flux to ensure they melted before the glaze or the article would be spoiled. The work of firing low temperature colours was carried out in a special kiln known as a muffle kiln, in which the wares were enclosed in an inner chamber or box (muffle) to shield them from smoke, and the heat was much less than in the main kiln. Whichever colours were used, the result depended on the purity of the ingredients as well as on the temperature of the firing. See Glazes; Kiln.

Cream-coloured Earthenware This was made in England in Staffordshire and comprised white clay usually mixed with calcined flints and covered in a lead glaze. By about 1762 Josiah Wedgwood was making his improved version of it and in 1765 accepted an order for some from Queen Charlotte, afterwards becoming Potter to the Queen and naming his product Queensware. Inevitably, Wedgwood had many imitators, both in Britain and farther afield, the factory at Leeds, Yorkshire, being the most successful.

Décor Bois The name *décor bois* has been given to a style of decoration apparently originating at Niderviller in about 1770. The surface is painted to represent boldly grained wood on which lies a sheet of paper bearing a landscape, the edge of the paper seeming to be curled realistically. Once introduced, *décor bois* was copied elsewhere.

Delftware To distinguish English-made tin-glazed pottery made in the manner of Delft, Holland, the English is usually spelt with a small initial ‘d’: delftware. The Dutch is referred to with a capital ‘D’: Delftware.

Enamels The pigments used for decorating. They are mixed with a flux so that they melt and adhere to the glaze before the latter is harmed by heat.

Encaustic painting The term employed by Wedgwood for his decoration on copies of ancient Greek vases. He achieved this with enamels, but correctly encaustic paintings were those executed in burnt-in waxes on wood panels.

Engraving Decorating pottery by engraving it on an abrasive wheel, in the manner of glass-cutting, was practised occasionally. Böttger's early Meissen red stoneware was ornamented with patterns or facets in this manner. Examples of late nineteenth century Wedgwood have been recorded with a brown glaze cut through to reveal the whitish body.

Faience Used on the mainland of Europe to describe certain types of tin-glazed earthenware. It is derived from the

Pottery, Methods and Materials (Continued)

town of Faenza, in Italy, which was formerly an important pottery-making centre. *Faience* is largely limited to Dutch and other wares made from the seventeenth century, while earlier Italian ones are known as *maiolica*. The word has occasionally been written *fayence*.

Flint When flint pebbles were burned they resulted in a white powder which was added to clay. The mixture produced a pottery lighter in colour than usual, and enabled it to withstand a higher kiln temperature so that it became harder. Flints were used in this manner in Staffordshire cream-coloured earthenware.

Glazes A shining glaze on pottery enhances its appearance and renders the article impervious to liquids.

Lead Glaze: the most commonly used glaze is akin to glass: a mixture of sand and lead oxide, the latter acting as a flux causing the sand to fuse in the heat of the kiln. Traces of iron were invariably present, so that instead of a colourless coating it was tinged with brown. Hence, a pure white pottery was not attained until about 1779, when Josiah Wedgwood made his pearlware. For this, in order to counteract any creaminess he added a trace of cobalt to the glaze. Lead glazes could be tinted when required, by adding suitable quantities of minerals to them.

Tin Glaze: if oxide of tin is added to the ingredients of lead glaze it becomes opaque. It sometimes has a tendency to show a pinkish hue, overcome by adding a little cobalt. The tin glaze was applied to articles made from red or buff clays, effectively giving them a coating of white on which patterns could be painted. This process was employed for *maiolica*, *faience* and delftware, all of which may be alternatively termed tin-glazed earthenware.

Salt Glaze: this was used for glazing stoneware. When the kiln had reached its greatest heat, a quantity of common salt was thrown into it. As a result of the chemical changes induced, the articles within were covered with an even thin coating of glaze. Its use ceased after about 1835 in favour of a glaze containing feldspar.

Greybeard See Bellarmine.

Hausmaler *Hausmaler* is a German term meaning literally a 'home painter', and is used to describe those men who bought undecorated wares from potteries and painted them in their own studios. This occurred in Germany, where there were a number of highly skilled craftsmen at Frankfort, Augsburg and elsewhere doing such work. In England the *Hausmaler* confined his attention to porcelain and is referred to as an Outside Decorator.

Incised Decoration Patterns cut into the surface were sometimes used on pottery. It was employed most effectively on Staffordshire salt-glazed stoneware between about 1740–80, when the cut designs were dusted with powdered cobalt. This decoration is often referred to as Scratch Blue. See *Sgraffiato*.

Ironstone China See Stone China.

Istoriato A type of painting in which the subject occupies the entire surface of a dish or other article. The *istoriato* manner is to be seen on sixteenth-century Italian maiolica.

Jasperware A very finely grained stoneware introduced by Josiah Wedgwood in 1775 was named by him jasperware. It was made in white as well as lilac-pink, sage-green, yellow, black, and best-known of all, pale blue. There was also a dark blue

Pottery, Methods and Materials (Continued)

Urbino maiolica *dish painted in the* istoriato *style with two men boxing, dated 1532.* Christie's.

and, in the early twentieth century, a deep red. The colours were normally solid throughout the ware, but between about 1777–80 the tint was applied only on the surface and the result was known as jasper dip. The best-known use of the material was for making relief portrait plaques, most familiarly in white on pale blue, but vases, candlesticks and many other pieces were made from it.

Kiln The two types of kiln employed were the high-temperature kiln at about 1200°–1400° centigrade, and the muffle kiln at 700°–900° centigrade. See Colours.

Kwaart A Dutch word for an extra coating of lead glaze sometimes added to Delft pottery and occasionally to English. The finished articles have a greater gloss and their colours are enhanced.

Lustre A type of decoration of a lustrous metallic appearance. Lustre wares were made in Spain and Italy in the fifteenth and sixteenth centuries, the former usually termed Hispano-Moresque because they were introduced into Spain by the Moors. In the late eighteenth century Josiah Wedgwood's son, Josiah II, introduced the making of teapots and other articles completely coated with a thin silvery film obtained from platinum. Elsewhere in England and Wales similar wares were made, in some cases patterned in colours in contrast to a silvery background. With the aid of gold, the so-called copper lustre was produced. In both instances the decoration could be painted, or achieved by resist: in the latter, the part to be left undecorated being covered with a shaped piece of paper, or painted with wax or varnish.

Maiolica The word is a corruption of the name of the island in the Balearics, Majorca. It was first used for the lustre-decorated pottery brought to Italy from Valencia in the fifteenth century, which came there via Majorca, but then came to mean ware made in Italy. This was tin-glazed earthenware painted in colours, duly imitated elsewhere in Europe.

Majolica A type of pottery introduced by Minton's in about 1850 was given the name Majolica. It was decorated with brightly coloured lead glazes, and while its name may be confused with that of *maiolica* the two wares are completely different in appearance.

Manganese A mineral used in pottery decoration which gives a brown or purple-brown colour.

Marbled Ware Coloured clays intermixed so as to have a marbled appearance. Compare Agate Ware.

Marks Marks denoting the source of

Pottery, Methods and Materials (Continued)

manufacture were used only occasionally on pottery. From the 1740s some of the Scandinavian concerns used a complex series revealing the name of the factory, the full date and the price. Later, in about 1770, Josiah Wedgwood began systematically marking every item from his manufactory, using an impressed stamp with his surname or that of himself and his partner. In the nineteenth century makers' marks became more common in all countries, although many of them took the form of initials or devices requiring research to unmask their identity. Between 1842 and 1883 English goods sometimes bore a lozenge-shaped mark with letters and numerals at the corners. It indicated that the design of the article had been registered with the Patent Office, but it does not mean that it was actually made in the year of registration. It should be stressed that marks can be very misleading, and should be used only to confirm other evidence of origin. They have always been, and will continue to be, an easy target for makers of fakes. Lists and reproductions of marks have been published. *Handbook of Pottery and Porcelain Marks*, by J. P. Cushion and W. B. Honey, deals with those of both Europe and the Orient, while *Encyclopaedia of British Pottery and Porcelain Marks*, by Geoffrey A. Godden, is confined to the British Isles. There are several pocket-sized booklets available containing selections of marks.

Mocha Ware A type of decoration found on pottery made throughout Britain during the nineteenth century. It features a series of tree-like dark brown or black shapes resembling those in Mocha stone, from which it acquired its name. The markings were produced from a mixture of stale urine, tobacco juice and turpentine.

Outside Decorator See *Hausmaler*.

Overglaze When decoration has been executed after the glaze on an article has been fired, it is known as overglaze decoration. It is sometimes termed on-glaze.

Paste Term used to describe the clay body.

Pearlware A white pottery introduced by Josiah Wedgwood in about 1779 to replace his Queensware.

Pottery A word used formerly to describe all kinds of fired ware, both pottery and porcelain, but now limited to non-porcelain varieties including stoneware.

Pressing Wares were sometimes made by pressing the plastic clay into shaped or carved moulds of baked clay, plaster or other material.

Printing See Transfer Printing.

Queensware After he had been patronized in 1765 by Queen Charlotte, Josiah Wedgwood named his cream-coloured earthenware Queensware.

Relief Decoration See Sprigging.

Resist See Lustre.

Rosso Antico Name given by Josiah Wedgwood to his unglazed red stoneware.

Sagger A fireclay container in which wares were placed for firing so that they were not harmed by flames and smoke when in the kiln.

Salt Glaze See Glazes.

Scratch Blue Type of incised decoration heightened with blue, used on stoneware for ornament and inscriptions.

Pottery, Methods and Materials (Continued)

Sgraffiato The term describes decoration scratched through a coating of slip to reveal the contrasting colour of the body. It is alternatively spelt *sgraffito.*

Slip A mixture of clay and water. It was used for attaching handles, spouts and other parts to vessels and to assemble the various sections of figures. Also, it was used for decoration; see Slipware.

Slipware When employed for decoration, slip was applied in two ways: the article could be dipped and entirely covered, as was usually done for *sgraffiato,* or the slip could be trailed on in the manner of icing a cake.

Sprigging Relief decoration of the type found on Wedgwood plaques and vases, for example, was performed by what was termed sprigging. The clay was pressed into a mould made of plaster or fired clay, which absorbed much of the water and allowed easy removal. The relief was carefully affixed in position with water or slip.

Stone China A hard earthenware put on the market in 1805 by Josiah Spode. In 1813 Miles Mason marketed a somewhat similar product supposed to contain iron slag as one of its ingredients, which he named 'Ironstone China'.

Stoneware When suitable clays are fired to a temperature of between 1200° and 1400° centigrade they become extremely hard and vitrified, so that they are impervious to liquids. Stoneware was made in red and grey until the late seventeenth century, and thenceforward it was improved to a near-white. The grey was coloured with washes of brown, or painted in blue or brown, and the whiter variety was sometimes decorated over the glaze in colours. The glaze used was sometimes a normal lead glaze, but more often was salt-glaze. See Glazes.

Throwing Pottery vessels can be thrown or formed on a horizontal revolving table or wheel, the potter manipulating the plastic clay with his hands.

Tin Glaze See Glazes.

Toby Jug Jugs in the form of a man, usually seated, were made in Staffordshire from the early 1760s. They acquired their name from Toby Fillpot, 'a thirsty old soul', whose beer-drinking exploits were

Staffordshire pottery Toby jug; he holds a pipe in his right hand and in his left a jug inscribed: SUCCESS TO OUR WOODEN WALLS.

Pottery, Methods and Materials (Continued)

commemorated in verse below an engraving of his ample form in 1761.

Tortoiseshell Ware The name given to mid-eighteenth-century Staffordshire pottery covered in brown, grey, green and other colours of lead glazes giving a mottled effect. They are invariably attributed to Thomas Whieldon (1719–95) but were doubtless made by many other potters.

Toys The term toys was applied in the eighteenth century to trifles of many kinds: scent bottles, snuff boxes, fob seals, and so forth. They were produced at several factories, but those of Chelsea porcelain are probably the best known.

Transfer Printing A process that involved engraving a design on a copperplate, which was then printed on a thin paper using a special ink. The paper was placed on the article to be decorated and the design rubbed on (transferred) to the surface, which was then fired in the normal manner. The process was in use on enamels by about 1750, and six years later was being employed at Liverpool by John Sadler (1720–89) and Guy Green (retired 1799), who decorated large quantities of locally made and Staffordshire wares. Transfer printing was at first executed over the glaze in red, black and purple, and after about 1759 in underglaze blue. About 1800 a new process, known as Bat printing, came into use. The copperplate was engraved in stipple, with the pattern in tiny dots, and was printed with oil in place of ink on to thin sheets (bats) of glue. The impression was transferred to the ware and then the oil pattern was dusted with powdered pigment. The result was a very fine and detailed design, and if executed in grey or pale purple and then overpainted in colour gave an appearance of handwork throughout. By the mid-nineteenth century a process for stipple printing in colour had been developed, and was used for Staffordshire pot lids and other articles. Following that, it became possible to make prints in colour by lithography, which gave a passable imitation of hand-painting.

Waster A broken or distorted piece of porcelain or pottery found at the site of a kiln, rejected because it was faulty and unsaleable. Such finds can provide valuable evidence of what was made at a particular place, but are not always conclusive because they can have been brought there for copying or some other purpose.

Willow Pattern A well-known Oriental scene, featuring a willow tree and buildings beside a bridge over a river, printed in underglaze blue on many makes of ware. It was engraved in the first instance by Thomas Minton (1766–1836) and is based on hand-painted decoration found on Nankin porcelain. There are numerous versions of the pattern that differ from each other in minor details, each maker apparently having his preference.

FACTORIES

In early times and later many potters worked on their own or on a small scale, so that their establishments could not be termed factories in the modern sense of the word. Nevertheless, a factory describes a place where articles are made, and it is adequate to cover the one-man business as well as the large company with hundreds of employees.

Pottery Factories (Continued)

Adams Several potters with this surname were active in Staffordshire in the late eighteenth/early nineteenth centuries. William Adams, of Tunstall (1746–1805), was a pupil of Wedgwood and after 1787 made cream-coloured earthenware and jasperware closely imitating those of his former master. William Adams (1772–1829) and his son William Adams (1798–1865), of Stoke, both produced blue-printed earthenware decorated with views of America for export to that country, and similar wares with English subjects for the home market.

Alcora, Spein A factory near Valencia was founded in about 1727 and employed as artists two Frenchmen. Some of the tin-glazed earthenware pieces made at Alcora are almost indistinguishable from French examples of the same period, but many show originality and superiority in their modelling and painting. Late in the eighteenth century figures and table wares were made in imitation of Wedgwood's Queensware. It has been written that Alcora wares produced between 1727 and 1749 'may be considered the finest of their kind made in Europe'.

Ansbach, Germany This Bavarian factory produced excellent *faience*, and is particularly noted for some with Chinese-style painting made in 1730–40.

Astbury There were a number of men with the surname Astbury working in Staffordshire during the eighteenth century. The best-known is John Astbury (1686–1743) to whom are attributed wares made in red clay with white ornamentation finished with a shining lead glaze. Among the articles in this category are teapots and small jugs, and figures of soldiers, musicians and actors.

Baddeley The Baddeley family operated potteries at Shelton, Staffordshire, from the mid-eighteenth century. They made stoneware and other types of goods and were responsible for several innovations. John Baddeley (died 1772) was acknowledged by Wedgwood as the foremost of his competitors.

Barnstaple, Devon At least one pottery in the town dated back to the seventeenth century. As with others in the North Devon area slipware was the principal production. From about the 1850s a family named Brannam owned the Litchdon pottery, often marking their wares with an incised signature and date.

Bayreuth, Germany Established in about 1713, the factory at Bayreuth, Bavaria, made several types of *faience*, including some particularly striking services with blue decoration of coats of arms. They also made a red earthenware with a dark brown glaze, which resembles stoneware. Many of the productions were marked, often with initials including a *B* for Bayreuth and the initials or name of the painter.

Bennington Vermont In the mid-nineteenth century there were two flourishing potteries in Bennington. Stoneware was produced at the Norton pottery, which was established in 1793 and endured for just 101 years. Both lead- and salt-glazes were used, including a mottled brown in imitation of that popularized at Rockingham. Between 1847 and 1858 another company was in operation, producing a variety of goods including a type of stone china which was named Granite ware and used for domestic articles.

Bentley See Wedgwood.

Berlin, Germany In the seventeenth

Pottery Factories (Continued)

and eighteenth centuries there were four earthenware factories in the Prussian capital. All of them used a reddish-coloured clay with a thin tin-glaze, and copied each other's productions. At one pottery a distinctive type of slip painting was executed on vases, and another, operating from 1797 to 1844, made cream-coloured earthenware.

Bethabara, North Carolina See Salem.

Bideford, Devon From the seventeenth century potters made wares from local clay and gave their products *sgraffiato* decoration. Large harvest jugs were a popular article and many of them bear humorous inscriptions as well as names and dates.

Bingham See Castle Hedingham.

Bologna, Italy Lead-glaze earthenware was made here from the fifteenth century, using various techniques among which was *sgraffiato* in conjunction with painting and coloured glazes. Decoration included borders of leaves, portraits and animals. A nineteenth-century firm made copies of early *maiolica*, on seeing which an English visitor in 1864 remarked 'a very useful lesson'.

Bovey Tracey, Devon The local beds of clay and lignite, the latter a type of coal, supported several potteries over the years. The Indio Pottery was active from 1766 until about 1840, making creamware and

Pottery dish printed in underglaze blue with a version of Willow pattern and marked on the back with the printed letters B T P Co; for the Bovey Tracey Pottery Company.

Pottery Factories (Continued)

stoneware, some of the former being decorated with transfer printing and the latter with 'scratch blue'. A proportion of the output was impressed with the alternative spelling of the name: *INDEO*. Another pottery was opened in 1846 and made domestic goods of Staffordshire type. They sometimes used a printed mark, *B.T.P. Co.*, for the Bovey Tracey Pottery Company.

Bristol Pottery-making in the area began in the mid-seventeenth century with the arrival at Brislington of some potters from London. The industry later removed to Bristol where, until about 1780, there were several factories making tin-glazed earthenware for local consumption and export. It is difficult to distinguish wares made at the west country port from those produced at London and Liverpool. None bear marks and not only did they apparently copy each others' styles but painters and potters went from one place to another. In 1786 a factory was established for making creamware and other Staffordshire varieties. In due course it came into the ownership of successive members of the Pountney family who carried on the business into the present century.

Brussels, Belgium A factory existed from the seventeenth century, and another started in 1724 included in its output some remarkable tureens in the form of animals, fishes, birds and vegetables. The tin-glaze tended to run and produce a marbled effect.

Burlington, New Jersey It is known only from documents that tin-glazed earthenware was produced at Burlington in about 1690. Clay for the purpose was shipped from England, and the products were sold in the area of manufacture as well as in Jamaica and Barbados.

Caffaggiolo, Italy A *maiolica* factory was set up in 1506 near Florence, and a proportion of its productions bear the arms of the local Medici family. Dishes and other pieces were finely painted in colours with triumphal processions, Biblical and mythological scenes, some within borders of grotesque animals and Cupids.

Cantagalli, Italy Ulysse Cantagalli established a *maiolica* factory at Florence in 1878. He made imitations of older wares and marked them with a figure of a crowing cock sometimes accompanied with the word *ITALIA*.

Castel Durante, Italy The *maiolica* made at Castel Durante, near Urbino, has been praised in modern times as 'among the most beautiful painted pottery ever made'. Probably dating from medieval times, the pottery achieved fame for its productions of the first decades of the sixteenth century. Its most distinguished pieces were painted by Nicola Pellipario, whose work in the *istoriato* manner is especially renowned. The locally-born engineer, member of a family of potters, Cipriano Piccolpasso (1524–79) wrote in 1556–9 a celebrated account of *maiolica*-making. The original manuscript in the Victoria and Albert Museum was translated into English and published in 1934 under the title *The Three Books of the Potter's Art*.

Castelli, Italy A number of potteries were in operation in the seventeenth and eighteenth centuries. Members of the Grue family were prominent during the latter period, and produced competently painted dishes, vases and plaques of which some bear their artist's signature.

Castleford, Yorkshire A factory was opened in about 1790 and made most of

Pottery Factories (Continued)

the current types of pottery. Best-known products are of near-white unglazed stoneware decorated in low relief and sometimes embellished with lines of blue. Some wares were marked.

Castle Hedingham, Essex Edward Bingham (1829–after 1909) was the son of a potter who produced such humble articles as flowerpots, but Edward had greater ambitions. By 1885 he had thirteen kilns from which he brought forth a variety of wares based on his conceptions of the past as well as direct imitations of ancient models. He gave his pieces colourful glazes and occasionally inscribed them with early dates, marking them with an applied pad showing a twin-towered castle or with an incised signature. The works closed in 1905 through failure of the local supply of clay, and after a further year Edward Bingham retired to America.

Chesterfield, Derbyshire Brown stoneware was made in this area at more than one pottery. The industry is known to have been in operation there since the sixteenth century.

Cistercian The name given to a very hard red pottery with a dark brown or black glaze sometimes decorated with white slip. It has been named Cistercian ware because fragments have been found on the sites of Cistercian abbeys. It dates from the sixteenth century.

Clews Ralph and James Clews of Cobridge, Staffordshire, made blue-printed earthenware, much of which was for the American market and bore views in that country. Following bankruptcy of the firm in 1835, James Clews went to America and set up a pottery at Troy, Indiana, but this too was unsuccessful. He came back to England and is known to have died in 1856. A printed mark was used bearing the words *CLEWS Warranted Staffordshire*, with a crown above.

Cockpit Hill, Derby Cream-coloured earthenware was made here from about the mid-eighteenth century, and it is possible that the products included other varieties.

Cologne, Germany The area about the river Rhine was rich in timber providing abundant fuel for making stoneware, which requires great heat to fire it. The history of potting there goes back to medieval times, but in the sixteenth century the factories built up a big export trade in salt-glazed wares. Bellarmines and other vessels were made in great quantities, some decorated with reliefs or impressed patterns and many styled to suit distant buyers.

Copenhagen, Denmark There were three factories active in and about the Danish capital during the eighteenth century. The earliest was the Store Kongensgade pottery, which lasted from 1722 to about 1770. Both coloured and blue-painted wares were made there and at the other establishments, while the latter also produced stoneware and cream-coloured earthenware.

Creil, France Staffordshire-type pottery of various kinds was made here from about 1794 until 1895. Cream-coloured earthenware was decorated with transfer printing, and some of the output was impressed with the name *CREIL*.

Crolius Members of the Crolius family were active in New York from about 1730 to 1870. A stoneware spouted pot decorated with blue flowers is inscribed by Clarkson Crolius (1773–1843) and dated *Feby. 17th 1798* (New York Historical Society).

Pottery Factories (Continued)

Delft*, *Holland At the height of its prosperity in the late seventeenth century the town of Delft had up to thirty potteries at work. The manufacture of tin-glazed earthenware then employed some 2,000 people and brought an international fame to the town. Few nations did not attempt, with varying success, to copy the quality of potting and painting and in England the name of Delft was attached to similar wares made at Lambeth and elsewhere. As the Dutch East India Company was active in importing Chinese porcelain, the Dutch potters had no lack of models to inspire them. They did not rely exclusively on the Orient; their native love of flowers lent itself to expression in decorative patterns, not least in wall-panels composed of tiles. In addition to tile-making, which was an important section of the industry, red stoneware was made in the early eighteenth century. Many of the potteries had individual marks.

Dutch Delft pottery wall-plaque painted in colours with a scene of a Chinese family at a meal. Christie's.

Davenport John Davenport established a pottery at Longport, Staffordshire in 1794. He made the current range of wares: blue printed and cream-coloured earthenware and cane-coloured stoneware. After John Davenport retired in 1830 and the business was continued by his sons, Henry and William, a heavy stone china with gaudy decoration was added to the list. The factory closed in 1887. Various marks were used, both printed and impressed.

De Morgan William Frend De Morgan (1839–1917) began by working on stained glass, but switched to potting in the 1870s and discovered a method of lustre painting. He built a pottery at Merton Abbey, Surrey, in 1882, six years later went to work in another at Fulham, and retired in 1907. De Morgan's productions are boldly and well painted and exemplify the artistic ideals of his friend, William Morris. Various marks were used.

Donyatt*, *Somerset At Donyatt and the nearby appropriately-named Crock Street there were potteries active from the seventeenth century. Cups, jugs and other useful wares in slipware with *sgraffiato* decoration were made for local sale. Many pieces are distinctively splashed with a green glaze, and dated examples are recorded.

Doulton John Doulton (1793–1873) and his partner John Watts made stoneware jugs and other articles decorated with small reliefs at a pottery in Lambeth. They also made spirit flasks bearing likenesses of politicians at the time of the Reform Bill of 1832. Henry Doulton (1820–97) joined his father in 1835 and ten years later leased premises where he could manufacture glazed stoneware pipes which he advocated for the carriage of London's sewage; a

Pottery Factories (Continued)

subject that had suffered neglect until successive outbreaks of cholera led to rapid change. Henry Doulton, however, had ideals above mere sewage pipes, and in conjunction with the Lambeth Art School he turned to the making of more artistic goods. The same stoneware as for the pipes was used, but was formed into decorative articles, and gradually a staff of painters and modellers was built up. Doulton stoneware, basically white or grey and coloured brown or blue in contrast, attained popularity, and by 1882 some 1,600 different shapes had been produced. Other varieties of pottery were also made, but the firm's name is synonymous with late nineteenth-century artistic stoneware. Almost all pieces were marked with the name *Doulton*, and often the initials of the decorator and modeller.

Dublin*, *Ireland A pottery here made tin-glazed earthenware from early in the eighteenth century and some plates dated 1735 are known. Later, a new factory was opened and appears to have continued until about 1770. Identified examples are not numerous and are painted in blue or purple with landscapes or Chinese scenes within elaborate borders. A few pieces bear inscriptions and dates.

Dwight John Dwight (1637–1703) was granted patents in 1671 and 1684 for the manufacture of stoneware. He carried this out at Fulham, where specimens of his productions and his notebooks were found in 1869. The notebooks were subsequently lost, but fortunately had been transcribed. See Fulham.

Elers Two brothers, David (1656–1742) and John Philip (1664–1738), came to England from Holland in the mid-1680s. One or both of them worked at potteries in London and Staffordshire, making red stoneware of Yi-hsing type. Traditionally the brothers are said to have introduced glazing with salt, but there is no proof of this. Their productions have not been positively identified, but it is widely accepted that carefully-finished red stoneware teapots, thinly potted and with neat relief decoration, were made by the Elers.

Faenza*, *Italy Faenza was a most important *maiolica* centre. The spread of its productions can be gauged by the fact that its name was adopted in the form of *faience* to denote all tin-glazed earthenware. The industry was flourishing as early as the mid-fifteenth century and continued until 1600, when it began to decline. There was revival in about 1700 and at least one factory was in production in the present century. The wares made in the prolific period were very varied, but generally of a high standard. Innovations included decoration incorporating human figures, which led to the *istoriato* style, and an attractive series of pieces decorated in white on a pale blue ground.

Frankfort*, *Germany The tin-glazed earthenware factory at Frankfort-on-Main was established in 1666. Its wares were well painted and potted, influenced by Delft and by Chinese porcelain, and are sometimes mistaken for productions of the former. Painting was in blue, blue and manganese, and sometimes in blue and yellow, while other colours were also used. Vases, jugs and dishes were the principal output, many of the dishes being of a nine-lobed pattern.

Fremington*, *Devon At this village, between Bideford and Barnstaple, red clay wares with *sgraffiato* decoration were made. In addition to useful articles like ovens and butter pots, ornamental pieces were made, some of them in variegated

Pottery Factories (Continued)

clays and with manganese glaze. The Fishley family were prominent from the late eighteenth century onwards and sometimes put their name to their productions.

Fulda*, *Germany Pottery was made at Fulda between about 1741 and 1758. It was finely painted in colours and sometimes embellished with gilding.

Fulham Fulham was once a village outside London, although it is now part of the urban spread. John Dwight began a pottery there for making stoneware, and some remarkably well-modelled figures and busts (mostly in the British Museum and Victoria and Albert Museum) were made there. It is not known who actually modelled them. Various small salt-glazed stoneware bottles, jugs and other items have been attributed to Dwight, as well as a number of red stoneware pieces. Eighteenth century productions included tankards, many of about quart size, with relief ornament, and partly stained with a brown wash before glazing. Many of them bear dates, names and inscriptions. The pottery continued in operation into the present century. See Dwight; De Morgan.

Glasgow*, *Scotland A delftware pottery is known to have been in existence here between 1748 and 1810. A few pieces of pottery with arms and inscriptions linking them with the area have been recorded. They have in common a style of painting described as 'spidery with nervous whip-like tendrils'.

Gubbio*, *Italy The lustre decoration on early sixteenth century Gubbio *maiolica* has given it an international fame, although that type of painting was probably first executed at Deruta. The artist Giorgio Andreoli, known as Master Giorgio (1465–?1553), was responsible for introducing lustre painting to the Gubbio pottery and not only did he embellish pieces made there, but potters from elsewhere sent their work to him for similar treatment. Dishes and other wares were made at Gubbio with embossed ornament to display the brilliant lustre. Giorgio's son apparently continued to operate the pottery from 1536, and the latest dated example recorded is 1557.

Fulham brown stoneware tankard with a hunting scene in relief, dated 15th July, 1729.

Habaner This is the name for peasant pottery of various kinds, tin-glazed and slip decorated, made from the late sixteenth century by the religious group known as Anabaptists, who were centred in a part of Czecho-Slovakia. *Habaner* is often employed as a term to describe folk pottery from Central Europe in general and not, as is strictly correct, only that of the Anabaptists.

Hamburg*, *Germany A factory for tin-

Pottery Factories (Continued)

glazed earthenware was operating in the mid-seventeenth century, producing jugs and other articles mostly painted in a bright blue. Some of the pieces bear real or imaginary armorial devices, and are dated.

Hanau*, *Germany This factory was founded in the late seventeenth century by some Dutchmen. Predictably, the earlier wares were similar to those from Delft, but after about 1740 they closely resembled productions from nearby Frankfort-on-Main.

Hannong See Strasburg.

Herculaneum This Liverpool factory was established in about 1793 and closed in 1841, having had a succession of owners. Stoneware and earthenware, both blue-printed and cream-coloured, were made. Marks used include the word *HERCULANEUM*, and after 1833 a cormorant, the so-called Liver bird.

Hesdin*, *France A small factory at Hesdin, south of Calais, operating in the late eighteenth/early nineteenth century made a speciality of tin-glazed chargers painted with half-length figures of men and women. The colours used were blue, manganese and yellow, and the articles have a deceptive look of being much older than they actually are.

Hispano-Moresque An opaque white tin glaze was used in the Near East for several centuries before it was employed in Europe. It reached there by way of the Moorish conquerors of Spain, and from Spain by way of Italy the glaze came into use throughout Europe. The Moors also practised lustre-painting, from whom the Italians learned the art. The pottery made in Spain by the Moors came from several centres of production from as early as the twelfth century and was continued for some three hundred years after that time. Examples are remarkable for their brilliant golden lustre, but few of importance are now to be found outside museums.

Höchst*, *Germany The Höchst factory, near Mainz, was established in 1746, and its pottery was of high quality. All kinds of wares were made, painted in overglaze enamels so that they can be mistaken for porcelain. The mark is a small wheel correctly with six spokes but often with fewer or more, from the arms of the Elector of Mainz. The original moulds were sold in the nineteenth century and used for making passable copies, also with the wheel mark.

Honiton*, *Devon In the eighteenth and nineteenth centuries *sgraffiato*-decorated slipware was produced for local sale.

Isleworth*, *Middlesex A small pottery flourished at Isleworth from about 1760. It is thought to have made wares that cannot be distinguished from those made in Staffordshire and elsewhere. The factory closed in 1825.

Isnik*, *Turkey At Isnik, south-east of Istanbul, a ware was made in the sixteenth and seventeenth centuries and exported to much of the Mediterranean area. It was made from a greyish clay decorated in strong colours of blue, turquoise, green, red and black, the red being noticeably of a bright tomato hue. The articles were given a thick glassy glaze, and ranged from tiles to tankards, dishes and bottles. All bear boldly-painted decoration, often of stylized floral motifs and sometimes of ships, birds and animals. Isnik pottery was once referred to as Rhodian, as it was erroneously thought to have come from the island of Rhodes.

Pottery Factories (Continued)

Jackfield, Shropshire Pottery is supposed to have been made at Jackfield since the sixteenth century. Mid-eighteenth century and later red clay wares with a shiny black glaze and unfired painting are attributed to the place, but are equally likely to have come from Staffordshire.

Lambeth, London Tin-glazed earthenware was made in London after two potters from Antwerp settled at Aldgate, in the City, in 1571. A century later there is documentary evidence that there was at least one pottery operating south of the river Thames, at Lambeth, and over the years other concerns came and went both there and at nearby Vauxhall. As no marked wares have been recorded it is usual to give the name of Lambeth as the origin of all surviving pieces likely to have had a London origin. Most pieces bearing the coats-of-arms of City Companies are understandably considered to have been London-made and the majority of pieces likely to have been made before 1700 are similarly attributed. After that date, especially in the case of the majority of plates and dishes, there is seldom any feature by which to tell apart the products of Lambeth, Bristol or Liverpool. By the early nineteenth century the making of tin-glazed ware in Lambeth was supplanted by salt-glazed stoneware. See Doulton.

Lambeth delftware pot in the shape of a seated cat, inscribed with the initials of the owner and the date 1671. Sotheby's.

Leeds, Yorkshire The principal manufactory at Leeds was founded in the early 1760s and carried on for a period of 120 years. Its best-known products were made in the years 1780–1820 and comprised cream-coloured earthenware in competition with Wedgwood's Queensware. The Leeds version usually has a slightly green tint in the glaze and articles with pierced decoration were favoured. Printed catalogues were issued, which help in identification as marks were not often used. A proportion of the output was left undecorated relying for appeal on its shape and relief ornament, but some was painted or decorated with transfer printing. Other pieces were sold to be painted locally and in Holland, with which country the pottery enjoyed a large export trade. Another concern was later established in the city, and having acquired the moulds used by the original firm made deceptive imitations from them. In many instances they took

Pottery Factories (Continued)

Butter dish, cover and stand of Leeds creamware, the pierced ornament typical of the factory. Sotheby's.

care to use a version of an impressed mark of earlier date: the words *LEEDS POTTERY* stamped crosswise, but with the letters composing the words in a straight line whereas their setting had been irregular in the past.

Linthorpe*, *Yorkshire The Linthorpe Art Pottery, Middlesbrough, was in operation from 1879 to 1890. The moving spirit was Dr. Christopher Dresser (1834–1904) who provided designs reflecting a visit to Japan and his liking for Near Eastern wares. Products of the pottery are unusual in shape and colouring; slip, painting and tinted glazes being employed for decoration. Marks used included the name of the firm, the impressed 'signature' of Dresser and the incised initials of decorators.

Liverpool*, *Lancashire There were numerous factories in and about Liverpool throughout the eighteenth century. Stoneware and all kinds of earthenware were produced, much of it for export to America and elsewhere. Attributions are possible in the case of some commemorative items: inscribed bowls made for ships' captains and pieces bearing local names. Tin-glazed earthenware from the area includes two initialled and dated mugs known to have been made in Liverpool for a Thomas Fazackerley and his wife in 1757 and 1758. The distinctive colours in which they are painted have been useful in allocating many other pieces to the same origin, but it is now known that others of similar appearance were made at Bristol. A few pieces of stoneware have been identified from names on them, but otherwise are no different from such goods made anywhere else in Britain. See Herculaneum.

Llanelly*, *Carmarthenshire The South Wales Pottery was opened soon after 1840, and manufactured wares similar to those then being produced in Staffordshire. The town being a small port meant that goods could be shipped without difficulty, and they were forwarded to Swansea and elsewhere for transhipment where required. Printed and impressed marks gave the name of the pottery, and between 1840 and 1855 sometimes included the surname of the owner, William Chambers. The business continued until about 1921.

Pottery Factories (Continued)

Lunéville, France Lunéville in eastern France was the site of a pottery which opened in about 1730 and continued throughout the nineteenth century. The more typical productions included large-sized decorated tin-glazed earthenware figures of lions and dogs; less remarkable was cream-coloured pottery in the English style.

Mafra At Caldas da Rainha, to the north of Lisbon, Portugal, a pottery was established by Manuel Mafra in 1853 and continued by his successors. The wares made were of earthenware covered, usually thickly, in coloured glazes, and impressed with the name of the maker. Examples from which the mark has been removed may deceive the unsuspecting into concluding that they were made in Staffordshire in the eighteenth century.

Malkin Samuel Malkin (1668–1741) made slipware at Burslem. His dishes have notched rims and the designs on them were given raised outlines serving to separate the tints of slip. Some of his work bears his initials and some is also dated.

Marieberg, Sweden This factory, near Stockholm, began to operate in 1760 following re-building after a fire which destroyed the newly-erected premises. The tin-glazed pottery was carefully painted in

Marseilles tureen and cover of tin-glazed earthenware. It is modelled with animal handles and finial, and finely painted with flowers and scrolls in colours. Christie's.

Pottery Factories (Continued)

overglaze enamels, and many of the shapes show French influence. Transfer printing was in use from 1766. The factory ceased to operate in the late 1780s. Painted and impressed marks were used, the latter including the initials *M B*.

Marseilles, France Several factories in the city made pottery from the late seventeenth century onwards. The best-known is the tin-glazed earthenware with fine enamel painting, similar to that produced at other French and French-influenced potteries. In the mid-century the establishment owned by the widow of Claude Perrin, known as the Veuve Perrin pottery, was responsible for wares of Rococo design, modelled and decorated with such skill and imagination as to rival porcelain.

Mason The Mason family were potters at Lane Delph, between Stoke-on-Trent and Longton, Staffordshire. Charles James Mason (1791–1856) invented and patented Mason's Ironstone China, and manufactured it in partnership with his brother and others between 1813 and 1854; a period that included bankruptcy in 1848, from which he emerged to start a further factory for a few years. The heavily-potted ironstone ware was made in quantity, and given printed basic decoration crudely coloured-in by hand in pseudo-Oriental patterns. Dinner and dessert services formed the major portion of the output, which also included fireplaces, bedposts and pairs of large vases. Printed and impressed marks were used.

Mayer The Mayers were a family active in the Staffordshire potteries, various members owning establishments at Shelton, Hanley, Longport and Tunstall from the 1770s onwards.

Metropolitan Slipware Red pottery decorated in white slip with inscriptions and dates between about 1630 and 1670 has been termed Metropolitan. It was given the name because it has been excavated in the London area, where it doubtless originated.

Montelupo, Italy Although it is known that Montelupo, in Tuscany, was a *maiolica* centre in the fifteenth century, it was not until later that wares of a distinctive pattern were made. In the 1700s large dishes depicting costumed figures of soldiers and others were decorated in bright colours with a strong yellow ochre prevailing.

Morley See Nottingham.

Moustiers, France Good tin-glazed earthenware was made at Moustiers, in the south of France, from the late seventeenth century. The earlier wares were decorated in blue in baroque style, often from designs by Jean Bérain. From about 1740, painting in a variety of enamels was continued until the last of the potteries closed in 1874.

Neale James Neale (1740–1814) was concerned in a pottery at Hanley from about 1778, most of the time in partnership with members of the Wilson family. Neale's made the usual range of Staffordshire wares, including some small-sized figures which were smoothly modelled so that they left their moulds without difficulty. Painting on them was carefully executed, with a purple-brown used for outlining rococo scrolls and square plinths. Several impressed marks have been recorded. See Palmer.

Nevers, France Italian potters became established at the end of the sixteenth century at Nevers, in central France, where local supplies of clay were available. Later, Frenchmen opened manufactories which reached a total of twelve by 1760. Vases

Pottery Factories (Continued)

and other pieces of early date resemble those of Urbino, but in the mid-seventeenth century distinctive wares included some large dishes painted in *bleu Persan* style, which was widely imitated. Other and later productions copied Delft and Frankfort shapes and their versions of Chinese decoration. At the time of the Revolution the Nevers potters made plates etc., inscribed with patriotic slogans, known as *faiences patriotiques* or *faiences populaires*. These and other Nevers productions have been continually copied.

Niderviller, France This factory in the east of the country was started in 1754, making tin-glazed earthenware similar to that of nearby Strasburg. Fine painting in enamels was applied to rococo shapes such as tureens, and groups and figures were produced. One type of decoration would seem to have originated at the pottery, the so-called *décor bois*. Wares in neo-classical taste were manufactured in the later eighteenth century, followed by English-style creamware.

Nottingham Nottingham was a centre for making stoneware from the late seventeenth century until 1800. Salt-glazed over a coating of brown slip, examples were noticeably thinly potted and a few surviving specimens bear inscriptions and dates. Double-walled mugs with pierced outside ornament are known to have been made by James Morley in about 1700, as a handbill of his has been preserved (Bodleian Library, Oxford), showing one of them, together with some of his other productions. Potters working in the area outside the city made wares of similar appearance.

Nuremberg, Germany Known to have been operating in the sixteenth century, the pottery at Nuremberg, in Bavaria, did not get into its stride until the early 1700s. Jugs, dishes and other pieces were made in tin-glazed earthenware, decorated in colours and often in complex patterns. Some of the wares were decorated by local *Hausmaler*.

Palissy Bernard Palissy (1510?–?1590) was a French potter whose reputation is legendary, much of it being based on his own writings. In his experiments to produce satisfactory coloured glazes he said that he went so far as to burn his own furniture to heat the kiln, although his wife's remarks upon this occurrence are unrecorded. Wares attributed to Palissy and his many followers are made of a whitish clay with coloured transparent glazes and sometimes modelled with frogs, lizards and ferns in full relief.

Palmer Humphrey Palmer had a pottery at Hanley, Staffordshire, where from about 1760 he blatantly copied Wedgwood's products. He went to the lengths of buying the latter's latest innovations as they appeared in order to reproduce them, which he did with some technical success. However, he was less able financially, and after 1778 his business was continued in partnership with James Neale. Palmer marked some of his productions with his surname.

Piccolpasso, Cipriano See Castel Durante.

Portobello, Scotland Several potteries were active at Portobello, north of Edinburgh, from the eighteenth century onwards. All of them made wares of Staffordshire types, which are often indistinguishable from the English-made products. Suitably dressed figures of Scotsmen and Scotswomen would appear to have been made at one or other of the potteries, and figures of lions and plaques

Pottery Factories (Continued)

bearing Biblical texts were also among the output. A few marks have been recorded.

Potter Christopher Potter was an Englishman who established a pottery in Paris in about 1790. He named it the *Manufacture du Prince de Galles*, but it was apparently no more successful than his attempt to obtain a monopoly in transfer printing.

Pountney See Bristol.

Pratt The Pratt family successively owned Staffordshire potteries, at Lane Delph and Fenton. Their name is associated with late eighteenth/early nineteenth-century figures and Toby jugs decorated in a range of muddy opaque colours including blue, orange, green and yellow. A few examples are recorded as being impressed with the name Pratt, but the numerous unmarked specimens may well have been produced by other imitative makers. In the nineteenth century F. & R. Pratt, of Fenton, developed the process of transfer printing with multi-coloured stipple engravings on the lids of pots. In this they were well served by the artist, Jesse Austin (1806–79) who worked with the Pratts from about 1846. Other firms also made and decorated pot lids, using a similar process but usually with less success, and F. & R. Pratt also employed it for decorating table wares.

Rhodian See Isnik.

Ridgway Members of the Ridgway family were actively concerned in the Staffordshire potteries from the late eighteenth century onwards. Job Ridgway (1759–1814) made blue-printed earthenware, and a later Ridgway turned his hand to jasper ware.

Rockingham, Yorkshire The factory was established in about 1745 and from 1787 to 1806 it was connected with the Leeds pottery. The wares made were of the usual types and have not been identified, as they bore no marks. After 1806 the concern came into the ownership of William Brameld and his family, who made blue-printed earthenware and other goods, of which many were marked with the surname. They used a manganese brown glaze that was sufficiently distinctive to have gained the name 'Rockingham glaze', whether employed there or elsewhere. The factory also introduced the 'Cadogan' teapot: a peach-shaped pot with no lid, filled through the base where a hole led to a tall tube within the pot, which originated in China. The Cadogan pot sometimes bears the name of Mortlock, a London china dealer, and it was also made by Spode.

Staffordshire pottery colour-printed pot lid made by F. & R. Pratt & Co., of Fenton. The subject is entitled 'The Truant'.

Rörstrand, Sweden With foreign technical assistance, the pottery was established as a successful concern by about 1740. Tin-glazed earthenware was produced, much of it decorated in blue and *bianco sopra bianco*. Baroque designs were replaced by

Pottery Factories (Continued)

rococo during the course of the 1740s and a greater range of colours was introduced. Later, creamware of English type was made. Various marks were used, sometimes comprising an abbreviation of the name of the factory and numerals giving the date.

Rouen, France There are records of potters working in Rouen, Normandy, as early as 1492, and in the sixteenth century Italian-style *maiolica* was being made there. In the late 1640s a fresh concern was established and until the end of the eighteenth century Rouen was an important French centre of the pottery industry. Large dishes, trays, ewers and other pieces of ambitious size were skilfully painted in blue and colours with complex patterns based on contemporary engravings or imitating Chinese and Delft prototypes.

Sadler and Green John Sadler and Guy Green were partners in a factory in Liverpool where pottery was decorated with transfer-printed patterns. Sadler is said to have invented the process in about 1750, and the two men used it on pottery made locally as well as on ware sent to Liverpool by Wedgwood and others in Staffordshire.

Saint Porchaire, France Pottery of a particular type was made here, a village to the south-west of Paris, in the mid-sixteenth century. The wares were made of a white clay decorated by means of impressed patterns filled with black, brown or reddish clays, the whole covered in a lead glaze. Ewers, saltcellars and other articles were made, some of them bearing the coats of arms of royalty and local notables. Specimens are mostly in museums.

Savona, Italy There were several potteries at work at Savona and other places near Genoa, where *maiolica* was made between the fifteenth and eighteenth centuries. Articles of all kinds were produced, and decorative treatments were equally varied. Many marks have been recorded, but there is uncertainty as to which particular factory may have used them.

Sceaux, France The Sceaux pottery, on the fringe of Paris, was started in the late 1730s or early 1740s, and produced tin-glazed earthenware of high quality. It was carefully decorated in enamels and is among the best of its type. Marks were used sometimes.

Sherratt Obadiah and Martha Sherratt owned a pottery at Burslem, Staffordshire, in the first half of the nineteenth century. They made figures and groups of rustic type which are mostly coarsely modelled and coloured. The wares are raised on flat bases with four or six short legs, with the name of the subject, often misspelt, impressed on the front.

Siena, Italy The city had potteries operating from the thirteenth century, but only pieces surviving from the early sixteenth century and later can be attributed with certainty. Tiles, dishes and drug jars of *maiolica* were painted in colours, many of them resembling those of Faenza and Deruta.

Simpson There were several men with the surname Simpson at work in Staffordshire potteries in the course of time. The best-known is Ralph Simpson, who made red clay chargers with slip decoration that included his name. It has been suggested that two men with the same names were involved in making the twenty or so surviving examples, or that he may have been a Ralph Simpson recorded as being born in 1651 and dying in 1724.

Pottery Factories (Continued)

Smith Sampson Smith (1813–78) was a potter at Longton, Staffordshire. From about 1850 he made simply-modelled and garishly-coloured figures and groups of celebrities of the time, as well as other goods for selling cheaply. These included pairs of seated dogs, some of which are marked in relief beneath the base *SAMPSON SMITH 1851 LONGTON.*

Spode Josiah Spode (1733–97) was apprenticed to Thomas Whieldon, and in 1770 established a pottery at Stoke-on-Trent, Staffordshire, which was duly continued by his son, also named Josiah (1754–1827). They manufactured earthenware of various kinds, particularly with blue transfer-printed decoration of good design and execution.

Strasburg, France This city in eastern France owed its eminence as a centre for tin-glazed earthenware to the activities of the Hannong family. Paul Hannong (1700–60) son of the founder, introduced in the 1740s enamelling and gilding of the type hitherto employed only on porcelain. First-class decorators were attracted to the establishment and its productions were widely copied. Both the shapes of articles and their colourful decoration influenced the output at Niderviller, Sceaux and elsewhere.

Sunderland, co. Durham A number of

Spode pottery plate printed in underglaze blue with a view of the bridge at Solaro in northern Italy. It was copied from a book published in 1797/8 and the plate was made about a dozen years later.

Pottery Factories (Continued)

potteries were active from the eighteenth century onwards. They made cream-coloured and white earthenware which was usually decorated with transfer printing and often further embellished with pink lustre. Similar goods were made at Newcastle, Gateshead, North Shields and South Shields, all of them supplying home demand as well as exporting to the mainland of Europe.

Sussex At Rye and thereabouts slipware was made in the late eighteenth century. A glazed redware impressed with patterns and inscriptions in printers' metal type filled in with white slip came from both Chailey and Brede, some pieces bearing early nineteenth-century dates. Apparently a county speciality was the figure of a pig, the animal's body forming a jug and modelled so that it would sit upright as well as rest on all fours, the removable lid serving as a cup.

Swansea, Glamorgan The Welsh seaport was a pottery centre for about 100 years from the 1760s. The Swansea Pottery and others of lesser importance made earthenwares of current types decorated with transfer printing and painting. The latter was sometimes very carefully executed and a few of the individual artists have been identified. Impressed and painted marks are recorded.

Talavera, Spain Tin-glazed earthenware was made at Talavera de la Reyna, not far from Madrid, from the early sixteenth century. Colours used there included a strong green, an orange-yellow, a dark purple and a blue. Battle scenes and bull-fighting vied with mythological and Biblical subjects as decoration.

Toft Many members of the Toft family were potters in Staffordshire from the seventeenth century onwards. Thomas Toft, in particular, made large slipware dishes bearing his name and dates between about 1670 and 1690.

Staffordshire slip-decorated charger with a trellis-pattern border enclosing a design of one uncrowned and four crowned heads of ladies, signed THOMAS TOFT. Christie's.

Turner John Turner and his two sons owned a pottery at Lane End, now a part of Longton, Staffordshire, between about 1756 and 1806. The father first established a concern at Stoke and after a few years removed to Lane End, where he and his successors made good quality earthenwares of many kinds. Much of the output was in imitation of Wedgwood's, and while some was sold through an agent in London a proportion went to Holland. The Napoleonic Wars put an end to the export side of the business, which was closed owing to bankruptcy.

Urbino, Italy Urbino is probably the most famed of *maiolica* centres, its importance dating from the early sixteenth century and lasting for about 100 years. A style of decoration based on some of Raphael's designs was sufficiently distinc-

Pottery Factories (Continued)

tive to have earned the name 'Urbino grotesques', in allusion to the patterns incorporating human and animal forms with flowers, leaves and scrolls. Members of the Pellipario family, known under various names, were among painters whose handiwork has been recognized.

Venice, Italy Venetian *maiolica*-making dates back to the fifteenth century. Much of the output reflects the Oriental influence seen in much else produced in the city, which was a meeting-place of the cultures of East and West. One particular style of decoration is distinctively Venetian; the use of a greyish-blue ground on which patterns are painted in dark blue and white.

Voyez John Voyez (1735?–?1800) was a modeller and carver who is known to have worked for Ralph Wood and Josiah Wedgwood, the latter finding him unreliable. Voyez turned to imitating Wedgwood's wares, especially his seals and intaglios.

Walton John Walton, of Burslem, Staffordshire, was active in the first decades of the nineteenth century. He made figures and groups, usually with a leafy tree as a background and support, brightly coloured in enamels. Many have a curved scroll on the front with the title of the subject, and some have a similar scroll at the back bearing the maker's name.

Wedgwood Josiah Wedgwood (1730–95) was one of a family active as potters. After some experience in the industry he was apprenticed to Thomas Whieldon for five years from 1754. In 1759 he began a highly successful career as a potter on his own. He was responsible for improving many of the traditional Staffordshire wares and devising fresh ones; additionally he was an excellent businessman and organized his manufactory on sound lines. He perfected a cream-coloured earthenware, duly named by him Queensware, in about 1762; by 1767 his black basaltes was launched, and eight years later the best-known of his compositions, jasper, was introduced. In 1762 Wedgwood met the Liverpool merchant Thomas Bentley, with whom he formed a fruitful partnership lasting from 1769 to 1780. Together they operated a newly-built pottery named Etruria, near Burslem, where the production was confined to vases and other purely ornamental pieces made of basaltes and jasper. Useful articles were produced at a separate establishment with which Bentley was not connected. Every advantage was taken by Wedgwood and his partner of artistic matters by which they might anticipate public taste, and every nuance of showmanship was put to the test. These factors, allied with a high standard of design and workmanship led to Wedgwood's deserved epitaph: He 'converted a rude and inconsiderable manufactory into an elegant art and an important part of national commerce'. His productions were copied in his own country and elsewhere, and the status his ability gave to Staffordshire still remains unimpaired. Wedgwood's son, also named Josiah (1769–1843), continued the business less successfully; not only did he lack his father's flair but the Napoleonic Wars caused a serious recession in trade in general. However, Josiah II was responsible for several innovations including the introduction of blue transfer-printing. The firm was active throughout the nineteenth century, living for much of the period on its past reputation. Josiah Wedgwood marked the great majority of his wares with his surname impressed, ornamental pieces of 1769–80 being stamped *WEDGWOOD & BENTLEY* or with the same words in relief on a circular disc.

Pottery Factories (Continued)

Whieldon Thomas Whieldon (1719–95) had a pottery at Fenton Low, Staffordshire, and is known to have made almost every type of ware current in his lifetime. He had a high reputation in his day and among his apprentices were Josiah Spode and Josiah Wedgwood.

Wincanton, Somerset A pottery was established at Wincanton in the 1730s and closed after a life of perhaps twenty years. A few specimens are recorded inscribed with the name of the town and dates between 1733 and 1748. Almost all the painting was in blue and manganese, and a favoured combination featured a ground of powdered purple-brown inset with panels painted in blue. This was not, however, exclusive to Wincanton.

Wood A number of members of the Wood family worked in Staffordshire during the eighteenth century. The most famous was Ralph Wood (1715–72) and his son of the same name (1748–95), who produced figures and groups decorated with transparent glazes. Not least, they probably made Toby jugs.

Wrotham, Kent Slipware was made in and about Wrotham in the seventeenth and eighteenth centuries. Many of the pieces are dated between about 1612–1740, and bear initials of one or other of the potters who worked there. They included members of the Richardson, Hubble, Ifield and Livermore families. It is most probable that the principal output was of domestic pieces that have vanished long ago, and only the more imposing specimens, made for commemorative or other purposes, have survived.

One of Josiah Wedgwood's copies of the Portland Vase, the Roman glass original of which is now in the British Museum. The pottery version was completed in 1793 after much experiment, and about twenty of this first series have been recorded. Several later issues of the vase have been made by Wedgwood's. Christie's.

Yi-hsing, China Teapots were the principal articles made from a red stoneware produced at Yi-hsing, inland from Shanghai, in Kiangsu province. The teapots came to the West in the late seventeenth century along with consignments of tea, and they quickly acquired a reputation for being the best articles in which to brew it. Copies were made in Holland, by Böttger in Meissen, and in England by the Elers brothers.

PORCELAIN

True porcelain is often referred to as 'hard paste', while imitations of it are known as 'soft paste'. A third variety, made in England, is called 'bone china'. All three are more or less translucent.

METHODS AND MATERIALS

Many of the techniques employed in making porcelain were common to pottery. The list of Pottery Methods and Materials should be used in conjunction with the one following:

Bleu Céleste A pale blue ground colour named literally sky-blue (*céleste:* celestial), introduced at Sèvres in 1753. It is known in England as turquoise-blue.

Bleu de Roi A dark blue ground colour introduced at Sèvres in about 1760 and supplanting *gros bleu.*

Bone Ash When burned, animal bones and other bones are reduced to a white powder. Bone ash was used as an ingredient of Bow porcelain from 1749, and later at other factories. After about 1800 it became a feature of the composition of most British wares. See Bone China.

Bone China Bone china is a compromise between hard- and soft-paste porcelains. It is made of china-clay and china-stone together with up to 40% bone ash, the latter resulting in an acceptable product at a reduced cost. Bone china was widely made from about 1800, traditionally at the instigation of Josiah Spode, and has remained a standard English porcelain with an international renown.

Bourdalou A chamber-pot for the use of ladies. It acquired its name from that of a French priest, Père Louis Bourdaloue (1632–1704), whose lengthy sermons were said to have caused his female hearers considerable personal inconvenience. The *bourdalou* was made at many factories, those from Sèvres and Meissen sometimes being ornately decorated.

Cabaret A word used to describe a teaset and tray for one or two persons, but it is not an old term for the purpose.

Café au lait A pale brown glaze resembling white coffee in colour employed as a ground on eighteenth century Chinese porcelain.

Celadon A pale greyish-green colour. The Chinese used it in the form of a glaze and efforts to copy it were made at Meissen. It is believed to have acquired its name from the grey-green costume worn by a shepherd named Céladon in a French play produced in the early seventeenth century.

China-clay Purified decomposed granite is a fine white clay known as china-clay, or *kaolin.* It is found in China and in various parts of Europe. In England, supplies came from Devon and Cornwall, and continue to do so.

China-stone Semi-decomposed granite is known as china-stone, and is composed of quartz, feldspar and a greenish variety of talc. It fuses when subjected to a high temperature. Like china-clay it occurs all over the world, and in England comes from Cornwall. It is also referred to by its Chinese name, *petuntse.*

Chocolate Chocolate became a fashionable beverage towards the end of the seventeenth century and in due course its

Porcelain, Methods and Materials (Continued)

imbibers were provided with suitable porcelain from which to take it. Chocolate cups are tall with a handle at each side and a cover to keep the contents warm. The saucers are of the *trembleuse* type, with a low gallery in the centre to prevent the cup tipping and spilling its contents.

Chrome Green A green enamel discovered at the end of the eighteenth century. Made from oxide of chromium, it replaced green made from copper and has a yellower appearance than the latter.

Clobber To overpaint a decorated article with a further pattern. This was sometimes done in Holland and elsewhere at a period when Chinese blue-decorated ware was unfashionable, the vari-coloured Western work seldom completely concealing the original design.

Commedia dell'Arte See Italian Comedy.

Dead Leaf Brown A mid-brown glaze, darker than *café au lait*, used on eighteenth-century Chinese porcelain.

Deutsche Blumen Flowers painted on porcelain in natural colours, realistically depicted, were termed *deutsche Blumen* in the eighteenth century. They were introduced at Meissen in about 1740 and the style was copied everywhere in due course.

Egg and Spinach The name given to a decoration found on Chinese porcelain in the form of random splashes of green, yellow and aubergine glazes.

Engraving Engraving by means of a diamond-point on Meissen and Furstenburg porcelain was executed by August Otto Ernst von dem Busch (1704–79), Canon of Hildesheim. He drew various subjects on the glaze, filling the fine lines with a black pigment so that they showed up. Some of the work is signed with his surname, and dated specimens have been recorded. Another dignitary of Hildesheim, Canon J. G. Kratzberg, did similar work.

d'Entrecolles Père d'Entrecolles was a French Jesuit missionary in China during the early eighteenth century. In 1712 and 1722 he sent back to Paris descriptions of porcelain-making as practised by the Chinese, together with samples of kaolin and *petuntse*. His letters were published in France in 1717 and 1724, stimulating activity to make porcelain in that country and farther afield.

Famille Jaune Chinese porcelain decorated with yellow predominating, which occurred during the K'ang Hsi period (1662–1722). The French term, like numerous others applied to Chinese wares, came into use in the nineteenth century when Albert Jacquemart first studied the subject.

Famille Noire Chinese porcelain decorated on a predominately black ground.

Famille Rose Chinese porcelain in which shades of opaque pink, or rose, appear in the decoration. The colour was first used at the end of the reign of the Emperor K'ang Hsi and has been employed ever since. Much of the porcelain exported from China to the West since about 1725 is sometimes collectively referred to as *famille rose*.

Famille Verte Chinese porcelain in which shades of green, with blue, yellow, manganese and red appear in the decoration. Albert Jacquemart applied the term to porcelain made in the reign of the Emperor K'ang Hsi (1662–1722), but it is sometimes used to cover a wider range of wares.

Garniture de Cheminée A *garniture de*

Porcelain, Methods and Materials (Continued)

cheminée is the term used to describe a set of five vases, comprising two open-mouthed beakers and three vases with covers. They were made in China for export to Europe, and were imitated by many pottery and porcelain makers in the West.

Gilding Occasionally gilding was executed on porcelain by laying gold leaf on a surface prepared with gold-size. Unfired, it soon wore away. Honey-gilding was much more durable, and involved grinding gold with honey and painting the mixture on with a brush. It was fired at a low temperature, could be burnished if required and resulted in a rich effect. The process was employed during most of the eighteenth century, being replaced in about 1780 by mercury-gilding. For this, an amalgam of mercury and gold was applied to the article, the heat of the kiln driving off the mercury to leave a thin film of gold. This, too, could be burnished, but its effect is seldom equal to that obtained with honey-gilding. Various other processes were introduced in the course of the nineteenth century.

Glazes Soft paste wares were finished similarly to pottery with a lead glaze and, very occasionally, with one containing tin oxide. Hard paste had a coating of powdered china stone and other ingredients.

Gros Bleu A rich dark blue ground colour employed at Sèvres. When imitated at Chelsea it was known as 'mazarine blue'.

Ground Colour A coloured background on which gilding might be executed. Equally, the ground could be broken with panels, or reserves, left in the white for further decoration. Chinese coloured grounds inspired the painters at Meissen and elsewhere, and there was competition between the principal factories of each country to produce the most beautiful colours. In addition to the plain grounds introduced at Meissen, Sèvres, Chelsea and Worcester, the last-named is renowned for its grounds patterned with overlapping scales of various colours. An increased range of coloured grounds was made possible by advances in chemistry that took place in the nineteenth century.

Hard Paste The name given to true porcelain, composed of china-clay and china-stone. Baked in a kiln to a temperature of 1300°–1400° centigrade, the result is a white and very hard material that is translucent, and breaks to reveal a moist-looking smooth fracture. It had been made in China continuously since the T'ang dynasty: A.D. 618–907, while in Europe it was first produced at Meissen in 1708. Compare Soft Paste.

Imari A port in Japan of which the name has been used to describe wares exported thence but actually made inland at Arita. The wares so-described were made in the eighteenth century and are painted in blue, iron-red and gold. The style was copied in China as well as in Europe.

Iron-Red A matt-surfaced bright red colour produced from oxide of iron and much used on Chinese porcelain, especially during the K'ang Hsi period.

Italian Comedy The Italian Comedy, the *Commedia dell' Arte*, was an impromptu theatrical entertainment popular throughout Europe during the seventeenth and eighteenth centuries. The various stock characters were played by professional actors who improvised their lines and action to provide amusement for the audience. The principal characters were the subject of sets of engravings, which in turn

Porcelain, Methods and Materials (Continued)

inspired models in porcelain at numerous factories. They included: the elderly *Pantaloon* who objects to the marriage of his daughter *Isabella* to *Cynthio*, preferring her to select the braggart and long-nosed *Captain* son of the *Doctor* and his wife *Ragonda*; while among servants of the foregoing were *Columbine*, *Harlequin* and *Punch*. All of them were known by alternative names. The best-known porcelain figures of these characters and others in the Comedy are those modelled at Meissen in the 1740s, most of them after illustrations in a book published in 1728. Less familiar but more remarkable is the series modelled at Nymphenburg in 1755–60 by F. A. Bustelli.

Japan Patterns See Imari, Kakiemon.

Jesuit China Porcelain made and decorated in China with Biblical scenes, allegedly to the order of French Jesuit missionaries in the country. The painting is usually in black with slight touches of red and gold.

Jewelled Decoration Shining jewel-like blobs of clear enamel over gold leaf or metal foil were used sometimes to decorate Sèvres porcelain from the early 1780s. Similar work had, in fact, been executed earlier in Germany, but the French examples are better known.

Johanneum A museum in Dresden in which is the Royal Saxon porcelain collection, started in the early eighteenth century. An inventory was commenced in 1721 and each piece in the collection had a number and symbol engraved on the back. The symbols each refer to the type of ware, and occasionally examples come on the market because duplicates from the Johanneum were sold in 1919 and 1920.

Japanese Arita porcelain plate with decoration in the Kakiemon style. Both the colouring and the pattern were copied in Europe. Christie's.

Kakiemon The Kakiemon family of Japanese potters has given its name to a type of porcelain made at Arita, Japan. It is sparsely painted in shades of green, red, blue, turquoise and yellow on a fine white ware. The colour-scheme, shapes and patterns were much copied in Europe.

Kaolin See China Clay.

Laub und Bandelwerk The German term means in English 'leaf-and-strapwork'. It describes a decorative motif much used on early eighteenth-century German and Austrian porcelain, comprising interlaced straps with formal foliage.

Lithophane Lithopanes are white porcelain plaques with designs impressed into them, made for holding to the light for viewing. They were made in the nineteenth century, especially at German factories.

Long Elizas An English translation of the Dutch *lange lijzen: lijzen* being the

Porcelain, Methods and Materials (Continued)

plural of an affectionate form of Elizabeth. Long Elizas are the willowy ladies who often appear on Chinese blue and white porcelain and were copied in England and Holland.

Marks From 1724 the blue-painted crossed swords of Meissen were used consistently by the factory on its wares, and in the course of time were imitated far and wide. Some factories used their own marks as well as that of Meissen, and when they used the latter seldom troubled to confine it to the type of goods likely to have been made there. Chelsea pioneered for a few years a small oval medallion with an anchor in relief on it, and in the course of time this sometimes fell off to leave a glaze-free scar where it had been. In the early nineteenth century, in England, the standardization of the porcelain body means that unless a piece bears a mark it is seldom possible to narrow down its origin to a particular source. In some instances however, pattern-numbers, which frequently appear, can be traced. It is worthwhile repeating, as with pottery, that marks on porcelain can be very misleading and should be used only to confirm other evidence. They always have been, and will continue to be, an easy target for makers of fakes and the downfall of many a tyro.

Mazarine Blue A dark blue colour used as a ground at Chelsea and Derby. At the time it was called mazarin, mazarine and mazareen blue, but the reason for giving it that name is not known.

Ming The Ming dynasty in China commenced in 1368 and ended in 1643, a period of some 275 years, during which seventeen Emperors came and went. Chinese porcelain having an appearance of age is often described loosely as 'Ming'.

Monkey Band A set of twenty or so figures of monkeys playing musical instruments, together with a conductor, first made at Meissen in about 1750. It was copied at Chelsea a few years later and was made again in Germany during the nineteenth century.

Nankin The Chinese port on the Yangtze river gave its name to eighteenth-century Chinese porcelain with blue decoration.

Parian An unglazed white porcelain introduced in the mid-1840s and used mainly for busts and statuettes. More than one Staffordshire maker claimed its invention as his own. Parian was quickly popular and was marketed over several decades by numerous firms. Wedgwood's called their version Carrara.

Pâte sur pâte *Pâte sur pâte* means literally 'paste upon paste' and describes decoration built up by painting and modelling slip, which was usually white on a coloured ground. The process was used at Sèvres and brought to England by Marc Louis Solon (1835–1912) who worked at Minton's from 1870. The process continued in use at the factory until 1939.

Petuntse French phonetic version of the Chinese name for china-stone (*pai-tun-tzu*).

Rose Pompadour A pink ground colour introduced at Sèvres in 1757 and noted in the factory records simply as *roze*. Soon after it was first used the name *rose Pompadour* was applied to it in England, and at a later date it became *rose Dubarry*.

Soaprock Soaprock, steatite or soapstone was used in the composition of soft paste porcelain at Bristol, Worcester and a few other English factories. It was obtained from the Lizard Peninsula, Cornwall.

Porcelain, Methods and Materials (Continued)

Soft Paste In contradiction to true porcelain or 'hard paste', artificial porcelain is known as 'soft paste'. It is basically a compound of glass and white clay, which fractures to reveal a dry-looking break that is rough and has a granular appearance like sugar. The first artificial porcelain was made in Italy between 1575 and 1587, when the Grand Duke of Tuscany, Francesco Maria de Medici, gave his patronage to a concern in Florence. The ware is known as Medici porcelain. Compare Hard Paste.

Trembleuse See Chocolate.

FACTORIES

Absolon William Absolon (1751–1815) was a china and glass dealer at Yarmouth, Suffolk. At the same time he ran a small establishment for decorating ware that he bought in the white from various factories. He signed some of his work with his name and town.

Amstel, Holland The Dutch factory at Oude Loosdrecht was transferred to Oude Amstel, near Amsterdam, in 1784. After a change of ownership it finally closed in 1820. While the hard paste porcelain was of good quality, the decoration was seldom of much interest. The usual mark was the word *Amstel* in script lettering in blue.

Ansbach, Germany Hard paste porcelain was made at the *faience* factory from 1758, when some Meissen workers were employed for the purpose. Figures and table wares were made, a peculiarity of the former being the outlining of eyes with red. The factory continued in operation until 1860, and some of its wares were marked with a capital letter *A*.

Arita, Japan Porcelain-making was unknown in Japan until some time in the sixteenth century, at the earliest. It was begun at Arita, in the province of Hizen, where suitable deposits of china-clay had been found. By the mid-seventeenth century much of the production was being shipped to Europe by way of the port of Imari, the trading station of the Dutch East India Company. The name of Imari has remained attached to dishes, vases and other pieces, some of them of large size, made of a greyish hard paste porcelain painted in a dull dark blue, red and gold. The patterns are usually in the form of panels of flowers, with chrysanthemums predominating. Another type, known as Kakiemon ware, was more carefully decorated in a limited palette on a good white porcelain. Again, much was sent to the West, where it was greatly admired and widely copied.

Barr See Worcester.

Belleek, Ireland This factory in County Fermanagh was established in 1857, and thirty years later had 200 employees. It produced parian and other kinds of ware, including much with a distinctive pearl-like glaze that has been described as glistening 'like wet barley sugar'. Vessels in the form of, or decorated with, sea shells were popular and were delicately modelled. Various marks incorporating the name of the factory were impressed or printed.

Berlin, Germany A newly-founded hard paste porcelain factory was bought by Frederick the Great in 1763 and endures to the present day. During his lifetime,

Porcelain Factories (Continued)

Frederick (died 1786) encouraged the concern to emulate the success of Meissen, and he was able to secure the employment of some craftsmen from there. Some important table services were produced as well as figures, all of excellent workmanship but usually lacking the vitality of Meissen. Biscuit busts, figures and groups were made in the early nineteenth century, and from about 1830 there was a large output of lithophanes. The mark used was a sceptre and at times in the nineteenth century the letters *K P M* for *Königliche porzellanmanufaktur*: Royal porcelain factory. Another establishment opened in 1752 lasted for only five years. It produced some good pieces during that time, although they are understandably now rather rare. The mark used was an initial *W*, in blue or impressed, for the surname of the proprietor, Wilhelm Kaspar Wegely.

Billingsley William Billingsley (1760-1828) was an arcanist and china decorator. He was born at Derby, learned his trades there and then alternated between painting and being involved in short-lived concerns. His decorating was more successful than much of his porcelain. See Pinxton; Swansea; Nantgarw.

Blanc de Chine The name given to a hard white porcelain made at Têhua in the province of Fukien, south-east China. It was produced from at least as early as the sixteenth century, and in the seventeenth and eighteenth centuries was exported in

Arita porcelain dish painted with the coats of arms of a Dutch couple who were married in 1667. Sotheby's.

Porcelain Factories (Continued)

large quantities to Europe. Some of the pieces were in forms to suit Western tastes, while others, particularly those moulded with branches of plum blossom in relief were imitated by factories in France, England and elsewhere. *Blanc de Chine* is sometimes referred to as Fukien porcelain.

Bloor See Derby.

Bonnin and Morris See Philadelphia.

Böttger Johann Friedrich Böttger (1682–1719) began his working career as an alchemist and made an early start trying to produce gold from base metals. Like innumerable others before and since he was not successful, but in the event he discovered how to make true porcelain, something known hitherto only to the Chinese. As a result the Royal Saxon Porcelain Manufactory was established at Meissen in 1710, but Böttger lacked the ability to exploit his success and he died from the effects of over-indulgence in drink only nine years later at the age of thirty-seven.

Bow The Bow factory was situated just outside London, on the Essex side of the river Lea, just opposite Stratford-le-Bow, which is in Greater London. The concern was established following a patent for making porcelain granted in 1744 to Edward Heylyn and Thomas Frye, a further patent being granted to Frye alone in 1748. The basis was an American type of china-clay, found in Georgia and known there as *unaker*, and it is assumed that the first Bow wares were some kind of artificial porcelain with *unaker* as one of the constituents. In addition, the 1748 patent specified the incorporation of bone ash in the mixture, which was the first recorded use of the material for china-making in England. Frye was manager of the concern, and being known otherwise as a painter and engraver probably had some say in its artistic direction. The earliest known dated examples of the factory's productions are seven pieces of various types dated 1750, and it can only be conjectured what may have been made prior to that year. Wares of 1750 onwards are usually recognizable by their shape and colouring, if any, and by the actual china of which they are made; this varies in colour from greyish to cream, is often only thinly glazed and specimens are not notable for their finish. Frequently present on Bow of all dates are pale brown stains where the glaze is extra thin, especially at rims. Colours used included a reddish-purple and an opaque pale blue, the former frequently appearing as an emphasis to moulding on bases of figures and groups. A large proportion of the

Bow porcelain figure of a man cutting wood, made in about 1755 and copying one designed earlier at Meissen. H. Spencer & Sons.

Porcelain Factories (Continued)

output was of table wares, much of it with blue decoration showing Oriental influence in the choice of both colour and subject. Ornamental pieces are sometimes of original design, but others are unsophisticated imitations of Meissen and other factories. Frye retired in 1758 and the factory continued in operation for a further fifteen years or so. Towards the end it is supposed to have been in the ownership of William Duesbury, and was finally closed in about 1775 or 1776. Various marks have been recorded on Bow, but none was employed consistently.

Bristol In addition to the numerous potteries in and about the city, there were two porcelain factories at one time or another in Bristol. The first venture was opened in about 1749 following the granting of a licence to obtain soaprock from a site in Cornwall; the soaprock to be an ingredient in the artificial porcelain that it was proposed to manufacture. A few specimens have been found on which is the word *BRISTOLL* in relief together with the date 1750. Two of these are figures of a Chinese Sage bearing slight decoration in underglaze manganese brown, which serves to link with them some other objects similarly coloured. Also ascribed to the Bristol venture are some blue-decorated sauceboats and various useful and ornamental articles with finely painted Oriental decoration. Some of the sauceboats, both blue and coloured, are also marked *BRISTOLL*, and have assisted in further attributions. The factory was, however, shortlived in the west-country port, for in 1751 the Bristol China Manufactory and all its secrets were purchased by the newly-formed Worcester Porcelain Company, and the former was closed in the following year. The kilns of the Bristol factory were in an old glasshouse once owned by a Mr.

Lund's Bristol cream jug. Made in the late 1740s at the factory that was bought and removed to Worcester in 1751. Christie's.

Lowdin, and for many years the ware was known as 'Lowdin's Bristol' to prevent confusion with other wares made in the city. More recently, it has become known as 'Lund's Bristol', after one of the original partners in the venture, a copper- and brass-merchant named Benjamin Lund. The second factory at Bristol was opened in 1770, when Richard Champion, a banker in the city, managed and then purchased William Cookworthy's enterprise started at Plymouth. It was the only English concern to make hard paste porcelain, and when Cookworthy's original patent for the process expired in 1773 its renewal was opposed by Wedgwood and others in Staffordshire. However, Champion was able to retain the sole right to use the materials in translucent porcelain, but the fight had been a costly one; he sold the patent in 1781 to the New Hall company and closed the Bristol factory. The wares made during the eleven years in which the Bristol hard paste concern was active included ornamental as well as useful pieces, many of them showing signs of distortion due to difficulties experienced in managing

Porcelain Factories (Continued)

the material. Colouring was sometimes inclined to be harsh, and designs were seldom outstanding. The marks used included imitations of the Meissen crossed swords and an *X*, usually in blue.

Buen Retiro, Spain The gardens of the Royal palace of Buen Retiro, Madrid, were the site of a porcelain factory transferred from Italy in 1759. In that year Charles III, King of Naples, succeeded to the Spanish throne, and brought the artists and workers from his factory at Capodimonte. Among the first products at Buen Retiro was a complete room-interior in porcelain for the palace of Aranjuez, which is signed by the artistic director José Gricci and dated 1763. Gricci designed many original figures and groups, and the factory also made table wares and snuff boxes. All are distinguished by their careful painting, and by the beauty of the porcelain itself; a slightly cream-tinted soft paste with a wax-like appearance. Sèvres and then Wedgwood provided inspiration, but from 1780 until the factory closed in 1808 little of interest was produced. The mark used was a fleur-de-lys, as at Capodimonte. See Naples.

Bustelli Franz Anton Bustelli (1723–63) was born at Locarno, Switzerland, and is thought to have acquired his skill in Italy. In 1754 he was appointed chief modeller at Nymphenburg, where he produced many highly individualistic figures. It has been pointed out that they 'invariably spiral upwards from exceptionally thin flat bases', and with great subtlety the support becomes part of the whole conception instead of intruding in the composition, as is more often the case.

Canton, China The port on the Pearl river was used for the shipment of goods to the West, and the various nations were confined to an area of the waterfront where each had its warehouse or *Hong*. Some of the porcelain made at Ching-tê Chên was decorated at Canton. The name is given to a class of nineteenth-century wares heavily painted with flowers and figures on a pale green ground, often additionally decorated with butterflies and

Figure of Julia, a character in the Italian Comedy, modelled by F. A. Bustelli for the Nymphenburg porcelain factory about 1755–60.

Porcelain Factories (Continued)

insects. In America, Canton refers also to nineteenth-century wares from China, but painted in blue with landscapes and other subjects, often of indifferent execution.

Capodimonte See Naples.

Caughley, Salop. The manufactory at Caughley (pronounced calfley), near Broseley, Shropshire, was founded in about 1775 by Thomas Turner (1749–1809). Reputedly the concern was on the site of an earlier pottery owned by Ambrose Gallimore, with whom Turner may have formed a partnership for the new venture. Turner had worked at Worcester, and much of the identified Caughley production closely resembles Worcester with its soft paste porcelain and blue decoration. This was painted or printed, with Chinese patterns predominating, often with only slight details to differentiate the one from the other. Even the marks were imitated, with Caughley using a capital *C* resembling the Worcester crescent. The concern was known at the time as the Salopian China Manufactory, and some of its output was less confusingly marked with the word *SALOPIAN* impressed or with a blue printed capital letter *S*. The company was purchased in 1799 by the nearby Coalport factory, and closed in 1814.

Chamberlain Robert Chamberlain had been employed as a painter at the Worcester manufactory. He left it early in the 1780s to set up his own establishment, in which he was joined by his son, Humphrey, and another partner, where they decorated wares bought from Caughley and other sources. Within a few years they had erected their own kilns and were making a soft paste porcelain in direct competition with that of the old-established Worcester company. While Chamberlain's ware is often just as well-painted as the other, the porcelain of its earlier years is decidedly grey in tint and inclined to be more heavily made. Later it was improved and there was less to choose between the two. In 1840 the rival firms were amalgamated, and by 1851 changes in partnership led to their trading as Kerr and Binns. Much of the Chamberlain output was marked with their name in full, painted in red script but occasionally impressed, and in the case of services it was the practice to mark only a few pieces.

Champion Richard Champion (1743–91) was a Bristol banker who managed and then bought Cookworthy's Plymouth hard paste manufactory. After selling the concern in 1781 he held a Government post, and then in 1784 emigrated to South Carolina where he died. See Bristol: New Hall.

Chantilly, France A soft paste manufactory was begun at Chantilly, just to the north of Paris, in about 1725. Until about 1750 the ware was covered in a glaze whitened with oxide of tin, in the manner of earthenware, which gave a smooth and perfectly white surface. This was neatly painted with sparse designs of Japanese type in the manner of Kakiemon. Later, a clear lead glaze was employed over a slightly cream-coloured body, and at the same time decoration was in the Meissen style, the naturalistically-coloured bouquets of flowers being painted on shapes inspired by Sèvres. Figures and other articles were made in addition to table wares, but all are scarce. A pattern used in about 1770–80 shows a small formal floral motif that was widely copied and became known as 'Chantilly sprig', and another depicting tiny cornflowers was equally popular. After 1803 a hard paste porcelain was made. The mark used at Chantilly was a French hunting horn in red, or rarely gold, and later in blue.

Porcelain Factories (Continued)

Chelsea, London The Thames-side factory was situated near Chelsea Old Church, at the corner of the present Lawrence Street and Justice Walk. The exact date of its establishment is unknown, but some existing cream jugs inscribed 'Chelsea 1745' suggest that it was in being in that year. It would appear to have been established by a silversmith born at Liège, Nicholas Sprimont (1716–71) and a French-born jeweller, Charles Gouyn (died 1781). When the latter retired in 1749 Sprimont gained the patronage of Sir Everard Fawkener (1684–1758), secretary to the Duke of Cumberland, son of George II. This was as near to Royal patronage as the factory attained, and contrasted with conditions at many establishments in Germany, and Sèvres in France, that were fully supported by heads of state. Although a proportion of useful wares was made at Chelsea, attention was soon concentrated on the ornamental and no pains were spared in making them the best of their kind. The output of soft paste porcelain can conveniently be divided into periods in each of which a different factory mark was used:

Up to 1749: a triangle was sometimes incised in the clay prior to baking. The ware has a glassy look, models often resemble current silverware, and much of the output was sold uncoloured.

About 1749–52: a small anchor in relief on an oval medallion was applied to articles, which are less glassy in appearance than those of earlier date. The range of models widened to include figures and busts of eminent persons and from about 1750 original figures were modelled by Joseph Willems.

About 1753–7: a small anchor was painted in red, sometimes very inconspicuously. A determined effort would seem to have been made to beat competition from Meissen, and many groups and figures from that factory were carefully copied as regards both modelling and painting. Small boxes, seals and scent bottles, so-called 'Toys', were made in quantity.

Chelsea porcelain figure of Isabella, an Italian Comedy character, modelled by Joseph Willems, about 1750. The original of the figure was a Venetian woodcut in a book published in 1598, which explains why the lady is depicted in a dress of that time. Sotheby's.

1758–69: a gold anchor was used as a mark during this, the final and most extravagant period of the factory's existence. Bone ash was added to the

Porcelain Factories (Continued)

ingredients permitting the making of larger and more complex models, while the glaze tends to be thick and often shows a greenish tinge. Highly decorative and costly table wares and vases were made, and large groups and figures with backgrounds of carefully-modelled flowering shrubs were no less colourful and eye-catching. The coloured grounds popular at Sèvres were imitated and occasionally equalled, and some striking large vases were modelled in the rococo style.

The factory was sold by Sprimont in 1769 and in the following year came into the possession of William Duesbury. He operated it in conjunction with his Derby porcelain manufactory, finally closing it in 1784. See 'Girl in a Swing'.

Ching-tê Chên, China Ching-tê Chên, in Kiang-si province, was the place of manufacture of the majority of Chinese porcelain. In the early eighteenth century Père d'Entrecolles described it as having 3,000 kilns with an estimated million persons engaged in the industry.

Coalport, Salop The factory was established in about 1796 by John Rose. Three years later he bought the Caughley concern, which lay just across the river Severn, closing it in 1814. In about 1820 Rose purchased the formulas and moulds used at Nantgarw and Swansea, adaptation of the Nantgarw body resulting in the manufacture of an improved bone china at Coalport. Throughout the nineteenth century the factory made currently popular wares of all kinds, many of them equalling the flamboyance of shape and decoration of anything on the market. Typical of the decade 1820–30 are vases and inkstands encrusted with flowers, while later came deceptive copies of Sèvres and other eighteenth-century porcelains. From 1800 to about 1850 the ware was alternatively known as Coalbrookdale china, and that name as well as *Coalport* was used as a mark. Other marks included imitations of the Meissen crossed swords, the initials *C D* in script, and a confusing printed crown with the inscription *COALPORT ENGLAND A D 1750*. The last mark came into use in the 1870s, and many owners have been disappointed to learn that their apparent antiques were made considerably later than 1750.

Cookworthy William Cookworthy (1705–80) was born in Devonshire, and after serving his apprenticeship set up as an apothecary in Plymouth. By 1758 he had discovered both china clay and china stone in nearby Cornwall, and ten years later patented the manufacture of porcelain with them. His Plymouth porcelain was a true hard paste product which he made from 1768 to 1770, transferring manufacture to Bristol in the latter year.

Copenhagen, Denmark A soft paste factory was in operation between 1759 and 1765. Hard paste was made at the Royal Copenhagen establishment from the mid-1770s, and continues at the present day. Frenchmen and Germans were concerned in the early days of both, offering their services as arcanists and in due course other men came as modellers and painters. The soft paste wares are rare, and surviving examples show the French influence of the immigrant who directed the factory during its short life. The long-lived Royal establishment reflects Meissen in shapes and decoration, most of the output showing the severe lines of the prevailing neo-classical style. Table wares ranged from simple patterns in blue to the celebrated *Flora Danica* service of over 1,600 pieces (Rosenborg Castle, Copenhagen), of which each

Porcelain Factories (Continued)

item is painted in colours with a flower native to Denmark. Biscuit was used for the reproduction of plaques and statuettes after works by the sculptor Bertel Thorvaldsen (1770–1844). From about 1800 the factory slowly declined and it was not until after the mid-century that it again became really active; new models began to be added to the repertoire and many of the old ones were revived. The mark in use continuously since 1775 is three short wavy lines in blue, representing the three Danish channels to the Baltic: The Sound, Great Belt and Little Belt.

Davenport The pottery factory at Longport, Staffordshire, started by John Davenport, began making bone china early in the nineteenth century. Production continued until the concern closed in 1887, and included wares of all types except figures decorated carefully and colourfully in current styles. Printed and impressed marks are recorded.

Derby Some soft paste cream jugs dated 1750 are thought to be the earliest surviving pieces of Derby porcelain. By 1756 William Duesbury, with the aid of a partner, acquired the factory and down to 1811 it remained in the hands of the Duesbury family. In that year it was purchased by Robert Bloor, fifteen years later there was a further change and the factory closed in 1848. The wares can be divided as follows:

To 1755: figures have been identified and have in common an area free of glaze round the lower sides of the base, the so-called 'dry edge', and have a funnel-shaped hole beneath.
1756–84: the range of figures was greatly increased as a result of much copying of Meissen, the factory advertising itself as 'the second Dresden'. White unglazed biscuit groups and figures were made from about 1770. Following Duesbury's purchase of the Chelsea factory in that year, the time from then until 1784 is referred to as the Chelsea-Derby period. Table wares were sometimes marked with a crown for Derby plus the Chelsea anchor. Figures seldom bore a mark but commonly were incised with *N^{o}* in script and a numeral referring to the model number.
1784–1811: the Crown Derby period,

Figure of John Wilkes, beside him a cupid holding a cap of liberty, made at Derby in about 1775.

Porcelain Factories (Continued)

when the mark of a crown over crossed batons with six dots and a script *D* was consistently applied. Well-made wares of all kinds with first-class painting and gilding gave the factory a high reputation.

1811–26: the Bloor period. In order to pay for the factory Bloor is said to have had all the ware that could be made, or could be found stored, decorated with quickly-drawn garish patterns. A proportion of good pieces continued to be produced, but the former standards were not attained. Bloor's name or a capital *B*, both with a crown, were used as a mark.

1823–48: small-sized figures, some decorated with 'lace' made by dipping real lace in slip, painted in bright colours and gold, were made. A version of the old crossed batons and a copy of the Meissen crossed swords were used as marks.

In 1850 some of the workmen from the closed factory opened one of their own, making small colourful figures and other pieces. It was called The Old Crown Derby China Works, and employed as a mark the one used immediately prior to the 1848 closure. A further enterprise, The Derby Crown Porcelain Company was opened in 1876, and following Royal patronage was permitted to change the name to The Royal Crown Derby Porcelain Company. This last firm duly bought its rival and the two still continue in business, making an almost unbroken link between about 1750 and to-day.

Doccia*, *Italy Successive members of the Ginori family have directed the Doccia porcelain factory, near Florence. It was founded in 1735, but it was some years before satisfactory wares were produced on a commercial scale. The material was at first greyish in tone, midway between true and artificial porcelain, and its glaze has been described as 'gluey'. From about 1770 it became whiter in appearance. Early table wares were decorated with the aid of stencils and ambitious versions of Chinese double-walled vessels were made. After the mid-century, Meissen and Sèvres styles were copied, and figures and groups, large and small were produced; some of the most dramatic having been modelled earlier by the sculptor, Massimiliano Soldani-Benzi (1658–1740). Widely known are table wares with mythological figures and garlands of flowers moulded in low relief, coloured brightly and with flesh tones stippled. The eighteenth-century versions of these pieces, marked with a star, are scarce, but in Victorian times the factory reproduced them in quantity, gave them Capodimonte marks and they were put on the market as old examples from the defunct Royal concern. Many more of the old Doccia pieces were reissued during the nineteenth century. See Naples.

Dresden*, *Germany The hard paste porcelain made at Meissen, outside Dresden, is often referred to in England as Dresden. During the nineteenth century there were a few firms in the city itself making or decorating wares imitating the earlier products of Meissen. Some of them used marks incorporating the word *DRESDEN*, others used the Meissen *AR* mark. This last was applied commonly to cups and saucers of a type that did not exist during the true currency of the latter mark.

Duesbury William Duesbury (1725–86) worked in London as an independent decorator (*Hausmaler*), painting wares by various makers. His private account book of the time has been preserved and printed. In 1756 in company with a partner he

Porcelain Factories (Continued)

bought the Derby factory and in 1770 that at Chelsea. He also played a part at Longton Hall and may have been concerned with Bow. His son, also named William (1763–?1797) owned the Derby concern after his father's death in 1786.

Du Paquier See Vienna.

Flight Thomas Flight (1726–1800) London agent of the Worcester Porcelain Company, purchased the concern in 1783, the management being undertaken by his sons, John (1766–91) and Joseph (died 1833). See Worcester.

Florence, Italy See Doccia; Medici.

Frankenthal, Germany In 1755 the French authorities forced the factory at Strasburg to close in order to protect the monopoly of Sèvres, so it was removed across the river Rhine and restarted at Frankenthal, near Mannheim. After seven years it ran into financial difficulties, and Carl Theodor, the Elector Palatine, ruler of the area, purchased it. The Napoleonic Wars of 1794–5 led to confiscation of the factory but it was duly run as a private concern until it closed in 1799. The hard paste wares were well made, with a milky appearance and much of the painting was of the highest quality. Table wares of all kinds were produced, and a number of good groups and figures. Various marks were used, the most common being the initials *C T* beneath a crown in blue.

Frye Thomas Frye (1710–62), born in Ireland, was in London by about 1729. He acquired a reputation as a painter of miniatures, an engraver and a painter of portraits. In 1744 and 1748 he was granted patents for methods of making an artificial porcelain, which were put into practice at Bow. He remained manager of the factory until retiring on account of ill-health in 1759.

Fukien See *Blanc de Chine*.

Fulda, Germany The factory at Fulda, north-east of Frankfort, was owned by the Prince-Bishop of Fulda and produced a good hard paste procelain. It was in operation from 1765–90, the output comprising table wares and figures; the latter modelled in an attractive blend of rococo and neo-classical. The mark used was the script letter *F*, in duplicate beneath a crown.

Fürstenburg, Germany Duke Carl I of Brunswick initiated experiments into porcelain-making at Fürstenburg. Although work began in about 1745 hard paste was not made successfully for eight years, and it was only in 1770 that the factory became free of financial and other difficulties. From then onwards, good table wares, groups and figures were made. Wedgwood's basaltes and jasper wares were imitated and a series of white biscuit busts and medallions was produced. The latter were impressed with a small figure of a running horse, while other wares had a script letter *F* in blue. The factory is still in existence and has continuously reproduced its old models, using a crowned *F* as a mark on them.

Giles James Giles (1718–80) was an independent decorator (*Hausmaler*) with premises in Berwick Street, London, from at least 1749. He is known also to have operated a kiln at Kentish Town and to have had trading premises in Cockspur Street. Some Worcester plates, given to the Victoria and Albert Museum by a descendant, demonstrate the types of painting executed in his workshop.

Ginori See Doccia.

Porcelain Factories (Continued)

Hancock Robert Hancock (1719?–1817) was an engraver who, after serving an apprenticeship at Birmingham, worked at Worcester and elsewhere making engravings for transfer printing. Later he lived in London and Bristol, dying at the latter place.

Herend, Hungary A hard paste porcelain factory was founded at Herend in 1839. Copies of Oriental and European wares of all kinds were made. The name *HEREND* was used as a mark, sometimes in letters 'so small as to be almost undetectable', or else a shield with the arms of Hungary painted in blue.

Höchst, Germany The factory at Höchst, near Mayence, was founded in 1750, but was in difficulty until 1765 when it began to receive a subsidy from the Elector. His son continued to support the enterprise from 1778, but it gradually declined in prosperity and closed twenty years later. The hard paste porcelain was used for well-painted table wares of rococo design, and for a large range of figures. Of these, the best-known are figures and groups of children modelled by Johann Peter Melchior (1742–1825), which are decorated attractively and posed on naturalistically-coloured grassy bases. The mark used was a wheel in red or blue. The original Höchst moulds were sold after the closing of the factory, and more than one firm subsequently made deceptive pieces from them.

Imari See Arita.

Kändler Johann Joachim Kändler (1706–75) studied sculpture and at the age of twenty-five, in 1731, began a career at Meissen which lasted until death. From 1733 he was chief modeller, and became responsible for designing most of the many figures and groups produced during the ensuing forty years. With Böttger he shares credit for the enduring fame of the factory.

Kakiemon See Arita.

Worcester porcelain bowl decorated in the workshop of James Giles with panels of birds and fruit reserved on a turquoise-blue ground. Christie's.

Porcelain Factories (Continued)

Littler See Longton Hall.

Liverpool, Merseyside There were several porcelain factories active during the second half of the eighteenth century. Attempts have been made to allocate to one or other of them soft paste wares that may or may not have been produced at Liverpool. The attributed pieces are mostly decorated in blue with Oriental patterns, and a number of printed specimens have been recorded. The more ambitious examples are reminiscent of Worcester, although lacking the quality of the material and the artistry of the ornamentation. Table wares would seem to have been the principal output, and it is likely that the major proportion was exported.

Longton Hall, Staffordshire A soft paste porcelain was made here from about 1750 until 1760, when a partner withdrew his support and the concern came to a sudden halt. The material was at its best of a greyish tint and often prone to be flawed in some way. Table wares in the form of leaves and vegetables were well modelled and brightly coloured, and some original figures were designed. Early examples of the latter are known as 'snowmen' figures because of their summary shaping and heavy bubble-laden glaze. Later figures are less clumsy but prove that the porcelain remained difficult to manage, and the crude colouring makes them more interesting to students of ceramic history than to collectors of objects of art. A strong blue colour, mostly employed for grounds, is known as 'Littler's Blue', after William Littler who invented it and was connected with Longton Hall for all or most of the factory's existence.

Lowdin's Bristol See Bristol.

Longton Hall porcelain mug painted in colours with imaginary buildings, the handle in the shape of a leafy twig. About 1755.

Lowestoft, Suffolk On the east coast of England this small factory made soft paste wares from 1757 to 1802. The material is very similar to that used at Bow, and it is traditionally said that one of the Lowestoft principals worked at Bow in order to learn their secrets. Table wares were the principal productions, either painted or printed in blue or coloured after Chinese originals. Figures have been identified following the excavation of fragments on the factory site. Interesting among Lowestoft's output are inscribed and dated specimens, many of which can be traced back to their original owners. Others were made for casual visitors and bear the legend *A TRIFLE FROM LOWESTOFT*. No factory mark was used, but occasionally the crescent of Worcester and the Meissen crossed swords were copied.

Ludwigsburg, Germany At Ludwigsburg, near Stuttgart, a hard paste manufactory was started by the Duke of Württemberg in 1758; the Duke stating

Porcelain Factories (Continued)

that such an establishment was 'necessary to the splendour and dignity' of his lands. The material varied in tint between grey and brown, and proved admirable for the making of figures of which a large number were produced during the lifetime of the factory. Some attractive miniature groups of figures depicted at market-stalls perhaps resulted from a visit paid to Venice by the Duke and are known as 'Venetian Fair' groups, but other figures of all the current types were made. Table wares were also produced. Marks varied from time to time and were copied at later dates.

Medici The first European soft paste porcelain was made at Florence, under the patronage of Francesco de' Medici, Grand Duke of Tuscany. Between 1575 and 1587 and perhaps for a little later, a translucent white ware was formed into vessels which, with a single exception, were painted in blue or blue and manganese. About sixty specimens, ranging from dishes to ewers in shapes used in *maiolica* of the time, have been recorded as surviving, the majority of them in museums. Most pieces bear the mark in blue of a dome, that of the Cathedral, S. Maria del Fiore, Florence.

Meissen, Germany The hard paste manufactory at Meissen, outside Dresden, was established in 1710 under the direction of J. F. Böttger. From its first experimental beginnings, it was encouraged in every way by Augustus the Strong, Elector of Saxony and King of Poland, who had a love of porcelain amounting almost to fanaticism. After Böttger's death in 1719, the concern was reorganized and with J. J. Kändler's appointment as chief modeller in 1733 an international renown was soon gained. Apart from imported Chinese and Japanese wares and a couple of small concerns in Europe (Vienna and Venice), Meissen had no rivals until the early 1750s, and by then the German factory had established a notable lead. From the start, the white material with its clear shining glaze was made into tablewares and figures; the former with a constantly changing series of patterns painted in an increasing palette of colours. Figures were likewise plentiful and imaginative in their design. Proof of success lies in the fact that very few factories, both in Germany and elsewhere, did not imitate the Meissen models, colours

Figure of Harlequin, from the Italian Comedy, modelled by J. J. Kändler in about 1740 for the Meissen factory. Kändler made several figures of the same character, this one being known as 'The Scowling Harlequin'. Sotheby's.

Porcelain Factories (Continued)

and marks. With the capture of Dresden by the army of Frederick the Great at the start of the Seven Years War (1756–63) the factory suffered losses from which it never fully recovered. Nonetheless, it continued to produce wares of a high quality, many of new design lacking the originality and vitality of the past. In the mid-nineteenth century there came a revival of many of the early models, which can confuse a present-day buyer into thinking they are genuinely of eighteenth century manufacture. Between about 1720–45 some of the output was sold undecorated and was painted by *Hausmaler*. Meissen marks range from the early use of the letters *A R* (for *Augustus Rex* and usually only on pieces for royal use or gifts) and *K P M* (for *Königliche porzellan-manufaktur*: Royal porcelain factory) to the crossed swords which came into use in 1724. The wares are often referred to in England as Dresden and in France as *Saxe* (for Saxony, the state of which Dresden was the capital).

Melchior Johann Peter Melchior (1742–1825) worked as a modeller at a number of German factories. His figures of children made at Höchst are distinctive.

Mennecy, France The factory was started at Paris in 1734, was twice moved outside the city and finally closed in 1806. The porcelain was of a creamy colour, soft paste, and with a bright glaze. All types of wares were made, but only Sèvres being permitted to use gilding, in common with that of other French factories Mennecy decoration was limited to colours for most of its period of activity. They included a pink and a blue that are characteristic of the concern. The mark was the initials *D V*, incised or painted, for the duc de Villeroy, the factory's patron.

Minton, Staffordshire The still-existing factory was started by Thomas Minton (1766–1836) and made porcelain between 1798 and 1811 and about 1821–5 before duly making it continuously. A good bone china was made and attention paid to the standard of modelling and workmanship, so that the firm consistently enjoyed a high reputation. All types of table and ornamental pieces were produced in current styles, the majority unmarked except for a pattern number and otherwise difficult to distinguish from the output of their competitors. Figures were sold coloured, in unglazed biscuit and in Parian. In 1870 the French decorator Marc-Louis Solon (1835–

Flower vase and base (jardinière) *decorated in* pâte sur pâte *by M. L. Solon. It was made at Minton's factory in about 1890 copying a shape originating at Sèvres in the 1750s.*
Victoria and Albert Museum.

Porcelain Factories (Continued)

1912) joined Minton's and introduced the *pâte sur pâte* technique which he had learned at Sèvres. Marks used included an imitation of the Meissen crossed swords, a version of the Sèvres mark with the letter *M* between two facing S's, and a printed globe encircled by *MINTON* or *MINTONS* which came into use in 1863.

Moscow*, *Russia Several hard paste porcelain factories were active in and about Moscow at various dates. Two of the principal ones owed their initiation to Englishmen: that of Francis Gardner, which was in the hands of members of his family from about 1765 to 1891 and that of Charles Milly, known as the Popoff factory, which flourished from the early 1800s to 1872. Both made good quality wares, including figures of Russian peasants in native costume.

Nantgarw*, *Wales The factory at Nantgarw, between Cardiff and Pontypridd, Glamorgan, was started in 1813 by William Billingsley who combined the skill of a flower painter with that of an arcanist. Financial and other troubles caused the removal of the concern to Swansea for the years 1814–16, after which it was re-established at Nantgarw until 1820. The soft paste ware was particularly beautiful, white and with a shining glaze, but liable to warp in the kiln and cause heavy losses. Painting was executed both at Nantgarw and Swansea, and much of the output was sold undecorated to be painted in London. The impressed mark usually employed was *NANTGARW* over *C.W.*, for China Works. Sometimes the glaze has flowed so thickly as to make the mark very difficult to see.

Naples*, *Italy The earliest factory in the city was started by Charles, King of Naples, in the grounds of his palace of Capodimonte. Five years earlier he had married a daughter of the Elector of Saxony, who brought with her an ample dowry of her father's Meissen porcelain. Charles duly set afoot efforts to rival his father-in-law's source of income and prestige, and succeeded in so far as he was able to make an excellent soft paste porcelain. It was a material with a yellowish cast and a smooth surface, that lent itself to the fine painting

Figure of an itinerant china-seller modelled by Giuseppe Gricci and made at the Italian Capodimonte factory in about 1750. Christie's.

Porcelain Factories (Continued)

it almost always received. Table wares and ornamental pieces were made, many of the former with unusual decoration in the form of battle scenes, or fruit piled against landscape backgrounds. Figures and groups were modelled in a lively manner, although many have noticeably small heads, and their colouring was often attractively slight. The mark used at Capodimonte was a *fleur de lys*, usually painted in blue but sometimes in another colour or gold, or the same impressed. Charles succeeded to the throne of Spain in 1759, when he took the entire concern, workers, clay and all, with him to Madrid, where they were established at Buen Retiro. A further factory was established at Naples in 1771 by Ferdinand IV. It was sold in 1807, restarted and finally closed in 1834. The material used was soft paste sometimes with a tin glaze to whiten it, but this became less necessary when the basic colour was improved. Table wares and ornamental pieces were made, the former including some very large services for presentation. One of these was sent to George III (much of it remains at Windsor Castle), with plates bearing careful paintings of ancient Etruscan vases and vessels in those shapes. The marks used were a crowned monogram of *R F*, for *Ferdinandus Rex* or *Real Fabbrica* (the latter for Royal factory), or the letter *N* crowned. This last was falsely used elsewhere, especially at Doccia.

New Hall, Staffordshire In 1781 a group of Staffordshire potters bought the Plymouth/Bristol patent from Richard Champion. From that date until about 1812 they made hard paste porcelain at premises in Shelton known as the New Hall, and after then turned to bone china. The output varied in quality between good and undistinguished, the best-known examples being decorated with tiny floral sprays. Printed patterns were also used and some examples received gilding. The majority of the output comprised teawares, the pots and jugs following the shapes current in silver. These unsophisticated wares would appear to have had their imitators and an attempt has been made to classify the 'cuckoos in the nest'. Prior to 1812 the factory used no marks except for a cursive *N* followed by the pattern number; after 1812 there was occasional use of a printed double ring enclosing *New Hall* in script. Production ceased in about 1830.

Niderviller, France The earthenware factory at Niderviller, near Strasbourg, also made porcelain from about 1765. The hard paste material was used for table wares in current French shapes with finely-painted decoration. A proportion of figures was made in white biscuit, sometimes with a slight trace of glaze on it, and in a few cases standing 60 cm or so in height. Various marks were used from time to time, some being painted and others incised.

Nymphenburg, Germany The south German factory at Nymphenburg, near Munich, was started in about 1753 with the aid of an arcanist from Vienna. The hard paste porcelain made from the beginning until about 1770 was noticeably of fine quality and very white, with a glaze sometimes showing a greenish tinge where it was thick. While the table wares were as good as any made at the time, it was the appointment of Franz Anton Bustelli as chief modeller that gave the factory an enduring reputation. Bustelli was employed there from 1754 until his death at the early age of forty-one. His series of sixteen figures of characters in the Italian Comedy, made between 1755 and 1760, his Chinese figures and his group of the Crucificion are outstanding as examples of what might be

Porcelain Factories (Continued)

achieved with porcelain by a gifted modeller. The mark most used was a small chequered shield, usually impressed and sometimes placed on the base or elsewhere on a figure where it could be seen clearly. The factory remains in operation.

Nyon, Switzerland Situated near Geneva, the Nyon factory was established in about 1780. Hard paste porcelain was made into table wares which were neatly painted in prevailing French styles. The mark used was a small figure of a fish roughly drawn in blue.

Oude Loosdrecht, Holland The Weesp factory was bought in 1771 by a pastor named Johannes de Mol, who transferred production to Oude Loosdrecht. Production was similar to that at Weesp, but the mark was changed to take the form of the letters *M O L*. Mol died in 1782 and two years later a purchaser removed the business to Amstel.

Paris, France Between about 1770 and the early years of the nineteenth century there were a number of small factories operating in Paris. All of them made hard paste porcelain which was carefully painted in the current Classical taste. Production was mostly confined to table wares. Marks were usually stencilled in red, often illegibly.

Petit In 1830 Jacob Petit (born 1796) purchased a factory for making hard paste porcelain that had been operating at Fontainebleau since 1790. The highly-glazed white material was modelled into clock cases, food warmers, vases and other pieces, which were usually thickly potted and highly coloured. A strong apple green and a purple-red were popular as ground colours, and gilding was not spared. The mark used was the initials of Petit in dark blue.

Philadelphia, Pennsylvania Soft paste porcelain was made in Philadelphia at a factory established by Gousse Bonnin (born ?1741) and George Anthony Morris (1742?–73); the former descended from a Huguenot family and the latter born in Philadelphia. The first wares came from the kiln in December 1770, and excavations carried out on the site in 1967–8 resulted in evidence of what was made. Some articles decorated in blue and not dissimilar from Bow and Lowestoft wares, traditionally attributed to the Philadelphia concern are now confirmed as having originated there. They include pieces with open-worked sides, two two-tiered dishes of shell pattern, and sauceboats. Some of them are marked with a capital letter *P* and others with a *Z*, despite 1771 newspaper announcements that 'all future emissions from this factory will be marked S'. In 1772 the owners found that they were unable to compete in price with imported goods and after a bare two years of existence the factory closed.

Pinxton, Derbyshire A soft paste porcelain factory was established at Pinxton in 1796, the partners being a local landowner and William Billingsley. The latter had been working nearby at Derby for the past twenty-two years, so there are some resemblances between the wares of the two factories. The Pinxton material was first a glassy soft paste, but after Billingsley left in 1799 the quality declined and it became slightly lumpy and greyish. Painting throughout was competent with the colouring often superior to the draughtsmanship. The factory closed in 1813 after a life of seventeen years. The mark sometimes used was a script *P* followed by a pattern number painted in purple.

Plymouth, Devonshire William Cook-

Porcelain Factories (Continued)

worthy opened his factory for making hard paste porcelain at Plymouth in 1768. It was the first in England to make true porcelain with china stone and china clay in the original Chinese manner. The constituents had to be fired at a high temperature and they proved difficult to manage, with many of the articles coming from the kiln warped, smoke-stained or otherwise damaged. Table wares, vases and figures were made, with decoration in a blue that was often blackish in colour, and with a crimson sometimes more like brown. The proportion of successful pieces was small but their quality excellent. In 1770, two years after he had started, Cookworthy transferred the enterprise to Bristol. The mark used at Plymouth was the alchemists' sign for Tin: resembling a figure four with the front upright curling over, painted in blue, red or gold.

Ridgway Various members of the Ridgway family, of Shelton and Hanley,

Pair of Bristol hard-paste porcelain figures of children and dogs, made in about 1775. Bearnes & Waycotts.

Porcelain Factories (Continued)

Staffordshire, made porcelain during the nineteenth century. They produced a bone china of good quality in current styles, differing little from that made by their contemporaries. Marks were used occasionally and took the form of the Royal arms or a crown denoting that the brothers John (1785–1860) and William (1788–1864) Ridgway were appointed 'Potters to Her Majesty the Queen'. In most cases, however, specimens bear only a pattern number. The Shelton factory came into the ownership of Brown, Westhead Moore & Co. in 1859, who carried it on as before.

Rockingham, Yorkshire The Rockingham Pottery began to make bone china in 1820 but ran into financial difficulties a few years later. In 1826, Earl Fitzwilliam, on whose Rockingham estate the works stood, came to the rescue and the re-established concern was enabled to continue in business until 1842. The soft paste porcelain was of excellent quality, usually ornately painted and gilt in the manner of the period. Table wares were the principal output, but figures were also made. Much that is traditionally attributed to the factory was made elsewhere, especially models of cottages and castles, and small figures of poodles with simulated hair which do not appear in any surviving list of Rockingham products. The usual mark used was printed in red and shows a winged griffin, the crest of the Fitzwilliam family, above the words *Rockingham Works Brameld* in script. Brameld was the name of the owners of the factory.

Saint Cloud, France The first establishment of importance in France to make porcelain was at Saint Cloud, just outside Paris. Soft paste wares were being produced before 1700 and were reported on favourably by writers at the time. The factory closed in 1766. The material was of a distinctly creamy colour, and was made into table wares and a proportion of figures. Moulded or applied decoration in relief was employed sometimes, two varieties being especially popular: overlapping scales, and branches of plum blossom copied from Fukien *blanc de Chine*. Painting on earlier pieces was in the manner of Bérain as seen on pottery of the time, later the influence of the Orient is seen in near-copies of Chinese *famille verte* and Japanese Kakiemon. Until the early 1720s the mark used was a sun with features and surrounded by rays, in blue; later came the painted or incised letters *S C* over *T*, the latter standing for the surname of the proprietor, Henri Trou.

St. Petersburg, Russia The Russian city of St. Petersburg, known also as Petrograd or Leningrad, was the seat of a factory making hard paste porcelain. It was started in 1744 and after lengthy experiments regular production began fourteen years later. Increased output came with the accession of Catherine the Great in 1762, when table wares and figures were made. Current European styles were imitated, with the influence of Sèvres increasing as the century progressed. Attractive figures of Russian peasants were made from about 1780, and in the early nineteenth century came pairs of heavily-gilt large vases painted with panels in colours. Marks were not used consistently, but several have been noted.

Samson The firm of Edmé Samson et Cie. was established in 1845 and since then has manufactured reproductions of the most popular output of many factories. A hard paste porcelain was used so that copies of Meissen, Oriental wares and Plymouth are at least correct in their

Porcelain Factories (Continued)

material, but the same was employed for Chelsea and other soft paste factories. Thus, the Samson versions of the latter are easily apparent to those able to differentiate between hard and soft pastes. The firm boasted that they put their own mark on all their wares, but this has been disputed and many specimens exist bearing forgeries of their appropriate marks.

Sèvres, France Experiments in making porcelain were carried out in 1738 at Vincennes, outside Paris. As a result a company was formed in 1745, with a staff including an eminent chemist, and the Royal goldsmith. In addition, the Vincennes venture was granted an exclusive privilege to make porcelain and to decorate it with human figures and gilding. With the patronage of both Louis XV and Madame de Pompadour prosperity was assured, and in 1756 a move was made to new premises at Sèvres, between Paris and Versailles. Financial difficulties then led to purchase of the company by the King, and it remained in Royal ownership until it was seized in the Revolution. The soft paste porcelain made was a beautiful material, skilfully and imaginatively modelled and painted, and it had from the start a reputation it has never lost. Many innovations in the way of vase shapes, figures and colours first appeared, or were improved upon, at Vincennes and Sèvres and were copied far and wide. For example, figures and groups in white biscuit were produced from 1751 and the so-called jewelled decoration was introduced in 1773, both quickly gaining popularity. From the beginning, the aim had been to make true porcelain, knowledge of the method being known from information supplied early in the century by Père d'Entrecolles, but it was not until 1769 that the essential clay and stone were found in France. Hard paste began to be made in quantity from the early 1770s, but it is the soft paste of Vincennes and Sèvres that has always been sought by collectors and, predictably, has received its share of attention from fakers. The mark used was two script letter *L*'s placed facing each other, from 1753 with a different letter of

Sèvres porcelain vase painted with a panel of warlike cupids reserved on a pink ground with gilding, and mounted on an ormolu base. The shape was known as a vase à oreilles *(vase with ears) and was first made in 1754.* Sotheby's.

Porcelain Factories (Continued)

the alphabet placed between them. Many painters' and gilders' marks have been recorded. Production continued throughout the nineteenth century; the porcelain remaining of good quality, its form and decoration following current styles with occasional innovations.

Sitzendorf, Germany A factory was founded at Sitzendorf, Thuringia, eastern Germany, in 1850. The output comprised figures of eighteenth-century pattern, many of them based on Meissen originals. The mark was some crossed lines in blue, which is often confused with the Meissen crossed swords.

Solon Marc-Louis Solon (1835–1912), worked at the Sèvres factory between 1862 and 1871. He then came to England, where he successfully introduced the *pâte sur pâte* technique at Minton's.

Spode The pottery founded by Josiah Spode was operated in due course by his son of the same name, Josiah Spode II (1754–1827). In or about 1800 he started to make a bone china, and is credited with having pioneered the introduction of the material that was duly adopted by his competitors. Spode's son, Josiah III (1777–1829) did not long outlive his father; the business was bought by a partner, William Taylor Copeland (1797–1868), and the firm remains to-day in the hands of the latter's descendants. Throughout the nineteenth century the wares produced at the Stoke-on-Trent factory were of good quality, with their design following current trends. Painting was well executed, with no lack of gilding on many examples. Various marks were used, impressed, painted and printed, all of which incorporated the names *Spode* or *Copeland* according to date.

Sprimont Nicholas Sprimont (1716–1771) was a silversmith of Flemish birth who came to England. He became manager and then proprietor of the Chelsea factory. A few pieces of silver bearing his mark have been recorded.

Swansea, Wales See Nantgarw.

Tournay, Belgium The Tournay soft paste factory was started in 1751, and was granted special facilities by the Empress Maria Theresa, in whose Austrian Empire the city was then situated. It became a large concern with hundreds of employees, much of whose output was of wares for everyday use. The material was at first greyish but was soon improved. Designs were based on Meissen and Sèvres, with painting in blue or colours which was often of good quality. Prior to closing in 1850, deceptive copies of Sèvres, Chelsea and Worcester were made. The mark used was at first a rough drawing of a tower, and then two crossed swords with small crosses in the angles.

Venice, Italy During the eighteenth century there were three porcelain factories in Venice: those of the brothers Vezzi, Nathaniel Friedrich Hewelcke, and Geminiano Cozzi. The Vezzi concern made a hard paste porcelain between about 1720 and 1727, with the help of a man who had learned of Böttger's methods when the latter was inebriated. The colour of the material varied, the glaze was clear and the output did not lack originality of design. Pieces were decorated with patterns in relief, as well as painted in blue or colours, and frequently reached the Meissen standard. Marks used were the word *Venezia* in full or abbreviated, painted in various colours or gold. The other two factories were of comparatively minor importance, but the products of the Cozzi

Porcelain Factories (Continued)

concern, which operated from 1764 to 1812 can sometimes be confused with those of Chelsea. Although the Venetian material is a hard paste and the two are not alike in appearance, Cozzi used for his mark a red anchor. It is larger than the Chelsea one, but sometimes traps the unsuspecting.

Vienna, Austria Not long after the pioneer effort of Meissen, hard paste porcelain was made at Vienna. The enterprise was started in 1719 by Claud Innocentius du Paquier with the assistance of an absconded Meissen employee, who left Vienna after a few years. Financial difficulties then beset du Paquier, but he managed to keep going until 1744 when the concern was bought by the state. Du Paquier's material was of a greyish tint, and was modelled into shapes that were often elaborate and owed much to German silverware of the time. Painting was often in red and black, in patterns of *laub und bandelwerk*, panels of figure subjects and imitations of Oriental designs. A proportion of the output was sold in the white for decoration by *Hausmaler*. After 1744 Meissen influence became noticeable, with coloured wares of all kinds, including many figures of original design. Later, the Sèvres coloured grounds were copied. In the nineteenth century, increasingly elaborate painting and gilding became the rule, and as has been remarked, the aim was 'show rather than taste'. The factory closed in 1864, but its later products were clumsily copied elsewhere. From 1744 a blue striped shield was the mark; it is sometimes read upside-down and referred to as the 'beehive mark'.

Vincennes See Sèvres.

Wall Dr. John Wall, see Worcester.

Wedgwood The Wedgwood pottery establishment made bone china between 1812 and 1822. Hand-painted and printed patterns were used on table wares marked *WEDGWOOD* in red, blue or gold. Manufacture of bone china was re-started in 1878, when the mark used was a small representation of the Portland Vase above the word *WEDGWOOD*.

Weesp, Holland A hard paste porcelain was made from about 1759. The productions copied those current in Germany and included both table wares and figures. In 1771 the concern was transferred to Oude Loosdrecht and from there to Amstel in 1784. The mark used at Weesp was an arrangement of two crossed swords and three dots, in blue.

Willems Joseph Willems (1716–66) was born at Brussels, and came to England in the late 1740s. He worked at Chelsea, modelling some important figures there between about 1750 and 1766. In the latter year he returned across the Channel to take up employment at Tournay, where he died six months later.

Worcester, Hereford and Worcester The factory started in 1751 when a company, mostly of persons living in the locality, purchased the small works at Bristol. The Bristol formula, which included in it a proportion of soaprock, was employed to make a soft paste porcelain that, according to a writer in 1763, 'has a good body, scarce inferior to that of Eastern China, it is equally tough, and its glazing never cracks or scales off'. Production was confined to table wares except for a short period, about 1769–72 when some figures were made. Decoration was always competently applied, whether painted or printed, the last-named process being in use at Worcester from 1756 or 1757. A great variety of designs was used, based on

Porcelain Factories (Continued)

Oriental, Meissen or Sèvres originals, together with coloured grounds copied from the last-named and Chelsea. The initiator of the factory is supposed to have been Dr. John Wall (1708–76) a physician and amateur artist, whose name has often been applied to wares made at Worcester between 1751 and 1783. The latter was seven years after the doctor's death, but a convenient date because in that year the concern was sold and the style of goods manufactured was changed. More accurately, the years 1751 to 1783 are termed First Period. In 1783 the firm was purchased by Thomas Flight, London agent of the company, and managed by his sons, John and Joseph. Soon afterwards one of the painters, Robert Chamberlain, left to start a rival factory, but a visit to the original works by George III provided compensation in the form of excellent advertisement and useful orders. Various changes in partnership led to an amalgamation with Chamberlain's in 1840, an alteration of name in 1862 to The Royal Worcester Porcelain Company, and later amalgamations with other rivals. From the early days of the factory, care was invariably taken to keep the output at a high standard as regards both potting

Worcester porcelain dish with a pierced border printed with a pattern in underglaze blue. It dates from about 1770.

Porcelain Factories (Continued)

and ornament, and this was maintained throughout the nineteenth century and later. In common with other Victorian manufacturers, the Worcester firm continually sought innovations, typical being their matt-surfaced ivory body, which was modelled into vases and other pieces with extremely intricate pierced patterns. The results of the painstaking labour involved in creating such exhibition pieces may not always be thought to have justified the means, but it cannot be denied that their effect is striking.

Zurich, Switzerland A porcelain factory was established near Zurich in 1763. For the first two years soft paste was made, and was followed by hard paste which continued in production until the concern closed in 1791. Table wares emulated current shapes and painted patterns, the latter being very carefully executed. Figures included some of miniature size, all of them comparing favourably with those made elsewhere at the time. As with the table wares, figures were meticulously painted. The mark used was the letter *Z* with a central horizontal bar, painted in blue.

3. GLASS

GLASS is basically composed of sand (silica) mixed with an alkali. When they are heated, the alkali helps the sand to melt and form the familiar material. Glass is usually thought of as being transparent, but it can be made translucent to the point of being nearly opaque.

Brief glossary of technical terms, mostly of foreign origin, used by glass-makers:

Annealing Freshly made glass objects contain high internal stresses that would cause them to fracture suddenly, unless eased by a slow cooling process known as annealing.

Batch The ingredients prepared and ready for melting.

Blowing-Iron An iron tube on one end of which is gathered molten glass, from which a hollow vessel can be made by blowing at the opposite end of the iron.

Bocca A hole in the side of a glass furnace allowing access to the pots of metal within.

Chair The combination chair and bench at which the gaffer sits. The chair is backless and has long flat arms, on the latter of which the blowing-iron or pontil can be rotated by rolling it.

Gadget A rod with a spring clip at one end for gripping a wine-glass or other vessel, an improvement on the pontil brought into use during the nineteenth century. Its advantage was that it did not leave a scar or pontil-mark.

Gaffer The leader of a small team of glassmakers. See Chair.

Leer A tunnel-like passage used in annealing.

Marver A slab of iron or marble on

Glass, Glossary of Terms (Continued)

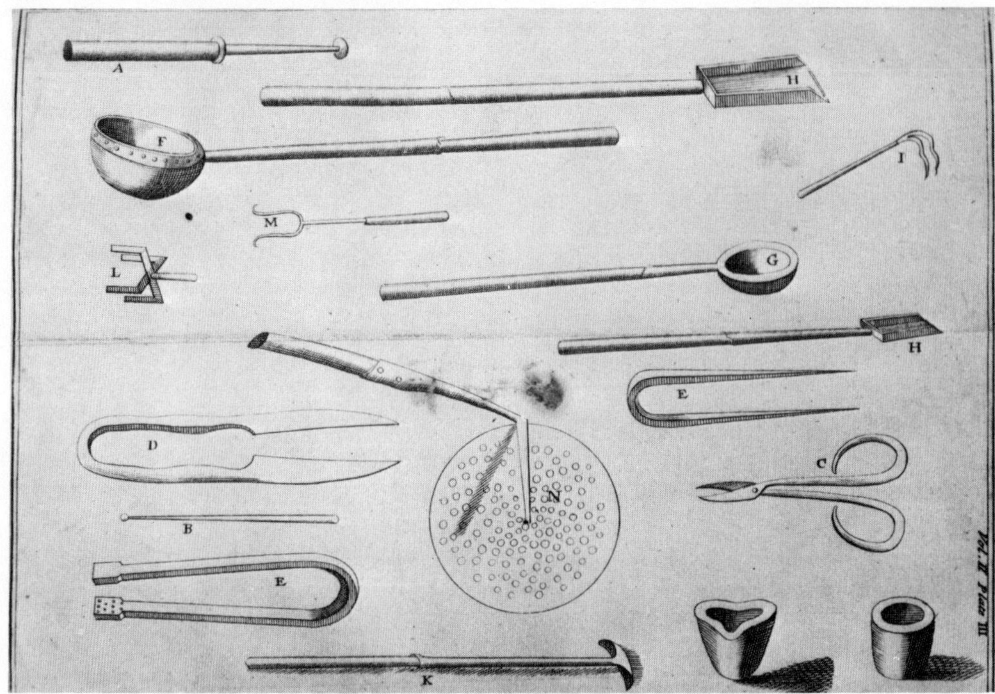

An eighteenth-century engraving showing glassmakers' tools, including at the top, left, a blowing-iron.

which the paraison is rolled to shape it evenly.

Metal Glass, either molten or in the form of finished articles.

Paraison The lump of molten glass taken from the pot on the end of the blowing-iron. It was then shaped roughly on the marver and blown.

Pot A large crucible in which the batch was melted in the furnace.

Pontil The pontil was an iron rod known also as a puntee or ponte. With a small lump of molten glass on the end it was stuck to an article while the blowing-iron was removed. Further processes and finishing could then be carried out and the pontil was finally broken away to leave a scar, the pontil-mark.

METHODS, MATERIALS, FACTORIES, AND ARTICLES

Acid Etching See Etching.

Agate Glass Glass coloured and worked to resemble the stone, agate.

Air-Twist Refers to the stem of a wine glass in which is enclosed a bubble drawn out to form a corkscrew-like silvery thread.

Glass; Methods, Materials, Factories and Articles (Continued)

Alkali Soda and potash were the principal alkalis employed in making glass. Soda was used in the Mediterranean area, being found in Egypt in the form of natron. Elsewhere it was obtained from plants such as Glasswort. Potash came from the ash of burnt bracken and beech trees; alternatively use was made of saltpetre in the form known as pearl ash. See *Barilla*.

Amelung John Frederick Amelung operated the New Bremen Glass Manufactory, near Frederick, Maryland, between about 1784 and 1794. Amelung came from Bremen, Germany, and the majority of his employees were from the same country, so the wares made were in the German style of the time. A few pieces from Amelung's factory have survived, all of them with engraved ornament.

Amen Glasses 'Amen' glasses gained their name from the Jacobite verses engraved on them, which invariably end with the word Amen. The verses vary in detail, but are a distortion of 'God save the King'. A typical example, in part, is:

God save the King I pray
God Bliss the King I pray
GOD SAVE THE KING
Send him Victorious
Happy & Glorious
Soon to Reign Over Us
God Save the King

God Bliss the Subjects all
And save both great and small
In ev'ry Station
That will bring home the King
Who has blest Right to Reign
It is the only thing
Can Save the Nation.

American Glass As early as 1608 there was a small glasshouse at Jamestown, Virginia, but its existence is recorded only in documents and none of its products have survived. A further attempt at the same place occurred in 1621, but was no more successful than its predecessor and the few others that were started during the seventeenth century. In the succeeding century some further enterprises were more fortunate, if only for short periods. One in southern New Jersey was started in 1739 by a German, Caspar Wistar, while another German, Henry William Stiegel set up glasshouses in Pennsylvania in 1763. Articles made by the foregoing have been preserved, and also some made by John Frederick Amelung, in Maryland, between 1784 and 1794. It was not until the first decades of the nineteenth century that the glass industry, like others in the country, began to achieve prosperity.

Amethyst Glass was given an amethyst colour by the addition of manganese to the batch. In England, amethyst glass of late eighteenth century appearance is usually termed 'Bristol', but it was also made elsewhere.

Annagelb Josef Riedel, who owned glasshouses in Bohemia in the early nineteenth century, devised an opalescent yellow glass. He named it *Annagelb* after his wife, Anna.

Annagrün Riedel gave the name *Annagrün* to a green glass, a variation of his *Annagelb*.

Aventurine Aventurine glass is of a brown colour with glittering tiny spangles, resembling a stone of the same name. It is alleged to have been made accidentally in Venice when some fine copper filings fell into a pot of molten glass, hence the name: *avventura* meaning chance.

Ayckbowm John Dedereck Ayckbowm,

Glass; Methods, Materials, Factories and Articles (Continued)

of German origin, was in England by 1772. Two years later he was at Limerick, Ireland, and dating from the 1770's are some decanters lettered in relief under the base: *J D AYCKBOWM DUBLIN.* In 1778 J. D. and J. H. Ayckbowm were adjudged bankrupt; their address was given as Back Lane, St. George-in-the-East, Middlesex, and their trade as 'glass-cutters'.

Baccarat The French glass factory began as the *Verrerie de Sainte-Anne*, at Baccarat, near Lunéville, eastern France, in 1764. In 1816 a concern making English-type cut glass was transferred to Baccarat from Vonèche, now in Belgium, and the output improved in both quantity and quality. A few years later a change of ownership took place, and the establishment became the *Compagnie des Cristalleries de Baccarat.* From the mid-1840s the factory was among firms making glass paperweights, those from Baccarat being identifiable by their patterns and colouring. A proportion include among their canes one bearing the initial letter *B* and dates between 1846 and 1858.

Bacchus Bacchus, Green & Green, Union Glass Works, Dartmouth Street, Birmingham, traded under that style from about 1818. In 1832 they were George Bacchus & Co., and following the death of George Bacchus in 1840 became George Bacchus & Sons. Twenty years later the same premises were owned by Stone, Fawdry & Stone, by which time it is probable that no member of the Bacchus family was concerned with the firm. In its heyday, from about 1840–55, the Bacchus concern was in the forefront of English makers, sharing in the renaissance of the industry that followed the repeal of the Excise Duty on glass in 1845. They had a large display at the 1851 Exhibition,

Baccarat glass paperweight, the millefiore *pattern in the interior revealed in windows cut in the white and turquoise-blue overlay.* Sotheby's.

including coloured, cut and engraved, and cased articles. The firm made paperweights for a short period, exhibiting some in 1848 and 1849, but perhaps found imported French ones too competitive and did not persevere with them.

Baluster A baluster-stemmed wine glass is one with the stem resembling the turned wood baluster or banister of a staircase. A true baluster is of pear shape, narrower at the top than at the base, while an inverted baluster is the opposite.

Barilla The alkali used by Venetian and other glassmakers was known as *barilla.* This was the name under which the soda-charged ash of Glasswort (*Salicornea herbacea*) was exported from Spain, where it grew in profusion in the region of Alicante. It was harvested when the berries had ripened, and after drying for a period the bushes were set alight. The liquid from the berries was allowed to settle and cool, when it formed 'a blue stone so hard it is

Glass; Methods, Materials, Factories and Articles (Continued)

scarcely malleable'. When prepared in Egypt and elsewhere in the Mediterranean area, the same substance was called *roquetta*.

Beilby William Beilby (1740–1819) and his sister Mary (1749–97), of Newcastle upon Tyne, decorated glass with coloured enamels. Examples are mostly undated but appear to have been executed between 1762 and 1778. The few signed ones bear the signature *Beilby pinxit*, with the exception of a decanter (Victoria and Albert Museum) and an armorial goblet (Fitzwilliam Museum, Cambridge).

Belfast A glasshouse was established at Belfast, northern Ireland, in 1781. It was operated by Benjamin Edwards, who had come from Bristol to Ireland some ten years before and continued to make glass there for the ensuing thirty years until 1811. After that his sons and various associates continued in the business at Belfast and other nearby places, changes in partnership alternating with periods of bankruptcy until a final closure occurred in 1850. Decanters marked *B. Edwards Belfast* have been recorded.

Bellingham John Bellingham is known to have been connected with the making of looking-glasses at Haarlem and Amsterdam, Holland. Between 1671 and 1674 he was manager of the Duke of Buckingham's glasshouse, Vauxhall, London.

Betts Thomas Betts was a glass cutter and retailer. From about 1740 he traded at The King's Arms Glass Shop, opposite Pall Mall, Charing Cross. His trade card announced that he

> Makes and Sells all Sorts of Curious Cut Glass such as Cruets, Castors, Salts, Lustres [chandeliers], Dessarts [dishes for sweets], Dishes, Plates, Punch Bowles, Cream Bowles, with Globes for Lanthorns.

Betts died in 1767.

Bimann Dominik Bimann (1800–57) was born in Bohemia and trained as a glass engraver. In about 1830 he settled at Franzensbad, a fashionable spa to the east of Prague. When visitors to the town were few, he worked elsewhere: in Gotha, Berlin and Vienna. Bimann specialized in portraits and landscapes, which he executed with great precision on drinking glasses, plaques and other articles. He signed his work with his initials, or with his name in full but variously spelt.

Bishop In February 1681/2, following the death of George Ravenscroft, Hawley Bishop or Bishopp signed an agreement with the London Company of Glass-Sellers. By this, he undertook to manage the Company's Savoy glasshouse.

Bohemia See Germany.

Bontemps Georges Bontemps (1799–1884), of Choisy-le-Roi, south-east of Paris, was a practical glassmaker who experimented in the making of clear and coloured sheet glass as well as optical glass. In 1848 he left France and joined Chance Brothers at the Spon Lane Glassworks, Birmingham. Bontemps assisted in their successful production of sheet and optical glass, and in 1868 published in Paris an important book on the industry, *Guide du Verrier*.

Bottles Bottles were usually made from a batch without decolourizer, so are almost invariably green or brown in colour. They were made in England from the mid-seventeenth century, being datable because of the custom of sealing them. This involved the addition of a seal of about 3–4 cm. diameter on the side or shoulder of

Glass; Methods, Materials, Factories and Articles (Continued)

the vessel, the seal bearing the name or crest of the original owner and often also the date. Others show the initials of a publican and his wife together with the insignia of their inn. From the information on seals, which were in use from about 1650 until 1830 it has been possible to chart the changing shapes of bottles over the years, and thereby to give approximate dates to unsealed examples. Bottle-making was a special branch of the glass industry and until the early 1820's each one was hand-made. Thereafter, machines of increasing complexity and efficiency were invented and brought into use.

Bowes Sir Jerome Bowes was a diplomat and businessman who acquired in 1592 from George Ravenscroft the final four years of the latter's monopoly allowing him to make 'Venice glasses'. Bowes was able to get this altered to give himself a monopoly on glass of all kinds as well as the sole right of importation. He died in 1616.

Bristol Blue Blue-coloured glass was made at one or more of the several glass-works active in Bristol during the eighteenth/nineteenth centuries. A number of specimens survive inscribed with the name of their maker, Isaac Jacobs. The colour was obtained by adding to the batch smalt, imported from Saxony through the port of Bristol, and it is likely that the name was applied to the colour and in time was given to the glass contain-

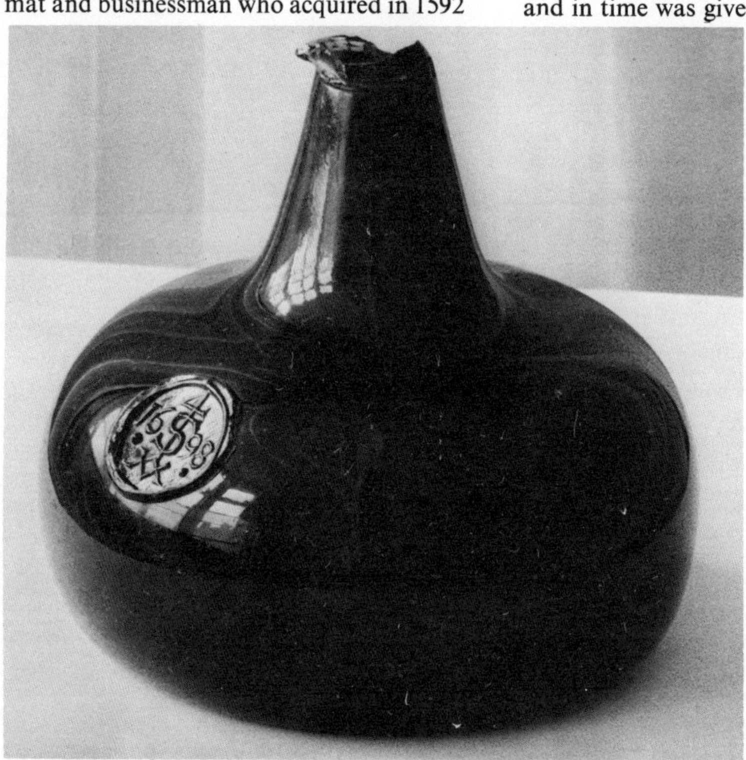

Wine bottle with a seal on the side dated 1698.

Glass; Methods, Materials, Factories and Articles (Continued)

ing it. Much more so-called 'Bristol Blue' is now in existence than could possibly have been made there.

Broad Glass The Broad, Lorraine or Cylinder process of making glass sheet involved blowing an elongated bubble; the ends were cut off and the remaining tube cut lengthwise. Opened out flat, it was finally annealed and polished. The Broad process was used in England in the seventeenth and eighteenth centuries, and Chance employed it for making the sheet glass used in building the Crystal Palace in 1851.

Broad Street In 1575 a glasshouse was established in Broad Street, in the City of London, by Jacopo Verzelini.

Buckingham George Villiers, Duke of Buckingham (1628–87) whose career was satirically said to have embraced 'chymist, statesman, fiddler and buffoon', also had an interest in the glass-making industry. He had a manufactory for mirrors at Vauxhall from about 1663, and although none have been identified it is not uncommon to find looking-glasses termed 'Vauxhall'. They may well have originated in that district of London, but not necessarily in the Duke's time, as there was a glasshouse there until about 1780.

Bull's-eye The name given to the thick, ridged piece of glass in the centre of a disc made by the Crown process.

Burmese Glass See Queen's Burmese.

Cameo Glass The Romans were skilful at cutting cased glass in the manner of natural stone. One of their *tours de force* in the technique is the Portland Vase (British Museum), which is made of a dark blue glass with a coating of white glass. There was a revival of the art in England during the second half of the nineteenth century, when among its practitioners were John Northwood and the brothers Thomas and George Woodall.

Cameo Incrustation Porcelain cameos in the form of heads of notabilities and other subjects, enclosed in glass, acquired an attractive silvery appearance. The process was patented and used by Apsley Pellatt, Jr., who named it Cameo Incrustation or *Crystallo-Ceramie*. It had been invented by a Frenchman during the late eighteenth century, and was still in use nearly a century later at Ford's Edinburgh glasshouse.

Cane The name given to the patterned rods used in the interiors of glass paperweights. They were made by fusing together the selected colours in the form of lengths of glass, which were then drawn out to the required diameter.

Cantáro A *cantáro* is a Spanish spouted-vessel for holding liquid.

Carré Jean Carré of Arras and Antwerp came to England in 1549 and tried to establish a glass house with the aid of some Venetians. The venture failed, but undaunted he returned in 1567 with some glass makers from Lorraine, France. The latter settled in the neighbourhood of Alfold, to the east of Chiddingfold, Surrey, where there was plenty of timber for potash and fuel, to make window glass. In 1570 Carré started a glass house at Crutched Friars, London, where he employed some Italians at making Venetian-style articles. In 1572, only two years later, Carré died and was buried at Alfold, his London business coming into the possession of Jacopo Verzelini.

Casing A vessel could be given one or more layers of contrastingly-coloured glasses, a process known as casing. The layers were then cut through to reveal the body, or to form a cameo in the manner of the Portland Vase. Casing is also known as flashing and as overlaying.

Casting The casting of glass to form plates larger in size than could be blown by the Broad process was introduced in France in 1688. In England, casting was used from 1773, when the British Cast Plate Glass Manufacturers were incorporated and established glasshouses at Southwark and Ravenhead. The latter, near St. Helens, Merseyside, had a casting-hall which was then the largest industrial building in England, and the town remains a centre of sheet-glass manufacture by the firm of Pilkington which absorbed the original company in 1901.

Chance Robert Lucas Chance managed the Nailsea glassworks, near Bristol, between 1810 and 1815. In 1824 he established the Spon Lane glassworks, Birmingham, where sheet glass was made with increasing efficiency over the years. Chance supplied the glass for the Crystal Palace built for the 1851 Great Exhibition. For this, nearly one million square feet of sheet glass were delivered, and during one fortnight of January 1851 no fewer than 63,000 panes for the roof, each pane 124·5 by 25·4 cm., were made by the Broad process. Georges Bontemps worked with Chance from 1848.

Chandeliers Lead glass proved especially suitable for making lighting appliances, the cut surfaces reflecting and magnifying the illumination. They were being made in England from at least 1714, when they were mentioned in a newspaper advertisement. Surviving examples date from about the mid-century and show that styles changed from time to time. In the eighteenth and nineteenth centuries the Venetians made chandeliers of clear and pale coloured glass, moulded and shaped in contrast to the glittering cut ornament used in England. In the past writers have referred to chandeliers as lustres.

Chinese Glass The making of articles in glass has been practised in China from some time in the Han dynasty (206 B.C.–A.D. 220), but whether the material was made in that country or imported from elsewhere is debatable. Blown glassware in quantity does not pre-date the reign of the Emperor K'ang Hsi (1662–1722), and the majority of surviving examples are of later date. Almost all are coloured, and treated in the manner of stone by being carved on the wheel. Snuff bottles and other pieces closely simulated agate, jade and other hardstones. Some of them were made of clear glass decorated with painting laboriously applied to the interior through the narrow neck.

Clichy The Clichy glassworks was founded at Sèvres and in about 1838 was removed to Clichy, a Paris suburb. Paperweights were made and were the only French ones shown at the 1851 Great Exhibition, where the firm also displayed overlay and other coloured articles for which they were awarded a prize. A proportion of the weights include a cane with a pink rose, a few have a letter *C* and none has been recorded with a date.

Clutha The name Clutha was applied to some glass made by the Glasgow firm of Couper and Sons during the 1880s and later. Use was made of metal displaying bubbles and streaks, and many of the pieces were designed by Christopher Dresser. Examples are marked *Clutha*, together with the initials or full name of the designer.

Glass; Methods, Materials, Factories and Articles (Continued)

Coaching Glasses Drinking-glasses with a short stem and no foot are called coaching glasses, hunting glasses or stirrup cups. They were made to be emptied quickly in a single draught.

Coin Glasses The term applied to drinking-glasses with a hollow stem holding a small coin. English examples with coins dating from the late seventeenth century onwards are recorded.

Colour-Twist The stem of a wine-glass containing coloured spirals is referred to as a colour-twist stem.

Cork In 1783 a glasshouse was established in Hanover Street, Cork. After numerous changes in partnership and the grant of awards from the Irish Parliament and the Dublin Society, the firm closed in 1818. Decanters are recorded bearing beneath the base in relief lettering the legend *CORK GLASS Co.*, and are decorated with moulded fluting and simple cut patterns. A water-jug similarly marked, moulded and cut is in the Victoria and Albert Museum. In 1815 another concern, the Waterloo Glass House Company, announced its opening. It made jugs and decanters very like those of the other company, but marked *WATERLOO Co. CORK*. It closed in 1835. A third glasshouse was started in Cork, the Terrace Glass Works, and lasted from 1818 to 1841. None of its products has been identified.

Crisselling A 'disease' of glass produced by an excess of alkali. It results in the article having a network of fine interior cracks, like a spider's web, and it may eventually completely disintegrate.

Crown Glass Sheet glass could be made by the Crown or Normandy method. It involved blowing a large-sized bubble, transferring it to a pontil opposite the place where the blowing-iron was affixed and removing the latter. Rapid rotation enlarged the gap left by the iron, and the bubble became a disc up to 120 cm. in diameter. Sheets of glass were cut from the disc to leave a central thick bull's eye where the pontil had been attached. Crown glass is usually noticeably misshapen: convex, with traces of the ripples induced by the rotation during manufacture. To this disadvantage is added the fact that only comparatively small pieces could be cut from the discs, but the material had a brilliant surface and did not require polishing.

Crystallo-Ceramie See Cameo Incrustation.

Cullet Waste glass, either from the glasshouse or as a result of breakage during use. It was noted in 1697 that 'Many hundreds of poor families keep themselves from the Parish by picking up broken glass to sell to the Maker'. Cullet was used in the batch to assist fusing.

Cutting Glass-cutting dates back to Roman times and was revived in Europe in the late sixteenth century. It was performed with the aid of wheels of metal or stone fed with water and an abrasive such as sand or emery. The cuts were usually polished by means of wood or lead wheels using a soft powder.

Cylinder Process See Broad Glass.

Danish Glass See Nöstetangen.

Davidson The firm of George Davidson and Co., of the Teams Glass Works, Gateshead-on-Tyne, was established in 1867. They were prominent as makers of pressed wares in slag glass, and also produced articles in a tinted metal with an

Glass; Methods, Materials, Factories and Articles (Continued)

opalescent edge, known as Pearline. Some of the output was marked in relief with a crest in the form of a demi-lion rising from what is known heraldically as a mural crown.

Davis, Greathead & Green Davis, Greathead & Green, of Stourbridge, had a large and varied display at the 1851 Great Exhibition. In 1874 the firm became John Davis & Co., ceasing trading in the late 1880s or early 1890s.

Decanters The wine decanter for use at the dining-table came into use in about the mid-eighteenth century. Shape and decoration of both the decanter itself and its stopper varied over the years. They were made in clear and coloured glass and in 1755 were advertised as being available with the names of their contents engraved on them. The rarest have had their names enamelled by the Beilbys and others.

Decolourizing The silica used in glass-making held impurities, mostly iron which gave the glass a green or brown tinge of varying intensity. To remove it, it was usual to add to the batch a small amount of oxide of manganese as a decolourizer.

Diamond-engraving From the sixteenth century glass was decorated by means of a diamond-point, both by professionals and amateurs. A variation was to stipple-engrave with innumerable tiny dots forming the decoration. The dots were made by gently hammering the diamond as it was held against the surface, and the effect has been described as being like 'a scarcely perceptible film breathed upon the glass'. See Greenwood; Verzelini; Wolff.

Door Stops Green bottle glass was used during the nineteenth century for making beehive-shaped door stops. Silvery-looking plant-like forms and bubbles were enclosed inside them, and some bear beneath the base the name of their maker: J. Kilner, of Wakefield, West Yorkshire. These door stops are sometimes referred to as Dumps.

Decanter enamelled in white with vine leaves and grapes and the name of its contents: CLARET. The insect on the neck was often used as a 'signature' by the Beilbys. Christie's.

Drawn Stem See Wine-glass.

Glass; Methods, Materials, Factories and Articles (Continued)

Dublin An Irishman named Charles Mulvaney started a glasshouse in Dublin in 1785, and after financial and other troubles it finally closed in 1846. Mulvaney stated in 1801 that his business was 'confessedly the most extensive in Ireland', but all that has been identified of his products are some decanters marked beneath the base *C. M. & Co.* Another concern was that of the Chebsey brothers, Thomas and John, who are said to have converted an iron foundry near Ballybough Bridge, Dublin, into a glasshouse in 1786–7. They went out of business in 1798, and it is uncertain whether they actually made anything other than sheet glass. A few other Dubliners whose connexion with glass was only in the role of retailers had their names put on articles, so that it might appear as if they were manufacturers. They were: *FRANCIS COLLINS, DUBLIN; ARMSTRONG, ORMOND QUAY; J. D. AYCKBOWM;* and *MARY CARTER & SON 80 GRAFTON ST DUBLIN.*

Dutch Glass See Netherlands Glass.

Edkins Michael Edkins (1734?–1811) is known to have decorated glass for a number of Bristol makers between 1762 and 1787. His business ledger (City Art Gallery, Bristol) records briefly the names of those by whom he was employed and when, what he did for them and how much he was paid for the work.

Enamel Glass was painted with coloured enamels: metallic oxides mixed with fluxes to ensure that they melted before the article to which they were applied itself started to melt. Enamel painting on glass was practised in many countries, in England the Beilbys being especially skilled in its execution. In the eighteenth century opaque white glass was termed enamel.

English Glass Immigrant French and German glassmakers are known to have been working in the south of England from the thirteenth century, making 'bottles, bowles, cuppis to drincke and such like'. In addition they made clear and coloured sheet glass for church and other windows. After an interval of two centuries came Jean Carré's attempts to start an industry, and following his death in 1572 his glass-house was taken over by Jacopo Verzelini. He made a success of the venture, and in due course was succeeded by a series of businessmen who organized glass-making in various parts of England. The Venetians had a very strong hold on world trade, with their glass competing everywhere in both quality and price. At the Restoration, the London-based Glass-Sellers' Company set out to break the near-monopoly, and to do so appointed George Ravenscroft as their official glassmaker. In 1673, after many experiments, it was announced that he had invented 'a particular sort of Christalline Glass resembling Rock Crystall, not formerly exercised or used in this our Kingdome'. The new material was glass of lead, or flint glass, which was soon adopted by most English makers and Venetian imports began to diminish. Of all the articles made from it the wine-glass is probably the best known, as it is among the more successful in displaying the metal at its most attractive. The forms of the vessel varied from decade to decade, permitting the maker ample scope in which to display his ingenuity and craftsmanship. An Excise duty levied in 1745 affected the industry, but although it was constantly increased the glassmakers managed to keep going. By the end of the century the art of cutting had been developed, English cut glass was widely acclaimed, and several firms had started glasshouses in Ireland where taxes were lower and competition

Glass; Methods, Materials, Factories and Articles (Continued)

could be met on more level terms. Finally, in 1845 the Excise was repealed, the trade was freed for the first time in 100 years and new types of glass began to be introduced. These were based on goods hitherto imported from Bohemia, France and Germany, with cutting replaced or supplemented by colour. Further impetus came from the increasing use of steam power, which assisted output and made cheap glassware available to a much bigger proportion of the public than ever before. The days of mass-production and design subordinated to the machine had come, although there was also a small and discriminating market to encourage better design and workmanship, and keep alive the spirit and the skills of the old craftsman.

Engraving Glass-engraving was executed with wheels, water and abrasives in a similar manner to cutting. It was usually performed by specialist workers and the results were more delicate than those attained by cutting.

Etching Decorating glass by eating away unwanted areas with acid was employed occasionally from the 1830s. The article was entirely covered in an acid-resistant varnish or wash, the design was pierced through this as required and immersion in acid did the rest; the depth of the work being regulated by the length of time during which the acid remained in contact. During the 1870s the process began to be used on a commercial scale.

Excise Duty In the mid-seventeenth century a duty was levied at a low rate on English glass. It was raised in 1695, when makers became liable for the payment of 20 per cent. on the value of all glass except bottles, the latter being charged at one shilling (5p.) a dozen, and it was enacted that the duty was to be in force only for five years. Although in 1696 this last was swept aside and the duty made permanent, the outcry was so great and so well organized that the whole was repealed in 1699. Then, in 1745, began the imposition of a duty that lasted for just 100 years, and was intermittently increased until it was in danger of completely stifling the industry. The duty was levied on the weight of ingredients, and in order to collect it effectively there were Customs officials stationed at every glasshouse. Thus, in effect, every action of managers and employees was supervised and all initiative and experiment discouraged.

Faceting Articles cut with diamond-shaped facets appeared in English glass in the first half of the eighteenth century. Facets were used on the stems of wine-glasses in about 1770.

Fairy Lamps Small bowls with out-turned rims, like miniature goldfish bowls, in clear and coloured glass, were used for outdoor illumination. Linked together with string they were suspended in rows, and their lighted cotton wicks resting in oil must have had a pretty effect. The trade name 'Fairy' was applied to small glass domes and bases for holding a night-light, a long-burning candle, used on dining-tables in the late 1880s.

Fire-polishing Glass articles heated at the furnace-mouth were held there just long enough to re-melt the surface and give it a brilliant shine. This was known as fire-polishing.

Firing Glass A wine-glass with a short stem and a noticeably thick foot is termed a firing glass, because it was used by a drinker to signal agreement and register applause by rapping with it on a table top. The noise produced by a roomful of

Glass; Methods, Materials, Factories and Articles (Continued)

convivial spirits would resemble that of musket fire.

Flashing See Casing.

Flint Glass Ravenscroft's improved glass was at first referred to as Flint glass, because one of the ingredients of the batch was ground flints. When flints were supplanted by sand the old name continued in use. Nowadays it is called Glass of Lead or Lead Crystal.

Flints English flints were used by George Ravenscroft and gave their name to his improved glass. They were prepared by calcining and then grinding them so that they became a white powder.

Flute Glasses Drinking-glasses with very tall tapering bowls were termed flutes, and were popular in the Netherlands during the seventeenth century. Two examples have been claimed as being of English make: one is engraved with a portrait of Charles II and inscribed '*God Bless King Charles the Second*' (Royal Albert Memorial Museum, Exeter), and the other shows the Royal arms and those of the Scudamore family (London Museum).

Ford's Glasshouse, Edinburgh John Ford's Holyrood glasshouse, at Edinburgh, made all kinds of glassware during the nineteenth century, including Cameo Incrustations.

French Glass From an early date, the French excelled at making sheet glass for church and other windows, and from the late seventeenth century pioneered casting as a means of making plate glass of large size. A century earlier, some Italian craftsmen had settled at Nevers, south-east of Paris, where they established glass-houses. Although all kinds of articles were made, the name of the town is especially attached to small figures made of coloured glass which can be mistaken for pottery or porcelain. It has been remarked that until the eighteenth century French glass remained so mediocre that no study has been devoted to it. However, soon after the mid-century a number of glasshouses were established, and within a few decades the position was righted. At first, the makers concentrated on wares in the English style, which it would seem they achieved with success; very little is firmly attributable to French makers, so it is presumably masquerading as English. In the early nineteenth century the production of a semi-transparent glass in pale tints, known as Opaline glass, proved very popular, and the introduction of paper-weights enclosing coloured canes led to imitations being made in many other countries. Although such paperweights were made slightly earlier in Venice and elsewhere, it was the French who perfected them and the French craftsmen who proved unequalled in their manufacture. Towards the end of the nineteenth century a number of men, prominent among them Emile Gallé, experimented with new techniques and styles which duly came to fruition and influenced glassmakers throughout the world.

Friggers Friggers is a glassmaker's term for articles made in his spare time, to give away to friends or to keep on his own mantlepiece. It is nowadays often used to include items that were produced commercially, such as rolling-pins and witch-balls.

Gallé Emile Gallé (1846–1904), of Nancy, in eastern France, designed and made vases and other pieces. He made use of numerous techniques, together or

Glass; Methods, Materials, Factories and Articles (Continued)

singly, and drew much of his inspiration from the Far East. Gallé rejected the mechanical perfection until then considered to be the true goal of a glassmaker, and exploited what would normally be thought of as imperfections: clouding, bubbles and asymmetry.

German Glass The most noticeable feature of German glass is the skill with which it was decorated with engraving. The craftsmen who had earlier worked with rock crystal transferred their attention to glass, and supplied their patrons with masterpieces. The material they used was developed in the late seventeenth century, and included chalk as one of its ingredients. This made a hard glass that could be manipulated into thick-walled vessels suitable for the lapidary. The most typical for this treatment was the *pokal*, a tall-stemmed goblet with a cover, but many other shapes of vessel received decoration in enamels that was sometimes less demanding of time and ability. In the last category were tall straight-sided beakers, some of which date back to the early years of the seventeenth century. An active glass industry existed in adjoining Bohemia (once in the Austrian Empire and now part of Czechoslovakia) where fuel and minerals were plentiful. In the nineteenth century, especially, the glasshouses in the region of Haida, north of Prague, were responsible for innovations that earned their makers fame at the time and later. See Bimann; Hyalith; Lithyalin.

Glass-Sellers' Company The Worshipful Company of Glass-Sellers, of London, was granted a Charter by Charles II in 1665. The Company engaged George Ravenscroft to seek a glass as good as, or better than, that imported from Venice and elsewhere.

Glasswort See *Barilla*.

Greenwood Frans Greenwood (1680–1761) of Rotterdam, but perhaps of English parentage, was a skilful amateur who decorated glass in stipple with a diamond-point. Some of his work is signed with his name in full or with his initials, and some is also dated.

Greener H. Greener & Co., of the

German drinking glass engraved with figures and an inscription, made at Nuremburg in the late seventeenth century. Sotheby's.

Glass; Methods, Materials, Factories and Articles (Continued)

Wear Glass Works, Sunderland, made pressed slag and other goods in competition with firms in the north-east of England. The founder of the business, Henry Greener (1820–82) had been employed at Sowerby's, of Gateshead, was in partnership for a few years with James Angus, and after the death of the latter built the Wear Glass Works. Greener's used a small mark in relief in the form of a demi-lion grasping a battle-axe.

Harris Rice Harris, of the Islington Glass Works, Birmingham, started in the business in about 1820, and later advertised as 'Flint and cut glass manufacturer'.

Group of glassware displayed at the Great Exhibition of 1851 by Rice Harris & Son, of Birmingham.

Glass; Methods, Materials, Factories and Articles (Continued)

As Rice Harris & Son, the firm displayed a variety of goods at the Great Exhibition, 1851, including moulded, cased and coloured glass. They are known to have made paperweights and two have been recorded bearing a cane initialled *IGW*, probably standing for Islington Glass Works.

Hyalith Georg Franz August Longueval, Count von Buquoy, owned glasshouses at Gratzen, in southern Bohemia. From 1820 they produced a dense black glass and another of sealing-wax red to which the Count gave the name Hyalith.

Incised Twist Wine-glass stems were made with narrow spiral reeding on the surface, resembling finely twisted cord, and these are termed incised twist stems.

Iridescence Much ancient glass, and some less old, that has been buried acquires a brilliantly coloured iridescence. Constituents of the soil result in the surface of the glass becoming finely laminated to produce a prismatic effect. Articles in this state should be carefully handled, as the surface tends to peel away in thin scales. Iridescence of a more durable nature can be achieved during manufacture, and was popular during the late nineteenth century.

Irish Glass Until the 1780s little glass was made in Ireland. The country was governed by Parliament in London, which prohibited the Irish from exporting their manufactures and the home market was too small to support a profitable industry. In 1780 the restriction was lifted, and as a result of the English duty being further increased in 1781, a number of Bristol and Stourbridge glassmakers came to Ireland. There, they were duty-free and could compete in all markets, but in 1825 Irish-made glass was made dutiable and the industry gradually perished. See Belfast; Cork; Dublin; Waterford.

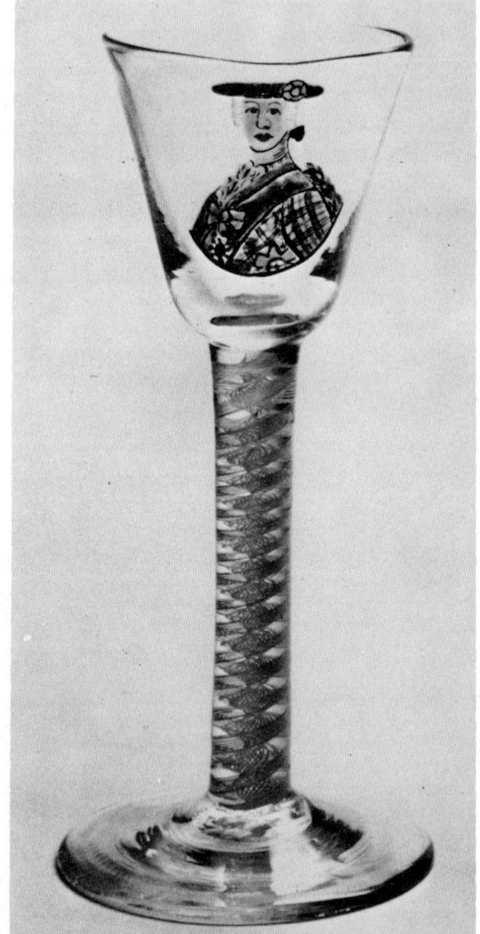

Wine glass, the bowl with an enamelled portrait of the Young Pretender. Sotheby's.

Jacobite Glasses The Old Pretender and the Young Pretender were the names popularly given to the son and grandson of James II, Prince James Francis Edward Stuart (1688–1766) and Prince Charles Edward Louis Philip Stuart (1720–88). Adherents to their cause considered that the two men should have been successively rulers of England, instead of which the great-grandson of James I, George I, had

Glass; Methods, Materials, Factories and Articles (Continued)

come to the throne. It is a complex story, with politics and religion equally involved, and with many of those who allegedly called themselves Jacobites being lukewarm in their allegiance. Numerous secret and semi-secret societies existed in the mid-eighteenth century, members of which drank toasts to 'The King over the Water', the two men being exiles, and for this purpose suitably inscribed glasses were provided. In many instances the engraved decoration carried hidden meanings with, for instance, a rose to represent the Old Pretender, a thistle for the Crown of Scotland, and a star alluding to the birth of the Young Pretender. Over the years there has been considerable debate about the meaning of the various emblems, and the significance of the Latin mottoes accompanying some of them. Although the majority of Jacobite glasses were engraved, a few were decorated in enamels and among them are some with a portrait of the Young Pretender. See Amen Glasses; Williamite Glasses.

Jacobs Lazarus (died 1796) and Isaac (died 1835) Jacobs were Bristol glass-makers. Isaac Jacobs advertised in 1805 that he had just completed his Non-such Flint Glass Manufactory, and in the following year he became Glass Manufacturer to His Majesty. Some blue glass plates and finger bowls with gilt decoration have been recorded, each bearing under the base the words *I. Jacobs Bristol* in gilt script lettering.

Kick A kick or kick-up is the indentation in the base of a wine bottle. It was formed by pushing up the base while it was still in a plastic state, thereby raising the pontil mark to where it could not affect the stability of the bottle or damage a surface on which it stood.

King's Lynn, Norfolk King's Lynn is the site of sand suitable for making glass, and had glasshouses operating from the late seventeenth century. One of them advertised its flint glass wares in 1747, and a number of surviving wine-glasses, decanters, tumblers and finger-bowls have been attributed to the town. They share the feature of horizontal ribs in slight relief.

Knop See Wine-glass.

Kothgasser See Mohn.

Kungsholm Glasbruk The Kungsholm Glasbruk, Stockholm, was started by an Italian in 1676 and although he left two years later the products were based on Venetian metal and styles for several decades. In the eighteenth century a German influence was noticeable, with vessels having thicker walls to withstand engraved decoration.

La Granja See Spanish Glass.

Latticino *Latticino* (*latticinio* or *lattimo*) glass has embedded in it fine threads of opaque white glass, 'lace glass' being an alternative name for it. The Venetians were particularly skilful in its making, and it was widely imitated in many countries at various dates.

Lead Glass Glass made as a result of George Ravenscroft's experiments and containing a proportion of lead oxide in the batch. It has a brilliant appearance and disperses light more effectively than other glass.

Lithyalin Friedrich Egermann (1777–1864) owner of a glass works at Blottendorf, near Haida, Bohemia, invented an almost opaque marbled glass in several colours which he named Lithyalin.

De Lysle Anthony de Lysle, a Frenchman, was in London by 1582, when he was

Glass; Methods, Materials, Factories and Articles (Continued)

described as an engraver of pewter and glass. It has been suggested that he was the engraver of some surviving glasses attributed to Verzelini.

Mildner Johann Joseph Mildner (1763–1808) of Gutenbrunn, Austria, decorated commemorative and other beakers. He specialized in insetting decorated panels in the sides and bases in the manner of *zwischengoldgläser*, so that the surfaces are flush and the joins virtually undetectable. Some of his work is signed and dated.

Milk Glass A white glass that varies between semi-translucent and nearly opaque and occasionally shows opalescence was made at many glasshouses, especially in Germany and Spain during the eighteenth century. Later, it was improved to become more even in tone and was much used for pressed wares in England. The older type is known in Germany as *milchglas* and in France as *verre d'albâtre*.

Millefiori The Italian *millefiori* means 'thousand flowers' and is the name given to close-packed coloured flower-like patterns in, for instance, paperweights.

Mirrors Sheets of glass suitable for silvering were made by the Broad process or by casting. In either instance, the surface had to be ground as flat as possible in order to reflect an undistorted image. Silvering was effected by covering a sheet of tinfoil with mercury, placing the glass on top and gently squeezing out the surplus liquid. After about 1840 this process was supplanted by one which deposited a thin coat of real silver on the glass. See Buckingham.

Mohn Samuel Mohn (1762–1815) and his son Gottlob Samuel Mohn (1789–1825) worked at Vienna and Dresden respectively, decorating beakers in the same manner as Anton Kothgasser (1769–1851) of Vienna. All three men painted with great delicacy making use of transparent colours, giving the appearance of watercolours, in place of the more usual opaque tints. Signed examples of their work are recorded.

Moulded Glass Moulded glass was made by preparing a mould into which glass was blown, any decoration on the mould being transferred to the surface of the article. Moulds were hinged or made to come apart to release the finished object, and a foot-operated hinged one for making bottles was patented in 1822.

Nailsea At Nailsea, near Bristol, a factory for making bottles was established in 1788 by a Bristol man, John Robert Lucas. In 1793 William Chance became a partner in the firm, and between 1810 and 1815 his son, Robert Lucas Chance was its manager. By 1840 Chance had opened a large glasshouse in Birmingham for making sheet glass, and the Nailsea establishment was used for the same product. The name of Nailsea has for some decades been applied to jugs, basins, flasks, rolling-pins and similar articles decorated with white and coloured stripes. It has been denied that most of these things came from there, as the factory only produced ordinary glass and not flint glass. More probably they made articles of tinted bottle glass with splashed white decoration, although it is known that such goods were certainly made at many other glasshouses.

Netherlandish Glass The glass made in the Netherlands, the countries now known as Holland and Belgium, was often closely similar in appearance to that from other areas. Until Ravenscroft devised his lead glass, that from across the Channel was often indistinguishable from English in both material and form. In the eighteenth

Glass; Methods, Materials, Factories and Articles (Continued)

Pair of cut-glass tumblers with zwischengoldglas *silhouettes by J. J. Mildner, of Gutenbrunn, Austria.* Christie's.

century German, Bohemian and English styles were followed, but in the latter instance examples lack the weight and sparkle of the prototypes. Decoration was often in the form of engraving, on the wheel or with a diamond; the stippled work of Greenwood and Wolff being outstanding on account of its individuality and excellent craftsmanship.

Newcastle upon Tyne Glassworkers from Lorraine and Venice are known to have settled in and about Newcastle by the seventeenth century. Their principal product was sheet glass, much of which was sent down the coast to London along with shiploads of coal. In the eighteenth century wine-glasses of good lead glass were made, many of them with distinctively graceful stems enclosing air twists or groups of bubbles. The Beilbys used Newcastle glass for their enamelling, and some of the Dutch engravers found it more suitable for their work than the comparatively lifeless material made in their own country. In the nineteenth century some cheap pressed wares were made at Newcastle, but more came from Gateshead on the opposite bank of the river Tyne. There, the firms of Sowerby and Davidson vied with each other, and with Greener of Sunderland, in producing immense quantities of such goods.

Northwood John Northwood (1836–1902) was largely responsible for the revival of cameo engraving, the type of decoration developed by the Romans and exemplified in the Portland Vase. Northwood not only copied that masterpiece in 1876, but designed and made many large and small vases, plaques and other objects using the same technique. Examples of the work are termed Cameo glass. John Northwood became Art Director at Stevens and Williams, of Stourbridge, in the early 1880s.

Glass; Methods, Materials, Factories and Articles (Continued)

Norway See Nöstetangen.

Nöstetangen In 1741, when Denmark and Norway were united under King Christian VI, a glasshouse was established under royal patronage at Nöstetangen, south-west of Oslo which was then named Christiania. Output was small and mostly in German styles, but twelve years later further glasshouses were built and two English craftsmen from Newcastle upon Tyne were employed in addition to Germans and others. Production was transferred in 1777 to Hurdals Verk and in 1809 to Gjövik Verk, the articles made at all three places including German and Newcastle types of vessels, pieces inspired by local silverware, and a proportion of coloured articles. Both lead and soda metals were used, with engraving and cutting being the favoured decoration. Gjövik closed in 1847.

Opaline A semi-opaque pastel-tinted or greyish-white glass made in France from about 1810. It became very fashionable and was imitated in other countries.

Opaque-Twist Refers to threads of opaque white glass forming a corkscrew pattern in a wine-glass stem.

Osler F. & C. Osler, who had a manufactory at Birmingham and a showroom in Oxford Street, London, were prominent at the 1851 Great Exhibition. They showed, among other articles, a pair of cut-glass candelabra standing 8 ft. (2.44 m.) in height and, on a smaller scale, busts of the Queen, Prince Albert and others in moulded frosted glass. Their principal exhibit occupied a central position in the building, and was described modestly as a 'large fountain, in cut crystal glass, 27 feet high'. Containing some four tons of glass, as well as a marble base and internal ironwork, it called forth epithets including 'stupendous' and 'striking' from writers at the time.

Pâte de verre *Pâte de verre* means literally glass paste. It comprised glass, white or coloured, powdered, blended and formed into a paste so that it might be moulded. The substance was used in ancient times, in the eighteenth century by James Tassie, and in the late nineteenth century by Emile Gallé and others.

Pellatt Apsley Pellatt and his son of the same name were successively owners of the Falcon Glassworks, Southwark, London. Pellatt Junior (1791–1863) patented and made Cameo Incrustations as well as other glassware in styles of the first half of the nineteenth century. The firm showed a wide range of its productions at the 1851 Great Exhibition, including a large chandelier and a display of the materials and equipment used in making glass. Pellatt wrote books on the subject of glass manufacture and its history, and was Member of Parliament for Southwark from 1852 to 1857.

Plate Glass The term applied to sheet glass made by casting.

Pontil-Mark The rough scar on the base of an article where it has been broken away from the pontil. In the late eighteenth century it became customary to grind the mark smooth.

Porrón The *porrón* is a Spanish spouted vessel. The drinker used it by raising the filled *porrón* above head-level, tipping it so as to direct a stream of wine into his open mouth.

Portland Vase The Portland Vase is without much doubt the most famous extant example of Roman glassmaking. It dates from the late first century B.C. or the

Glass; Methods, Materials, Factories and Articles (Continued)

first century A.D. and is made of cobalt blue glass cased in white. The flat base is of the same date and decorated in the same cameo technique as the vase, but the latter originally probably terminated in a point and the base is a subsequent addition. The subject of the cameo engraving round the vase has been debated since the first printed theory of 1642, but modern scholarship suggests that it depicts the myth of Peleus and Thetis. The vase was recorded as being in the Barberini Palace, Rome, in 1642, and was sold in about 1780 by the last member of the Barberini family. It was duly acquired soon afterwards by the Duchess of Portland, who died in 1785. The vase then came into the possession of her son, the Duke of Portland whose son, in turn, lent it to the British Museum. There it remained undisturbed until 7 February 1845, when a young man threw something at its showcase and smashed the vase to fragments. The culprit, who pleaded intemperance was fined £3, and the numerous bits and pieces of glass were carefully re-assembled. In 1945 the Portland Vase was acquired by the British Museum, where it remains. The vase was copied in pottery by Josiah Wedgwood between 1786 and 1790, and in glass by John Northwood in 1876.

Pressed Glass Pressed glass was made in a mould bearing the pattern and shape of the outside of the required object. Into the mould was placed a quantity of molten glass, and then a plunger in the form of the interior shape of the object was lowered into the glass-filled mould. It pressed the glass into shape, and the object was then removed for annealing. The process was developed in the United States in the mid-

Pressed glass ornament in the form of a woven basket, made in opaque pale blue glass by Sowerby's, of Gateshead-on-Tyne.

Glass; Methods, Materials, Factories and Articles (Continued)

1820s and came into use in England soon afterwards. Pressed glass was shown at the 1851 Great Exhibition, and later in the century was made in quantity in the Newcastle upon Tyne area and elsewhere.

Prunt A button of glass usually with a patterned surface used for decoration on, for example, the *römer*.

Queen's Burmese A matt-surfaced glass shading from pink to yellow was given the name Queen's Burmese Ware in 1886 by its makers in England, Thomas Webb & Son. Under the name Burmese glass it had been patented in the United States in 1885 and was made by the Mount Washington Glass Co., of New Bedford, Massachusetts, whose gifts of some dishes was accepted by Queen Victoria and followed by an order for a large teaset. Before the American firm had had time to make and deliver the set, Webb's had acquired a licence to make Burmese glass to the original name of which they added the royal title. Some Queen's Burmese Ware was left undecorated, but much of it was enamelled and gilt. Pieces are recorded bearing Webb's name and other details etched beneath the base.

Ravenscroft George Ravenscroft (1618–81) was born at Hawarden, Flintshire, and is reputed to have owned ships and traded with Venice. In 1673, at the age of fifty-five he began glassmaking at a glasshouse in the Savoy, London, and a year later succeeded in producing an improved type of glass for which he was granted a patent. The Company of Glass-Sellers then engaged him to continue his researches on their behalf, using a glasshouse at Henley on Thames for the purpose. In June 1676 the Company announced that an earlier defect in much of the new glass, a defect known as crisselling, had been cured, and

Glass posset pot made by George Ravenscroft and with his seal at the base of the spout. Posset was a drink made from curdled milk and other ingredients, which was popular at the date this piece was made—in about 1675. Sotheby's.

that henceforward all articles in the new metal would be marked with a seal. The announcement gave no further details, but during 1676 it was stated that from that date the seal would depict a raven's head; a punning allusion to the maker's name. Ravenscroft's glass was made from English flints and potash in place of the pebbles and *barilla* used in Venice, and to counteract the lower fusibility of the flints he added lead oxide. Then he replaced flint with sand, but the name Flint glass remained in use alongside Glass of Lead and Lead Crystal. At present about twenty articles are recorded with a small glass seal, about 7 mm. in diameter, showing in relief a rather blurred impression of a raven's head.

Richardson The firm of W. H., B. & J. Richardson, of Stourbridge, made all varieties of glassware in the nineteenth century. Their display at the 1851 Great Exhibition included cut, engraved, frosted, coloured, and gilt articles, opal glass and black glass. As regards the cut examples it was noted at the time that 'the beauty and variety of the cutting in the whole of these works cannot fail to secure to them unqualified admiration'. One of the Richardson brothers, Benjamin (died 1887), was known in Stourbridge and district as 'the father of the glass trade'.

Rolling Pins Glass rolling-pins were made at numerous glasshouses throughout the nineteenth century. They were in white, coloured or variegated glass, and some of the plain ones were decorated in unfired ordinary paint of which traces have often worn away completely. Their purpose has sometimes been seriously argued, suggestions put forward including their use as containers for salt, tea or rum.

Römer The *römer* is a drinking-vessel with a globular bowl raised on a tall and wide stem, the latter bearing prunts. It was favoured in Germany and the Netherlands.

Rupert's Drops If small pieces of molten glass are dropped into water, each sets in the shape of a pear with a long tail. Not being annealed, the drops are highly stressed and if the tail is broken off one the remainder of it explodes into thousands of tiny pieces. They are known as Rupert's Drops because of the interest taken in them by Prince Rupert (1619–82), a nephew of Charles I.

Russian Glass There were glasshouses in Russia during the eighteenth and nineteenth centuries. Their productions followed German styles, and in many instances were decorated with engraving.

Saint-Louis The *Cristallerie de Saint-Louis*, in Lorraine, was founded in 1767, and for the first decades of its existence enjoyed Royal protection. English-type lead glass was made there from the early 1780s, and the factory was among those producing Opaline after it had become fashionable. Saint-Louis made paperweights and while 1845 is the earliest dated example recorded, they may well have been making them prior to that year. Some of the paperweights are not only dated but bear the initials *S L* over the numerals.

Salviati Antonio Salviati established a glasshouse at Murano in the 1860s, where he produced articles in old Venetian forms. The opening of a showroom in St. James's Street, London, provided a good outlet for selling and stimulated interest in old glass. Some of Salviati's copies were sufficiently good to deceive collectors of antiques, although it is not thought that that was the maker's intention.

Savoy Glasshouse The Savoy, Strand, London, was the site of a palace until the building was burnt in 1381; a theatre, a hotel and a street on part of the site commemorate the old name. In July 1673, George Ravenscroft opened a glasshouse 'in the Savoy at the Riverside'. Another, active a few years later was described simply as 'The glasshouse in the Savoy'.

Schwanhardt Georg Schwanhardt (1601–67) and members of his family were highly skilled glass engravers who worked at Nuremberg, Germany.

Sealed Glass Glass seals bearing devices, similar in appearance to seals of sealing-wax, were used by George Ravenscroft from 1674. Seals of larger size, about 3–4 cm. in diameter, were used on wine bottles between about 1650 and 1830.

Sheet Glass See Crown Glass.

Ship's Decanters Decanters for use on board ship were made with bases of large

Glass; Methods, Materials, Factories and Articles (Continued)

diameter so that they would perhaps remain upright despite the motion of a vessel.

Silesian Stem The name Silesian was given to a type of wine-glass stem current in England for a short period from about 1715. It was ribbed, with facets at the wide upper end, the facets sometimes bearing raised inscriptions like 'God Save King George'. The stem acquired its name because it is thought to have been introduced into England from Silesia; alternatively it is said to have been current in Hesse and Hanover.

Silvering See Mirrors.

Slag Glass Slag glass was the name given to a marbled coloured glass used for pressed articles from about 1875 by firms in the Newcastle upon Tyne area. It acquired its name because one of the ingredients of the batch was slag, which is waste material separated during smelting and readily obtainable from local ironworks.

South Jersey See Wistar.

Sowerby Sowerby & Co., of the Ellison Glass Works, Gateshead, were prominent makers of pressed glass wares in the late nineteenth century. In 1882 it was reported that they had between 700 and 1,000 employees and their weekly output was 150 tons of goods. The Sowerby mark was a crest in the form of a peacock's head.

Spanish Glass Sixteenth- and seventeenth-century Spanish glass showed Venetian features in its decoration, although many of the forms were strictly local. The *cántaro*, among others, was ornamented with thin threads of glass, pinched edges and occasionally bands of *latticino*. The metal was tinted, but this was because of impurities and it was not deliberately coloured. In 1728 a glasshouse was established at La Granja de San Ildefonso, near Segovia, which specialized in making mirrors but also produced other goods. Forty years later, a German was put in charge of the glasshouse and cut, engraved and gilt articles were made, many of them lacking any especially Spanish characteristic.

Stevens and Williams Stevens and Williams, of Brierley Hill, near Stourbridge, were active throughout most of the nineteenth century producing good quality articles in current styles. John Northwood was Art Director of the firm from early in the 1880s.

Stiegel Henry William Stiegel (1729–85) settled in Pennsylvania where he arrived in 1750 from Cologne, Germany, and began his career by starting an ironworks. In 1763 he opened a glasshouse at Manheim, to the east of Philadelphia, which was duly expanded until in 1773 the over-ambitious Stiegel was declared bankrupt and the venture ceased. During the decade in which he was active Stiegel produced all kinds of wares from window glass to tumblers and other domestic goods. Some of the latter were made of coloured metal blown into moulds which impressed the vessels with an overall diamond pattern, and others were painted in enamels in the current German style.

Stipple Engraving See Diamond Engraving.

Stourbridge Stourbridge, West Midlands, about a dozen miles to the west of Birmingham, has been a centre of the glass industry in England since the nineteenth century. Emigrants from Lorraine settled there in the sixteenth century, and it gradually supplanted London.

Glass; Methods, Materials, Factories and Articles (Continued)

Stuck Stem See Wine-glass.

Sunderland See Newcastle upon Tyne.

Swedish Glass The most important glasshouse was the Kungsholm Glasbruk, at Stockholm, which was founded in 1676 and was in operation until 1815. Other establishments of smaller size came and went during that time, but in most instances based their output on Kungsholm where German styles predominated.

Tassie James Tassie (1735–99) and his nephew William Tassie (1777–1860) made portrait medallions similar to the ceramic ones of Josiah Wedgwood, but they used a white glass paste (*pâte de verre*). Their 1791 catalogue lised 16,000 items, and eight years later this had increased to 20,000. After 1840 they were succeeded by John Wilson.

Venetian Glass Glassmakers were active in Venice as early as the eleventh century, and two hundred years later the industry left the city for the island of Murano. This occurred because of the constant threat to Venice of fires spreading from the glass-furnaces, whereas on the isle such conflagrations would be confined. The industry was strictly regulated, and severe penalties were prescribed to prevent the emigration of workers and the spread of secret knowledge. Venetian glass was esteemed throughout the civilized world, the various importing nations each engaging in efforts to equal or excel the famed *cristallo*. The soda-alkali metal was slow in cooling, allowing the craftsman time in which to manipulate it into the characteristic ornamented shapes. By the seventeenth century, despite the stringent laws, many Venetians had ventured into other countries where they assisted in establishing glasshouses and working in them. As a result, it is often difficult, if not impossible, to distinguish Venetian-style wares made in one or other European country from those made in Murano. As the maritime power of Venice faded, so did its industries and by about 1700 the glass monopoly was no longer effective. In the mid-nineteenth century there came a revival on a much smaller scale than in the past, with Antonio Salviati and others making articles in the old styles.

Verzelini Jacopo Verzelini (1522–1606) was of Venetian origin and is supposed to have reached England from Antwerp in 1571. Four years later he was granted a privilege to make glass for the period of twenty-one years, which he began to do by establishing a glasshouse in Broad Street, in the City of London. Without doubt the majority of the glass made in London by Verzelini would have been indistinguishable from Venetian of the time, but a small group of surviving examples is attributed to him. They comprise some tall-stemmed goblets, each of which is decorated with diamond-engraving and bears a date between 1577 and 1586. All are initialled with the exception of one with the names John and Joan Dyer (actually, *JOHN JONE DIER*), and two are engraved with the motto of the Pewterers' Company: *IN GOD IS AL MI TRVST*. This last has resulted in the suggestion that the glasses were ornamented by Anthony de Lysle, a Frenchman who was in London by at least 1582 and who was described at the time as an engraver on glass and pewter. Verzelini would appear to have prospered, for he retired from business in 1592 and went to live at Downe, near Orpington, Kent. He died there, and is commemorated in the church by a brass depicting him with his wife and nine children.

Glass; Methods, Materials, Factories and Articles (Continued)

Walking-Sticks Glass walking-sticks were made of clear and coloured glass, with and without internal twists in white and colours.

Waterford, Ireland The Waterford Glass House was established in 1783 by two Irish merchants, George and William Penrose. They employed as manager John Hill, of Stourbridge, who brought with him from England a number of craftsmen as well as a good knowledge of the industry. The name of Waterford remains synonymous with cut glass and much of it was made there, although only in very rare instances is it possible to state the origin of examples. Certain shapes were apparently an Irish speciality, for example large-sized oval and boat-shaped bowls which were usually raised on a foot with a moulded underside. The latter was often given a pattern of radiating furrows, which earned it the name 'lemon squeezer' foot on account of a likeness in appearance to that article. Decanters, jugs and finger-bowls are recorded with raised lettering beneath their bases, reading *WATERLOO CO. CORK.* The Waterford factory continued in operation long enough to display its products at the 1851 Great Exhibition, but it failed in that very year and the stock and equipment were disposed of.

Webb Thomas Webb & Son, of Stourbridge, were active from the early decades of the nineteenth century, and it has been stated that between 1837 and 1900 their pattern books record some twenty-five thousand different items. They made cut and coloured wares of all kinds, and in 1886 bought the English rights to manufacture Burmese glass, which they marketed under the name Queen's Burmese Ware. The Woodall brothers were in charge of the Webb cameo workshop, which had a large output. Most of the firm's productions were unmarked, but occasionally an etched mark incorporating the name was used.

Drinking glass engraved in diamond-point with a hunting scene, inscribed JOHN JONE DIER and dated 1581, probably made at Jacopo Verzelini's London glassworks and engraved by Anthony de Lysle.
Victoria and Albert Museum.

Glass; Methods, Materials, Factories and Articles (Continued)

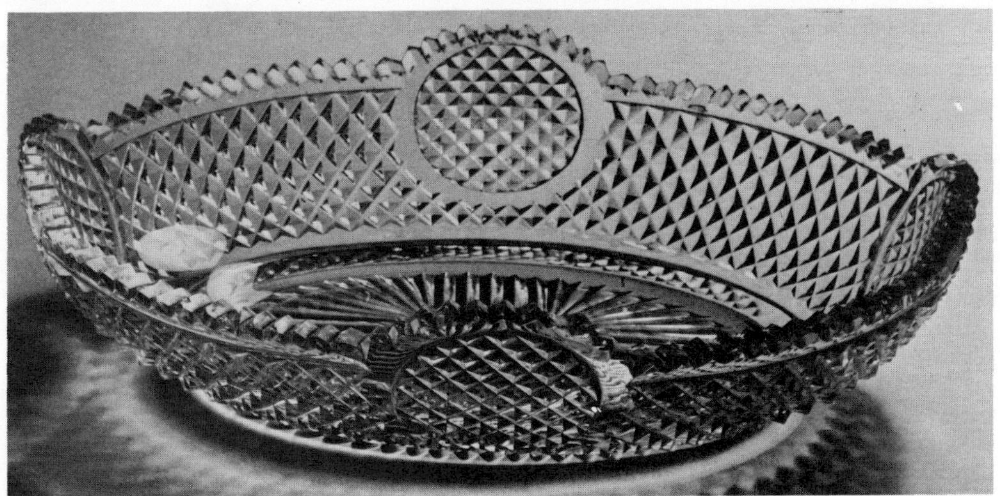

Oval glass dish with cut decoration in the manner of Waterford, about 1820.

Whitefriars Glassworks The Whitefriars Glassworks was situated in the City of London, where it remained in operation until as recently as 1922, when the business was transferred to Wealdstone, Greater London. During the eighteenth century they made chandeliers and much else, and in the second half of the nineteenth century were prominent as makers of articles in the taste of William Morris and his followers.

Williamite Glasses Williamite glasses bear representations of William III or related wording, commemorating not only the memory of that monarch but the existence of Englishmen and Irishmen opposed to the Jacobites. Surviving examples depict the King, sometimes on horseback, and are often inscribed with references to his success in defeating James II at the battle of the Boyne in 1690.

Wine-Glasses The wine-glass is an object on which the glass-maker was able to exercise his skill and imagination, and one in which the qualities of Lead glass were exploited. Surviving English examples, dating mostly from the eighteenth century, show great variety in their bowls, stems and feet, and the many ways in which these were combined. The glasses can be divided into two basic types: two-part or drawn stem, and three-part or stuck shank; the former having the stem drawn out from the bowl while still in a plastic state and then having the foot attached, and the three-part comprising bowl, stem and foot made separately and put together. A selection of bowls and stems is illustrated here, the stems being shaped as balusters, with knops (protuberances) or with straight outlines; in some instances employing the foregoing singly, and in others in combination. Stem styles varied in other ways, with changing fashions for interior ornament, such as air-twist, opaque-white-twist and colour-twist, and externally there were cut faceting and a rope-like incised twist. The dates when they were current are approximately:

Air-twist 1735–70
White-twist and colour-twist 1745–80
Cut facets 1750–1810
Incised twist 1750–60

Glass; Methods, Materials, Factories and Articles (Continued)

Group of eighteenth-century drinking glasses: (left to right) firing glass engraved on the bowl with Masonic devices; faceted stem; two with Newcastle type opaque twist stems. King & Chasemore.

The foot varied comparatively little, the main types being the plain foot and the folded foot. The first-named is the more common of the two, the folded foot fitting its description by having the outer edge turned underneath. This gave added strength where chipping was likely to occur, but when glass became more expensive following the Excise duty of 1745 the folded foot went out of fashion. It is found occasionally on later glasses. The nineteenth-century wine-glass lost its individuality with the exploitation of new processes and machinery, and a gradual diminution in the craftsman's role.

Wistar Caspar Wistar (1695–1752) was born in Germany and set up in business in about 1720 as a maker of brass buttons at Philadelphia. In 1739 he established a glasshouse at Wistarberg, New Jersey, both of which enterprises were continued by his son Richard (d. 1781) after the death of Caspar in 1752. All kinds of glass were made, including vessels in tinted metal ornamented with contrastingly coloured loops or 'lily pads'. Articles of the type, made by the Wistars or their later imitators, are referred to as being of South Jersey type.

Witch-balls Hollow glass globes, clear or coloured and usually silvered on the inside, were made at many glasshouses and at all periods. Known as Witch-balls, many legends have become attached to them.

Wolff David Wolff (1732–98) lived most of his life at The Hague, Holland. His stipple engraving on glass vies in skill with that of Frans Greenwood. Signed and dated examples are recorded, the latter between about 1780 and 1795.

Woodall The brothers Thomas and George Woodall were in the forefront of engravers in the fashionable cameo style of

Glass; Methods, Materials, Factories and Articles (Continued)

the last quarter of the nineteenth century. They worked mostly with Thomas Webb and Son, of Stourbridge.

Yard of Ale The yard of ale was a one-yard long (91·4 cm.) trumpet-mouthed vessel with a hollow bulb in the base. The bulb meant that it would not stand upright when rested, so the contents had to be drained at a single gulp. The unsuspecting drinker raised the glass to his lips, and as the vessel rose above the horizontal the remaining contents squirted in his face because of air entering the bulb.

Zwischengoldgläser *Zwischengoldgläser* means literally between-gold glasses. They were beakers or goblets decorated with a pattern in gold leaf, which was protected by means of an outer glass made precisely to size, and fitting so that its presence is almost undetectable. The glasses were made in Bohemia in the first half of the eighteenth century. The technique was revived in part at a later date by J. J. Mildner.

Pink and white cameo glass plaque carved with Venus and Cupid by George Woodall, about 1890.
Corning Museum of Glass, Corning, N.Y.: photo, Sotheby's.

4. SILVER

METHODS, MATERIALS, FACTORIES AND ARTICLES

Adam Robert Adam (1728–92) made designs for silver for some of the clients whose houses he built and decorated. A selection of the designs was engraved in the three-volume *Works in Architecture of Robert and James Adam*, published between 1773 and 1822, and others are in the form of the original drawings now mostly in Sir John Soane's Museum, London. Adam's designs included candlesticks, dishes and racing cups, the latter of classical vase form with suitable ornament, not all of which were carried out.

Alterations See Forgeries.

Ambassadorial Plate In order to represent their sovereign and country in a creditable manner it was usual for ambassadors to foreign lands as well as certain important Government officials, to be loaned a quantity of silverware. The amount varied according to the position of the borrower, and in the case of a Lord Chancellor could be 4,000 oz. The plate was supplied by the Royal Jewel Office, each piece being engraved with the sovereign's arms and insignia. Despite this clear mark of ownership, it became customary during the eighteenth century for the silver to be retained. Despite occasional complaints no official action was taken until 1815, when the various foreign embassies were provided with plate that remained in them for use by successive occupants. In 1839 the practice ceased with regard to other persons. It explains the reason for the presence of Royal arms on pieces of silver, and makes it clear that not everything so-marked was made for a sovereign's personal use.

American Silver Immigrant silversmiths from England were working in Massachusetts by the mid-seventeenth century, doubtless producing wares in the style of their native land. Similarly the first American-born craftsman, Jeremiah Dummer (1645–1718) of Boston, did most of his work in the same vein. New Amsterdam, which came into English hands in 1674 and was duly re-named New York, predictably showed a preference for pieces of Dutch inspiration in both shape and decoration. In both instances, American examples show a gap of between twenty and thirty years between their making and that of their European prototypes. John Coney (1656–1722) of Boston, for example, made sugar boxes of Charles II type in about 1690, and the immigrant Dutchmen of New York worked with a comparable time lag. Before the mid-eighteenth century there had been occasional signs of French influence, but by that date it had, like the Dutch, been largely replaced by English. No hall-marking system operated in America, with the brief exception of one in Baltimore that lasted from 1814 to 1830. See Revere.

Andirons See Fire-irons.

Apple Corer Most surviving examples date from the eighteenth century. Many were designed with the blade unscrewing so that it could be reversed into the handle, making it safe to be carried in the pocket.

Argyll The Argyll, or Argyle, apparently owes its name to a Duke of Argyll, perhaps Archibald, the third Duke, who succeeded to the title in 1743. It was a gravy or sauce container designed to keep

Silver; Methods, Materials, Factories and Articles (Continued)

the contents hot at the dinner-table, by means of either hot water or a heated iron. Many examples resemble tea- or coffee-pots in external appearance, but with a removable lid instead of the usual hinged one and an orifice for filling in the case of the water-filled variety.

Assaying To assay or test (from the French, *essayer*: to test) the purity of silver a small amount was wrapped in lead and put in a crucible made of bone ash and known as a cupel. Heating to a high temperature caused the lead and any other impurities to oxidize and be absorbed by the crucible. The silver remaining was weighed, its weight was compared with that of the original amount and the discrepancy represented base metal that had been alloyed with the sample assayed. See Hall-marking.

Auricular Style This style, known in Dutch as *kwabornament*, incorporates fleshy curvaceous shapes bearing a resemblance to the human ear, and enjoyed a limited popularity in the seventeenth century. It was much used in the Netherlands by members of the van Vianen family and a few other silversmiths, while in England it made a fleeting appearance in the work of Christiaen van Vianen. See Netherlands.

Australian Silver As the nineteenth century progressed an increasing number of silversmiths became established in Australia. German and English names were allied with wares revealing the influence of those countries, with added variations to suit local buyers. Figures of aboriginals, emus and kangaroos were cast or chased as decorative adjuncts, and the large emu egg was transformed into ornamental cups, vases and coffee-pots with the aid of silver

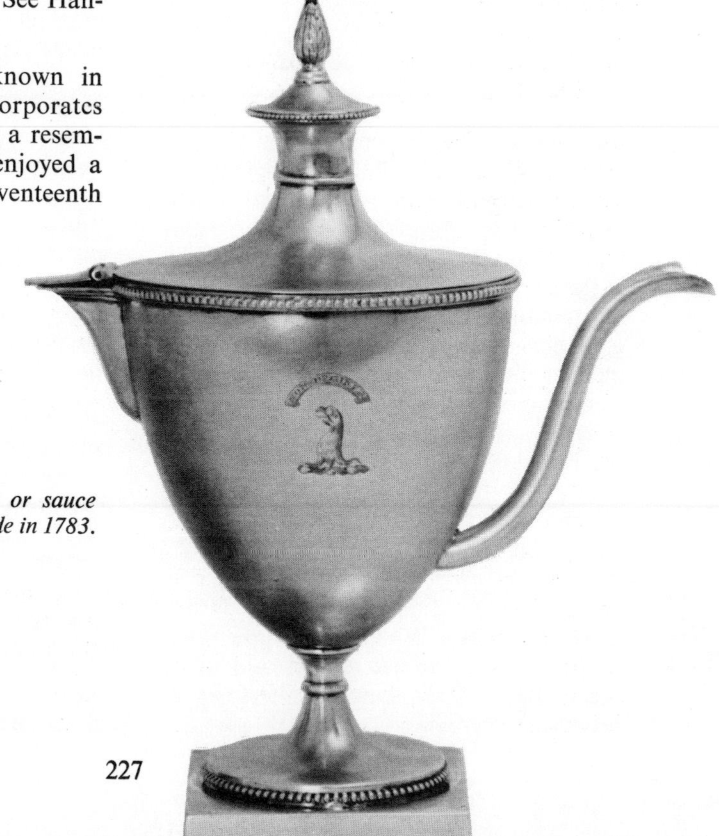

Silver argyll used for keeping gravy or sauce hot at the table. This example was made in 1783. Sotheby's.

Silver; Methods, Materials, Factories and Articles (Continued)

mounts. Makers were to be found first at Sydney, and in due course at Hobart, Adelaide, Melbourne and a few other centres of population. No hall-marking system existed, but most of the silversmiths stamped their work with their surnames or initials and their town name. Some added English-looking cyphers, and others used stamps depicting kangaroos or emus.

Basket Baskets, usually for holding bread at the table, took a number of forms. Although they were made earlier and examples have been preserved, most survivors date from the eighteenth century. The majority are oval in outline, and almost all have their sides pierced in patterns approximating, more or less, to woven basketry. Exceptional examples take the form of large seashells. Some baskets were made without handles, but others have hinged ones or a pair of small fixed handles.

Bateman The Bateman family were active as silversmiths in the late eighteenth/early nineteenth century. Its most famed member was Hester Bateman (1709–94) wife of John Bateman who left her a widow at the age of fifty-one when he died in 1760. She continued his business of maker of gold chains, expanding it successfully to include silverware and in 1790 handing it over to her sons, Peter (1740–1825) and Jonathan (1748–91); the latter's share in the business being taken over by his wife Ann (1749–1814) from 1791. Ann's son, William (1774–1850) joined the firm in 1800, and his son, also William (1800–?1874) was apprenticed to his father in 1822. The productions of the family between about 1760 and 1820 are characterized by restrained design and ornament, much of the latter in the form of bright-cut engraving.

Beaker The shape of the beaker goes back at least to medieval times, and it has been suggested that its shape is owed to that of an animal's horn cut short for conversion into a drinking vessel. Examples of English make survive from many dates, but it was even more popular in Germany, the Netherlands and elsewhere on the mainland of Europe.

Bell Bells of various types and made of various metals survive from very early times. Silver examples of more recent date, mostly of the eighteenth century, include bells forming part of an inkstand, others for use at the table, and those that ornamented the canopy carried over a sovereign at his or her coronation.

Birmingham The city was for long an important centre for making goods in all metals, including silver. The latter had to be sent to the nearest assay office, Chester, or to London for hall-marking, which involved delay and expense as well as possible damage in transit. In 1773, at the instigation of Matthew Boulton, an assay office was opened in Birmingham. Its distinctive mark was, and remains, an anchor. A large proportion of the silver wares made at Birmingham comprises small articles, such as snuff and other boxes.

Boulton Matthew Boulton (1728–1809) of the Soho Works, Birmingham, was one of the foremost eighteenth-century manufacturers of high quality metalwares. He began silversmithing in 1765 and produced articles equal to those of London in style and finish. Boulton was responsible for the opening of an assay office at Birmingham.

Bowls See Monteith; Punch Bowl; Sugar Basin.

Silver; Methods, Materials, Factories and Articles (Continued)

Brandewijnkom *used in Holland for drinking brandy or other spirits, made at Sneek, in Friesland in the north of the country, in 1648.* Christie's.

Boxes Boxes for many purposes were made of silver, although it is not always possible to be certain of the original use of examples. One or more boxes formed part of a toilet service, while ladies had small boxes to hold patches and men had them for snuff and tobacco. An inkstand often held boxes for pounce and wafers, and in the late seventeenth century sugar boxes were used at the table. See Vinaigrette.

Brandewijnkom The *brandewijnkom* is a small bowl raised on a low base and with two flat handles. It was popular in the Netherlands during the seventeenth century, at the same time as the comparable English porringer, Scottish quaich and French *écuelle*. *Brandewijnkom* means brandy-bowl, which explains the purpose of the vessel.

Bright-cut Bright-cut ornament shows burnished facets and is a type of engraving popular from the late eighteenth century.

Britannia Standard At the Restoration in 1660 there arose a great demand for silverware, much having been melted earlier during the Civil War, and silversmiths turned to Sterling silver coins as a source of supply for the metal. There followed a shortage of coin, while much remaining in circulation was clipped, the edges not having been milled and issued only roughly shaped. To prevent the abuse, the Government in 1697 raised the standard for wrought silver to 11 oz. 10 dwt. in each pound (Troy weight, one pound = 12 oz.), and ordered finished articles to bear a special mark in the form of a seated figure of Britannia. Hence silver of this superior purity became described as being of 'Britannia' standard. In 1720, silversmiths were again allowed to make articles to the old Sterling standard, but Britannia standard remained optional and continues to be.

Buckle Silver shoe-buckles were worn during the late seventeenth century and the following century. A fashion for extra

Silver; Methods, Materials, Factories and Articles (Continued)

large buckles in the 1780s caused wearers, it was said, 'to buckle them to the shoe with a false strap' to prevent them falling off.

Butter-Dish Among the most pleasing of these are late eighteenth-century examples made in Ireland. They have pierced sides and covers and inner glass liners, with a seated cow to form a knob handle and indicate the contents.

Buttons Buttons were made of silver, gilt and chased or engraved as required. Designs found on them include crests, coats-of-arms, initials and sporting subjects.

Caddy Spoon A spoon with a short handle was found suitable for taking tea from the caddy in which it was kept. Surviving examples date from about 1770 and many were made at Birmingham. Their designs were very varied and involved the use of many techniques including chasing, piercing and engraving. Caddy spoons have been recorded in the form of miniature jockey caps, seashells, and bunches of grapes resting on vine leaves, as well as in more appropriate patterns.

Cage-work A style of ornamentation in which a pierced and chased metal 'cage' enclosed an object, usually made of glass, stone or porcelain, but occasionally of silver or silver-gilt. Caged silver cups and tankards were made in the late seventeenth century, and a hundred years later small glass perfume bottles and other toys were caged in gold.

Canadian Silver Surviving eighteenth-century Canadian silver is scarce, although it is known that a number of silversmiths worked there. French influence is apparent in what remains, but much of the output was of small items to barter with Indians as the tide of immigrants moved westwards. Jesuit missionaries gave their converts rings engraved with the sacred initials *I H S*, but these are no less rare than other articles made in the country.

Candlestick and Candelabrum Few English examples dating before the Restoration are known to exist, but from 1660 onwards surviving candlesticks enable

A nine-light candelabrum modelled with rococo scrolls and cupids, an example of the nineteenth-century revival of the style current during the preceding century. It was made in 1836 by Robert Garrard, a prominent silversmith of the time, and weighs nearly 800 oz. Christie's.

Silver; Methods, Materials, Factories and Articles (Continued)

changes in style to be traced. The drip pan descended the stem until it disappeared altogether by about 1700, when turned stems on octagonal bases were popular; their simple shaping according with that of other silver wares and the plain lines of much furniture of the time. The rococo of 1740 onwards saw an increasing elaboration in ornament and the reappearance of drip pans. By 1755–60 the assymetrical excesses were disappearing and being replaced by the comparative severity of the neo-classical, with the Corinthian column, with or without embellishments, being popular as a candlestick. In the Regency, the many current motifs were employed in conjunction or singly, while later in the century most of the earlier styles were revived. Candelabra dating from before the mid-eighteenth century are now rare. Their design follows that of candlesticks, and many of them are enlarged versions of the latter with arms to hold two or more candles. Sometimes there is a central socket for a candle, with a removable finial for when it is not in use. See Chamber Candlestick; Taper Stick.

Canteen Pocket-sized sets of knife, fork, spoon and other implements were made for use when travelling. Some had silver cases that served as drinking vessels, while others fitted into containers of leather or of wood covered in shagreen.

Cartagloria Frame Italian *cartagloria* frames were intended to stand on altars and display cards on which were inscribed prayers. Many old examples have been converted into looking glasses.

Caster A few casters for sugar and spices have survived from the sixteenth century, and vary greatly in shape. Those of the later years of the seventeenth century were straight-sided with a spreading foot, and a pierced domed top held in place by a bayonet joint. Soon after 1700 a change came, and the caster was raised on a low pedestal foot with rounded or faceted sides to the pear-shaped body. Usually they were in sets of three, one sometimes being unpierced and intended to hold dry mustard; the bayonet fixture was replaced by a simple push fit. By about 1740 the body of the article bulged more than hitherto and both body and cover were often chased with rococo ornament, while this in turn was supplanted by a caster on a taller pedestal foot with decoration limited to a little engraving. By the end of the eighteenth century, the silver caster was a comparative rarity, its place at the table being taken by one of cut glass with a silver top. See Cruet Frames.

Casting Solid portions of articles were cast in fine sand and then carefully finished by hand before being soldered or bolted in place.

Cellini Benvenuto Cellini (1500–71) was an Italian metal-worker and silversmith. He not only wrote treatises on his art but also recorded his life and loves in his memoirs, which have been translated into several languages. Cellini executed commissions for Popes Clement VII and Paul III, and travelled to Paris and Fontainebleau at the command of Francis I. Most of his work has disappeared, but there remains a magnificent gold salt made between 1540 and 1543 for the French King (Kunsthistorisches Museum, Vienna).

Chamber Candlestick Chamber or hand candlesticks were made with the nozzle set in a handled pan, and often fitted conveniently with an extinguisher of matching design. Surviving examples date from the second half of the seventeenth

Silver; Methods, Materials, Factories and Articles (Continued)

century onwards and vary in pattern from decade to decade.

Chamber-Pot Silver chamber-pots survive from the seventeenth century, although their earlier existence is recorded in documents. See Forgeries.

Chandelier Chandeliers are listed in old inventories as 'lustres' or 'branches', and it is known that many were in the Royal palaces in the early eighteenth century. One of about 1700 remains at Hampton Court, and another from St. James's Palace is now at Colonial Williamsburg, Virginia. They were never commonplace, and were supplanted in the mid-eighteenth century when glass was found to be very effective for the purpose.

Channel Islands Silver Silversmiths are known to have been working on Jersey during the seventeenth century, but little survives except spoons. The Royalist sympathies of the Islanders and the fact that a mint operated there during the Civil War, would have induced most owners of plate to give it up in aid of the King. In the eighteenth century both Jersey and Guernsey supported silversmiths, and in 1835–45 the metal was mined on Sark. A few shapes of articles are peculiar to one or other of the islands: christening cups were made wide and shallow on Jersey, but those from Guernsey are less wide and deeper in comparison. Most of the recorded pieces are small in size, and rarely bear any decoration apart from an owner's initials. By the end of the eighteenth century most of the wants of the Islanders were supplied from London and the local craft was declining.

Chasing Chasing was a method of decorating by embossing a pattern with a hammer and punches. It could be performed on the front surface or the back and when on the former is known as flat chasing, which may sometimes be confused with engraving. Chasing differs from engraving in that it does not involve the removal of any metal; it only pushes or 'chases' it into the required form.

Cheese Scoop Cheese scoops of shovel-like form were made from the late eighteenth century, and were given wood or ivory handles. Some have sliding devices to remove the cheese from the rounded blade, but others leave this problem to the user.

Cheese Stand Stands designed to hold all or part of a round of cheese resting on its side were made very occasionally in the eighteenth century. One, made in 1760 is in the Victoria and Albert Museum, and is known to have been invoiced to the original owner as a 'Cheese plate'.

Chester The assay office at Chester was in operation from sometime in the fifteenth century until 1962. The town mark varied from time to time, but usually included the three garbs (sheaves of corn) of the Earls of Chester.

Chinoiserie European versions of Chinese scenes were engraved on silver from the late seventeenth century onwards, and occasionally copies of porcelain jars and other articles were made in the metal. In about 1750 there was a vogue for articles designed with Oriental motifs, when pagoda roofs, pendent bells and figures of Chinese men and women made an appearance in the round or in low relief. A further revival of interest in the same theme, with similar results, occurred in about 1820.

Chocolate Pot Chocolate was first taken as a drink in Europe in the mid-seventeenth century, and in England an

Silver; Methods, Materials, Factories and Articles (Continued)

advertisement offering it for sale appeared in 1657. Most silver chocolate pots follow the design of coffee pots, including having the handle at right-angles, but differ in having a subsidiary tiny lid in the top of the principal one. This was for inserting a special rod, known as a molionet or molinet, to stir the contents prior to pouring. Surviving chocolate pots usually have either tapering straight sides, or a pear-shaped body and low foot. Very few would appear to have been made in England after about 1710, although an exception is one complete with its molionet in the Ashmolean Museum, Oxford. They continued to be produced in America until the 1720s.

Chocolate pot made in 1771; it differs from a coffee pot in having a small lid at the top of the normal one so that a stirrer could be inserted without the contents becoming chilled. Sotheby's.

Coaster The coaster is a circular low-rimmed stand for a bottle or decanter, referred to in the past as a bottle stand or bottle slide. It made its appearance in the 1760s. Coasters are occasionally entirely of silver, but most examples have wood bases inset centrally with a disc of silver, bone or mother-of-pearl. The rims are variously ornamented with casting, piercing, engraving and chasing, and the most exotic examples of about 1820 are gilt. After 1830 the upper edge of the rim turns outwards and is decorated with floral and other patterns. Coasters were sold in pairs and sets, and it is often found that the marks are difficult to decipher because of damage to them during the finishing when the wooden bases were fitted. Double coasters were also made, some taking the form of a ship's jolly-boat and others having wheels to enable the port to be passed with greater ease.

Coffee Pot As early as 1637 there was a Greek at Balliol College, Oxford, who drank coffee, but it was not until thirteen years later that a coffee house was opened in the same city. London had one two years later and by 1700 there were four hundred in the capital alone. This was despite the fact that Charles II had tried to close them down in 1675 because they were resorted to by those 'who devised and spread abroad divers false, malicious and scandalous reports'. The earliest known silver coffee pot is one of 1681 (Victoria and Albert Museum), with tapering straight sides and a tall conical lid; the spout is straight and the handle in line with it. In the 1700s the same general shape persisted, but the handle was occasionally at right angles to the curved spout and the body was faceted. Later came the pear-shaped body raised on a low foot, the latter increasing in height as the century progressed.

Silver; Methods, Materials, Factories and Articles (Continued)

Cream and Milk Jug Small jugs for cream or milk, called creamers in America, were made from about 1710 onwards. Numerous styles, plain and fancy, came and went during the century and it is probably correct to say that broad-lipped examples were for cream. The various shapes, whether raised on feet or pedestal bases, overlapped so much in date that it is impossible to lay down a chronological order, and dating must usually be gauged by ornamental design and marks. The odd-looking, but appropriate, jugs in the form of cows, which were a speciality of John Schuppe, of London, were made between about 1755 and 1775.

Cruet Frames holding sets of casters and bottles were made from the first decades of the eighteenth century. The earlier type, sometimes termed a Warwick, had a series of rings above a platform raised on feet, while at the end of the century the frames were usually oval with a pierced and bright-cut gallery. In most instances they have a central handle by which to carry them complete with their contents.

Cupel A crucible made of bone ash used in assaying.

Cup Cups of various kinds have been made in silver for many centuries and in most countries. Elizabethan and early seventeenth-century examples were usually on tall and slender bases, were fitted with covers and frequently derived their design from German sources. In the mid-century came the more practical two-handled porringer or caudle cup, again usually with a cover and sometimes additionally with a matching stand. They were made between about 1650 and 1720, and then supplanted by more imposing two-handled covered cups that were purely for display; they varied in shape as well as ornament, demonstrating the virtuosity of designer and maker, the beauty of the metal and the good taste and wealth of the owner.

A late seventeenth-century silver tankard with cut-card work on the lid and handle. Christie's.

Cut-card Work Cut-card work was a form of decoration that often served also as a reinforcement. A sheet of silver, shaped and usually pierced, was soldered to the body of an article; for instance, at the junctions of the handle and spout in the case of a coffee pot. Cut-card decoration was in use in the late seventeenth/early eighteenth century.

Decanter Wagon Coasters conjoined and sometimes fitted with castors so that they could be moved easily about the table, were made in about 1800. They sometimes took the form of a boat.

Dinner Service Silver dinner services with matching plates, dishes, tureens and other components were made during the eighteenth century. In the first half of the

Silver; Methods, Materials, Factories and Articles (Continued)

century rims were moulded or gadrooned, but later came the reed-and-tie and more complex patterns. In most instances the owner's coat of arms was engraved on borders, and large pieces sometimes had the arms cast and applied.

Dish Cover A domed cover was used for keeping a joint of meat hot when it was brought to the table or while the joint awaited further carving. They were made in various sizes, but are seldom earlier than about 1800.

Dish Cross The dish cross was an X-shaped support for a dish, adjustable to the size of the latter and fitted with a central spirit-lamp to keep the contents hot. They were made from about 1730 until the end of the century.

Dish Ring These rings, 15–20 cm. in diameter and about 10 cm. in depth are sometimes called Potato Rings. They were made in small numbers in England in the early eighteenth century, but the Irish examples of the 1770s onwards are the more plentiful and best known. They were used to support a bowl of steaming potatoes, or equally one of punch, at the same time protecting the table surface from heat. The dish ring was usually skilfully decorated with piercing, chasing and engraving.

Dog Collar Privileged pets wore collars made of silver and some have survived.

Douter See Extinguisher.

Drawback See Duty.

Drinking-Cup Tall-stemmed cups closely resembling wine glasses were made from the sixteenth century, and only went out of use when Ravenscroft's glass successfully supplanted them. Late eighteenth/early nineteenth century examples are almost always inscribed to the effect that they had been awarded as prizes.

Dublin Dublin silversmiths were required to mark their wares from 1605, but as 1638 is the first year from which an example has survived it is assumed that the earlier injunction was ignored. Marks used include a crowned harp and a figure of Hibernia, the latter in a seated position making her liable to be confused with Britannia. See Britannia standard.

Dutch Silver See Netherlands Silver.

Duty In England, a duty of 6d. an oz. (2½p) was levied on most silverware made between 1719 and 1758. It was re-imposed in 1784, with some few exceptions, and to prevent abuses a special mark was ordered to be stamped on every article assayed after 1st December of that year. It showed that the duty had been paid, and took the form of the king's head in profile in incuse (sunken), but two years later the opposite was adopted and the head of George III in relief was employed. The duty was abolished after April 1890, and until then the heads of successive sovereigns were used as marks. If such marked plate was exported a repayment of the duty, known as drawback, was allowed, and when this took place a further mark was stamped to prevent an article from circulating as if tax on it were paid. The extra mark was a figure of Britannia, but unlike that used to denote Britannia standard or Hibernia on Irish silver, the drawback Britannia is standing and in incuse. The drawback mark has been found hitherto on fewer than a score of pieces, and it is stated that it was seldom used because of the damage caused to articles when it was stamped and the delay while it was done.

Silver; Methods, Materials, Factories and Articles (Continued)

Duty Dodgers Any duty has its evaders, and pieces of silverware on which statutory duty had not been paid are called duty dodgers. Evasion occurred mostly between 1719 and 1758, when no special mark was in use to show that payment had been made. The method employed by the nefarious was to cut out the marks from a trifling article that had already been stamped and neatly affix the piece removed in the base of the undeclared item. A piece that has been tampered with in this way is usually only detected if suspicions are aroused, when it is then found that the marks are not on the true base but on a piece of silver fitted over it. Thus, the marks might be taken from an object weighing 2 or 3 oz. and transposed onto a larger and heavier one, thereby saving what was at the time a worthwhile sum of money. The practice was not confined to lesser makers, for men like Paul de Lamerie were not above it as exemplified in a gilt ewer of 1736 in the Victoria and Albert Museum.

Écuelle The *écuelle* is a shallow bowl and cover, the bowl with two flat handles, and an accompanying dish. It was introduced in France in the early seventeenth century, and while most examples originated in that country a few were made in England and elsewhere by immigrant Huguenot silversmiths.

Edinburgh Silversmiths have been active in Edinburgh for many hundreds of years, their town mark being in use since the sixteenth century. It was taken from the arms of the city, and shows a triple-towered castle accompanied from 1759 by a further stamp of a thistle.

Egg Cup Sets of egg cups in frames were made from the mid-eighteenth century onwards, some of them being complete with spoons. More complex and comprehensive was the egg-boiler. It comprised a lidded water-vessel containing a frame for the eggs; this was raised on legs between which was a spirit lamp, and the whole was topped by an hour-glass.

Embossing See Chasing.

Enamel Gold and silver luxury articles were sometimes ornamented with coloured enamel. There were several types:

> *Champlevé:* in which the surface was cut with a series of hollows to form a pattern. Into each hollow was placed a separate colour.
> *Cloisonné:* in which a series of *cloisons* (French: walls) of metal wire were affixed to the surface to form the desired pattern. Again, each enclosed area was coloured differently to make the design.
> *Basse taille:* in which a pattern was engraved and then covered in transparent enamel.
> *Plique à jour:* in which *cloisons* were mounted on a thin base and filled with transparent enamel. The base was then ground away to produce a decoration resembling a miniature stained-glass window.

Miniature portraits were sometimes painted in enamel on thin plaques of gold.

Engraving To engrave silver is to remove some of the metal by means of a tool. The process was used to ornament articles, as well as to give them marks of ownership in the form of initials, crests and coats of arms, or to add commemorative and other inscriptions. In the past, initials were often in threes, that of the surname on top, and in Scotland it was customary to place the motto over the crest instead of below as in England. Most of the engravers have re-

Silver; Methods, Materials, Factories and Articles (Continued)

mained anonymous, but the names and productions of a few are known from the signatures on their work. The artist William Hogarth served his apprenticeship with a London silversmith, and it is thought that he may have been responsible for the fine engraving on the Walpole Salver (Victoria and Albert Museum).

Entrée Dish Entrée dishes and covers were made from the second half of the eighteenth century and took many shapes. In many instances they were topped by a ring handle, removable so that the cover could be reversed and used also as a dish. Those dating from after 1800 were occasionally provided with stands holding spirit lamps, or were constructed with a compartment to hold hot water.

Epergne The epergne was a centrepiece designed to stand on the dining-table. It was not only decorative but functional, because it was fitted with bowls and baskets to hold sweetmeats, pickles and other delicacies. It came into use in the 1730s and allowed designers and makers scope for their imagination, many of those made in the rococo style being particularly extravagant in appearance.

Silver epergne with pierced baskets for holding sweetmeats and other dainties at the dinner table, made in 1770.

Silver; Methods, Materials, Factories and Articles (Continued)

Ewer and Basin The ewer and basin was essential at the table prior to the introduction of forks in the seventeenth century. The ewer held perfumed water which was poured into the basin, so that diners could cleanse their fingers after using them for eating. Surviving early examples vary in shape and ornament, while those of post-seventeenth century date, intended for display rather than use, are often of flamboyant pattern.

Exeter Some surviving examples of sixteenth century silver prove that craftsmen were working in the Exeter area at that period, and it is probable that they were active much earlier. The assay office in the city was opened in 1701 and closed in 1883, using as a mark a triple-towered castle not unlike that of Edinburgh.

Extinguisher A conical object for placing on top of a candle to extinguish the flame. Most chamber candlesticks have a slot provided for an extinguisher, the latter being fitted with a peg to hold it in place. Another type was of scissors-like form, and is sometimes known as a douter. Douters are similar in appearance to sugar nippers, but the ends which squeeze the wick are flat-surfaced.

Filigree Filigree, manipulated wire and small beads of metal, was used to form decorative panels and complete articles. In the late seventeenth century it was fashionable in many countries, and in Italy the silversmiths of Genoa were masters of the technique. In a revival of filigree work during the nineteenth century, there was a big output of it in India. Owing to their delicate nature, articles made of filigree would seldom withstand stamping. Consequently, marked pieces are few, and it is only occasionally possible to be certain of the origin of examples.

Fire-Irons Sets of fire-irons comprising poker, tongs and shovel, made of iron and covered in beaten silver, were made in the later seventeenth century. Additionally, andirons, pairs of bellows and fire-pans were similarly ornamented. Examples are to be seen at Ham House, Surrey, and Knole Park, Kent (National Trust).

Fish Servers Slices with shaped flat blades for serving fish were made from about 1740. They are identifiable by their outline, piercing, and engraving, which feature fishes or other appropriate emblems, their handles being often of silver or ivory. In the nineteenth century the slice was usually given a matching fork, and the two items were sold in velvet-lined cases.

Flagon The term flagon once described a type of large bottle with a stopper and usually two handles, but nowadays it applies to a vessel, resembling an over-tall tankard with a hinged lid, that used to be known as a livery pot. The pots were made in pairs from the late sixteenth century, sometimes straight-sided and sometimes of pear shape, often chased and engraved and not infrequently gilt. Presumably they were made as much for display as for use, and many were presented in the past to churches. See Jug.

Forgeries Forgeries of old silver are few in number in comparison with the quantity of genuine pieces. They may be divided into two varieties: forgeries of marks, and forgeries of actual articles wholly or in part. The former was done to save payment of duty, to avoid assaying when use of poor metal would not have passed scrutiny, or to attempt giving a modern copy an age it does not possess. It was achieved by cutting the marks from an old piece and transferring them, but

Silver; Methods, Materials, Factories and Articles (Continued)

An early eighteenth-century monteith with chasing of flowers and some of the scrolls added later.

this is usually revealed by traces of soldering where the marked portion has been inserted. Suspicions can often be confirmed by breathing on the area, which will reveal clearly if such tampering has taken place; although the more advanced fakers plate over the join and make it more difficult to detect. Occasionally castings are made of old objects, such as spoons, marks and all, but the latter lack the sharpness of the originals and normally deceive only beginners. Additions to articles and changing of their original purpose render them liable to further assaying and marking, but this has not deterred the unscrupulous from clandestinely adding an extra handle to a chamber-pot to convert it paradoxically into a loving-cup; turning a small tankard into a milk jug by the addition of a spout; or making a tea caddy into a teapot by giving it a spout and handle. These and similar tricks are, fortunately, only rarely encountered, but the Victorian habit of chasing plain Georgian pieces was so widespread that examples abound. As such handiwork has not changed the original purpose of the article and it is properly marked it is not illegal, and can only be condemned on aesthetic grounds or because monetary value is affected. An untouched piece is more highly esteemed by most people, who prefer it to one that has been 'improved'.

Silver; Methods, Materials, Factories and Articles (Continued)

Fork In England the fork did not gain general acceptance until the late seventeenth century, when its convenience was lauded by travellers who had used it in Italy. Many of the earlier examples had three prongs, but there are no hard and fast rules as to whether there should be three or four at any particular date. Forks were often made of steel with silver handles, the silver being thin and filled with a composition so that it kept its shape.

French Silver Old French silver is scarcer than that of almost any other European country. In 1689 and 1715 there were calls for citizens to give up their silver, so that it might be melted to pay for wars. Records of what once existed and the little that now remains make it clear that many examples of great craftsmanship were lost forever. The French silversmiths did, however, supply foreign clients, and examples of their work remain in countries other than France. Charles II gave his favourite, Frances Teresa, Duchess of Richmond and Lennox, a superb fifteen-piece toilet service made in Paris in about 1670 (Royal Scottish Museum, Edinburgh), and parts of an enormous dinner service made for Catherine the Great of Russia in 1770 are to be found in museums in various countries. The classical lines of Régence wares were replaced by rococo assymetry largely through the influence of Juste-Aurèle Meissonier, whose engraved designs circulated widely and initiated changes throughout Europe. A further melting of silverware took place following the Revolution, but after a decade or so the craftsmen were hard at work again replacing it in the new Empire style.

Furniture Silver furniture was fashionable in many countries during the last quarter of the seventeenth century. In the majority of instances the articles were made of wood or iron covered in sheets of chased and engraved metal, but parts were sometimes cast in the solid. English-made examples are at Windsor Castle, and there is a suite of candlestands, table and wall mirror at Knole Park, Kent (National Trust). Another suite, but of walnut overlaid with chased plaques of silver, is in the Metropolitan Museum of Art, New York. Such furniture was made for display rather than use, although this may not have applied to a bed made in 1674 for Nell Gwynn. It contained more than 2,000 oz. of silver and cost about £900, but has since disappeared; no doubt into the melting-pot. A like fate befell the many silver furnishings that were once at Versailles, but the throne and footstool made in London in 1731 for the Empress of Russia remain at the Hermitage Palace, Leningrad. In the 1720's English silversmiths made tripod stands for tea-kettles, but these would never have been numerous and only a very few survive. See Kettle.

Gold and Gilding This precious metal has always been esteemed for its scarcity, as well as for the facts that it is resistant to attack by most chemicals, does not appreciably tarnish and is extremely malleable. Like silver, gold is too soft to use in its pure state, so it is alloyed with silver and other metals to give it durability. Its purity is determined in carats: pure gold being 24 carat; and it is rated according to the proportion of alloy in it. Thus, 22 carat gold contains that amount of metal plus 2 carats of alloy to make a total of 24, and 9 carat gold is in the proportion of nine parts to fifteen. From 1477 to 1576 the standard for English gold was 18 carats, from 1576 to 1798 it was 22 carats, and from the latter year both 18 and 22 carat were made legal. In

1854 the total was increased by the addition of 15, 12 and 9 carat, and distinctive marking was introduced. Gold could be applied to the surface of silver articles in order to give them a richer appearance and prevent tarnishing. Pieces finished in this manner are described as silver-gilt, and if gilded only in part are termed parcel-gilt.

German Silver From the sixteenth century for a period of about two hundred years German silversmiths were to the fore in making ceremonial cups, which influenced the design of those made in other countries. These objects, made mostly for display, took varied forms and were usually provided with covers. Some of them are classified into types: the *Traubenpokal* resembling a bunch of grapes, the *Akleibecher* or 'Columbine Cup' with a likeness to the Columbine flower or *aquilegia*, and the *Munzpokal* inset with coins. Outstanding are the cups modelled as animals which, like the foregoing, were copied extensively in the nineteenth century. In the eighteenth century and later, German silver mostly followed French patterns, and although of good craftsmanship most of it is not of especially distinctive design.

Hall-marks Marks certifying the purity of the metal on which they were stamped were introduced in the year 1300. From 1363 it was further required that the maker should add his own mark, and by the mid-sixteenth century a system had evolved that remains in operation. It comprises the heraldic lion passant guaranteeing the standard of the silver; a date letter, changed annually, so that the wardens responsible for assay can be traced in case of complaint; a hall-mark, a leopard's head for London, an anchor for Birmingham, etc., varying according to which assay office tested the article; and, between 1784 and 1890, the sovereign's head to denote that duty had been paid. Between 1697 and 1720 the Britannia standard replaced the Sterling standard, and special marks were required to indicate the fact. The system of date letters comprised twenty letters of the alphabet (J, U, W, X, Y and Z were not employed), so that an 'A' would be re-used every twenty years. To prevent confusion, the style of each alphabet was altered and the shape of the outline of the punch also varied, but despite these aids ambiguities arise especially when marks are worn. There was no uniformity in the letters used at the various offices, each alphabet varying in character as well as in the year during which it began to be stamped. The system is difficult to explain fully, but it worked well, and although it was instituted to safeguard the buyer and prevent fraud it had a secondary role in aiding the collector. Following only brief experience, there should be little or no difficulty in accurately dating the majority of specimens normally encountered. It may be noted that up to 1790 there was confusion as to which among the numerous small articles needed to be assayed, stamped and have duty levied on them. In that year it was ordered that anything weighing under 5 dwt. should be exempt, and could be sold bearing no mark or just that of the maker. However there were a few exceptions that were of insignificant weight but which had to conform to the rules for heavier pieces.

They were:

Mounts for bottles in cruet frames.
Buttons and certain types of studs.
Bottle tickets (now known as Wine-labels).

Silver; Methods, Materials, Factories and Articles (Continued)

Patch boxes.
Salt spoons, ladles and shovels.
Tea strainers and caddy spoons.
'Pieces to garnish Cabinets or Knife Cases, or Tea Chests [caddies], or Bridles, or Stands, or Frames'.

In theory, all the above should have the appropriate full set of marks, but in practice they sometimes bear only the maker's mark or a lion passant or nothing at all. Date letters, makers' marks and other marks are fully described and illustrated in *English Goldsmiths and Their Marks*, by Sir Charles James Jackson (second edition 1921, but reprinted in 1949 and later). The date letters only may be found in an inexpensive pocket-sized booklet, *British Assay Office Marks*. See Britannia Standard; Duty; Sterling Standard.

Honey Pot Pots in the shape of woven straw beehives (skeps) were made between about 1790 and 1825, many of them with a finial in the form of a bee.

Ice Pail Ice pails, alternatively known as wine coolers, were made from about 1700. They were normally sold in pairs,

Inkstand with chased auricular decoration in the manner of Christian van Vianen. It bears the London date letter for 1639. Christie's.

Silver; Methods, Materials, Factories and Articles (Continued)

but sometimes in longer sets, and each had a detachable collar and inner liner so that the ice cooled the wine-bottle without coming into direct contact with it.

Indian Silver Most Indian-made silverware is below Sterling standard, ranging between 800 and 900 parts of the pure metal in a thousand. A number of English craftsmen worked in Calcutta, Madras, Bombay and elsewhere, supplying goods in English style to English residents, some of the makers establishing large workshops staffed by trained natives. Marks approximating to those current in England were used, but apart from showing the name or initials of the maker so that he may be identified they have no other significance.

Inkstand Inkstands, or standishes, date from the early decades of the seventeenth century, one of the first being an example of 1630 fitted with an inkwell, pounce pot with sand for blotting ink and roughening parchment, and a box for holding wafers used in sealing letters (Museum of Fine Arts, Boston, Massachusetts). In the mid-century there was a fashion for low rectangular lidded caskets holding the essential accessories, the whole article raised on feet and sometimes with a carrying-handle on the top. This last variety is often referred to as a Treasury inkstand, because a number of them were issued to the Treasury by the Jewel House in 1686. In the early eighteenth century a further type became fashionable, with the inkwell and pounce pot, sometimes accompanied by a wafer box, arranged on a shaped tray and occasionally completed with a small bell. The tray variety endured in one form or another, with a solid or a pierced gallery, with silver or cut glass fittings, down to the days when the universal possession of fountain- and ball-pens made the inkstand superfluous.

Irish Silver Silver was fashioned in Ireland in ancient times, but it was not until the seventeenth century that the craft was established on any scale. Surviving examples generally date from the Georgian period, with most pieces following English models. A few articles were a speciality of Irish silversmiths, although it cannot be said that they were the exclusive makers. Such pieces include the so-called strawberry dishes, and dish- or potato-rings. Manufacture was carried on at several towns, some of which had their own marks, but the assay office was at Dublin.

Italian Silver The silversmiths of Rome who had been active from early times, reorganized themselves in 1509, built a church in the city and dedicated it to their patron, St. Eligius. The Renaissance coincided with this event, and the craftsmen embodied features of the new style in the objects they made for ecclesiastical and secular use. Many of the latter were for the numerous foreigners visiting the city from time to time, who took back with them their purchases to be admired and imitated. Later Roman silver followed rather than initiated styles: baroque, rococo and neo-classical being employed with local modifications. In addition to the range of objects made elsewhere, those for religious use included holy water stoups, *cartagloria* frames and crucifixes. Other Italian cities also had their silversmiths, whose quality of workmanship was not invariably as high as at Rome and whose styles of ornament were not usually as up-to-date. Turin was strongly influenced by France; Genoa made a speciality of filigree work but also produced goods in other techniques; Venice often followed English styles, and Naples became noted for pairs of vases filled with flowers, all in silver or silver-gilt.

Silver; Methods, Materials, Factories and Articles (Continued)

Jug Pairs of jugs, differing little in appearance from flagons, were made from about 1700 onwards. In fact, it seems to be modern practice to call a jug a flagon if it was made prior to that date, as well as to refer to it as a ewer if it is, or was, accompanied by a basin. The eighteenth-century jugs were made with and without domed covers, and usually have pear-shaped bodies on squat moulded bases, short spouts, and scrolling handles. Often they were termed beer jugs, which is apparently confirmed by the presence on some of ornament including barley and hops. Most examples, however, bear a minimum of decoration apart from an engraved coat of arms, and their original use remains uncertain.

Kettle As eighteenth-century teapots were of small size they required frequent re-filling with hot water. The large kettle complete with a charcoal-burner or a spirit-lamp and a stand provided the answer. In general shape and decoration the teapot was the inspiration, although the larger surface to be covered was a challenge sometimes accepted by the chaser who gave vent to his imagination. A few kettles were made complete with a tripod stand, all of silver, of which there are examples in the Victoria and Albert Museum, London, and the Metropolitan Museum of Art (Untermyer Collection), New York.

Kovsch The *kovsch* is a Russian ladle with a boat-shaped body and a short handle at one end. Examples exist in silver and gold and some are elaborately decorated with chasing, enamel and other ornament.

Kwabornament See Auricular Style.

Ladle The familiar type of ladle with a bowl and a curved handle dates from the first decades of the eighteenth century. They were often made to accompany sauce boats; later they were given handles matching the patterns of table silver. Large-sized examples were for serving soup, and others were for punch; the latter

Late nineteenth-century Russian silver kovsch *ornamented with* cloisonné *enamel.* Phillips.

type usually having a handle of twisted whalebone, silver-tipped at the top, and a shaped silver bowl inset in the base with a coin. Late in the eighteenth century small ladles with pierced bowls were made for serving sugar. See *Kovsch.*

De Lamerie Paul de Lamerie (1688–1751) was born in the Netherlands and came to England with his parents in 1689. He served an apprenticeship to a silversmith and recorded his own mark in 1712, becoming the leading maker of his time. Lamerie's work is invariably of high quality as regards finish, and he did not spare metal in its production.

Livery Pot See Flagon.

Marrow Scoop The marrow scoop was a double-ended channelled implement for scooping the marrow out of bones. They were made from sometime in the first half of the eighteenth century, and the number of surviving examples proves the popularity of eating the delicacy.

Mazarine A flat oval strainer to rest in a dish for meat or fish, allowing gravy or other liquid to run through. How it acquired its name is uncertain, but it would appear to have no connexion with the French statesman, Cardinal Mazarin. The mazarine was made from the last years of the seventeenth century, and some examples are attractively pierced and engraved with fishes and nets.

Meissonnier Juste-Aurèle Meissonnier (1675–1750) was born at Turin, Italy, but spent the major part of his life in France. He combined the talents of an architect with those of a painter, sculptor and silversmith, and was an early and influential exponent of the rococo style. His published designs, issued in about 1745, include some for silverware, among them an exuberant suite of a table centrepiece and two tureens designed and made for an Englishman, the Duke of Kingston, in 1735.

Miniatures Miniature copies of everyday silver articles made mainly between the 1680s and the 1750s have been recorded. Only a small proportion is fully marked and thus can be precisely dated. In the nineteenth century quantities of miniatures, not only of objects like teapots and tankards but of horses and carts, sledges and sedan chairs, were exported from the Netherlands. Many of them were made from sheet silver decorated with raised patterns bearing no relation to the finished articles.

Molinet See Chocolate pot.

Monteith An account written in 1683 provides positive evidence of the purpose of the monteith. It reads:

> This yeare in the summer-time came up a vessel or bason notched at the brim to let drinking vessels hang there by the foot, so that the body or drinking place might hang into the water to cool them. Such a bason was called a Monteigh from a fantasticall Scott called Monsieur Monteigh who at that time or a little before wore the bottome of his cloake or coate so notched: U U U U .

The monteith resembled a punch bowl, but with a scalloped rim, the latter sometimes being made removable. In this way the vessel was given a dual role and might be employed as a cooler or for punch, at will. Recorded examples date from the early 1680s and they were seldom made after about 1730.

Mounts In the fifteenth and sixteenth centuries it was not unusual for any esteemed curiosity to be given silver or

Silver; Methods, Materials, Factories and Articles (Continued)

silver-gilt mounts. They not only enhanced its appearance but often converted it into an article of use rather than merely an ornament, although it is doubtful that any of them were actually used. Chinese porcelain was especially favoured in this way, the earliest example being a vase of about 1300 which was turned into a ewer by means of enamelled silver-gilt mounts about fifty years after it was made (National Museum of Ireland, Dublin, although the mounts are now missing). The earliest piece with English mounts is a bowl presented to New College, Oxford, in 1516, and the earliest hall-marked specimen is a jug of 1550 (Museum of Fine Arts, Boston, Massachusetts). Pottery, ostrich eggs, coconuts, rock crystal, jasper, and nautilus shells were likewise treated. Occasionally, silver mounts are found on objects such as knife boxes and tea caddies and, very rarely, on larger articles. See Furniture.

Mug Mugs, holding about a half-pint of liquid, date from the late seventeenth century. Their shapes varied; straight-sided, pear-shaped or round-bottomed with a low foot, and occasionally others are met with. They continued to be made throughout the eighteenth and nineteenth centuries, in the latter of which they were commonly presented as christening gifts. Many good plain mugs have been given chased ornament at a later date, and others have had spouts added to convert them into jugs.

Mustard Pot Mustard was often used in its dry powdered form in the seventeenth and eighteenth centuries, and it is conjectured that unpierced or blind casters from those times were employed for the dry variety. Lidded squat pots date from the 1720s, often being shaped like a small tankard, and by the end of the century they were oval with pierced sides and blue glass liners. They were for wet mustard.

Nef The nef took the form of a ship, and was used at the table for display or as a salt. They were made in Germany, France and other countries, but none has so far been recorded as of English origin. A typical example is the Burghley nef (formerly at Burghley House, Northamptonshire, but now in the Victoria and Albert Museum), which is of parcel-gilt silver with the hull formed from a nautilus shell. It bears the Paris mark for 1482. Old nefs are very few in number, and their ranks have been greatly swelled by numerous examples made in Victorian times that usually look more aged than they are.

Netherlands Silver Up to the end of the sixteenth century Netherlands silversmiths produced little that differed appreciably from wares made in Germany and elsewhere. During the seventeenth century, however, there came to the fore a group of craftsmen whose work was outstanding, and was well received in England. The most important was Christiaen van Vianen (1598–?1666), member of a talented family of silversmiths from Utrecht. Christiaen became an exponent of the so-called auricular style, and by 1630 had come to the attention of Charles I. He would seem to have resided in England between 1633 and 1647 and again for a few years after 1662. His commissions included one in 1634 to supply a set of altar plate for St. George's Chapel, Windsor, but in the troubled times of the Civil War it disappeared. Some other pieces of his workmanship have been recorded, but they are few in number. An interesting feature of van Vianen's English work is that it does not bear hall-marks, only his engraved signature, probably because he enjoyed Royal patronage. In

Silver; Methods, Materials, Factories and Articles (Continued)

1650 Christiaen van Vianen published a volume of engravings of designs made by his father Adam (1565?–1627), which increased the family's reputation and spread knowledge of the style they had played a major part in developing. See Auricular Style; *Brandewijnkom*; Wager Cups.

Newcastle upon Tyne Silversmiths were working at Newcastle in the thirteenth century, but the earliest recorded examples of local craftsmanship are dated some four hundred years later. An early assay office did not endure, in 1702 another was established and this closed in 1884. The town mark took the form of three castles set in a shield; the castles being single castellated towers, set two above a single one, they are not easily confused with the marks of Exeter and Edinburgh.

Niello *Niello* was an amalgam of sulphur, lead, silver and copper used as a filling in engraved work. After being applied, it was melted and the excess polished away to leave the design in black contrasting with the shining silver. Niello was much used in Russia in the nineteenth century for decorating boxes and other objects.

Nutmeg Grater The nutmeg, a spice imported from the East, was much favoured for adding to beverages in the seventeenth and eighteenth centuries. For this purpose the hard nut had to be powdered, and a small grater, with a compartment to contain the nut also, was often carried in the pocket. Specimens of the grater have survived from the time of Charles II onwards, and take a diversity of forms, some of them additionally incorporating a corkscrew.

Parcel-gilding See Gold and Gilding.

Pap Boat The pap boat was used for feeding a child, and was a small oval bowl elongated at one end to form a lip. It was made between about 1710 and 1830, and while most were quite plain some were given ornamental rims and other decoration. It is not unknown for pap boats to have been given feet and a handle in order to convert them into more saleable sauce boats.

Pipe Silver pipes for smoking tobacco are known to have been made occasionally during the seventeenth and eighteenth centuries, their bowls following the pattern of contemporaneous clay pipes. It is understood that, contrary to expectation, the silver pipe gives a satisfactory smoke and the bowl does not get unduly hot. That useful accessory, the pipe stopper was also made of silver, sometimes resembling a seal but also in the form of a finger ring bearing a raised button for packing down the tobacco in the small bowls used in the past.

Pomander A small container for per-

French early seventeenth-century enamelled silver-gilt pomander, the sections each engraved with the name of the aromatic herb it was intended to contain.
Parke-Bernet Galleries, New York.

Silver; Methods, Materials, Factories and Articles (Continued)

fume or spices which was suspended either from a necklace or a girdle. They were usually fancifully designed and often took the form of a segmented globe, each segment sometimes engraved with the name of its contents. Such pomanders were made in Germany, France and the Netherlands between about 1550 and 1650. After an interval, their place was taken by the vinaigrette.

Porringer See Cup.

Portuguese Silver Much ecclesiastical silver is to be seen in Portuguese cathedrals and churches, but marking was haphazard and precise dating is not always possible. One of the most striking examples is the Belem monstrance, made in 1506 from gold brought back from India by the navigator, Vasco da Gama (Museo de Arte Antigua, Lisbon). Some surviving dishes of the fifteenth/sixteenth centuries, bearing Lisbon and Oporto marks, show that bold chasing was a favoured form of decoration, examples being bordered with distinctive studs and studded bosses. Later articles follow varied European trends in design, with variations to suit local tastes. After the Duke of Wellington had driven the French army out of Portugal in 1808, the Portuguese decided to present the Duke with a large dinner service as an expression of their gratitude to him. Fifty-five boxes containing the service were landed in England in 1816, and their contents may be seen at the Wellington Museum, Apsley House, London. The service is in the then-fashionable classical style, the centrepiece, depicting the Continents thanking Victory, standing on a plateau 7·84 metres in length which is peopled with dancing nymphs as well as being fitted with candelabra.

Potato Ring See Dish Ring.

Punch Bowl The drinking of punch began after Charles II came to the throne in 1660, and bowls made purposely for serving it survive from the 1680s. They vary in their decoration, some have covers and some have two handles. In diameter they range from 30 to 45 cm., and a number of the bowls have removable notched rims to convert them into monteiths. Silver punch bowls were supplanted from the mid-eighteenth century by the importation of increasing numbers of Chinese porcelain examples, which were less expensive and although breakable had the attraction of being colourful.

Quaich The quaich is a Scottish shallow-bowled drinking vessel with two flat handles, not unlike the French *écuelle* but without a cover. It was often made of wooden staves in the manner of a barrel, and some silver ones are engraved in simulation of this construction. Surviving silver quaichs date from the seventeenth century onwards.

Reed-and-tie A pattern in imitation of reed stalks tied at intervals with ribbon often used as a border on plates, dishes, etc., in the later eighteenth century.

Revere Paul Revere (1735–1818) born at Boston, Massachusetts, is probably the best-remembered American silversmith, although he did not confine his craftsmanship to that metal. He worked also as a copperplate engraver, and as part of his activities as a patriot was responsible for building a gunpowder mill. He was given a posthumous fame by the poet Longfellow, who wrote of Revere's ride from Charlestown to Lexington in April 1775, to warn of the coming of British troops from Boston. Poetic licence romanticized the event so that the poem is less than accurate, but the silversmith-horseman is an American legend along with George Washington

Silver; Methods, Materials, Factories and Articles (Continued)

and Buffalo Bill. Numerous examples of Paul Revere's silverware have been preserved. They include a set of six tankards bought in 1772 by the Third Church of Brookfield, Massachusetts (Henry Francis du Pont Winterthur Museum, Delaware), other pieces of greater and lesser importance and interest in American museums, and a small gold urn made by Revere in 1800 to contain a lock of George Washington's hair presented by his widow to the Grand Lodge of Massachusetts and still in the ownership of the Lodge.

Salt and saltcellar Salt was expensive in the past, and because it was known to be beneficial to health it was treated with respect. For use at the table, it was placed in elaborate silver and silver-gilt containers, some of such complex pattern that it might trouble a guest to find the contents. Some salts were made with covers, and others were topped by upright legs to support a linen napkin. The more modern variety of salt container, the small open saltcellar, began to appear in the seventeenth century. It varied in shape but had a central depression; being known as a trencher salt because it was placed beside the dish or trencher instead of in the centre of the table as was the standing salt. Other names for the same or similar articles are table salts and saltcellars, all of which followed current styles throughout the eighteenth and nineteenth centuries.

Salver A small flat dish with a low border, with or without one or more feet, is known as a salver or waiter, the terms being interchangeable. According to a description printed in 1661, the salver is '. . . broad and flat, with a foot underneath, and is used in giving Beer, or other liquid thing to save the Carpit or Cloathes from drops'. They survive from the mid-seventeenth century, with plain or ornamented borders, round, trefoil, octafoil and semi-rectangular, these last being neither round nor square but a combination of both. Many bear engraved armorials of varied elaboration, the outstanding example being the Walpole Salver (Victoria and Albert Museum); measuring 45 cm. in width it is more accurately termed a tray. Salver or tray, it was made in 1728 by Paul de Lamerie from the Exchequer Seal of the Chancellor, Sir Robert Walpole, and the engraving is attributed to William Hogarth.

Sauce Boat and Sauce Tureen Sauce boats were first made in about 1720, when they were oval in shape with a handle at each side and a pouring lip at either end. After about 1730 they were given a single lip with a handle at the opposite end, but as before the base was oval and moulded. Ten years later this last type was more usually supported on feet, often in the form of short cabriole legs with lions' paw terminations comparable to furniture of the time. The bowl was frequently plain until the rococo style became general, after which cast and chased ornament was common. From 1765, the neo-classical style affected the sauce boat by transforming it into a tureen with cover and stand, usually a miniature of the soup tureen and matching other pieces of a dinner service. In the nineteenth century earlier types were copied.

Saucepan The silver saucepan is often referred to as a brandy pan, but it is probable that its use was not limited to the heating of spirits. Most surviving examples are of eighteenth century make, have wooden handles, and can be with or without pouring-lips and covers.

Scandinavian Silver Scandinavian silversmiths were largely influenced by French and German work. In the eighteenth

Silver; Methods, Materials, Factories and Articles (Continued)

century a two-handled bowl for drinking spirits, of a type similar to the Netherlands *brandewijnkom*, was popular; in Sweden it was known as a *dopskal*, in Norway as an *oreskaal* and in Denmark as an *orekovsken*. The best-known pieces are the lidded tankards dating from the seventeenth century, which were often purchased by visitors to Scandinavia and taken back to their homes as souvenirs. The tankards have cylindrical bodies supported on three feet, the latter sometimes in the form of partly-opened pomegranates, while the lids are inset with a contemporaneous coin. A variant, the peg tankard is of similar appearance, but with a series of short pegs fitted down one side of the interior. The user was required to drink until the liquid was exactly even with a peg, with over- or under-drinking leading to a forfeit.

Early eighteenth-century Swedish silver tankard, the lid inset with a coin and the feet and thumb-piece in the form of pomegranates.

Sconce A sconce, known alternatively and more descriptively as a wall-light or wall-candlestick, was a candle holder with a backplate of silver to act as a reflector. Sconces were usually supplied in sets of four or more. Although they are known to have been in existence during the reign of Henry VIII, the earliest surviving examples date from the second half of the seventeenth century. The silver backplate was often given chased decoration, sometimes with a central engraved coat of arms. Alternatively, the arms were cast and affixed with bolts and nuts.

Scottish Silver Most Scottish silver of early date was melted by order of Mary Queen of Scots in the late 1560s, the solid baptismal font sent to her by Queen Elizabeth I of England being included. Surviving early seventeenth-century examples include a number of racing trophies, but from the mid-century onwards more has been preserved. Most pieces show a similarity to those being made at the time across the Border, but with differences in design and ornament to distinguish them. From 1485 the Edinburgh silversmiths appointed a deacon and a searcher to supervise the craft and ordered suitable marks to be stamped on work. The marks were to include not only that of the maker but also one for the deacon, as well as a date letter and a town mark. In addition to the principal assay office at Edinburgh, silver was stamped also at Canongate (now incorporated in the capital city), Glasgow, Aberdeen, Dundee and a few other places.

Scratched Weight See Weights.

Seal Box The large wax seal attached to an important document was often given the protection of a silver box. The box usually bore on its lid a chased or engraved representation of the seal it contained. While most seals were circular, some were oval or otherwise formed and the shapes of the boxes varied accordingly.

Sheffield An assay office was opened in

Silver; Methods, Materials, Factories and Articles (Continued)

Sheffield in 1773, in the same year as that at Birmingham. The mark used was, and remains, a crown, which was sometimes stamped from a punch bearing also the date letter. This practice of a single mark in place of two was confined in England to the Sheffield silversmiths.

Skewer Early eighteenth-century meat skewers were of rectangular section and tapering, with a ring or other handle. By the 1780s they had become diamond-shape in section with terminals similar to earlier examples. Nowadays they seldom, if ever, appear at the dining-table, but make very useful letter-openers. As well as meat skewers some 35 to 40 cm. in length, there were smaller ones about 15 cm. long for game.

Snuff Box The habit of taking snuff was at first satisfied by each person grating his own tobacco. By the late seventeenth century the ready-ground article, snuff, was on sale and boxes were made to contain it for carrying in a pocket. Many were made of tortoiseshell, sea-shell and other materials in silver mounts or wholly of silver ornamented with chasing or engraving. Others were of solid gold, set with precious stones, enamelled or otherwise ornamented. The most lavish of these last were of French make, but fine examples were also produced in Germany, England and other countries.

Snuffers Prior to about 1820 candles had wicks which were not self-consuming. They curled over as they burned and quickly caused guttering with its accompanying flow of hot wax and cloud of black smoke. It was essential for such candles to have their wicks trimmed at regular intervals, and for this purpose a scissors-like snuffer was employed. They differed from a conventional scissors only in having a small box on one of the blades, in which the cut-off ends of wick were contained. A pair bearing the arms of Henry VIII and the Archbishop of York has survived, and a mid-sixteenth-century pair is in the Victoria and Albert Museum. Those dating from about 1700 are less rare and sometimes retain their original stands. Usually the stands are flat with or without a handle on one side, but between about 1685 and 1725 there was a fashion for pedestal stands to hold the snuffers upright.

Soap Box The eighteenth-century ball of soap, or wash ball, was sometimes given a silver container. This was of spherical shape raised on a moulded foot.

Spanish Silver The most spectacular Spanish silver was made for use in cathedrals and churches. An example is the *custodia* (monstrance) commissioned in 1501 for Leon cathedral, which took twenty-one years to complete, stood 2 metres in height and was melted down in 1809 to help in vanquishing Napoleon's forces. Secular pieces were made, and followed shapes and styles common elsewhere in Europe. French craftsmen came to Spain following the accession to the throne in 1700 of Philip V, who was a grandson of Louis XIV. The principal silversmithing centre was Madrid.

Spoons Spoons are among the oldest surviving examples of silverware, the Coronation Spoon (Westminster Abbey) dating to the twelfth century. During the ensuing five hundred years a number of patterns were introduced and became popular. The bowl varied at times between round and fig-shape, but the greatest variations were in the knop; the termination of the handle. The best-known comprise figures of the Master and twelve

Silver; Methods, Materials, Factories and Articles (Continued)

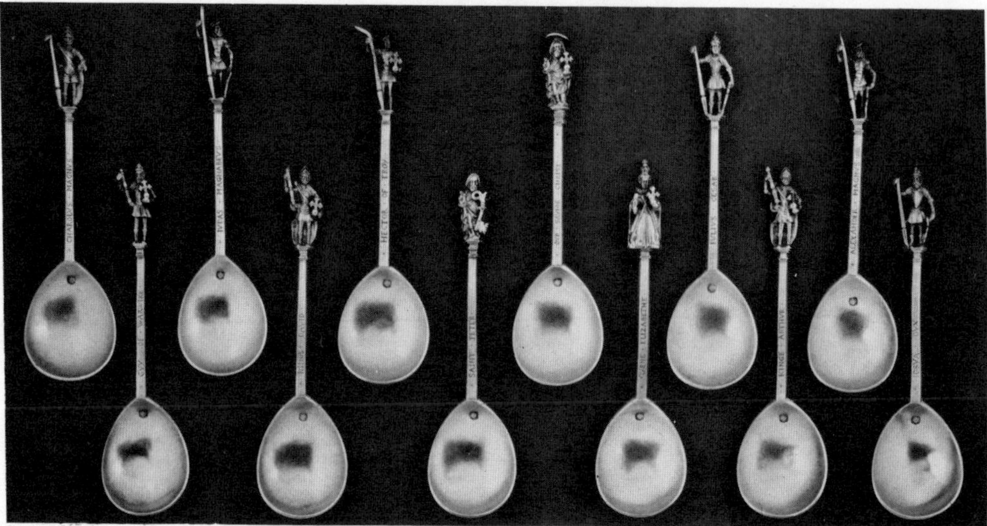

Set of silver-gilt spoons with their tops modelled as the Nine Worthies of Christendom and Queen Elizabeth I, Saint Peter and Christ. They are stamped with the date letter for 1592. Christie's.

Apostles, of which a few complete sets are recorded. Other knops, of which the names are mostly self-explanatory include:

Buddha
Diamond Point
Dog-nose
Lion sejant—a lion seated.
Seal top—a circular flat top.
Slip top—the end cut off at an angle.
Trefid—with two notches in the rounded top.
Wavy—like the foregoing but not notched.
Wrythen—in the form of a sphere spirally fluted.

Eighteenth- and nineteenth-century patterns, many of which remain in production, include:

Fiddle—in outline resembling that of a violin.
Threaded Fiddle—as above, but with a narrow moulded border.
Hanoverian—broadening and rounded at the top where it thickens and turns upwards, often with a decorative reinforcement in the shape of a so-called rat tail under the bowl.
Old English—similar to the preceding but with the top turned downwards.
King's—cast with a shell within two scrolls and with two anthemions.

Spoons made for particular purposes include the familiar tea, dessert and table spoons. In addition there were the following and others:

Basting spoon—of large size and probably used at the table for serving.
Feeding spoon—with the bowl covered to leave only a small space at the front of the bowl.
Strainer spoon—known also as Mote Spoons, these have the bowl pierced and a pointed knop; the former for straining tea leaves and the latter to clear the strainer inside the teapot.
Salt spoon—with a shovel-shaped or round bowl and small in size.

See Caddy Spoon.

Silver; Methods, Materials, Factories and Articles (Continued)

Spoon Tray Until the mid-eighteenth century tea spoons were accommodated in a small dish or tray, usually oval in shape and sometimes with a scalloped rim.

Sterling Standard Sterling silver contains not less than 11 oz. 2 dwt. of fine silver with 18 dwt. of alloy in every 12 oz. of gross weight. The standard was first established by Edward I in the year 1300.

Stirrup Cup Silver stirrup cups, to contain a drink taken while on horseback prior to a day's sport, were made from the 1760s. Some were in the shape of a fox's mask realistically engraved, others represent a greyhound's head and rare examples are in the form of the head of a hare.

Storr Paul Storr (1771–1844) was born in London, son of a silver chaser, and spent his working life in the capital. He served an apprenticeship to a silversmith, and in 1796 set up his own workshop in Air Street, Piccadilly, removing in 1807 to Dean Street, Soho. Storr had for some years been working for the Royal silversmiths, Rundell, Bridge & Rundell, of Ludgate Hill, and in 1811 became a partner in the firm. Rundell's clientele included not only George IV but many noblemen and persons of wealth and position in London and the provinces, so that Storr's workshop was kept fully occupied. The taste of the day was for large pieces in the classical style, often gilt, and the comparative elegance of preceding decades was shunned. A prominent architect and designer wrote in 1806 of 'massiveness, the principal character of good plate', and for the remainder of the century most of the silverware produced satisfied this criterion. The quality of pieces marked with Storr's initials is invariably high, whether they were made purely for display or for everyday use. In 1820 Paul Storr resigned from Rundell's, and after acquiring a new workshop, formed a partnership with James Mortimer in order to retail his productions from premises in New Bond Street. Storr & Mortimer became Mortimer & Hunt following Storr's retirement in 1838, and eventually changed to Hunt & Roskell.

Soup tureen, cover and stand made by Paul Storr in 1807. It is modelled with Egyptian and other motifs in the current Regency style and weighs altogether more than 300 oz. Sotheby's.

Strainer Various kinds of strainers were made at different times. They include those for lemons and oranges, as well as mote spoons for straining tea leaves. The former were in existence by the sixteenth century, an inventory of 1533 listing 'A strayner of golde for orrenges'. The few examples surviving from the years before 1700 have a single tubular handle, but those of later date were given two flat handles that were often scrolled and ornamented.

Strawberry Dish Circular dishes with scalloped edges ranging in diameter from about 10 to 25 cm. are commonly termed strawberry dishes, although they doubtless had numerous uses. The dishes were made during much of the eighteenth century, many of them bearing the marks of Irish silversmiths.

Sugar Basin The sugar basin or bowl was usually provided with a lid and was first made at the end of the seventeenth century. The early examples were topped by a knob, but later the lid was given a circular raised rim in the centre of the top. It was thus reversible, standing on its rim and perhaps serving as a spoon tray. While many of the basins and lids were circular in form, some especially attractive octagonal ones are known. Alternatively, sugar was kept in a box or casket, frequently oval in shape and decorated with chased ornament, dating from about 1660–80. Similar boxes were made in America for some years afterwards. A century later sugar was brought to the table in an open basket with a hinged handle.

Sugar Tongs The earliest contrivance for handling sugar was a miniature version of a pair of fire tongs, the hinged turned arms ending in hollowed oval grips. From about 1715 a version resembling scissors was made, with the arms shaped as a series of scrolls, the grips often modelled as shells, and the hinge a convenient surface for engraving with initials, a crest or a coat of arms. A variant was modelled as a stork, its long beak being well adapted to its purpose. These scissors kinds are generally referred to as sugar nippers, and were supplanted from about 1770 by tongs with straight arms joined to an arched springy back. The arms were occasionally elaborately pierced, or were more often engraved with bright cut ornament.

Sweetmeat Dish Small dishes for holding sweetmeats were made from the early seventeenth century onwards. Some of them have two handles and closely resemble wine tasters. Baskets or small bowls with swing handles were in use from the eighteenth century, some of them being suspended from the arms of epergnes. Others, without handles, have sometimes been parted from such centrepieces, but were also made separately.

Tankard The lidded tankard is known to have existed from at least the fourteenth century, but the earliest recorded survivor dates from the reign of Elizabeth I. Most existing examples were made after the Restoration, when the majority were of plain cylindrical form, with a flat lid and a decorated thumbpiece by which to raise it. Some examples were supported on squat feet, while most had their bases edged with mouldings. In the second quarter of the eighteenth century the lid became domed, and the base of the body curved inwards above a spreading circular foot.

Taper Box A coiled wax taper for melting sealing wax was contained in a cylindrical box, sometimes forming one of the items on an inkstand but occasionally found separately. Alternatively, the coil could be accommodated on the upright post of a taper stand, which also held a scissors-like grip to hold the wax vertical. Other taper stands had the post set horizontally but the grip operated in a similar manner. These two latter types are sometimes referred to as wax-jackets.

Taper Stick The taper stick was a

Silver; Methods, Materials, Factories and Articles (Continued)

Engraved silver tea and coffee service made in 1856 by the London firm of Barnard.

miniature candlestick holding a small-sized candle, used at the writing desk for melting sealing wax. It was made from the late seventeenth century onwards and follows the patterns of full-sized examples.

Tea Caddy Containers for tea leaves began to be made early in the eighteenth century. They were at first termed 'cannisters', the term caddy being adopted in due course from the Malay *kati*: a weight of about 1 1/5 lb., by which tea was sold in the East. Caddies varied in form like all other silverwares, the earlier examples being often of rectangular shape with circular domed lids. They were sometimes supplied in twos or threes for holding different teas, each being engraved with the name of the variety, and were provided with a fitted polished wood or shagreen-covered box. Mid-eighteenth century caddies were of rococo form, chased and engraved with Chinese ornament, while later ones bore bright-cut decoration and were fitted with small locks.

Teapot Tea and tea-drinking were introduced into England in the first half of the seventeenth century. In 1658 an advertisement announced:

> That excellent and by all Physitians approved China Drink called by the Chineans Tcha, by other nations Tay, alias Tee, is sold at the Sultaness Head, a cophee-house in Sweeting Rents, by the Royal Exchange.

Two years later, Samuel Pepys noted in his diary: 'I did send for a cup of tea, a China drink, of which I never drunk before'. The earliest existing teapot bears the date letter for 1670, and if an inscription engraved on it did not state the purpose for which it was used it would be mistaken for a coffee pot. It stands 34 cm. in height, has a tapering cylindrical body and domed cover, while the handle is set at a right-angle to the spout (Victoria and Albert Museum). Examples that are indisputably teapots survive from the early years of the eighteenth century, and in the following

Silver; Methods, Materials, Factories and Articles (Continued)

decades, although they varied in shape and ornament, they were invariably of small size. As the cost of tea decreased, so it was used in larger quantities and the pot was of greater capacity. The vessels reflect successive changes in style, and in numerous homes over a long period the silver teapot was regarded with the highest esteem.

Tea Set Matching services of teapot, milk jug, sugar basin and other items were first made in the early eighteenth century, but were uncommon before about 1775. Then, they sometimes included a coffee pot and an urn, and occasionally a tray. During Victoria's reign the teaset reached the peak of its popularity.

Thimble The earliest surviving gold, silver, and silver-gilt thimbles date from about 1700, although they are recorded as having existed long before. They continued to be made in the eighteenth and nineteenth centuries, but can seldom be dated with precision as their small size and light weight exempted them from hall-marking.

Toasted Cheese Dish A dinner-time savoury of cheese grilled on toast was prepared and served sometimes in a silver dish especially made for the purpose. It took the form of a rectangular tray holding six or eight small removable pans and often was fitted with a container for hot water to keep the contents warm. It had a lid and a handle, and one particularly appealing example, dated 1804, has small figures of mice reaching up at each corner.

Toasting Fork Forks on which bread might be toasted in front of an open fire have existed since at least the time of Elizabeth I. Surviving examples vary both in date and design; the prongs being two or more in number and sometimes being hinged. The handles were made of silver tubes to telescope conveniently when not in use, or of turned wood.

Toast Rack The toast rack came into use in the late eighteenth century. It was often constructed with wire divisions, the central one with a ring handle on top. Others were cast with patterns.

Tobacco Box See Snuff Box.

Toilet Service Sets of silver and silver-gilt articles for use at the dressing table survive from the late seventeenth century. These, and others of later date, varied in their contents which numbered from ten to thirty items. They included a framed looking-glass with a strut support, rectangular and circular lidded boxes, brush-backs, scent container, jewel caskets and pin cushions. Probably all the sets formerly had their own fitted cases for use when travelling, but in the majority of instances these only survive with sets dating from the mid-eighteenth century onwards. From the 1760's many of the articles were made of glass, cut and mounted in silver.

Toys The old meaning of this was a trifle, not necessarily a child's plaything, and such luxuries as silver- and gold-mounted seals and scent bottles would be described as toys.

Tray The tray grew from the salver and is a larger version of the latter, usually with handles by which to carry it.

Trowel A silver or gilt trowel was used for the ceremonial laying of foundation stones. The custom dates from the early nineteenth century, and examples were engraved with details of the occasion.

Tumbler Silver tumblers gained their name from their rounded bases, which returned them to an upright position if they

Silver; Methods, Materials, Factories and Articles (Continued)

were tipped over. Many were awarded as prizes at cock-fighting contests and horse races, and they were made from about 1660 until the end of the eighteenth century.

Vase Large decorative vases were fashionable during the late seventeenth century. They served as alternatives to those made of Chinese porcelain or European pottery, being decorated with chasing and engraving instead of with painting in colours. The purpose of the silver vases would seem to have been purely decorative.

Van Vianen See Netherlands Silver.

Vinaigrette A small lidded box with an inner pierced cover under which was a sponge soaked in an aromatic liquid. The vinaigrette came into use during the last quarter of the eighteenth century and was a revival of the Elizabethan pomander. The boxes were variously decorated, some with views of familiar buildings such as Windsor Castle, and many were made in Birmingham. Their vogue lasted for about a hundred years.

Wager Cup These frequently take the form of the figure of a woman holding aloft a cup which swings freely. The woman's skirt also forms a cup, and both containers had to be drained in order to win the wager. A seventeenth century English example is recorded and was copied at a later date, but they were much more popular in Germany and the Netherlands.

Waiter See Salver.

Wall-light See Sconce.

Warming Pan The circular warming pan, with a hinged pierced cover and a long wooden handle, was usually made of brass or copper. A few silver examples have survived from the late seventeenth/early eighteenth century, and perhaps it is not surprising to learn that Nell Gwynn owned one in 1674.

Warwick Vase The Warwick Vase is of marble, and was discovered in 1770 in a lake near Hadrian's Villa, Rome. A large object, no less than 1·78 metres in diameter, it was purchased by the Earl of Warwick who duly built a special conservatory for it in the grounds of Warwick Castle, where it remains. Small-scale silver copies of the vase were made by Paul Storr from 1812 onwards, a number of them being supplied in pairs for use as ice pails.

Wax-jack See Taper Box.

Weights Silver is weighed according to Troy weight, which is listed below together with its equivalent in grammes.

Pound	Ounces	weights	Grains	Grammes
1	12	240	5,760	373·242
	1	20	480	31·103
		1	24	1·555

In using Troy weight it is the practice to abbreviate pennyweight to *dwt*, and however heavy a specimen may be its weight is never expressed in pounds or *lbs.* It is invariably quoted in ounces and pennyweights (*oz.* and *dwt.*), and in the past the weight of an article was often engraved beneath its base. Such 'scratched weights', as they are termed, are usually greater than the actual weight today, and testify to the industry of butlers, housekeepers and others in polishing away some of the metal in getting a good shine.

Wine Cistern The wine cistern held water, in which were placed bottles of wine for cooling their contents. Examples survive from the late seventeenth century onwards, and others that have subsequently vanished are noted in old documents. They varied in size as in weight, the largest of all

Silver; Methods, Materials, Factories and Articles (Continued)

measuring 1·67 metres in width and weighing over 7,000 oz. It was made in London in 1734, bought by the Empress Anne of Russia, and is now in the Hermitage, Leningrad (copies in the Victoria and Albert Museum, London, and Metropolitan Museum of Art, New York). The cisterns were oval in shape and most of them were raised on moulded low bases, although a few were given four legs. One of the later examples was made for George IV in 1829 (Windsor Castle), and weighs little less than the one in Russia. It was supplied by Rundell, Bridge & Rundell, whose partner, John Bridge, was eager to be present at a Royal dinner. His wish was granted by William IV, and the silversmith was permitted to be in the room 'hid during the dinner behind the great wine cooler'. The same vessel was used in 1842 at the christening of the future Edward VII, when the cistern was filled not with several gallons of Jordan water, but with mulled claret.

Wine Cooler See Ice Pail.

Wine Funnel Surviving examples are seldom of earlier date than the second half of the eighteenth century. The funnels were often fitted with strainers and sometimes had a matching salver, although ornament was seldom more than a gadrooned rim in each instance.

Wine Label The wine label, known in the past as a bottle ticket, came into use in the 1740s. The first examples were of simple outline, often just an oblong engraved with the name of a wine within a ruled border, and fitted with a chain. As the years passed, they increased in variety with crescents, shields and more complex designs, sometimes with the name pierced. During the nineteenth century the labels were occasionally cast or chased with appropriate Bacchic themes, while others were formed as cut-out names or initials. The various patterns have been divided into as many as nineteen distinct varieties, with a twentieth headed 'Miscellaneous' for those not allocated elsewhere. Many of the names found on labels refer to beverages now long out-dated: wines such as Vidonia, Lissa and Masdue, among numerous others. On the other hand, some of the names were deliberately invented to deceive, either in attempts to hoodwink thirsty servants or to mislead prying visitors: thus, gin could be concealed as Cream of the Valley, Old Tom, or more simply as Nig. Similar silver labels, of smaller size than the foregoing and differently engraved, were made for hanging on sauce bottles, and others have been recorded suitably lettered for use with toilet waters.

Wine label cast with vine leaves and grapes and with cut-out lettering for PORT, made in about 1810. Christie's.

Silver; Methods, Materials, Factories and Articles (Continued)

Wine Taster Wine tasters are recorded as having been in existence in the fourteenth century, but surviving specimens are no older than the 1600s. Some English examples exist, and take the form of shallow basins with domed centres against which may be seen the colour of the wine. Small two-handled bowls dating from the late seventeenth century are also sometimes claimed to be wine tasters, but it is no less likely that they were intended to hold sweetmeats. This confusion may have arisen because they bear a resemblance to silver wine tasters made in France and elsewhere.

York As assay office was active in York from the fifteenth century and marks are recorded from 1560 to 1712. Activity apparently recommenced in 1779 and final closure took place in 1858. The mark from 1700 was five lions passant arranged on a cross.

5. COPPER, BRONZE, PEWTER AND OTHER METALS

Africa See Benin.

Agricola Agricola, the Latin form of his surname, was the pen-name of Georg Bauer (1490–1555), a German scholar. He was the author of *De re metallica*, published in 1556, dealing with mining and metallurgy and illustrated with woodcuts. The book has been translated into English.

Ale and Spirit Measure Liquid measures have been made in bronze as well as in copper. The most familiar are the pear-shaped copper ones with tinned interiors, which were made in sets ranging in capacity from five gallons down to a Drop. Most old copper measures date from the nineteenth century, but there are many reproductions on the market made for collectors rather than for serious use.

Ale Warmer Vessels for mulling or warming ale were made in several forms. One is shaped like a boot, the toe part to be put among the burning coals or logs, while others are conical with an iron handle. These last were common in the west of England and earned the name of 'donkey's ears'.

Alms Dish The term applies to dishes, both shallow and deep, which may have been made for collecting alms but were equally suitable for other purposes. The dishes were made of brass embossed with religious and other scenes, and with Gothic lettering. The letters are often only decorative, having no meaning and employed to fill a border instead of scrolls or other motifs. The dishes were made in the late fifteenth century in the area of Nuremberg, Germany.

America Most of the needs of colonists were imported during the first half of the eighteenth century, but a number of men made and repaired metal goods for local clients. Thus, in 1744, John Halden advertised in New York that he made and sold all kinds of copper and brass wares and that he 'gives Ready Money for Old Copper, Brass, Pewter or Lead'. By 1768 Thomas Pugh, 'Brass and Bell-Founder,

Copper, Bronze, Pewter and Other Metals (Continued)

from Birmingham', was also established at New York, and announcing that he 'Makes and casts all sorts of Work in the Brass founding Way'. Pewterers were active at a much earlier date, with the probability that spoons and small objects were being made at Jamestown, Virginia, by 1610. Later in the century, a Londoner, Richard Graves, established himself at Salem, and three others were working at Boston, both places in Massachusetts. Pewter continued to be made until the alloy was replaced by the harder Britannia metal after about 1800, but many of the men who manufactured the new product continued to describe themselves as 'Pewterers'. Cast iron was employed for making stoves, garden furniture and, from about 1850, for complete buildings of up to five storeys. Tinned sheet iron was imported and made into boxes, jugs and other useful articles, which were japanned to make them more decorative while keeping them rustproof. After independence from English rule following the Declaration of 1776, the new United States set about establishing industries to make goods that had hitherto been brought ready-made across the Atlantic. At the same time exploitation began of the vast mineral deposits abounding in many parts of the country.

Andiron Andirons or fire-dogs were used on a flat hearth to support burning logs, and although it is considered that the andiron was the more imposing of the two it is nowadays usual to find the words used interchangeably. The earliest surviving examples date from the fifteenth century and were of iron. In the sixteenth century they were occasionally decorated with silver, and a hundred years later this became less rare. Brass was used most often, sometimes in the form of spheres on the iron uprights, and some rare andirons are decorated with coloured enamels. Sixteenth- and seventeenth-century Italian andirons were cast in bronze with elaborate pedestals supporting figures, while French eighteenth-century metalworkers used ormolu for their variety of dogs (*chenets*) which rise to only a fraction of the height of many others. In America, iron was also used and sometimes embellished with brass. A pair of andirons made by Paul Revere (Metropolitan Museum of Art, New York) is of brass, each supported on a pair of cabriole legs with ball and claw feet above which is a tall shaped column decorated with spiral reeding.

Antimony A metallic mineral sometimes found in its pure state, but for long known in the form of Stibnite: sulphide of antimony. Antimony is alloyed with copper and tin to produce Britannia metal.

Aquamanile An aquamanile, literally a hand-washer, is a water-container, usually of bronze or brass and dating between the twelfth and fifteenth centuries. The aquamanile was employed at the dining table in the days before forks came into use, the diner cleaning his fingers by pouring water over his hands from the vessel into a basin. Most surviving examples are of eccentric design, typical being those in the shape of a lion which pours from its open mouth and has its tail curled to form a handle. Aquamaniles were made mostly in the Netherlands, in the region of Dinant.

Argand Aimé Argand (1755–1803) was born at Geneva, Switzerland, and trained in France as a chemist. In the early 1780s he devised an oil-burning lamp which was subsequently given his name. It had a tubular wick so that air in the centre assisted combustion, and a glass chimney to increase the draught; both improve-

Copper, Bronze, Pewter and Other Metals (Continued)

ments resulted in a much brighter light than had hitherto been attainable. A noticeable feature of Argand lamps was the oil reservoir, which was placed at a slightly higher level than the burner, so that oil reached the latter by gravity; the thick oils then in use would not otherwise have been soaked up in sufficient quantity to keep the flame alight. Argand had great difficulty in marketing his invention in Paris, so came to England and patented it in London in 1784. He arranged with Matthew Boulton for its manufacture, but within a few years his patent was declared to be invalid in law, and the inventor finally died in poverty. The lamps were made in large numbers in numerous materials, and were frequently improved in later years. See Carcel Lamp; Moderator Lamp.

Oil lamp of Argand type with a raised reservoir (on left) shown at the Great Exhibition, 1851.

Argentan Argentan is an alternative name for German silver and Nickel silver.

Ashtadhatu An alloy employed in north India, and composed of copper, zinc, lead, tin, iron, mercury, silver and gold.

Bath Metal Another name for Prince's metal. See Tobacco boxes.

Battersea Battersea was a village south of the river Thames, opposite Chelsea. For a brief period it was the seat of a manufactory of enamels which, until modern research clarified the position, gave the name of Battersea to more articles than could ever have been produced there. The establishment was started in 1753 to exploit the decoration of enamelled copper articles by means of printed patterns, a process that was already in use at Birmingham. Early in 1756 the principal promoter of the concern, Sir Stephen Janssen, became bankrupt, the works closed and dispersals by auction soon followed. From advertisements of the latter it is possible to glean information about the types of articles produced:

> . . . Snuff-boxes of all sizes ana of great variety of Patterns, of square and oval pictures of the Royal Family, History and other pleasing subjects . . . Bottle tickets with chains for all sorts of liquor, and of different subjects, watch-cases, Toothpick-cases Coat and Sleeve Buttons, Crosses and Curiosities . . .

Many of the above articles have been identified.

Bauer Georg Bauer, see Agricola.

Bedstead Bedsteads made of metal became popular in the mid-nineteenth century, when they supplanted those of wood. The use of brass and iron for the

Copper, Bronze, Pewter and Other Metals (Continued)

purpose was advocated principally on grounds of hygiene, insect pests finding metal less inviting as a shelter. Nevertheless, makers of the new articles tended to copy the old, and made their products with careful imitations of intricate carving that must have harboured dirt and germs almost as well as wood had done. While some of the examples were of a modern design, there was a continued demand for the four-poster type. An example was displayed at the 1851 Great Exhibition, where visitors saw:

> A four-post bedstead clothed in green silk, the metal work in the renaissance style, with figures, foliage and scroll-work introduced.

Most later nineteenth-century bedsteads were not made of solid brass, but of iron tubing covered in brass foil, polished and lacquered to prevent tarnishing.

Belgium See Netherlands.

Bell-metal The composition of bell-metal was formulated so that the product gave a good musical note when struck. The proportions of the ingredients varied according to the size of the finished bell and the sound it was required to produce, but was in the region of eighty parts of copper to twenty parts of tin. In the past, bell-founders worked on the spot, travelling from site to site within an area of where they lived. Their art relied greatly on experience: the heat of the makeshift foundry had to be gauged without the aid of instruments and the shape of the finished bells often varied from maker to maker. Portable bells, for use at the table or elsewhere in a house, were made in Italy and other countries from the fifteenth century. Surviving examples are of elaborate design, but are scarce and were frequently copied at later dates. Simple types of bells, to hang round the necks of flocks that they might be located by ear when they strayed, were made from sheet bronze. A rectangular piece was bent over to form a U-section, the ends pressed in and rivetted, and a handle and clapper fitted. Most of them are devoid of ornament but sometimes specimens with punched designs are found. It is only occasionally possible to date bells of this type with accuracy, nor can they usually be assigned to a particular country.

Benin Craftsmen of the Bini tribe, of Nigeria, Africa, were extremely skilful workers in bronze. Although it is considered that they were already highly proficient by the fifteenth century, it was not until the very end of the nineteenth century that knowledge of Bini artistic achievements became known in Europe. This sprang from a British diplomatic blunder resulting in bloodshed, followed in 1897 by a punitive expedition. After capturing the capital, Benin City, the troops found an enormous quantity of bronzes of a quality of design and execution never suspected as existing in Africa. Some of the figures are of Portuguese soldiers, who accompanied traders from that country to Nigeria during the sixteenth century following an initial visit by João Alfonso d'Aveiro in 1485. Other bronzes show an *Oba* (King of Benin), his attendants and Bini warriors and traders, as single figures and groups. Important collections are to be seen at the British Museum, London, Museum of Primitive Art, New York, and at some of the bigger museums on the mainland of Europe.

Bidri Bidri, which is sometimes referred to as Biddery, is an alloy of copper, lead, tin and zinc, taking its name from the town of Bidar, to the north-west of

Copper, Bronze, Pewter and Other Metals (Continued)

African Benin bronze figure representing a Queen-Mother or one of her attendants, dating from about 1550. Bearnes & Waycotts.

Hyderabad, India. Articles were made of the metal and inlaid with silver, the ground being treated with chemicals to produce a contrasting black surface.

Bilston The town of Bilston is in an area of south Staffordshire, to which is assigned, along with neighbouring Wednesbury, a large number of enamelled copper articles dating from the 1750s. The industry continued in being for a period of about eighty years.

Birmingham The Midlands city has for long been the English seat of metal manufactures. The absence of guilds and their restrictions on enterprise encouraged the industrious, and from the late seventeenth century onwards the city grew in size and importance. Numerous branches of metalworking have been carried on there, not least in interest being that of John Taylor, who was described in 1755 as 'the most considerable maker of gilt-metal buttons, and enamelled snuff boxes . . . he employs five hundred persons in these two branches . . .' Slightly later in date was Matthew Boulton's Soho Works, where coins were minted and the metals employed for numerous purposes ranged from copper and its alloys to silver. Later again was Elkington's, where electro-plating was first practiced. Birmingham's output of goods relied for a long period on the labours of out-workers, men who worked in their own homes or who hired space in a communal workshop, selling their finished goods to a merchant each week and then buying further raw materials. The system was still current in the 1850s, but was gradually replaced by the modern factory, in which the materials are supplied and regular wages paid by the employer.

Bolsover Thomas Bolsover (1704–88) is credited with the discovery of Sheffield plate. This event is said to have occurred in 1742, when he accidentally found that a piece of copper clamped against some silver had become fused together after

Copper, Bronze, Pewter and Other Metals (Continued)

being heated. Bolsover made buttons and buckles by the process, which he and others improved over the years.

Boulton Matthew Boulton (1728–1809) succeeded to his father's business of manufacturing metal articles on the latter's death in 1759. He removed the concern to new premises at Soho, to the north of the centre of Birmingham, which duly became one of the showplaces of industrial England. Boulton's success was largely due to his application and initiative, and his partnership with James Watt in 1775 was responsible for the commercial success of the steam engine. In addition to building the engines, the Soho manufactory produced a wide range of goods, including Sheffield plate, ormolu and cut steel and, in fact, innumerable objects in many kinds of metal.

Brass An alloy of copper and zinc. It was produced in England from the late sixteenth century and duly became a monopoly of a body with the grandiloquent title of The Governors, Assistants and Societies of the City of London of and for the Mineral and Battery Works. Brass varies in colour according to the proportions of the ingredients; the less zinc present the redder the colour, and when there is overmuch zinc it is greyish and liable to be fragile.

Brasses See Monumental brass.

Britannia Metal An alloy of which the basis is tin, copper and antimony. It came into use in the late eighteenth century, reaching its peak of popularity in the 1850s. Britannia metal is akin to pewter, but harder and amenable to being made into thin-walled articles by means of spinning. Examples followed current silver patterns, but those of the earlier years are scarce and the later more plentiful pieces include a large proportion of florid design. Sheffield was the centre of manufacture, with the firm of Dixon among the more prolific in output. They and others usually stamped wares with their names in full, often with a series of numerals indicating a pattern number; hence many an owner has cherished a teapot stamped 1397 in the belief that it was made in the fourteenth century. Many pieces were originally electroplated with silver, although often the thin deposit of precious metal has vanished long ago, leaving the only trace of its former existence in the letters EPBM: Electro-plated Britannia metal. In America Britannia metal began to be used soon after 1800, and nowadays is loosely described there as pewter.

Britannia metal sugar container in the shape of a coal scuttle, with a shovel for serving.

Bronze Bronze is an alloy of copper and tin, varying in their proportions and resulting in a product that is fairly readily melted, casts well, is hard and takes a good

Copper, Bronze, Pewter and Other Metals (Continued)

finish. It is known to have been used from at least 2500 B.C. when it was employed for many of the purposes later fulfilled by iron and steel. In less ancient times the metal was cast into figures and groups; a form in which the artists of several nations became highly skilled. In England there are the recumbent effigies of Henry III and his queen, Eleanor, the gates to the chapel of Henry VII and the screen round his tomb (all in Westminster Abbey), the first-named being the work of an English craftsman, William Torel, active A.D. 1300. While the Italians had earlier been leaders in creating works of art in bronze, from the late seventeenth century the French excelled in using the material in another manner: in the form of ormolu.

Buttons Although the humble button must have existed far back in time, surviving specimens pre-dating the eighteenth century are very scarce. A number of men specialized in their manufacture, most of whom had premises in Birmingham. Not least among them was Matthew Boulton, who was visited at his Soho works in 1774 by Samuel Johnson. The Doctor recorded '. . . we went to Boulton's who with great civility, led us through his shops. I could not distinctly see his enginery. Twelve dozen of buttons for three shillings!' Various types were produced at various dates, the most elaborate being made of small concave discs soldered together and fitted with a shank. Others were in a single piece cast in one with the shank or eye, while by 1825 they were being given shanks of canvas; and gradually the entire manufacturing process became mechanized. Many of the cheaper buttons were of cast pewter, and despite Dr. Johnson's remarks Boulton is known also to have made buttons decorated with steel facets that sold at 140 guineas (£147.00) a gross. In America, imports from England supplied much of the market prior to about 1800, although Caspar Wistar, who reached the country in 1717 and turned later to glassmaking, is known to have manufactured buttons at Philadelphia with success. His son, Richard, advertised from the same city in 1769, seventeen years after his father had died:

> He also continues to make the Philadelphia Brass Buttons, well noted for their Strength, such as were made by his deceased Father, and are warranted for seven Years.

Brass was not the only material in use or fashion across the Atlantic. Advertisements in Boston, Massachusetts, newspapers between 1747 and 1757 mentioned 'white and yellow mettle Coat and Breast-Buttons, white stone and other kind of sleeve buttons', 'best double gilt Regimental Coat and Breast Buttons, and a Variety of a cheaper Kind for the Country Sale, best London made Silver Sleeve Buttons, set with Brilliant Stones, and all other sort of Sleeve Buttons', and 'Coat and Jacket Buttons, Bath Metal & other sleeve Buttons'. In 1772 a news item reported:

> A Person came Passenger with Capt. Jenkins who carried on the Button-making Business, and has bro't over the Materials for making all sorts of gilt Buttons.—A Manufacture not known by any in America.

Candle Mould Moulds in which to make candles were of pewter and of tinned sheet iron (tinplate), sometimes in the form of a multiple mould to produce as many as a dozen candles at a time. Many of the devices comprised a set of tubes held together at top and bottom, or, as was described in 1855:

Copper, Bronze, Pewter and Other Metals (Continued)

> The moulds used . . . are of pewter, and consist of two parts; namely, a hollow cylinder of the length of the candle open at both ends, and nicely polished on the inside; and a small metallic conical cap with a hole in the centre for the wick.

A wick was affixed down each tube and held in place while the heated wax or tallow was poured in. On cooling, the candles were removed after the mould containing them had been momentarily warmed.

Canton Enamel The city of Canton, China, gave its name to painted enamels, most of which were made for export to Europe and were often decorated to suit Western tastes. The technique was similar to that employed at Limoges and elsewhere, with the articles made from thin copper coated with an opaque neutral-tinted all-over layer of enamel prior to the final painting. The Chinese learned it from French Jesuit missionaries who were in the country, and first practised the art from about 1710.

Carcel Lamp A variation of the Argand lamp, in which oil was pumped through to the wick by clockwork. It was invented in 1800 by a Frenchman, B.-G. Carcel.

Casting Metal wares could be cast or founded by pouring the molten material into a mould prepared according to the degree of heat involved. In the case of iron it was usually of sand and clay. The resulting pattern would be a simple relief without undercutting, of which the iron fireback is a good example. See *Cire Perdue*.

Cast Iron See Iron.

Chandelier Early churches are recorded as having been lighted by two types of hanging chandelier, which were: the *polycandelon*, a circular plate pierced with holes to contain vessels, each of which held oil and a wick; and the *corona*, which was a simple ring of iron on which were spikes for candles. By the fifteenth century more sophisticated-looking devices were being used on the mainland of Europe, and were duly imported into England. They were made of brass, and had a central stem ornamented with figures from which sprang curved arms with candle-holders. Because both Henry IV and Richard I, in the fifteenth century, forbade the importation of what were termed 'hanging candlesticks' it is assumed that they were then being brought into England, where someone was making them and required protection from competition. It would seem that the prohibition was sometimes ignored, because there are subsequent records of foreign chandeliers hanging in English homes. They were probably of Netherlands origin, whence came many seventeenth-century examples with gracefully scrolled arms springing from a stem composed of a series of spheres. Close copies were made in England both at the time and later, most of them destined for churches and public buildings. From signed examples it has been learned that there were makers active in both London and the provinces. In France, gilt metal chandeliers ornamented with shaped pieces of natural rock crystal were made from the seventeenth century, until the glass-makers were able to successfully replace the stone with glass that gave an acceptable glitter. A similar course of events took place in England. In the eighteenth century the French made chandeliers of ormolu, which were again fashionable in France and England in Victorian times.

Chestnut Roaster A chestnut roaster

Copper, Bronze, Pewter and Other Metals (Continued)

A mid-eighteenth-century French ormolu chandelier hung with cut rock-crystal drops. Parke-Bernet Galleries, New York.

usually takes the form of a brass box with a hinged pierced lid, and a long handle. Examples of a date earlier than the nineteenth century are scarce.

China The Chinese have made objects of bronze for many thousands of years, and surviving specimens of early date are highly esteemed. Almost all of them have been excavated, and as a result of lengthy burial have acquired a surface colouring that adds to their attraction. Bronzes of similar type were made in succeeding periods, although not necessarily as forgeries; the Chinese have always revered the past and each generation tended to imitate the possessions as well as the ways of its ancestors. In more modern times, however, with the high value placed on genuinely old examples, the excavated

Copper, Bronze, Pewter and Other Metals (Continued)

ones have occasionally been forged: the patina being carefully applied with wax and paint, and natural ageing accelerated by immersion in cess-pits. In addition to cast and chiselled decoration, gold and silver wire were sometimes effectively inlaid, and gilding and parcel-gilding were also employed. The Chinese were adept at enamelling on bronze and copper, using *champlevé*, *cloisonné* and painting techniques with success. The last-named variety they learned from Europeans in the early decades of the eighteenth century, the city of Canton being the centre of the industry and giving its name to the product. See Paktong; Tutenag.

Cire Perdue Artistic bronzes were often cast by the *cire perdue* (lost wax) process, as in contrast to straightforward casting it would reproduce complex undercutting. Briefly it involved the sculptor's executing his work in wax over a core of clay, the latter having been shaped roughly to the outline of the projected object. The finished. model was enclosed in a clay casing in which holes were provided for the introduction of the molten bronze, the escape of gases and the release of the melted wax. The latter operation was first performed, the metal was poured in to replace the wax, and when cooled the clay casing and core were broken away. The object had then to be given the desired finish by filing and chiselling away imperfections, and suitably toning the surface. For each bronze the sequence had to be repeated from start to finish. The *cire perdue* process has been in use over many centuries in all parts of the world.

Coal Scuttle Coal containers of brass or copper were used in the 1760s, and possibly prior to that time, and like later scuttles they were accompanied by scoops. A helmet-shaped scuttle was shown at the Great Exhibition, 1851, where it was announced as being 'of new and simple design'. Also on display were 'Copper coal scoops, exhibiting the changes in their patterns during the last 70 years'.

Colza Oil Obtained from the seeds of a certain type of kale, Colza oil is a yellowish liquid. It was much used in lamps in the late eighteenth/early nineteenth century.

Company of Mines Royal The Company of Mines Royal was founded in 1568 to work English copper deposits. Two years earlier, as a result of negotiations conducted by Queen Elizabeth I's Secretary of State, Sir William Cecil, German miners were brought to England and commenced operations at Keswick, Cumberland (Cumbria). A later attempt to extract copper in Cornwall met with little success. In 1693 an Act of Parliament allowed freedom to all who wished to mine, and the monopoly of the Company terminated.

Copper The pinkish-red metal, copper, has been known to mankind since remote ages. It occurs in many parts of the world in both a pure state and as an ore, and in the past the principal European sources were at first Germany and Sweden. Then, in the late sixteenth century operations began tentatively in England with the encouragement of the Company of Mines Royal, which commenced work in Cumberland (Cumbria). In about 1580 mining, which had been carried on in North Wales in Roman times, began to be undertaken in Cornwall in conjunction with a smelting works at Neath, in South Wales. The venture made a halting start and it was not until the final years of the seventeenth century that activity increased enough to bring commercial success. The business expanded throughout the succeeding century, with national output increased for a

Copper, Bronze, Pewter and Other Metals (Continued)

few years after deposits of the metal had been found close to the surface (and to the smelting works) at Parys Mountain, Anglesey. By that date, the more easily worked Cornish ores were exhausted and underground tunnelling had become essential, but this was dependent upon efficient pumps to clear the water that otherwise flooded the workings. For this purpose, James Watt's steam engine, manufactured at Matthew Boulton's Soho works, proved the saviour, with the first installed in 1777. It was the turn of Devon to give output a fillip in Victorian times, and the opening of the Devon Great Consols mine, near Tavistock, which began operating in 1844, started a wave of speculation. In 1846 the mine sold 13,300 tons of ore and the £1 shares were valued at £800 apiece. The prosperity did not last, and from 1865 onwards, steamships were able to bring ore from South America at prices with which the Devon and Cornish miners could not compete. The metal was occasionally used on its own, but in most instances it was alloyed to produce a material that was more easily worked and resulted in better articles. In the eighteenth and nineteenth centuries it was most commonly found in its pure form in the kitchen, where copper pans were to be found in daily use. They had to be coated internally with tin or food-poisoning would result, and newspapers of the time continually reported the occurrence of cases.

Crusie The simplest type of oil lamp took the form of a small bowl to hold the oil, with a lip at one end in which rested the wick. A double variety, with a similar bowl hanging below the other to catch any drips, was known in Scotland as a crusie, in Cornwall as a chill and in the Channel Islands as a crasset. Crusies were made of copper or any other available metal, and were used in the remoter country areas in many parts of Europe as well as the British Isles.

Curfew The curfew is a domed cover resembling a quarter of a sphere in shape and with a handle, usually made of brass or copper decorated with embossed patterns. A few eighteenth-century examples are recorded. The curfew gained its name from the French *couvre-feu*: literally, cover-fire, because its purpose was to keep the air from reaching a fire so that it would remain glowing overnight until revived in the morning.

Curtain Holder The curtain holder or hold-back secured drawn curtains neatly at each side of a window. It came into use in the second half of the eighteenth century, was made of gilt or lacquered brass and continued to be manufactured throughout the Victorian period.

Cut Steel Steel, highly polished after being chiselled and faceted was known as cut steel. The work was executed in many countries including Russia (at Tula) Italy and England. In the latter, it was for some time in the eighteenth century a well-known local industry at Woodstock, in Oxfordshire, where a visitor in 1778 noted that she 'saw some scissors at fifteen guineas [£15.75] a pair, very curious no doubt, but not answerable to the price: sword-hilts and stars for the nobility are beautiful . . .'. The industry became centred in Birmingham, where Matthew Boulton included the making of cut steel jewellery among his many other activities.

Damascening Inlaying iron, steel, copper or brass with gold or silver, or with both, is known as damascening. It acquired its name from the city of Damascus,

Copper, Bronze, Pewter and Other Metals (Continued)

in Syria, where the art had been practised for many centuries. In Europe, damascening was executed in Milan during the sixteenth century, where the armourers often decorated their work with gold and silver inlay.

Dinanderie See Dinant.

Dinant Dinant, a town on the river Meuse, in the Netherlands, was once noted for its brass wares, and such was its fame that products of the area acquired the name *Dinanderie* to describe them. Simple domestic articles were made, while more ambitious pieces such as lecterns and large candelabra were provided for ecclesiastical use. In 1466 Dinant was besieged and stormed by Charles the Bold, who acted in the name of his father, Philippe le Bon, and those of its inhabitants who escaped slaughter settled elsewhere.

Door Knocker Some of the oldest surviving door knockers are on the doors of cathedrals and churches. That on the north door of Durham Cathedral, in the shape of a stylized lion's mask with a ring in its mouth, once assured sanctuary to criminals, who could not be arrested on reaching and grasping it. The malefactor had also to toll a special bell, wear a particular robe and carry out other prescribed regulations, but the entire procedure was abolished by an Act of 1623. More prosaic examples, for the doors of houses, came into use during the eighteenth century, and were varied in pattern. Most of them were made of brass, ranging in design from a clenched fist to arrangements of husks and urns, and in Regency times Nelson's triumphs were commemorated in knockers formed as dolphins. In the course of the nineteenth century cast-iron knockers became common, many of them reproducing earlier patterns while others were of Gothic inspiration.

Iron door knocker shown at the 1851 Great Exhibition by a London firm of manufacturers.

Dutch Metal A name for a variety of brass more or less resembling gold in colour. Other alloys with a similar property were named Mannheim Gold, Similor and Pinchbeck.

Electroplate Depositing a thin layer of silver on a base metal by the use of electricity, known as electroplating, was exploited commercially in 1841. In that year a factory was opened for the purpose in Birmingham by George Richards Elkington. The process soon ousted Sheffield Plate, and brought silver-surfaced wares within the reach of many. Electroplating was not limited to silver, but was equally usable with gold, or any other metal, and the base could also be varied. Silver was applied to German silver, known as Nickel silver, and pieces so treated were stamped EPNS, for Electro-plated Nickel silver. Gold was plated on copper or on silver, in the latter instance the articles being termed silver-gilt.

Electrotype Electrotyping is a variation of electroplating, and with its aid it is possible to make exact copies of objects of many kinds. A mould of plaster or some other suitable material is made and smeared with blacklead, which is a conductor of electricity and receptive to plating. A deposit of metal is then built up on the cast until it is of the required thick-

Copper, Bronze, Pewter and Other Metals (Continued)

ness, and if it is of base metal it can then be electroplated with silver or gold. The process has been used to make reproductions of articles that would not otherwise have been accessible. An instance of this occurred in 1880, when a party of experts left England, having learned accidentally of the existence of some unrecorded English silver in the Kremlin, Moscow. Among those who journeyed to Russia was a member of Elkington's staff who was duly responsible for making electrotypes of 300 items, some of which were English. The Kremlin treasures were next seen in 1908 and then there was an interval of a further fifty years before another English expert examined them. The electrotypes proved their worth in place of opportunities to inspect the originals. (Some of the Moscow electrotypes are in the Victoria and Albert Museum, London, and others are in the Metropolitan Museum of Art, New York.)

Elkington The firm of Elkington was founded by George Richards Elkington (1801–65) and remained foremost as makers of electroplated wares from their introduction in 1841. The process had evolved during the preceding decade, while Elkington, the son of a spectacles maker, was apprenticed to his uncles who were silver-platers at Birmingham. In 1841 a new factory was opened to exploit the process, which was gradually improved by the purchase of other patents. Elkington had his cousin Henry (died 1852) as a partner and in 1842 was joined by Josiah Mason, to make the style of the firm Elkington, Mason & Co. They licensed a number of others to use their methods, and their commercial success was due no less to general business efficiency than to maintenance of high standards of workmanship.

Enamel *Cloisonné* enamelling was practised in Europe, but it was in the Far East, first in China and then in Japan, that it was widely and very skilfully employed for decoration. The Chinese started to use it in the fourteenth century, having acquired their knowledge from examples of European and Western Asian craftsmanship. Surviving Japanese specimens are no older than the seventeenth century, although a few potentially more aged ones have been the subject of argument, and most are of comparatively recent date. The *champlevé* technique was used in the Middle Ages on the mainland of Europe for decorating ecclesiastical articles, and was at other times employed by the Chinese and in England (see Surrey Enamel). The late fifteenth century saw a further technique, the introduction of what are termed painted enamels. The town of Limoges, in west-central France, became the centre for such work and gave its name to it. In the eighteenth century, in Germany, in England at Birmingham, Bilston and Battersea the same process was used. At Canton, China, it was imitated successfully.

Escutcheon The plate framing a keyhole was usually made of brass, polished or gilt, pinned or screwed in place. The escutcheon reached the height of exuberant design in the rococo, and soon afterwards it almost disappeared. Its place was taken by a narrow brass strip in the shape of the key-end inset in the keyhole. Sometimes it was flush with the surface, but earlier types had a raised and rounded rim.

Ewer and Jug Ewers and jugs for holding water, usually for making it available at the table for hand-washing, but also for other liquids for other purposes, survive from the thirteenth century onwards. They were made in many countries of bronze and other metals, decorated with cast

Copper, Bronze, Pewter and Other Metals (Continued)

Eighteenth-century Chinese figure of a quail made of gilt metal decorated with cloisonné *enamel.* Phillips.

ornament, damascening and stamped patterns. See Aquamanile.

Fender The fender is a device for preventing burning coals or embers from damaging the floor of a room. It usually takes the form of a shaped length of metal some 20 cm. or so in height, with an iron base-plate to keep it standing upright, placed across the opening of the hearth. The fender was usually of brass or steel, pierced, engraved and polished, and it came into use from about 1700 when coal ousted wood fuel; the former requiring to be burned at a height where a draught might aid combustion, but also being liable to accidental and potentially dangerous spillage. Cast brass fenders displayed at the Great Exhibition in 1851 included one modelled with vine leaves and bunches of grapes. Then and later less costly examples were made in cast-iron.

Fireback The fireback was made of cast-iron and rested at the back of the fireplace. Its purpose was to reflect heat from the fire into the room, while protecting the rear of the fireplace, and it provided a convenient surface for ornamentation. This was in the form of patterns in relief, sometimes with dates, initials and even short inscriptions. Early examples were wider than they were high, but by the mid-seventeenth century this had been reversed and they were of 'tombstone' shape. They were made with the arms and initials of sovereigns from Henry VIII to James II, while others depict Biblical subjects, the defeat of the Spanish Armada and other national events of importance. Iron firebacks were made in the Netherlands, in many instances with a close resemblance to English examples.

Firedog See Andiron.

Fire Irons The early fireplace required tools such as a poker, tongs and a brush, and with the coming of coal a shovel was added. Matching sets of fire irons were uncommon before the end of the eighteenth century, but by 1851 visitors to the Great Exhibition saw a display by a Birmingham firm comprising:

> Highly polished steel fire irons, with engraved burnished steel pans, and diamond, octagon, and hexagon cut, twisted, fluted, and scolloped shanks; with cut steel, ormolu, bronzed, silvered, and gilt, china, glass, pearl, and ivory heads.
>
> 'Pokerettes'; with octagon, sexagon, and twisted shanks, and cut steel grips.
>
> Coal vase tongs; with octagon, sexagon, and twisted shanks.

Copper, Bronze, Pewter and Other Metals (Continued)

Firemark From the end of the seventeenth century it was possible for a houseowner to insure against loss by fire, and to show that he held a policy the insurers gave him a suitable plaque to affix to the front of the building. This acted as an advertisement, and in the event of fire the Company's brigade would recognize their own mark and take appropriate action. Firemarks varied in shape and size, averaging 25 cm. in height, and were made of iron, lead, copper and brass, often coloured and gilt. Each bore the name of the insurers and an insignia, and in some instances was stamped with the number of the policy.

Footman A kettle stand for use in front of a fire. The footman was made of metal, often brass, ornamented with piercing and sometimes also engraved. It was a type of trivet, and the two are scarcely distinguishable from one another.

German Silver An alloy of copper, nickel and zinc which has a silvery appearance and originated in Germany. Some of it was taken to Sheffield in 1830 and within a few years it replaced the copper formerly used in Sheffield plate. German silver was later known as Nickel silver and is very similar in composition to Paktong and other alloys. The letters EPNS stamped on articles stand for Electro-plated Nickel silver.

Germany Germany, with its great sources of minerals, has long been famous for its miners and metal-workers. German miners came to England in the time of Elizabeth I in order to exploit English ores and teach mining methods. Examples of metalwork dating back to the tenth century are to be seen at Hildesheim, near Hanover, which was a centre of craftmanship, but later the workers at Nuremberg and Augsburg gained supremacy. From these cities came bronze figures and groups rivalling those of Italy, as well as finely-made engraved iron caskets with elaborate locks and keys. Solingen, near Düsseldorf, in the Rhineland, was for a long time famed far and wide for sword and knife blades. Ormolu mounts for porcelain and furniture were made in Germany during the eighteenth century, and are sometimes difficult to distinguish from those of French origin.

Gilding Copper, bronze and brass were usually gilt by the process known as fire-gilding. The article was carefully finished, coated with an amalgam of gold and mercury, and then heated to drive off the mercury. The work was completed by polishing the highlights with an agate burnisher. Poisonous fumes were given off as the mercury became hot, and their dangerous nature affecting the health of the craftsmen eventually led to the virutal abandonment of fire-gilding. See Ormolu.

Gloucester Candlestick The Gloucester candlestick (Victoria and Albert Museum) is one of the most famous examples of English metalwork. It dates to the twelfth century, an inscription engraved on it reading 'The devotion of Abbot Peter and his gentle flock gave me to the Church of St. Peter at Gloucester'; it is known that in the year 1104 Prior Peter was elected Abbot of the monastery of St. Peter, Gloucester. In some way, the candlestick came into the possession of the cathedral at Le Mans, France, and then in the nineteenth century was found to be in private ownership in the same town. Following further changes in ownership its adventures ended in 1861 when it was bought for the museum. The candlestick was cast in bell metal, in a complex pierced and relief pattern of what has been termed 'a fantastic ballet of men, monkeys

Copper, Bronze, Pewter and Other Metals (Continued)

and monsters'. It stands 50.5 cm. in height and doubtless once formed one of a pair made for use at the altar.

Gong The metal gong with its vibrant tone originated in the East. It makes an occasional appearance in an orchestra, but was once a very familiar sound in the home when it summoned the hungry to the table.

Gouthiere Pierre Gouthière (1732–?1813) was born at Bar-sur-Aube, in north-eastern France, the son of a saddler. By 1758 he married the widow of a master-gilder and had himself become a master craftsman. He worked as gilder to many of the great silversmiths of the time, but it is on his work as a chaser and gilder (*ciseleur-doreur*) of ormolu that his fame rests. Among his numerous important clients was the Duc d'Aumont, for whom he mounted rare specimens of marble, and he was among the eminent specialists employed on Marie-Antoinette's jewel coffer: the coffer is lost but is known from existing documents and from its appearance in the background of a painting of the Queen. Because of the high reputation he enjoyed in his lifetime, it has become a habit to attribute to Gouthière every well-finished piece of ormolu in the Louis XVI style, but his surviving authenticated works are few in number. Among them is a large clock dated 1771, and a perfume-burner formerly belonging to the duc d'Aumont and purchased by Marie-Antoinette after his death in 1782 (both pieces in the Wallace Collection, London). Gouthière became bankrupt in 1788, was finally ruined by the Revolution and died in poverty.

Grate The grate came into use following the introduction of coal for room-heating. Not only did the grate raise the fire above the level of the hearthstone allowing a

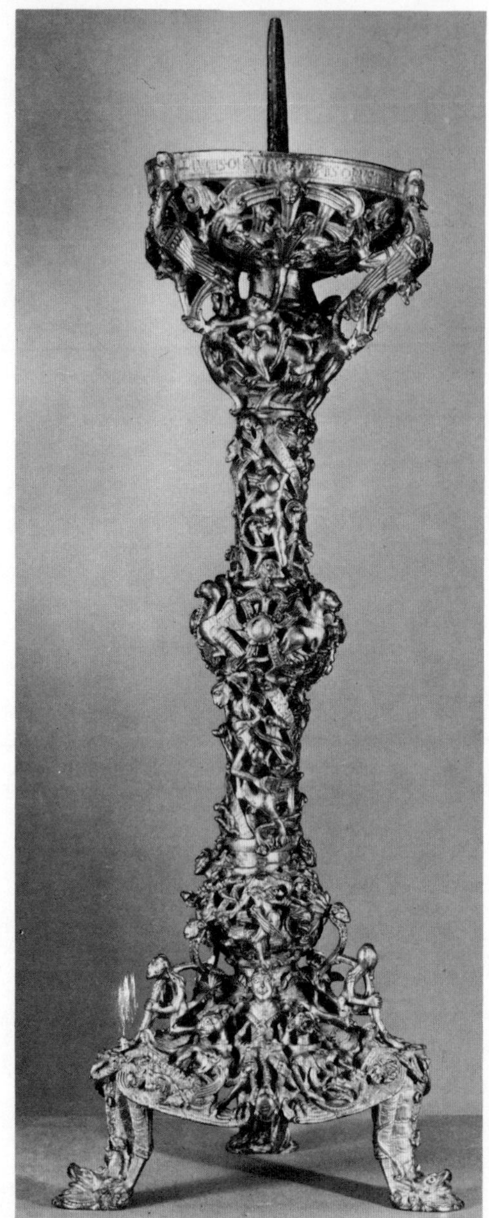

The Gloucester candlestick: a twelfth-century English candlestick made of gilt bell metal given in the early 1100s to the church of St. Peter, Gloucester. Victoria and Albert Museum.

Copper, Bronze, Pewter and Other Metals (Continued)

draught to encourage flames, but it confined the fuel so that the flames spread without trouble. Coal began to be used in the early seventeenth century, but its employment was not general until after the Restoration and then only in towns and cities. While the body of the grate was constructed of iron, the front was usually decorated with polished and pierced steel or brass. Exceptionally, metals like Paktong were employed for the purpose, a visitor to a fashionable house in 1771 noting one that had cost the owner £105. For the first three-quarters of the eighteenth century, the dog grate, which was completely free-standing, held its own. It was followed by the Bath stove or hob grate extending completely across the hearth and, in effect, a flat decorated plate with an opening at the top for the coal and another at the bottom for ashes. Soon afterwards experiments began with the burning of anthracite coal, resulting later in a totally enclosed slow-combustion stove with mica windows to provide a note of visual cheer. The American scientist and statesman, Benjamin Franklin, devoted some of his investigations towards room heating, and some years after his death in 1790 his name was applied to various types of grates.

Gun Metal An alloy of copper and tin results in gun metal, which was developed for the making of gun (cannon) barrels and was occasionally used for other articles. It has a similar appearance to bronze.

Hame A pair of hames forms a part of the collar worn by a draught horse. Some of them are made of wood and others are of brass, curved and shaped somewhat like a horn.

Hanukah Lamp The Jewish festival of Hanukah is celebrated in December to commemorate the defeat of the Syrians in 165 B.C. after they had suppressed worship in the Temple at Jerusalem. It involves the use of a lamp with eight wicks or eight candles, each of which is lighted in turn. Eight-branched candelabra were made for the purpose in various countries of Europe, many of them made of brass and some suitably inscribed in Hebrew.

Hold-Back See Curtain Holder.

Horse Brass The horse brass is to-day more often seen hanging on a wall than on the harness of the animal for which it was made. The origin of the brass has been traced back to the Bible, where there occurs mention of ornaments on camel's necks. That being so, it is probable that horses also wore amulets of some kind and these were forerunners of horse brasses. The more immediate precursors were perhaps small bronze plaques, cast, engraved or enamelled with the name and arms of the owners of an animal, worn in battle for identification. There gradually evolved a custom of decorating animals employed on routine labours in a similar manner, and from being made individually for each buyer they were duly produced commercially. Some two thousand different designs have been recorded, and a full-decked horse in full harness might plod along carrying a display of brassware weighing as much as 7 lb. A few of the different types are:

> *Bells:* these were arranged in up to four tiers, comprising the Lead with five bells, the Lash with four bells, and the Body and Thill with three bells apiece. The bells in each tier were tuned differently and the resultant chord gave a warning of approach while driving away evil spirts.

Copper, Bronze, Pewter and Other Metals (Continued)

Ear brasses: one was suspended behind each ear.

Face brasses: one or more were suspended down the forehead.

Flyer: this was a small frame enclosing a swinging miniature brass or a bell, some being surmounted by a tuft of red, white and blue bristles. The Flyer was mounted on the head of the horse, and it was known also as a Terret or Swinger.

Runner brasses: three were at each shoulder.

Martingale brasses: the martingale is a strap running from the collar down between the forelegs, and as many as ten brasses were on it.

Hunneman Charles Hunneman was a Boston, Massachusetts, coppersmith, active in the late eighteenth century. Warming pans bearing his name have been recorded, and he is one of the few American metalworkers of the time whose products have been positively identified.

India Bronze statuettes were made in India many centuries ago and have been produced continuously since then. The complex mythology of the country, and those adjoining, led to the making of images of the Buddha and the many other deities involved in worship, the various schools of makers giving their work characteristic treatment. While the religious significance of the personages is only occasionally appreciated outside the area where they were made, the artistic excellence of the best examples has a universal appeal. Many of the similar figures and groups from Tibet were gilt and some additionally inlaid with turquoise, but comparable work was exported from China and the precise origin of specimens is not always certain. Domestic articles of brass and copper were also made in various parts of India, especially during the nineteenth century when much of it was bought by visitors. See Bidri.

Iron Iron is the most plentiful of all metals and extremely versatile. It is divisible into two varieties for artistic purposes: cast and wrought. The first is, as its name implies, formed by pouring the molten metal into prepared moulds, and the result is a strong material that is unmalleable and, being brittle, may fracture under stress. It was used for many purposes as diverse as heavy firebacks and delicate jewellery; the latter a nineteenth-century product at which the Germans excelled. Wrought iron, on the other hand, is of similar composition to the other but contains less carbon, which permits it to be malleable and of great strength. These properties mean that it can be wrought, i.e., hammered and twisted into desired shapes and, additionally, if two pieces are heated and hammered together they will become one: a process known as welding. Wrought-iron was suitable for decoration by engraving and damascening; from it were made ornamental gates and railings, as well as door-knockers and suits of armour. In the past those who worked with iron enjoyed a respect recorded in the words of a sixteenth-century Italian, Vannoccio Biringuccio:

> Were it not for the lesser nobility of the material, I would say that the smith working in iron should rightly take precedence over the goldsmith because of the great benefits that he brings to mankind.

Islam The Mahommedans were skilled metalworkers. Some of their work executed in the thirteenth and fourteenth centuries is now almost all in museums. Typical is a candlestick with a deep base and short

Copper, Bronze, Pewter and Other Metals (Continued)

A Syrian (Islamic) candlestick damascened with intricate patterns made in about the years 1250–60. Christie's.

neck, of brass finely inlaid with intricate patterns in silver made for an inhabitant of Baghdad in about 1300 (Victoria and Albert Museum). Excellent work continued to be produced later in the way of damascened iron and embossed brassware, although much of indifferent quality was made for tourists.

Italy If for no other artistic productions, Italy would be celebrated for works executed in bronze. The first sign of the Renaissance was the pair of bronze doors by Lorenzo Ghiberti (1378–1455) at the Baptistery, Florence, for which his design was selected in a competition held in 1402. In addition to that and other large-scale works, the later fifteenth century saw a revival of interest in small copies of antique statues as decoration in the home. Original works in the classical style were also made, and continued to be produced by a number of renowned craftsmen, who included Andrea Briosco, called Riccio (1470–1532); Jacopo Tatti, called Sansovino (1586–1570); and Giovanni Bologna (1524–1608). The works of these men and other masters of the art have been copied frequently, much research has been devoted to the Italian bronze and its full appreciation is only achieved after careful study.

Japan Japanese metalworkers were unequalled for their skill, but the finer points of their best productions are only rarely

Copper, Bronze, Pewter and Other Metals (Continued)

appreciated by Westerners. The making of armour, combining the greatest strength with the least weight, was no less an art than the making of swords. In fact, the sword and its decoration is a study in itself, with the various items of sword-furniture, *tsuba*, *menuki*, *kashira* and other pieces, the subjects of specialized collections. Metal-inlaying and other techniques common in the West were all practised by the Japanese, and in addition they used a number of alloys, often in conjunction with iron. These included *sentoku*, like a yellowish bronze; *shakudo*, a mixture of bronze and gold treated with chemicals to turn it black; and *shibuichi*, copper and silver alloyed and pickled to become a silver-grey. Vessels were made in gilt bronze for use in temples, and for secular purposes there were all kinds of boxes, vases and candlesticks among much else. Figures of animals were made in both bronze and iron, the latter often being realistically articulated. It is not always easy to date the work, even though many examples bear signatures, as it was common to copy earlier pieces for century after century.

Japanning See Pontypool Ware.

Jugs See Ewer and Jug.

Kettle Copper kettles for heating water were imported from Holland in the early eighteenth century. A London maker advertised in 1741 that his own products 'exceed any that come from Holland or any other place', and gave the price of those he then had in stock:

Three-pint tea kettles and lamps at 10s. [50p.]

Two-quart tea kettles and lamps at 13s. [65p.]

As these were complete with lamps they must have been intended for use at the tea table by those who did not possess similar articles made of silver. The maker quoted above further referred to the fact that his kettles were brown in colour, so they were presumably finished with a process that made them resemble bronze. This is borne out by a mention in 1768 that a charge of 6d. was made for 'Browning'. The same source referred to tinning costing 2s.6d., which meant that the interiors of kettles were coated with tin to prevent poisons in the copper tainting the water; a wise precaution. Most surviving copper kettles are of nineteenth-century date; being functional articles their pattern has not changed much over the years and many of them are erroneously thought to be much older than they really are. Brass kettles, of a pattern similar to the copper ones, were very popular at the end of the nineteenth century.

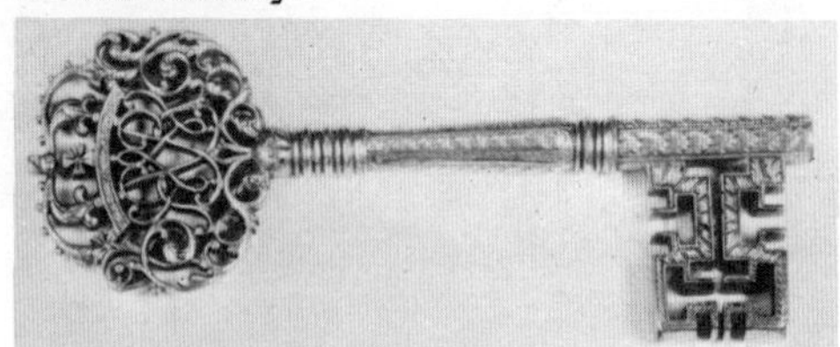

A late seventeenth-century English Chamberlain's key of gilt bronze. Sotheby's.

Key While most old keys were carefully made, the majority of them were functional objects with little or no decoration. Exceptions were the keys made in France between about 1550 and 1650, when the bit (operative end) was just as elaborately made as the bow (top). In addition the tubular section, the hollow shank joining bit and bow, was often shaped internally. Such keys, made by apprentices at the end of their training, were masterpieces to show the skill of the craftsman and not intended for use. Comparable to the foregoing were the

Copper, Bronze, Pewter and Other Metals (Continued)

Chamberlain's keys made in England as well as in other countries in the seventeenth and eighteenth centuries. In them, the bow was usually of gilt brass elaborately pierced with a device, the key being a badge of office to be worn ceremonially with a silk rosette. Monarchs and noblemen had the bows of keys pierced with their insignia in much the same way as they had their crests and coats of arms engraved on silver or carved on furniture. In the nineteenth century decorative keys were provided for the ceremonial opening of important buildings, such keys having silver or silver-gilt bows, suitably inscribed to record the event and sometimes embellished with coloured enamel. They were duly presented to, and retained by, whoever had officiated at the occasion.

Lantern A lantern is a lamp for outdoor or indoor use which has the light-source protected from draught. Those for outdoors were portable, of simple sturdy construction, and seldom bore any ornamentation. Indoor lanterns were more decorative, and usually to be found in an entrance-hall where the opening and closing of a front door would test their efficiency. Metal-framed examples survive from the eighteenth and nineteenth centuries, their designs following prevailing styles. While many of them were for central suspension others were made to be affixed to a wall.

Latten Brass supplied in the form of thin sheets. There were three varieties: black latten, unpolished; roll latten, polished on both sides; and, shaven latten, a thin foil.

Lectern Ecclesiastical lecterns were made of metal from the time of the Middle Ages, but surviving English examples date mostly from the sixteenth century and later. Many are in the form of a column supporting the figure of an eagle, of which the outstretched wings support the Bible at a convenient height for reading. From time to time its place has been taken by pelicans, winged lions, gryphons and other strange birds and beasts. Most examples to be seen in cathedrals and churches are made of brass.

Locks The French excelled at lock-making, as they did at making keys, producing both with elaborate ornamentation. This began in the fifteenth century, and a typical lock of the period has the side of the case decorated with an applied pierced iron tracery of Gothic design resembling a church window of the period. German and Spanish craftsmen vied with the French and occasionally equalled them. At that date it was the practice to affix the lock to the outside of a chest, but towards the end of the sixteenth century the lock was fitted within. For that reason there was then little point in ornamenting the lock-case, and attention was devoted to the complexity of the mechanism and its finishing. This was particularly true of the German smiths, at Nuremberg and elsewhere, who made iron coffers with highly elaborate locks revealing their mechanisms when the lids were opened. At about the same date, French apprentices were required at the termination of their period of service to make a lock and a key that worked, and in addition demonstrated their maker's artistic ability. Locks for house doors were sometimes very ornate, being made to screw to one side of a door so that their decoration remained visible. Such locks were made in many countries, the English industry being centred in the Birmingham area from the late seventeenth century. After about 1800 the lock was only rarely decorative, its function as a security device being more important than its appearance. In any case, by that date the mortice lock, which was fitted within the thickness of the door, had come into general use, with only a keyhole at either side to betray its presence. To compensate for this, Robert Adam and others designed gilt metal lock-plates with hinged keyhole covers.

Mannheim Gold See Prince's Metal.

Marquetry The principal exponent of the practice of incorporating metal in marquetry on furniture was the French cabinet-maker, André-Charles Boulle (1642–1732). Brass was most frequently employed, but sometimes pewter and copper occur. The method of making the layer of marquetry was to glue together thin sheets of, say, brass and tortoiseshell, which were then marked with the desired pattern. This was cut through with a fine saw, with the result that there were two complete panels, each the reverse of the other. The one with a pattern in tortoiseshell on a ground of brass was known as *première partie*, and the other, with brass designs against tortoiseshell, as *contre partie*. Such work was executed by Boulle during much of his long lifetime, and continuously afterwards by his numerous followers. In the 1740s there was a limited fashion in England for mahogany furniture inlaid with engraved brass, and some examples of high quality have survived.

Milk Pails Many old drawings and engravings show eighteenth-century milkmaids with cylindrical metal pails. Examples of similar pattern, made of copper, rivetted up the side-joint, with the base similarly fitted in place and with a brass swing handle are used at the present day for logs and coal, but few, if any, date from the eighteenth century.

Mirrors Sheets of polished metal served as small-sized mirrors, the ancient Chinese using bronze for the purpose and casting the backs with decorative patterns. In England, the alloy speculum was used and a few seventeenth-century examples survive.

Monumental Brass Engraved brass or latten monuments exist in larger numbers in England than in any other country, although their numbers have been reduced over the centuries by vandalism and neglect. They originated probably in the Netherlands and the oldest surviving example (Verden, near Hanover) dates from the early thirteenth century. The shaped brass was affixed in a shallow hollow cut to receive it in a slab of stone placed usually over the grave of the deceased. The earliest English monument has been stripped of its metal, the indentation in the stone being all that remains in commemoration of a man who died in 1208 (St. Paul, Bedford). From later in the same century the brass of Sir John d'Aubernoun, who died in 1277, remains complete (Stoke d'Abernon, Surrey), the full-length figure depicted in armour. Such brasses have been of considerable assistance to historians and others, revealing not only details of costume at various dates, but providing information about medieval and later art. By the mid-seventeenth century the dead were no longer commemorated in that manner, and at the same time many brasses then in existence were despoiled of their metal either for conversion into instruments of war or because of religious prejudice. The Victorian engraved brass plaques which are to be found in great numbers in many old churches are seldom a worthy substitute.

Mortars The mortar is a bowl, often made of bronze or bell-metal but some-

Copper, Bronze, Pewter and Other Metals (Continued)

times of marble or some other strong material, used for pounding foodstuffs, chemicals and anything else requiring to be reduced to a state of fineness. Metal mortars survive from the fourteenth century onwards, and were made in many countries. The most interesting examples are those moulded with bands of decoration, inscriptions, and names and dates. It is probable that many mortars were made by bell-founders because examples have been recorded bearing the names of such men.

Mosaic Gold An alloy of copper akin to Bath metal and others.

Nickel A metal, greyish-white in colour, very soft and ductile, used as an alloy in German silver and Paktong.

Ormolu The word has come to mean gilt bronze, the bronze having been cast, chased and finished with gilding and burnishing. Ormolu was used in the eighteenth century for making corner-pieces, feet and other attachments, which protected as well as embellished pieces of furniture. It was used in this manner especially in France, but also in England and other countries. Ormolu was employed for mounting porcelain of all kinds, a fashion at a height in the late 1760's, when Josiah Wedgwood mentioned it in a letter:

> Mr. Boulton tells me I should be surprised to know what a trade has lately been made out of vases at Paris. The artists have even come over to London, picked up all the old whimsical ugly things they could meet with, carried them to Paris, where they have mounted and ornamented them with metal . . . Of this sort I have seen two or three old China bowls, for want of better things, stuck rim to rim, which have had no bad effect, but looked whimsical and droll.

Ormolu was used also in Paris and London for clock cases, candlesticks and other decorative objects. See Boulton; Gilding; Gouthière.

A Chinese pot and a pair of Meissen swans and cygnets mounted in French ormolu in the mid-eighteenth century. Sotheby's.

Paktong Paktong was an alloy of copper, zinc and nickel, taking a high polish and resembling silver, imported into England from China in the eighteenth century. It was used to make candlesticks, grates and other articles, and was popular because it resisted tarnish. At the time it was often confused with Tutenag, which was zinc from the same source, and old writers used the latter word when they meant Paktong.

Palais Royal The Palais Royal, Paris, was built by Cardinal Richelieu in about 1630, its later inhabitants including the duc d'Orléans, Philippe Égalité (1747–93). In the early nineteenth century part of the

Copper, Bronze, Pewter and Other Metals (Continued)

building became a series of shops which were very popular with the thousands of foreign visitors who came to the city following Napoleon's downfall. Some of the souvenirs purchased in the *boutiques* were small articles of mother-of-pearl or glass mounted in gilt metal. They were principally items for the writing- or dressing-table: candlesticks, ring-stands, letter-racks, and so forth.

Panchalouha An alloy used in India, composed of copper, brass and white lead sometimes with the addition of silver and gold.

Pewter Pewter is a grey-coloured alloy of tin with varying quantities of lead, copper and other metals. Its composition has altered over the centuries, and from country to country as well as from maker to maker. In England the Worshipful Company of Pewterers, of London, was incorporated in 1474 to regulate the craft. In due time there were three kinds of pewter in England, and a mid-eighteenth century writer classified them thus:

> *Hard metal:* the most durable, and used for dishes, plates, spoons, better quality tankards etc. [It was stamped with an X below a crown, and it was said]' . . . this hard metal may be easily known by its nearly resembling silver'.
> *Trifle metal:* used for commonplace dishes and plates, public-house tankards, and other ordinary articles in daily use.
> *Lay metal:* used for chamber-pots, wine measures, &c.

The writer continued:

> The Trifle and Lay metal are easily distinguished from each other: for the Trifle metal has a coarse resemblance of the Hard metal; and the Lay metal looks almost as coarse as lead.

In addition to the use of the crowned X on pewter of appropriate quality, the makers used other marks or touches closely resembling those stamped on silver; a procedure that doubtless deluded the unsuspecting into thinking the ware was made of precious metal. The important touch was that of the maker, which he was required to register with the Company by stamping it on a touch-plate in their keeping. The plates in use prior to the year 1666 were lost in the Great Fire of London, but there remain at Pewterers' Hall five plates, of which the earliest was in use from 1668, impressed with a total of 1,090 touches. By means of the Company records it has been possible to identify many of the pewterers, and although they did not use date-letters, as did the silversmiths, it is

Early eighteenth-century English pewter flagon with a hinged lid and scroll handle.
King & Chasemore.

possible to date articles approximately from a knowledge of the working spans of the makers concerned. Several provincial towns in England had their own Companies, the Pewterers' Guild of York and that of Bristol being active by the fifteenth century. Farther north, in Scotland, the Incorporation of Hammermen of Edinburgh was in being in 1496, and some of the touchplates on which its members recorded their stamps have survived. A covered measure of distinctive shape, known as a tappit-hen was peculiar to Scottish pewterers. It was made in several sizes to hold quantities that had been standard in the country prior to the Union with England of 1707. The measures were:

4 Scottish gills = 1 mutchkin (¾ of an English pint)
2 mutchkins = 1 chopin (1½ English pints)
2 chopins = 1 pint (3 English pints)

In America, pewter is known to have been made since early in the seventeenth century, but for many decades the makers had to rely on a supply of ready-made articles which they melted and re-fashioned. Existing eighteenth-century examples show various European influences in their design. Makers used personal marks stamped on their products, but these did not have the authority of a legally constituted Company behind them and anyone could use whatever kind of touch he pleased. In England, on the mainland of Europe and in America pewter passed out of favour in the late eighteenth century, when cream-coloured earthenware became available in large quantities and at low prices. English pewter touches are reproduced and identified in H. H. Cotterell's *Old Pewter, its Makers and Marks* (1929, reprinted 1963), and conveniently and inexpensively in a paperback, *English Pewter Touchmarks*, by Radway Jackson, 1970. See Britannia metal.

Pinchbeck Pinchbeck is an alloy composed of zinc and copper, but the exact proportions appear to have varied according to the maker. It was devised by a London clock- and watch-maker, Christopher Pinchbeck, who died in 1732, his son, Edward, announcing in the same year that he did not sell 'one grain of his curious metal, which so nearly resembles gold in colour, smell, and ductility, to any person whatsoever' and that he was the sole supplier of articles made from it.

Pipe-stopper Cast brass pipe-stoppers of many patterns, often of topical interest, were made in the eighteenth century and later.

Poker See Fire Irons.

Pontypool Ware Tinned plates of thin iron were japanned by coating completed articles with coloured varnish, baking them to about 140° C. and then further painting and varnishing them. The work was done at Birmingham and elsewhere during the eighteenth century, but nowhere with greater success than in Wales, at Pontypool. The industry was started there by Edward Allgood in about 1730 and after he retired thirty years later it was continued by one of his sons, while another opened a factory in opposition a few miles away at Usk. All kinds of articles were made including candlesticks, trays and tea and coffee urns, which were available in many colours as well as simulated tortoiseshell. The Allgoods would appear to have ceased working in about 1820, but before that the term Pontypool had become applied to goods of the kind produced elsewhere. In America, similar articles were made from tinplate imported from

Copper, Bronze, Pewter and Other Metals (Continued)

England, and the industry is said to have been started in the 1740's in the Connecticut River Valley. In both countries the ware largely ceased to be made during the second half of the nineteenth century. In France a similar product was known as *tôle peinte* (literally, painted sheet-iron), a term in use nowadays in the United States to describe such objects whatever their country of origin.

Powder Flask Powder flasks were made of copper and brass, and large numbers survive from the mid-nineteenth century. Their sides are decorated in relief, many of them appropriately with sporting subjects. They were used with the muzzle-loading guns of the time, which required to have a measured quantity of powder poured down the muzzle before a bullet was rammed home and the weapon was fired.

Prince's Metal A type of brass named after Prince Rupert, nephew of King Charles I. Like Bath metal, Mannheim gold and several other alloys with a superficial likeness to gold, Prince's metal was used for making small-sized articles such as pocket boxes, buttons and watch cases.

Russia See Tula.

Samovar A type of tea urn used in Russia and often made of brass and copper. It has an internal arrangement for keeping the contents hot.

Saucepan Surviving eighteenth-century saucepans resemble in shape those in use nowadays, but were often made of copper with tinned interiors and have iron handles held in place with rivets. The tinning was intended to prevent poisons in the copper contaminating food, but it was found that the tin used often contained just as much harmful lead. In 1756 a prize was offered to anyone who could devise a method in which only pure tin played a part, and eventually a safe process was employed.

Scuttle See Coal Scuttle.

Sentoku See Japan.

Sheffield Plate A man named Thomas Bolsover (1704–88) is credited with the discovery of the process, duly named Sheffield plating because the industry was centred in the South Yorkshire manufacturing town. Bolsover found that copper and silver would fuse together under heat, and that if pieces of them were so treated and then rolled out the result would be a sheet of silver-coated copper. In the same way a silver-copper-silver sandwich could be made, and this was successfully formed into useful articles. The raw edges revealed the method of construction and were unsightly, but it was a simple matter to solder along such places silver wire or other ornamentation. Many of the articles made in Sterling silver were executed in Sheffield plate, and as they contained only a fraction as much of the precious metal they could be sold very competitively. In the 1830s the process was adapted to using German silver, which did not reveal the distinctive pink colour of copper when the surface wore away. Finally, the process was completely superseded in 1841 by the newly-devised electroplating.

Skillet Long-handled saucepans on three short legs were called skillets. They were usually cast in bell-metal, and examples survive from the fifteenth century when they were made with rounded sides, and the seventeenth century when they had become straight-sided. The handles are sometimes cast with the founder's name or with a moral reminder such as: *YE WAGES OF SIN IS DEATH.*

Skimmer The skimmer was used to skim cream that rose to the surface of a

Copper, Bronze, Pewter and Other Metals (Continued)

pan of milk. Some of them had a circular and slightly concave bowl, pierced with holes and affixed to a long handle; the latter being of iron, while the bowl was of brass. Other patterns are among surviving examples, but few are older than the nineteenth century.

Snuffers Snuffers for trimming the wicks of candles were made in the eighteenth century and later. Many were of steel, but iron and brass were also employed, and there were numerous varieties. Most of them were designed to collect the wick trimmings in a little box on top of the cutters.

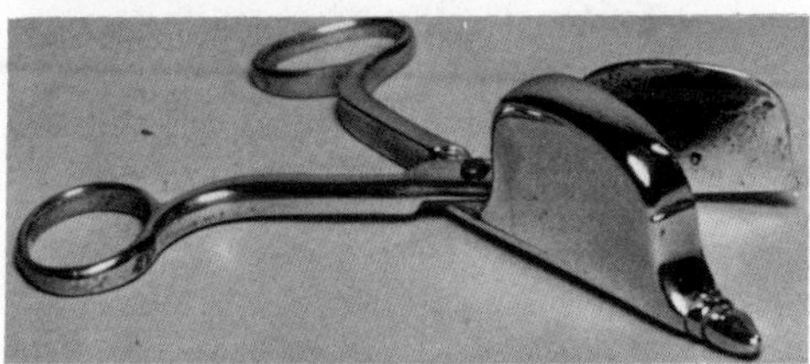

Pair of brass candle-snuffers dating from the first half of the eighteenth century.

Spain Spanish craftsmen were active in the past, and some of their more ambitious productions are to be seen in cathedrals in that country; for example, the great bronze candalabrum at Seville and the pulpits of the same metal at Burgos and Toledo. Later, Italian and German influences were often so strong that Spanish work is barely distinguishable from that of the other lands.

Speculum An alloy of tin and copper with small quantities of other ingredients which made a silvery metal. It took a high polish and was used for small-sized mirrors. Speculum was referred to by past writers as Steel, but it has no connexion whatsoever with the other metal of that name.

Spelter An alloy consisting mostly of zinc. It was used during the nineteenth century for making inexpensive copies of bronzes, and spelter, which is of a greyish tint, was suitably coloured to assist the deception. It is a brittle metal.

Spinning A process involving fitting a lathe with a shaped wooden core. As the latter revolved rapidly, a sheet of metal was pressed against it and gradually acquired the shape of the core. It was suited to making hollow articles, such as bowls and teapots, and was introduced in England in the 1780s. Spinning could not be used with all metals, but was highly successful with Britannia metal.

Spoons Old spoons are normally thought of as being made of silver, but many more were of pewter and various kinds of brass. Although they once existed in quantity, their comparative cheapness meant that they were treated casually and were lost or discarded without thought. They are now rarer than their silver counterparts which they followed in pattern.

Steel Steel is iron containing a small percentage of carbon, giving it the properties of being extremely hard and strong and adaptable to numerous uses. It was only very occasionally employed for artistic purposes. Steel was the name given also to Speculum. See Cut Steel; Tula.

Surrey Enamel In the seventeenth century objects were made from brass, ready cast with hollowed-out patterns to be filled with coloured enamels. The finished effect was similar to that achieved by the *champlevé* process, but in that instance the hollows were cut by hand into a flat surface. Various articles decorated in the manner have survived, including candlesticks, andirons, and stirrups. Although the work was done on the mainland

Copper, Bronze, Pewter and Other Metals (Continued)

of Europe as well as in England, it is referred to as Surrey enamel. There is no convincing explanation as to how or why it acquired the name.

Tin Tin is a bluish-white metal that was seldom used on its own, but was important as an alloy with copper to make bronze. The English source of supply was Cornwall, in the far south-west of the country, where the Phoenicians had voyaged for the metal in pre-Christian times. The country continued to provide sufficient tin for the whole country until the end of the nineteenth century.

Tobacco Box Brass, and less often copper, was used for making boxes to carry tobacco in the pocket. Eighteenth century Dutch examples are often of oval shape and engraved with scenes and inscriptions, the latter sometimes indecent. German boxes of the same period mostly originated at Iserlohn, a town near Dortmund, which was a centre of metal-working comparable to Birmingham in England. Many of the Iserlohn boxes are of a narrow oblong shape with rounded ends, the tops decorated with battle scenes in low relief. English boxes were decorated with a crest or other indication of ownership, but do not seem to have survived in such numbers as those from Holland and Germany. Matthew Boulton is recorded as having made a quantity of tobacco boxes to the order of the East India Company, they were made 'of Bath metal, which admitted of being struck when hot in very handsome forms; they could not have been made of brass at half the money'.

Tôle Peinte See Pontypool ware.

Trivet The trivet was usually a three- or four-legged metal stand for placing in front of a fire, on which could be stood a kettle, plates or anything else requiring to be kept warm. It was made of iron or brass, the legs sometimes shaped into a cabriole-like curve and the top ornamented with a pierced design. An alternative pattern of trivet was made to hang on the front bars of a grate. See Footman.

Tsuba The oval-shaped hand guard fitted to a Japanese sword. The *tsuba* was frequently made of iron, pierced, inlaid and otherwise the subject of skilful ornamentation.

Japanese tsuba, *sword guard, made of iron inlaid with gold and silver.* Christie's.

Tula The town of Tula, one hundred miles south of Moscow, was the site of the Imperial arms manufactory, founded in the early years of the eighteenth century. In addition to making pistols and other weapons, the craftsmen produced articles for peaceful use, such as furniture and ornaments. They were made of burnished steel, inlaid with copper, brass, gilt bronze and silver.

Tutenag was the name given to zinc imported into England from China. The name was also applied erroneously to articles of Paktong.

Warming Pan The warming pan was used to take the chill off a bed, and took the form of a circular, lidded pan affixed to a long handle. The pan held glowing charcoal, and was ventilated by means of holes in the hinged cover. It was apparently introduced in the late sixteenth century and was made of copper or brass with an iron handle. Later, the handle was of ebonized wood. Copper containers of various shapes replaced the foregoing in the nineteenth century. They were filled with hot water, and although the occasional leak must have occurred they would surely have been less dangerous than the older type. See Hunneman.

Weights and Measures Standard English weights and measures were legalized in 1495 and each district possessed a set. They were made of bronze or brass, suitably stamped and inscribed, and a number are still owned by authorities up and down the country. The English standard pound weight was lost when the Houses of Parliament in London were destroyed by fire in 1834, and at the same time the yard measure sustained damage and was mislaid until 1891.

Wool Weight For many centuries wool was the product on which the English economy was based; the raising of sheep, spinning and weaving were occupations giving employment to thousands, and export of the raw wool and finished goods brought foreign money to the exchequer. The trade was of such importance to the nation that it was subject to careful supervision as well as taxation and for this purpose standard bronze weights were provided at the various marts. The weights were shield-shaped, cast with the arms and initials of the reigning monarch and each had a hole at the top so that it could be suspended from a beam scale. They were replaced on the occasion of each coronation and it was forbidden for outdated ones to be used. The weights were for 7 lb. and 14 lb. and at the back of each was a circular depression of varying size where surplus metal had been removed during testing against the standard. Also, each weight bore the impressed marks of the Founders' Company, who gained in the sixteenth century the right of sizing and stamping those made within the City of London and three miles around. In the eighteenth century the importance of wool declined in the face of competition from cotton.

Zinc Zinc is a bluish-white metal and was usually obtained from ore known as *lapis calaminaris* or Calamine. This was found in England in Derbyshire and Cumbria but on the mainland of Europe the principal sources were near Liége and Dinant in the Netherlands, and in Germany. The most important use of zinc was to alloy it with copper in the making of brass, but it also formed the major constituent in spelter. Zinc imported from China was known as Tutenag.

INDEX

Note: Page numbers of references in the text are shown in Roman numerals; those of references to captions of black-and-white illustrations are shown in plain italics; those to illustrations in colour are shown in bold italics.

A

B

C

D

I

J

O

P

T

Y

Z